# The Bill McKibben Reader

# THE BILL McKIBBEN READER

## Pieces from an Active Life

## Bill McKibben

A Holt Paperback

HENRY HOLT AND COMPANY · NEW YORK

Holt Paperbacks
Henry Holt and Company, LLC
*Publishers since 1866*
175 Fifth Avenue
New York, New York 10010
www.henryholt.com

A Holt Paperback® and 🜨® are registered trademarks
of Henry Holt and Company, LLC.

Library of Congress Cataloging-in-Publication Data

McKibben, Bill.
  The Bill Mckibben reader : pieces from an active life / Bill McKibben.
    p.   cm.—(A Holt paperback)
  Includes index.
  ISBN-13: 978-0-8050-7627-1
  ISBN-10: 0-8050-7627-1
  1. Environmental protection—Citizen participation.   I. Title.
  TD171.7.M38   2008
  333.72—dc22                                        2007039609

Henry Holt books are available for special promotions and
premiums. For details contact: Director, Special Markets.

First Holt Paperbacks Edition 2008

Printed in the United States of America

1   3   5   7   9   10   8   6   4   2

To William Shawn

# Contents

# The Bill McKibben Reader

# Introduction

Looking backward, one can usually discern a trail—find a logic for what at the time seemed spontaneous decisions. These pieces come from the first quarter century of my writing life, all written in the passion of a particular moment, the grip of a new experience or idea. They lack the coherence that a more systematic thinker would have produced—they are the products of a reporter's imagination, restless and fast-moving. But seen in reverse I can force a certain unity on them. Which is a pleasurable and conceited thing to do with one's life.

As I was digging through mounds of old clips, I looked at a few essays I'd written for my college newspaper, *The Harvard Crimson*. Mostly I covered City Hall in Cambridge—the police beat and so on. But we were nothing if not full of ourselves, and so we also felt no compunction in taking on the largest subjects of the day. The night that Ronald Reagan was elected president in 1980, I wrote the news story, got grimly drunk, and spent the next day in bed. When I rose, I wrote three thousand words, most of them jejune, that in retrospect defined the ground I'd cover in the years to come. The election of Reagan was not just a rejection of a hapless

Jimmy Carter; it was the choice for a kind of pretend America where we would agree that we didn't have to face any limits, change any habits. Our commitment to a careening growth economy (just two years after Carter had hosted a reception for E. F. "Small Is Beautiful" Schumacher at the White House) set in motion the events that would punctuate my adulthood, and which are still playing themselves out—we lurched toward a society *whose only measure was individual success*. It's in defiance of that trend that I've spent the succeeding years writing, often quixotically; it's that trend whose meaning we can now read in every cubic meter of atmosphere, in every tick mark on the rising thermometer.

For me personally, though, the years after college were delightful. Through a series of flukes I found myself fresh out of college as a staff writer at the *New Yorker*. I was the youngest person on the staff, and no one else was as interested in the low-paying and (in those days) anonymous job of writing the "Talk of the Town." For me it was heaven, a license to explore the most entertaining city on earth. These were the last years of William Shawn's editorship, and we became great friends—our difference in years was so great that instead of the fraught father-child relationships he had with so much of the staff, I got to enjoy the much easier grandfatherly version. And his only real requirement for "Talk" pieces suited me as well—I could write about anything, provided it didn't involve celebrities or newsmakers. So for five years I churned out oddball thousand-word essays, often three a week, on a man who played spoons in front of the public library or a compulsive author of letters to the editor. For reasons best known to him, he also let me write short political essays for the "Notes and Comment" section at the front of the magazine—for a while, Jonathan Schell and I alternated weeks, and it was from him that I learned how great reporting could produce critical thinking. It was a liberating reprieve from the twin straitjackets of "objective reporting" and "punditry."

(Mr. Shawn, to whom this book is dedicated, also gave me

another gift. He asked me—before it became a cliché—to chronicle New York's emerging homeless problem by living on the streets. I did so for considerable stretches—one result was the piece in this book about a single day in that period. Another result was the chance to meet my future wife, Sue Halpern, who was a homeless advocate and writer.)

After five years of this charmed life, upheaval arrived in the person of Si Newhouse, who bought the magazine and soon forced Mr. Shawn to resign. I quit the same day—at the time it seemed like high principle at a high cost, but in retrospect it was clearly a blessing. Not only did I avoid the demoralizing decade that followed at the magazine till David Remnick arrived to right the ship, but I also escaped what was in some ways a velvet prison—a writing sinecure so cush that it trapped many an author over the years. The best part for me was the escape route—I'd grown up a good suburban child, and become an urban reporter. But one of the last things I did for the *New Yorker* was a long piece about where everything in my apartment came from—water, electricity, you name it. It began to open my eyes to the *physicalness* of the world, the fact that even Manhattan depended on nature, and consumed it, for its existence. (The degree of surprise that this caused me defines, I think, the meaning of American suburbia.) At about the same time, through yet another fluke, I spent six winter weeks at a writing retreat at Blue Mountain Lake, New York, deep in the heart of the Adirondacks. I fell in love with winter and with wilderness and, months later, when the time came to leave the *New Yorker*, that's where Sue and I headed. We bought a cheap house way, way out in the biggest woods in the American East (at that time the Adirondacks were cheap, and we were in a particularly poor and remote section) and began to learn how to live a new life, at home in nature.

My love affair with those wild mountains was so intense and instant—I knew I'd found the right landscape for me, just as I knew I'd found the right woman—that it set the stage for what followed.

Always an omnivorous consumer of journalism, I'd begun reading the occasional reference to something called the "greenhouse effect." The more I studied what little science was available, the harder I was hit by the realization that this world I had suddenly woken up to was just as suddenly in mortal danger. *The End of Nature* sprung, in less than a year's time, from that realization. It was the first book for a general audience about global warming and hence contained much reporting on the subject, but its heart was a lament for the notion that wildness was vanishing—that every last place had been touched by a human hand.

The book was both successful—it's now in twenty-four languages—and scorned; *Forbes* magazine ran a review with a headline urging its readers not to buy it, and Rush Limbaugh went on the attack. But its main meaning for me was to set the task that has dominated my writing and thinking life since: how to come to terms practically, culturally, economically, theologically, politically, and emotionally with this most enormous problem humans have ever faced. The years that followed were in one sense odd. I hoped very much that I'd been wrong about global warming, but with each new scientific report and each new year of record warmth I also felt an undeniable and slightly shameful vindication. I kept tugging at the problem from different directions—in "What's On" and *The Age of Missing Information* I tried to figure out why our information culture made it so hard for us to come to grips with real challenges, and for "If You Build It, Will They Change?" and *Hope, Human and Wild* I traveled the world looking for alternate models. It was also a time of great personal joy—we had a new daughter, Sophie, and we were living in our gorgeous corner of a gorgeous world. Though there were no other writers close to hand (with the vital exception of my wife), I was also finding a literary community—"nature writers" such as Terry Tempest Williams, Rick Bass, David Abram, Barry Lopez, Gary Snyder, Wendell Berry, and the like, who became friends and whose work inspired and taught me. It's been a great privilege to be a small part of that movement, to understand the possibilities for a literary life defined by commitment and service to place and planet.

At the turn of the century we shifted seventy miles east from the Adirondacks to the Green Mountains of Vermont. The cultural distance was further than the topographical—from Appalachia to New England. For me it meant the pleasure of a loose relationship with Middlebury College, and with writers such as John Elder. Perhaps drawing on those experiences, my own work became more insistently focused on the gulf between individual and community—focused, in a sense, on the same choice we'd made in that fateful Reagan-Carter election. I've come to think that the solution to our environmental problems has more to do with rebuilding working communities even than with reworking our engines and appliances: the essay "(Tod) Murphy's Law" and my most recent book, *Deep Economy*, are efforts to make that case, and also to explore the ways that community might provide some of the pleasure that seems so rare in a consumer economy devoted to the quick and easy.

In recent years my life has taken another turn too. In despair at the lack of political action about global warming, even in the face of ever more dire science, I've turned increasingly to helping organize Americans to demand change, "Speaking Up for the Environment" an early example. After spearheading a successful march across Vermont in August of 2006, I began working with half a dozen incredibly talented recent graduates of Middlebury to organize a pair of nationwide protests. Step It Up, as we've called our efforts, has been a success—in April of 2007 we organized 1,400 demonstrations in all fifty states, the biggest day of grassroots environmental protest since Earth Day 1970. I'm as proud of that work as of anything I've written. Indeed, I have become a student of a new genre: the e-mail designed to set protest in motion.

I hope that some of the pieces in this book move you to reflect, or better yet to laugh. Taken as a whole, however, I hope they help move you to act.

# · I ·

## AT HOME
## IN NATURE

# · 1 ·

## A Carefully Controlled Experiment

—*The Nature of Nature* (Harcourt, Inc.), 1994

June 29—It is a warm, close afternoon, and I am stringing twine around a small patch of the forest behind my home.

Why am I stringing twine around a small patch of forest? Because, by God, I am through with being a dilettante. This morning I finished writing a magazine article on the oldest trees in the eastern United States—seventeen-hundred-year-old bald cypresses in North Carolina swamps, Massachusetts hemlocks nearly half a millennium old, the magnificent tulip poplars of the Smokies. I spent most of my time in these groves peering up slack-jawed and thinking my usual liberal-arts-type thoughts: "Cathedral grandeur," say, or "That's *tall*," or "Whoa!"

As I wrote the article, however, I noticed, and not for the first time, that the best interviews I conducted were with the field biologists, the people who were down on the ground carefully studying the life of these places, finding reasons to save them. A Mr. Duffy had demonstrated that even after a century clear-cut areas lacked the wildflowers of the ancient forest; a Mr. Petranka had patiently proved that large-scale logging could cut salamander populations 80 percent. And Stephen Selva, a biologist I met in

Maine whose license plate read "LICHEN," had discovered a species that seemed to exist in only two places in the world: eastern old-growth forests and someplace in New Zealand. "It's sort of the spotted owl of the East," he explained. "Unfortunately, it's a lichen."

Thus the string. Because of my admiration for these people, I have pledged to be more systematic in my study of the natural world. No longer will I indulge in those daily hikes where I stride as quickly as possible to the top of something in order to gaze out enraptured on an Adirondack vista. Instead I will study my backyard plot. The time has come to develop the left—or is it the right?—side of my brain, whichever one it is that science lives in.

I intended to build a ten-foot-square research plot, but an old white pine has turned it into a slight rhomboid. First observation: my plot has a lot of mosquitoes today. I estimated density: thick. Question for further research: what brand of mosquito repellent do real biologists use? Tomorrow will be a good time to actually start an inventory of the flora and fauna of my stand.

· · ·

July 5—The mosquitoes have been joined by the most intense heat wave since the 1940s. Day after day it tops ninety degrees, even here at fifteen hundred feet. My plot is within sight of my pond, a flawed research design.

· · ·

July 9—There's a maple tree on one corner of this plot. It's fourteen and a half inches around at breast height. Its leaves appear healthy.

About six feet up the trunk, however, a piece of rusting fence wire sticks jaggedly out. The rest of the fence has disappeared. Here is a puzzle common in the eastern forest. What can be logically deduced from this rusting piece of wire?

What can be deduced is pasture. It is easy enough to imagine the man who strung the fence. He must have arrived here late in the nineteenth century and cut down the big hemlocks so their bark could be used by the local tannery. Perhaps he found enough spruce to justify borrowing a team of horses and hauling it out. And then he decided to farm, as his parents had farmed in Massachusetts or in Ireland, not completely aware of how thin the soil was, perhaps hoping that the first ninety-day growing season was a fluke. But the second? And the third? Day after day, pulling stones from the field—the biggest heap is ten yards east of my plot—all the time wondering if he was throwing good labor after bad.

I can see that farmer's son deciding to leave, to take his chances in the cities to the south or the fields to the west, and the farmer growing older, unable to maintain his spread. The forest sidling back in on his field—the pines daring to rise a few inches and then exulting in their sunny freedom and shooting up with the spreading shape of a field tree. Is this a hard thing or a sweet one?

A woman grew up in this tiny valley in those days. Jeanne Robert Foster was so beautiful that she managed to get to New York City, where she became a Gibson girl, and then a poet, a friend of Pound and Picasso and Joyce. She wrote about the mountain poverty of those farms where she had grown up, places redeemed only by hardscrabble religion and the beauty of the hills. One poem tells of walking such a field, three miles from my plot, with an old farmer who had grown desperate at the decay. "I must find a man who still loves the soil," he says,

> *Walk by his side unseen, put in his mind*
> *What I loved when I lived until he builds*
> *Sows, reaps, and covers these hill pastures here*
> *With sheep and cattle, mows the meadowland*
> *Grafts the old orchard again, makes it bear again*
> *Knowing that we are lost if the land does not yield.*

There is true human sadness at the work of a generation dissolving. I know old men in my town who will not drive out this way; it pains them too much to see the fields they cleared grown back in. Yet there is, at my feet, the remains of a trillium that bloomed a month ago, nourished by the sun that filters into this woods before summer closes the canopy, an old occupant who has reclaimed her home.

The fence has rusted away, leaving this one small strand of wire as a memorial to the momentary and (in the larger scheme of things) gentle touch of a particular human being on this particular landscape. A testimony to the recuperative power of any spot where it rains. This quadrant of mine has sojourned briefly in civilization, but it has not been civilized.

· · ·

July 14—I am tired, and in sitting down to rest against the maple tree on the southeast corner of my plot I fear I have crushed several maple saplings. There are twenty-three of them spread around me, and a couple of hemlocks that have been browsed so thoroughly by white-tailed deer that they have pretty much given up. Is the destruction caused by my rear end on the maple saplings philosophically comparable to the damage done by hungry deer?

I have pretty much given up on the word "wild." Here in this one small place, the quality of the sunlight is affected by the thinning ozone, the temperature reflects our industrial society's emissions of carbon dioxide, the rain falls with a noticeably acid taint. And the deer—they've been nurtured for years by a state conservation department eager to please hunters, their predators largely exterminated save for the rifle and the Ford. Are they wild anymore, or are they a human creation? We need a more honest word to describe places where people are not in total control yet have their thumb on the scale.

· · ·

July 20—Still, the idea of "wild" haunts this place. Due east of my plot, clearly visible today through the leaves, is a small mountain—not one of the hundred highest even in New York State, but the dominant peak in this area, a mountain that I love. And I am not alone in that love. A man whose name should be more widely known, Howard Zahniser, had a summer cabin not far from here, with a view of the same angle of this mountain as my plot affords. From there, he wrote many of his telling speeches on behalf of wilderness, and planned the two decades of lobbying that culminated in the federal wilderness statute finally enacted in 1964. The law—the most progressive and the most philosophical that Congress has ever passed—sets aside "untrammeled" land where man is "only a visitor." His son, Ed, maintains that the choice of words was careful, and paid off in the 1970s, when eastern lands were added to the national wilderness system. "Most of those lands were not pristine, but had recovered from human use to the extent that Congress found them now untrammeled," he writes.

So it is with my study site. There is no denying that most of the Nikon-triggering grandeur in this country is west of the Mississippi, in tracts more nearly virgin than these Adirondacks. But there is something about this plot, standing for all the other recovering places, that speaks well for human humility. People have taken a step back here, and the land has responded.

• • •

August 8—Some unscientific animal has stolen the string demarcating my research area. By now, however, I know it well enough not to mind.

Any one piece of ground exists in many different dimensions. When my dog visits me here, she concentrates on the dimension of smell, and doubtless has made many valuable observations to which I am not privy. I am working today on sound, trying to separate the noises that filter back to this spot. There is the sound of Mill Creek falling over the lip of a beaver dam, a spectacular piece of engineering that has built for us a new wetland in recent years. An occasional fish jumps in that swampy pond, slipping back into the water with a gurgle. Once, in response to some alarm, a beaver slaps hard, and the sound echoes lazily; only once, on this humid afternoon, does some bird let go a snatch of song.

Most of the sound is constant, more flowing—a ceaseless pulse of insect warble that I normally tune out with ease, but now, listening hard, find deeply reassuring. Trills, occasional tiny buzz-saw riffs, oscillating chirps blended together into high-pitched waves. It is life, pure and simple—life without the stories that come attached to the beaver slap or the birdcall or the gears grinding every so often on the nearest road. It is life on automatic, the deep life that our lives emerge from and skate across and subside back into.

· · ·

August 26—The moon is working back toward full tonight, bleaching my study site in its soft wash of light. There's an old birch tree here, and I like to rub its trunk—the smoothness of the paper, the random weave of bumps and gashes, the peelings that it sheds as it grows. It is like holding a cast-off snakeskin—like holding time.

· · ·

September 5—Most of the leaves in my plot are still green, the deep leathery green of old age. A few have turned, scarlet premonitions of the approaching explosion. It's still summer, but it feels like 3:00 A.M. in the city, the last moment when it's still night, when it's maybe fifteen minutes from becoming morning, right at the point where "out late" turns into "up early." Everything inside this plot—and all that I can see outside it—has moved further along on its journey these past couple of months. The saplings are a little taller, the birch somewhat shaggier, the dead maple a bit more rotted, the old rot a little more like dirt and nearly ready to nurse the next round of seeds.

This morning over breakfast, I read an article in the paper about an economist who figures that most Americans will change careers eight times in their lives to keep up with the rapid pace of technology. And they may move to new towns or new parts of the country that often, probably trading in a husband or wife along the way. The last century has been an experiment in how much we can speed up society before the strains prove unbearable. The next century, if the scientists are right about phenomena like climate change, will test whether nature can manage a similar acceleration, whether systems geared toward repetition can handle enormous variability. Will beech trees still survive on this spot if the temperature increases three or four degrees? Probably not. Autumn starts to take on a different meaning—not just one spot along the endless cycle of natural time; but perhaps a metaphor for the slow expiration of the natural when it is forced into linear, human time. Autumn, implying May, is bittersweet; this new fall would be simply bitter.

. . .

September 12—A chipmunk, working without visible grant support on a careful study of nut production, has taken over my quadrant and is angered when I come to visit. Time for me to leave, to take down my corner posts and resume my meandering—I'm not cut out for the cutthroat world of science.

Without the string, with the poles gone, my study site blends back into the anonymous woods. But the scientific method has appealed to me greatly. Look low, look carefully. And know globally—the small and the subtle refer constantly to the overarching, the huge issues of the moment are reflected in the duff and the mushroom and the sapling. The war (and the courtship) between humans and the land can be read on this ten-foot-by-ten-foot (give or take) patch of grown-in pasture, and the chances for truce (or for marriage) assessed. I should close, I know, with questions for future research, suggestions for these scientists who will probe more deeply. How do we want to live? What matters to us? What does a tree say as it stands in the forest?

# · 2 ·

## Consuming Nature

*—Consuming Desires* (Island Press), 1999

To be under siege from a cloud of blackflies is to feel your sanity threatened. In and out of your ears they crawl, biting as they go; in and out of your nose, your mouth, the corners of your eyes. If you've covered up everything but your hands, they will start there and crawl to your wrists, leaving welts wherever they feed. I went out to the garden one spring evening without my shirt tucked in tight enough, and when I came in five minutes later my wife described to me the perfect row of bites, twenty or thirty of them, that ran along the narrow gap of skin that had winked open when I stooped to weed.

Blackflies hover in a cloud about your face and move with you for miles, so great is their need for your warmth and company and blood. Every writer of the mountainous North has tried to describe their voraciousness—"winged assassins," "lynch mobs," "jaws on wings." Here in the Adirondack Mountains of upstate New York they constitute their own season, one that lasts as long as spring or high summer or fall color (though not as long as winter). For six or seven weeks, from before Memorial Day to after the Glorious Fourth, the paradise of a town where I live, an enormous expanse of mountain and river and stream and lake and pond, is a paradise flawed. Most of the land here is protected by the state constitution, proclaimed "forever wild," but the legislature has never managed to resolve away the blackflies.

It's not that no one's tried. As early as 1948, local towns seeking to extend the tourist season were spraying DDT from helicopters and tossing chunks of it into the streams. Rachel Carson put an end to that by 1965 (and by the early 1990s the first eagles were finally returning to the Adirondacks to nest, their eggs' shells again thick enough to allow them to hatch). In subsequent years, some towns used malathion or methoxychlor, sprayed usually from the air but always in the face of opposition. Then, more recently, some scientists began experimenting with a more natural method of control, a naturally occurring bacteria called *Bacillus thuringinsis*, which had been used for many years for organic control of garden pests. The *israelensis* subspecies, from the deserts of the Middle East, is highly specific for mosquitoes and blackflies. And so there was soon a small Adirondack industry of private contractors who would bid for the right to treat streams each spring, killing off the blackfly larvae in ways that appealed to both environmentalists and tourist-seeking local businesses.

But our town had never gone in for BTI, as the treatment is known, in large part because it is a frugal place, with the lowest property taxes in the region. No one ever brought the question up, and so spring after spring we had blackfly season, hard on the heels of mud season. Then, suddenly, that changed. A petition circulated demanding that Johnsburg join the list of towns that treat their streams. The movement may have started one morning at a Rotary Club meeting in Smith's Restaurant, at which a local realtor got up to complain that she'd lost a sale when she could not even get a couple from car to house, the flies were so thick. Sandy Taylor heard her and agreed to help write a petition.

Sandy Taylor and her husband, Jim, moved here not long ago from the South and before that the Midwest, where Jim had worked for the Monsanto Company for many years. They are exactly the sort of people who revitalize communities by moving into them. Before long Sandy was helping to organize our town's new library, the first in its history. The Taylors became mainstays of Rotary, of the church, of the theater group. They represent everything that is good about a certain American civic ideal, a spirit that is in many ways foreign to this backwoods spot. And it's not as if they are environmentally unaware or unconcerned; Sandy worked for many years as a guide at the biological research station run by Washington University in her hometown, St. Louis. "Our happiest memories as a family," she told me once, "are the camping trips we used to take."

But for her, as for most people, blackflies were not a desirable part of nature. "I can't garden, and I can't walk in the woods without all this protective paraphernalia, which is uncomfortable and hot and irritating," she told me. "My legs become a mass of bites that don't go away till August." Soon several hundred people had signed the petition she helped draw up, and the town board was busy drafting a set of specifications so it could put the job out for bids. Local innkeepers predicted that the cost might well be covered by the taxes paid by vacationers who would otherwise stay away. It looked like a done deal, as if our town would soon join the twenty-one other Adirondack communities that treat their streams with BTI.

Against most expectations, however, opposition began to form. It was not particularly organized—there was no official group, no "Save Our Flies" contingent. Instead, questioning letters started appearing in the local newspaper. Some of the comments concerned cost. "This is going to cost us $40,000, my share will be $56, and I don't even know if it's going to work," said one resident. Others questioned the effectiveness of the plans: Johnsburg covers a vast area, most of it deep wilderness, and since blackflies will migrate a good distance in search of the blood they need to lay eggs, all those streams would have to be treated, which some experts said was a dubious proposition.

But most of the opposition was unexpectedly philosophical. For one thing, the messages of thirty years of ecological thinking had begun to penetrate people's minds. The fact that there are millions of blackflies around Johnsburg in the spring, several residents pointed out, means that *something* must eat them for dinner. Fishermen testified that they had slit open trout bellies to find them crammed with blackflies; others worried about birds, or about bats, or simply about whether it was prudent to muck around with Such Vast Systems.

And there were the people who said, This is not such a big problem. Sure, a few days a year, when there's no wind, it gets bad, and so I wear my bug veil or I stay indoors.

And there was something more yet. A surprising number of my neighbors said—not always loudly, often a little backhandedly, maybe with a shade of embarrassment—that somehow the blackflies were a part of life here, one of the things that make us whatever it is that we are. Could we still have the Black Fly Ball at the local tavern, someone wanted to know.

. . .

I once did an odd experiment in which I found the largest cable television system on earth, which was at the time a hundred-channel operation in Fairfax, Virginia, and got people to tape for me everything that came across all the channels during the same twenty-four-hour period. I took my 2,400 hours of videotape home to the Adirondacks with me and spent a year watching it, trying to figure out what the world would look like were that one's main window on it. And what I found, amid the many lessons that spewed forth from the six home shopping channels, the four music video channels, the three sports channels, was this one overriding message: *You are the most important thing on earth.* You, sitting there on the couch, clutching the remote, are the center of creation, the heaviest object in the known universe; all things orbit your desires. This Bud's for You.

This is, of course, the catechism of the consumer society—the elevation of each one of us above all else. Sometimes it is described as "human nature," usually by people who would argue that you can't do anything at all about it. But of course in other times and other places, people have managed to put other things at the center of their lives—their tribe or community, their God, nature, or some amalgamation of these. Sometimes that's been all to the good: visit an Amish community. Sometimes it's meant pogroms. All I'm saying is that there have been other choices on offer.

Whether that still is true, however, I'm not sure. We have grown up in a culture so devoted to consumption—grown up so solid in the understanding that we define ourselves through certain patterns of consuming—that I doubt very much we can truly shake our conditioning. How else would we behave? From "real needs"? Save for the relative few of us who ever experience actual hunger or actual involuntary exposure to the elements, that sense of reality is as hard to summon as a sense of what it felt like to be chased by saber-toothed tigers. Poor people are just as interested in brand names as anyone else, just as devoted to the various cults (convenience, comfort, identity) of this central religion as anyone else.

And so it is no real stretch to say that the drive to eliminate blackflies from the small rural town where I live is simply one more manifestation of our deep consumer urge. We want to consume bite-free air; we want to consume our cedar decks and our pools and our gardens free of any complication or annoyance. We want to consume them *when* we want (not just on windy days) and *how* we want (bare-chested, with no damn bug veil). Jim Taylor spent the latter part of his career at Monsanto managing the AstroTurf division—managing the metaphor, fair or not, for conversion of the natural into the convenient.

· · ·

But what about those of us who oppose the blackfly treatment, we exemplars of biological virtue, eager to sacrifice ourselves for the sake of that great order Diptera and its thirst for our blood? How do we explain our escape from the great consumer faith into which we were baptized?

Mainly, I think, we do so by saying that we are just consumers, too. Why do I not want blackfly larvae killed in Mill Creek where it runs past my house? Partly because I don't want the biology of the stream tampered with but at least as much because I live not in Generic Suburban America, where everything is supposed to be convenient, but in the Rugged Frontier Adirondacks, where everything is supposed to be a challenge. At some level, I fear that I like blackfly season for the same reason I like winter and bad roads: because it heightens the adventure of living here. I consume inconvenience, turning it into a pleasurable commodity; it becomes the fuel for my own sense of superiority. I don't feel special because I own a particular brand of clothing, drive a particular make of car, smoke a particular brand of cigarette; I feel special because I have a crappy car, because I wear old clothes all the time, because it's a twenty-mile round-trip to get a quart of milk. I *like* it when people call up from the city to talk and the power has just failed, or a blizzard has just struck, or the temperature has gone to thirty below. I feel larger because of all that, I think; it pumps me up the way a Nike shoe, a Rolex watch, an in-ground pool, a Ford Explorer is supposed to pump us up. Blackfly season is a test, something to endure; I come out of it feeling tougher, stronger—which means, I think, that I'm a superconsumer, too. Blackfly season is about *me*.

And in this, I imagine, I am not alone. The shift toward voluntary simplicity now under way in some small corners of American culture is in some ways simply a shift toward a new self-image. Instead of defining ourselves by what we buy, we define ourselves by what we throw away.

There is clearly a sense in which this slightly submerged consumerism is more twisted than its straightforward counterpart. Elimination is a logical human response to blackflies, BTI a giant and efficient version of the timeless slapping hand. Wanting to consume fly-free air is, at some level, extremely logical. Finding a way to consume fly-*filled* air is more than a little nuts.

· · ·

So is it all just a toss-up? If ours is an age of endless irony, when nonconsumption is just another form of image building, does it make any difference how we live? Can you say that one path is better than the other? Can you say we shouldn't kill all the damn blackflies?

You can, I think, though you have to say it carefully, aware that your own sense of superiority is more than a little absurd.

The first argument is clear: even if the main reasons why you defend blackflies or recycle your dental floss have to do with you, they nonetheless benefit the rest of creation. Whereas normal consumption is almost by definition costly to the earth, this more rarefied form is almost by definition cheap and undamaging. This is a great practical virtue, since the results of normal, everyday consumer life now threaten to wreck everything around us. I've spent much of the past ten years writing about global warming, which is nothing more than the sum total of our lavish devotion to convenience, comfort, and power transmuted into several extra watts of solar energy per square meter of the earth's surface. It is human desire translated into planetary physics, and unless we can get those desires under some kind of control, the physics will turn impossible. By this analysis, though it may be bizarre to consume by not consuming, doing so is like supplanting heroin with methadone; one's cravings are stilled with minimum damage to the underlying system.

And yet there is something more to it than that. By its very nature, this kind of somewhat silly nonconsuming puts us in harm's way—raises the possibility that we will be exposed to forces that might actually change us, might begin to erode some of the conditioning we've carried since near birth. An example: when I lived in

New York City, I helped start a small homeless shelter at my church and spent many nights there. This was classic nonconsumer behavior, robbing me of many hours I might have spent in restaurants, bars, movie theaters, and boudoirs. But of course I did not do it primarily because I was a good Christian; I did it because I wanted the sense of being a slightly sainted fellow. Over time, however, the mere fact of being there began to change me in certain small ways. I learned that in some fashion it made me feel peaceful to do the small daily tasks of that place—changing the sheets, cooking the soup, delousing the pillowcases. It was one of the paths to learning not to resent housework, one way to cease the innate consumer desire for a maid (or a mother). In fact, I sensed, counterintuitively, that this work made me happy—a revelation that would not have surprised any of the long chain of gurus and Christs and other cranks down through the ages but certainly shocked my suburban soul. Having been exposed to some deeper (if transient) joy, I was marginally less of a sucker for the various ersatz appeals of popular culture.

Sometimes now I help with the campaign to return wolves to the Adirondacks. They were wiped out here in the last years of the nineteenth century by people who thought of them in the way realtors now think of blackflies—as an annoyance standing in the way of progress. I try not to pretend to myself, any more than I have to, that my main interest is with the wolves themselves or even with the health of the forest, which badly needs a top predator. I know that what I want is to hear a wolf howling in the woods because it will make this place, and my life here, feel yet more romantic. I will consume that wolf howl, just as my predecessors consumed the quiet of their suddenly wolfless nights. But once the wolf is there, its howl will also carry certain other, less obvious messages; and there will be the remote chance of an encounter with this other grand representative of creation, an encounter that might go beyond mere consumption. I saw a grizzly bear one recent summer in Alaska, not far away on a muddy bank on a foggy night, and the sheer reality of that encounter shook some small part of me out of the consumer enchantment into which I was born.

Blackflies accomplish this, too, in a subtler way. They remind me day after day in their season that I'm really *not* the center of the world, that I'm partly food, implicated in the crawl and creep of things. They are a humbling force, and even if for a time I can involve them in my self-aggrandizing myths, they still exert a slow and persuasive pressure of their own. Over the course of a decade, living in a place dominated by high mountains, wild winters, summer storms, trackless forest, and hungry insects has in fact warped me in certain ways. I am not the same person who came here. I am still a consumer; the consumer world was the world I emerged into, whose air I breathed for a very long time, and its assumptions still dominate my psyche—but maybe a little less so each year. And perhaps they dominate my daughter just a little less than that. There are times when I can feel the spell breaking in my mind—the spell of the advertiser on the tube, even the spell of the mythmaker in my mind. There are times when I can almost feel myself simply being.

. . .

At least for this year, Johnsburg decided not to use BTI. Instead, a questionnaire is being sent out with the tax bills. If the town were to treat the streams, it asks, would you be willing to give the workers access to your land? I think quite a few people—by no means a majority, but probably enough to make the plan unfeasible—will say no. Like me, they'll probably do it without quite knowing why. But it's one small sign for me that the enchantment is wearing off, that the incantation sung over our cradles by the television set may be less permanent than some think. A sign that spring may be coming—and with it the biting flies, by God.

# · 3 ·

## Human Restoration

*—The Return of the Wolf* (Middlebury College Press), 2000

The Hilton Hotel on the slope below the state capitol in Albany, New York, houses an endless rotation of people who would like the Empire State to behave in some particular way. One day it's the snack food dealers demanding lower taxes on potato chips, the next it's landlords fulminating against rent control, the next it's paving contractors with lists of new roads to build. They pass through in groups, distinguishable by name tag, feeding on buffets and open bars and trays of shrimp; when they meet a legislator they either shyly flatter or browbeat him depending on his seniority or vulnerability. They press the flesh, rub shoulders, build new relationships or reestablish old ones, elect leaders, and then they migrate on, back to the daily grind of selling Fritos or bitumen.

I've seen timber wolves exactly once in my life—a pair of them, in the downstairs ballroom of this very Hilton in the fall of 1996. An environmental group called Defenders of Wildlife was sponsoring a wolf conference at the hotel, with experts from all over the nation. "We chose Albany as our conference site in order to draw attention to our proposal to restore the eastern timber wolf to the

Great Woods of the Northeast," wrote the president of Defenders. In other words, they wanted something from the government too: permission to stick wolves back into, say, the Adirondack Park in northern New York, where I live, or the Maine Woods, or the White Mountain National Forest, or Vermont's Northeast Kingdom. Even though they were more earnest than the snack dealers, the Defenders came with the same sorts of apparatus—charts, polling surveys, the implicit promise that there might be a political payoff for those who supported such works. And they came with props—a pair of captive-born wolves from a wolf center somewhere out West. The conference organizers were savvy enough to know that two or three reporters might cover a conference full of papers on topics like "Evaluating Vasectomy as a Means of Wolf Control" and "Tracing the Life History of a Dispersing Female Wolf in Northern Wisconsin," but that every TV station in the neighborhood could be counted on to send a camera if there were living wolves to shoot.

Some functionary ushered all the reporters and camera crews into the subterranean ballroom; everyone plugged in their mikes; speeches were heard and literature distributed. And then, finally, a pair of handlers ushered in the wolves themselves. And suddenly everything changed. A cold front blew in, cutting the damp human-flavored air. The wolves showed next to no interest in the dais full of whirring motordrives and humming videocams; though they were on leashes, the room was theirs by right and they explored it thoroughly. One saw a thermostat high on a wall, and lifted up on his hind legs to look at it, stretching his long body till his muzzle reached the dial. The other stretched out on the carpet a moment. Those deep unselfconscious stretches, almost more feline than canine, declared them masters of the terrain—none of the tense jostling of photographers eager for a tighter shot, none of the favor-begging of the environmentalists. They were simply there. Not larger than life. It's just that human life seemed a bit smaller in their presence. They were life-size. They fit their skins. They didn't charge the air. They relaxed the air.

. . .

Since I've now exhausted my firsthand knowledge of wolves, let me move on to a topic I know something more about: a forest without wolves. I've spent some time in the New England forests, but my real experience is confined to the Adirondacks, a range of mountains that bulges out in a great dome from northern New York. Bordered roughly by Lake George and Lake Champlain on the east, Lake Ontario on the west, the St. Lawrence on the north, and the Mohawk valley on the south, the Adirondack Park covers a swath of land larger than Glacier, Grand Canyon, Yellowstone, and Yosemite national parks combined. On a map of the eastern United States, it's the large patch of green in the upper right-hand corner; if you fly over it in a light plane, that green patch on the map becomes a green patch of ground—unbroken trees as far as the eye can see, none of the clearcuts that checkerboard Oregon or Washington or Maine. It's just trees and mountains and lakes and rivers, interspersed with small towns scattered every ten or twenty miles.

What makes it interesting, however, is less its current beauty than its scarred past. Remember these two dates: 1899 and 1907. In 1899, St. Lawrence County paid the last bounty in northern New York on a dead wolf; as far as anyone knows, that was the last *Canis lupus* to lope through these mountains. Her death marked the symbolic end of an era of spasmodic destruction that had begun in the early nineteenth century, a space of six or seven decades that saw a nearly primeval forest cut over, burned, plowed, and polluted with great ferocity. People had come late to the central Adirondacks—the Indians used the mountains only as a seasonal hunting ground, and the first European didn't climb the range's highest peak until 1837, a generation after Lewis and Clark had returned from the Pacific. But when they came, they came with a vengeance. The first images of environmental destruction chiseled into the national imagination were lithographs and early photos of bare Adirondack hillsides sliding into creeks, of moonscape vistas from high peaks.

The epic destruction coincided with the birth of what we'd now call adventure tourism, as city dwellers rode the rails to escape the Industrial Revolution for a few weeks and enjoy this accessible paradise. (The first public building on earth with electric light was the big hotel on Blue Mountain Lake; that should give you some sense of it.) These tourists helped spur the efforts to protect the forest, which also gained support from downstate tycoons worrying that deforestation would silt in the economically all-important Hudson River, which rises in these mountains (an insight they gained at least in part by reading bestselling proto-ecologist George Perkins Marsh, the Vermont polymath who was then midwifing environmental science). Together they passed landmark laws creating the forest preserve, and began the slow task of buying land within that six-million-acre park. It's murky work trying to fix the right date for the end of the park's decline—while the state constitution was amended to draw a "blue line" around the Adirondacks in the 1890s, the most destructive logging may not have taken place until the early years of the twentieth century. But 1899 will do—the last wolf howl strangled, the wildness of the place seemingly gone. No bears were left, or almost none; no mountain lions, elk, or lynx. The Adirondacks had been subdued.

And then, eight years later, in 1907, something happened that seemed unimportant at the time. State officials released a few pairs of beavers from Yellowstone Park in a couple of drainages in the southernmost part of the Adirondack Mountains. The beaver had been extirpated too—trapped out for its pelt, its habitat cut down, dried up, dammed for mills. But now a few people were interested in bringing the beaver back. And it took. With protection from game wardens, the animals started to spread north, back into forests that were slowly recovering—many of them forests the state had bought, or taken over for nonpayment of taxes, forests protected as "forever wild" under the state constitution, where no human could cut a tree. The law did not apply to beaver, of course, and before long the early succession white birch were lying on the ground beside one pond after another, before long the dams were backing up trickles into wetlands on a thousand watersheds, before long the tail slaps of nighttime warning were cracking out across three thousand ponds.

This was the beginning of Adirondack restoration, one of the earliest such efforts anywhere. From 1907 on, people were trying not just to protect what was left of the Adirondacks, but to recover some of their original character. A great experiment was under way: could you unscramble an egg? Bruce Babbitt, Bill Clinton's gregarious secretary of the interior, insisted that restoration must be the hallmark of twenty-first-century conservation; in recent years he has already helped take out a few big dams. But for the Adirondacks (and in a subtler way for much of the eastern forest), the twentieth century has already been a restoration epoch. So what news do we have to share?

When I think about restoration, as I said, I begin by thinking about beavers. I try to imagine what these woods would be like if someone had not trucked the beavers out from Wyoming and let them go in a couple of streams. It would be much quieter, I think—the noisiest places I know in the woods are murky small sunlit ponds backed up by some intricate dam or another, algal places filled all summer with every kind of buzzing and droning and croaking. The beaver waddled back into the Adirondacks trailing life of infinite variety behind him. That's the first thing, obviously; restoring animals means restoring processes.

Other creatures wandered back too. I know old men in my town who can remember the first bear they ever saw, sometime in the 1930s. Now there are trees enough to hide them by the thousands: they hoot from the ridges by night, they leave great piles of berry-colored scat on the trail and wide claw tracks on the smooth-skinned beech. Every once in a while they get so lost in their eating that they don't hear you coming and then they finally do and crash off through the undergrowth, making your heart beat hard. I can't imagine this landscape without bears; it would seem *lean*, austere. Restoring animals means restoring the spirit of a place.

As the animals have returned, the forest has returned; ghost flora conjuring up ghost fauna and vice versa. About half the Adirondacks now belongs to the state as inviolate wilderness; the other half is in private hands, used mostly for timbering, but under fairly tight forestry laws that prevent the abuses common elsewhere. There is enough land that the moose wandered back about a decade ago, somehow crossing the highways and lakes that separate us from New England.

People reacted to the return of the moose in an interesting way. When big environmental groups, with tacit support from the state, proposed reintroducing the huge animals, many local residents hated the idea. In public meetings they worried aloud that the moose might spread disease to the deer herd, and that Adirondackers would surely die in collisions with the beasts (the haunch of a moose is just about windshield-high). And so the state backed off. But just about the same time, the moose began reestablishing themselves, and no one complained at all about that. In fact, people loved it—when a moose is spotted in our town, the phones begin to ring as everyone shares the news. Nature was simply taking its course, and that didn't seem to bother anyone.

If the wolf would simply walk back in—if a pack from Algonquin Park in Ontario would simply decide to wander south a few hundred miles—then I suspect they too would be greeted with open arms. But that isn't going to happen, because big highways, broad stretches of open farm valley, and the St. Lawrence River all stand in the way. The wolf, killed off by people a century ago, needs people to bring it back. Which is a problem.

Even two decades ago, the idea of reintroducing wolves here would have been a nonstarter, ludicrous. But it's easy to underestimate how successfully environmentalists have shifted people's thinking, at least about animals. The Red Riding Hood crowd is smaller now, and mostly older. At least as many people have some Farley Mowat story stashed away in their hearts. When Defenders of Wildlife commissioned a poll in 1996, a huge majority of New Yorkers, and a substantial majority of Adirondackers, favored bringing back the wolf.

That doesn't mean a restoration would happen easily, though. Among the park's political powers, there is little support for reintroduction. County governments have passed symbolic resolutions prohibiting the release of "dangerous predators" within their borders; various barroom heroes have boasted to the newspapers that they would kill the creatures if they ever appeared. Some of their arguments have been pretty tenuous; a great deal of concern is expressed for the almost nonexistent livestock of these forested mountains, for example. The visceral opposition comes mostly from people who don't want to be pushed around from outside, who don't want someone else telling them what to do. In the words of a leader of the Adirondack Association of Towns and Villages, approached by a reporter on the day that Defenders first suggested a reintroduction: "I don't know much about it, but I'm sure we're against it." Against some outside notion of what constitutes the proper forest.

No one even knows if a reintroduction would be successful—the first reports from biologists cast doubt on the ability of the Adirondacks to support a pack, in part because they fear too many would be shot. But the deeper debate goes on outside the facts. What constitutes a wilderness restored? Is the process begun in 1907 still under way, or has it reached its limit? How far can restoration go in a place where human beings live? Because, of course, what makes the Adirondacks interesting, besides its scarred past, is its peopled present. This is not like Yellowstone, where you need to worry about the surrounding ranchers; here, wilderness and human settlement are completely interwined.

We know that human beings can wipe out most other large

creatures; we know that if humans set aside a large enough wilderness they can save most creatures (though we're only beginning to appreciate how large, and how intact, that land must sometimes be). What we don't know—and it's a fairly important question for a world of six billion people headed for ten—is whether in the modern age you can have small but complete human settlements amidst intact wilderness. That's the experiment the Adirondacks, without exactly knowing it, undertook a century ago; that's the experiment that environmentalists have begun in many tropical regions within the last decade. It's still a new experiment. The results are only starting to trickle in.

Often, in the winter, I'll be out skiing on some backcountry lake and come across the stomach, the head, the hooves, and some of the skin of a deer. That's all that's left a day after the coyotes have chased it out on the ice, the whitetail's skinny legs windmilling till they snap. When the coyotes eat their fill, the ravens descend, and so on down a long cafeteria line.

One way of asking if a place has been restored is to ask if its biology works, if something is missing that causes something else to be out of balance, and so on. If you visit my in-laws' house in suburban Connecticut, the answer couldn't be clearer. They have no rosebushes left. Pie plates dangle from their shrubberies in an effort to keep the deer at bay. Does and fawns browse with utter unconcern in the backyard; if you run out to chase them away, they look at you with unconcealed contempt. Since you can't hunt very well in this land of cul-de-sacs, and since there are no predators, and since people have created a smorgasbord of browse with their lawns and gardens, it is deer heaven. As Richard Nelson makes clear in his classic book *Heart and Blood: Living with Deer in America*, most of America is now deer heaven for just such reasons: "By 1991 an estimated 1,500 whitetails lived within the city limits of Philadelphia. That is more than the total number of deer inhabiting the state of Pennsylvania in 1900."

But in the Adirondacks you don't see so many deer. They are

there—on many lakes you can see a good browse line, where they've nibbled the lower branches of the shoreline hemlocks to the same height as they stood on the ice—but three things have kept their numbers in some kind of check. First, there's not a lot of opening in the forest; without clear-cuts, and with three million acres of the park off-limits to any logging at all, sunlight doesn't reach the forest floor in sufficient quantity to grow great pastures of browse. Second, humans hunt them. And third, in these mountains the coyote has grown into something like a wolf.

Coyotes are supposed to be lone scroungers, loping through the world looking for an easy meal. They are superbly adaptable (a biologist I knew once said, "when the last man dies there will be a coyote howling over his grave"), but we don't think of them as a top predator. In the absence of the wolf, however, that may be how they have evolved in parts of the American East. Our coyotes are big, they have learned to hunt in packs, and they eat a lot of whitetail—the 1,200 coyotes now living in the Adirondacks may consume 12,000 deer annually. So if you have a wolf substitute, why do you need a wolf, especially if it might mean Government Restrictions of some kind?

The biological answer is not completely clear. Wolves and coyotes aren't identical; coyotes haven't learned how to kill beaver as efficiently as wolves do, for instance, and so beaver numbers are booming (just ask the road crews who spend half the year draining flooded roads). And despite the fears of the sportsmen, wolves might actually benefit human hunters; if the biologists are right, they will chase off lots of coyotes, perhaps enough to actually diminish the wild deer kill. But it's not an overpowering argument. The mountains like wolves, as Aldo Leopold pointed out so memorably, but they have probably come to appreciate the coyote as well.

There's a kind of theological argument too, of course. Wolves were here, and we chased them out, so we should invite them back. Amen, hallelujah, thanks be to Noah.

I've felt the power of this kind of reasoning. A few years back I spent some time on the Alligator River National Wildlife Refuge on the Atlantic shore of North Carolina, an aggressively nasty place. Old pine plantation, absolutely flat, gridded with dirt roads that ran at right angles, microwaved by the sun, guarded by nine kinds of things that fly and bite, and two or three that slither and bite. I'm sure that if you grew up there you might develop some slight affection for the place, but every tourist I saw was heading swiftly for the Barrier Islands. Yet something incredible hung in the air, for it was in this place that *Canis rufus*, the red wolf, had been resurrected.

Red wolves once ran across much of the continent; they may have made it up into the Adirondacks. But by the 1980s, just a few were left in the United States, hanging out in Texas. They weren't going to hang on many years more, so federal officials hauled the last ones into zoos. This strand of DNA, this voice on the land, this particular fancy of creation, seemed to have run its course, and not just in one place, like the Adirondack beaver, but every place. Forever. But the environmentalists and the feds hadn't quite given up, and they found a piece of land in eastern North Carolina, in the former range of the red wolf, to reintroduce them into the world. In 1987, the Fish and Wildlife Service opened some cages and released four pairs of captive-born adult red wolves. By the mid-1990s, ninety-four pups had been born in the wild. These were fourth- and fifth-generation wild wolves.

I didn't see them—I only see the wolves in hotel ballrooms. A Fish and Wildlife worker drove me around the refuge for long hot hours, sticking rank bait in traps as he tried to catch some study animals that needed new batteries in their radio collars. I didn't hear them howl or bark; I just heard their beeping transmitters as I held the antenna out the window and we tried to home in on them. But that didn't much matter—it was the simple fact that these wolves existed that mattered. For a while the red wolf had not existed; it was alive in a zoo somewhere, but that was nothing more than keeping its DNA on ice. It hadn't existed as part of the sweet battle and concert of life bumping up against other life, and now it did again. God smiled.

For the timber wolf in the North Woods, though, the case is not so clear. Wolves live other places—lots of them in Alaska and Canada, healthy and well-established populations in Minnesota and Wisconsin, the new packs roaming Yellowstone. They have become accepted in most of those places, just as the red wolf has become accepted in North Carolina. Long caravans of cars go out on nighttime wolf-howling expeditions. In Minnesota, they named their damn basketball team for them, and tens of thousands of people visit the International Wolf Center in Ely, a hard-to-get-to little town hard by the Canadian border that now boasts daily plane service from the Twin Cities. At least on this continent, wolves seem safe as a species.

So if the wolf doesn't need to be here, and the deer don't need them here, who needs them? Might it be the same species that needs cable TV, high-speed modems, hair transplants, twenty-one-speed mountain bikes, frappucinos, frappucino grandes, frappucino tres grandes? Could it be the same species that needs two-thousand-square-foot houses and monster trucks and 17-gigabyte hard drives? Could be.

· · ·

The world as we now know it is shaped by human desire, especially by the incredible needs developed by the affluent West in a single century. Those needs shaped the landscape in obvious ways—the suburbs with their endless circling roads are desire poured from the back of a cement mixer, the desire for convenience, comfort, privacy, individuality. And now those needs shape the landscape in more insidious and permanent ways. You can read our desires, our needs, in every cubic meter of the air, and in every upward inching of the thermometer. Our needs for mobility, for elbow room, for never getting too hot or cold or bored, all require the consumption of gas and oil and coal, and that endless combustion fills the atmosphere with carbon dioxide. Spring comes to the northern hemisphere a week earlier now than it did two decades ago, because of our needs. The warmer air holds more water vapor, and hence severe storms are twenty percent more common—that's our appetite at work. The warmer oceans expand, and glacier melt pours more water into the sea; the scientists say that the Atlantic and the Pacific will be a couple of feet higher before this century is out, thanks to our needs. We are machines for generating needs and then generating technologies to fill those needs (and sometimes the other way around). So what might it mean to say we need the wolf?

We need something new to consume. We need wolf howl, we need the little frisson that comes with thinking: there's a wolf pack out here in these woods where I'm spending the summer. This kind of symbolic consumption is old news, of course. Folks buy Durangos or Blazers or Pathfinders or Dakotas or Tahoes or Expeditions or the other behemoths of the sport utility tribe knowing full well they'll never take them off road. The extra fifty horsepower and thousand pounds of steel and eight inches of clearance give them rights to a certain image. You can buy it for two bucks in a pack of Marlboros. In the same way, I'd like wolves in my backyard because I'd like to think of my backyard as wonderfully rugged. The more rugged my backyard, the more rugged I can claim to be. I live with wolves, or I vacation with wolves, hence I am close kin to Kevin Costner. It rubs off. That's how consumerism works in an age when we're light-years past food and clothes and shelter.

In Abruzzo, Italy, where an active recovery plan brought the wolf back from the edge of extirpation (in a park one-sixtieth the size of the Adirondacks), 2,500 tourists a year used to visit Civitella Alfredena; now they've opened a wolf museum and 100,000 come annually. Wolf tourism is one of the big advantages cited by the environmentalists who want to reintroduce the animals, but there's something a bit creepy about it. The biologists at Algonquin say it doesn't damage the wolves to have organized howling parties out night after night in the summer, but who knows? It might damage the howlers—it's only an inch away from paying some sleazeball aquarium owner for the chance to swim with their dolphins and caress their blowholes. It's consuming, literally, the time and the attention and the wildness of another creature for some little jolt in return. For a story to tell when you get back from your trip. *It's about you.* The wolf becomes one more thing to experience, to own in some way or another. We live in a culture capable of taking a Civil War battlefield and transforming it into a theme park. We live in a culture fully capable of taking a wolf howl and turning it into a commodity.

But maybe we still live in a culture capable of more than that.

· · ·

Most Civil War battlefields haven't been handed over to the theme-park developers, thank heaven. Many of them, in the custody of the Park Service, lie in that fast-suburbanizing corner of Maryland and Virginia and Pennsylvania, curious eddies of open space in a tide of pavement that has swept by on all sides. They have very little to do with that culture—the battlefields speak not to convenience or comfort, but to honor, obedience, glory, to that whole compound of older martial virtues now mostly mysterious to us. When we stroll Bloody Angle or the Sunken Road, when we climb Seminary Ridge, we visit powerfully different ideas of what we might be. Men gave their lives here for the Union? For Virginia? It's not that these were necessarily wise ideas—it may be far better to think of Virginia as an interchangeable place with San Jose or Tampa, a place to live until it's time to move. Glory and honor and obedience have caused their share of pain over the years. But the mere existence of these spots helps keep these alternate conceptions of human life alive and real.

I grew up in Lexington, Massachusetts, and I spent my summers in a tricorne hat, giving tours of the Battle Green. Some part of my political restlessness comes from endlessly reciting the story of the eight men killed on that common, men who inhabited a moral universe profoundly different from the moral universe of the twentieth-century Boston suburb that was otherwise shaping my soul. I remember the night in 1973 when I was twelve and I saw my father and five hundred other good suburbanites arrested because they refused to leave that Green during a protest of the war in Vietnam. They might have behaved the same way on some anonymous patch of ground, but they might not have, too; for an evening, two centuries of time collapsed, and Captain Parker's admonition to his troops ("If they mean to have a war let it begin here") nerved up another militia. We journey to Rome, to Mecca, to Benares, to Antietam, to Birmingham, and to the shiny black wall of the Vietnam Memorial with the sense that something there might change us. A pilgrimage, by definition.

So if we should be wary of how our endless neediness might shape our encounter with the wolf, we should be equally open to the idea that the wolf might be one force able to help us to reshape our endless neediness. The encounter with history at a battlefield or a shrine might be like the encounter with real wildness in a forest or a mountain or a seacoast; each might hold the power to break us out of the enchantment under which we now labor, the enchantment of things, an enchantment that is quite literally wrecking the world.

In fact, I would go further than that. Contact with the natural world is one of the two forces potentially powerful enough to break through the endless jamming static of our culture and open us to other, wider possibilities. (The other force is contact with the nonpossessive forms of love, be they found at Fredericksburg or in Mother Teresa's hospice.) I have seen this effect in enough people, myself sometimes included, to be confident of its truth. Show me an environmentalist who did not start with an encounter with the more-than-human world, and I will show you an exception to the rule. And try to find someone who has had such an encounter without it changing her politics, her priorities, her very sense of self.

This encounter need not be wild in the traditional sense—it need not involve Gore-Tex. Consider E. O. Wilson and his ants, or Rachel Carson wandering her short stretch of the Maine coast. Consider the bird-watchers of Central Park, necks eternally stiff from their involvement in the modest life above them. For those of us with thicker shells, however, some starker wildness, some drama, helps kick the message home. John Muir, on his Thousand Mile Walk to the Gulf, found himself fixated on the notion of alligators; later, in his exuberant first summer in the Sierra, a season that defined forever our grammar of wildness, it was earthquakes and windstorms as well as sunny afternoons and butterflies that helped him understand that "we are now in the mountains and they are now in us, making every nerve quiet, filling every pore and cell of us."

I've had some of the same sense of dissolving into the world on days when I've stood staring at grizzly tracks in Alaskan mud. But I felt it much more one day in the woods behind my house. I was wandering along, happy for the exercise but lost as usual in some plan, lost as usual in my own grandness. Suddenly, the fiercest pain I've ever felt boiled up my torso toward my face. I whirled, staggered downslope, cracked into a tree, fell; by now I could see the yellowjackets coating my T-shirt. I ran, flicked, ran; eventually they were gone. But I could tell I was reacting to their venom. Hives popped out across my upper body. All I could think of for a minute were all the risks I'd heard dismissed by comparing them with bee stings: "you're less likely to die by tornado/plane crash/shark attack." But as I jogged back through the woods the few trailless miles to my house, I found those thoughts replaced by another almost overpowering urge. The urge to pray, and not a prayer of supplication but a prayer of thanksgiving. The trees had never looked more treelike, the rocky ridges more solid and rich, the world more real. The drama had somehow taken me out of myself, and though the sensation faded as the weeks passed, it has never disappeared altogether.

As I tried to describe the experience to others, I would say it was the first time I had felt a part of the food chain. But that was glib. In some way it was the first time I'd felt a part of any chain other than the human one. The first time I glimpsed the sheer overpowering realness of the world around me, the first time I'd realized fully that it was something more than a stage set for my life.

. . .

A healthy wolf has never attacked and killed a person in this country—yellowjackets are several orders of magnitude more dangerous, and let's not even discuss the Durangos and the Blazers and the Pathfinders. In a way, though, it's almost too bad that news is spreading of their benign image, almost too bad that people are starting to think of them as cuddly. Too bad because it's not true (on the basis of my hotel ballroom encounter, I will say I have rarely seen a being more aloof), and too bad because some of their power to shake us from our enchantment comes from their dramatic image.

Beavers just happened to be extirpated from the East; it was their poor luck that fashion found a use for the skin with which evolution had equipped them. But wolves were extirpated systematically, based on our understanding of their wolf nature. No creature save perhaps the snake has been more unremittingly vilified—the little pigs cowering in their shoddy homes, Little Red Riding Hood deceived by the granny-killer, werewolves snarling from page and screen, the very language making them the image of poverty ("the wolf at the door") and of the predatory male.

As much as anything else, that's the reason we need to invite them back in. Not to make it up to them—wolves roam outside the culture of victimhood—but because it is hard for us to do so. It would be a meaningful gesture.

You must remember that the Adirondacks, the Whites, the

Greens, the North Woods of Maine are four or five or six hours' drive from Madison Avenue, from the epicenter of the idea that everything should be easy. They are four or five or six hours north of the first suburbs on the planet, those ever-expanding monuments to the goddess convenience. They are due north of the megalopolis, of the notion that humans might survive in an entirely human corridor. They are, in other words, within range of the problem that needs solving.

I've been circling the exact nature of that problem, for it is daunting to search out the central point of a culture, but to state it as clearly as I can: we believe too firmly that we, each of us as individuals, are the most important things on earth. This belief is so strong in us that we begin to imagine that things we have not created are not quite real. Thus, we can fret with real worry about dangers to the economy (the chance, say, that the Y2K computer bug might damage it) but we cannot muster the same concern for the natural world, which seems to us more abstract. Certainly we cannot muster enough concern to actually change the ways in which we live so as to protect that natural world. Only the largest jolts break through that shell, allow us to feel small in any way. Look at the few books about the natural world popular at the moment; invariably they concern climbs up Mount Everest (and only deadly climbs at that), or storms producing hundred-foot boat-eating waves; consider the vogue for adventure travel. How much has changed even in the course of a hundred years, since the time that gentle John Burroughs, with his stories about woodchucks and chickadees, reigned as the most popular writer of any sort in the nation.

Which in turn reminds us of how new this particular problem is, at least in certain ways. Humans have always tended toward selfishness, always thought too much of themselves—that's the message from the Buddha, from the Christ. But for most of human history, we had other problems too. No one living in the Adirondacks a century ago, or in any part of America fifty years before that, was in any danger of forgetting that the world was real, any more than someone inhabiting the delta of Bangladesh at the moment is likely to forget. Our forebears faced the very real problem of individual survival—of getting food on the table—and so, even with the benefit of hindsight, it seems wrong to condemn them for chasing the wolf away. Theirs was still the age-old problem that humans are slow and hairless and dull-sensed.

But that's not *our* problem. In this country, at this moment, our problem is somehow reining ourselves in, figuring out that each one of us does not reside at the exact center of the universe. We marinate in that idea—the idea that there should be no limits placed on us. And we have the technology to annihilate those limits at least temporarily. That is a dangerous combination. Many of the dangers of our moment—environmental, societal, psychological—flow from that sense that we're all that counts.

· · ·

By now the conceit of this essay should be apparent. It's not wolves that stand in need of restoration; wolves, though chased to the fringes of the continent, have managed to retain their essence. Even tied on leashes in the windowless basement ballroom of a slightly shabby hotel they were what they were.

People, on the other hand, especially the subspecies that inhabits the Western world, and especially the troop of them that has grown up on the eastern edge of North America, find themselves badly out of balance, operating under the influence of a spell. An intoxication, with ourselves. It's an intoxication that will likely grow deeper as the next few decades progress. Our unthinking consumption of resources has now reached the point where we are changing the global temperature, and with it the speed of the wind, the size of storms, the pace of the seasons. When we see the formerly natural world, we see ourselves. Our morally casual manipulation of genes may mean that within a very short time most of the organisms that we see around us will reflect our desires—will reflect us. We may be entering a period of overwhelming and un-avoidable loss, of species extinction so profound that it may leave us with a planet almost empty of other meanings. The enchant-ment that prevents us from recognizing our peril as a peril, spiri-tual as well as pragmatic, and from making the changes necessary to correct—that enchantment is our problem.

Happily, any child's bookshelf provides a series of recipes for dealing with dangerous enchantments. It's not the kisses of princes that will wake us up in time; our culture is one long wet kiss. But maybe the howl of a wolf might help, the howl of a wolf echoing out over the hills of the East.

# · 4 ·

# Enoughness

*—Resurgence,* March/April 2005

Last evening, on the longest day of the year, I took a walk in a meadow near my home.

At the edge of the meadow a path opened into the woods, and I followed it perhaps a hundred yards to the bank of a small stream where I rested on a rock and watched the brook flow. Then I walked back.

Nothing spectacular happened. No large animal jumped out to demonstrate its majesty. The flora was beautiful but unremarkable: buttercups, Queen Anne's lace, daisies, lupins. The sky didn't crackle with summer lightning; the sunset was only streaks of purple, some rosy glow on the underbellies of the clouds. A few mosquitoes made their presence known. It was simply a lovely night.

And simply the sort of scene that we have evolved with for hundreds of thousands of years, that has made us who we are, that we can't be fully human, or at least fully sane, without. The sort of scene whose absence in our lives is now making us slowly crazy. If there is a pertinent modern question, it is "How much is enough?" The consumer societies we have created posit that the only possible answer is "More." And so in pursuit of more we have turned ourselves into tubby folk, raised the temperature of the planet one degree with a further five degrees in prospect, countenanced the ever deeper gulfs between rich and poor, and so on. And in the process made ourselves . . . happy?

But say you're in a meadow, surrounded by wildflowers. Do you find yourself thinking, "They could do with some more wildflowers over there"? Do you glance up at the mountains on the horizon and think, "Some more mountains would be nice"? Do you lie on the rock by the brook thinking, "This brook needs more rocks"? Does the robin in that tree chide herself for not tripling the size of her nest? I think not. Nature schools us in sufficiency—its aesthetic and its economy demonstrate "enoughness" at every turn. Time moves circularly through the natural world—next spring there will be wildflowers again. Not more wildflowers: second quarter output for 2005 will show no year-on-year gain. Growth only replaces, since the planet is already accomplishing all the photosynthesis that's possible. It offers the great lesson of being simultaneously abundant and finite.

Interdependent, too. The emergent science of ecology is easily summed up: everything's connected. Field biologists using sensitive detectors have discovered that the needles of trees near Alaskan rivers owe their nitrogen to the carcasses of salmon that die along the banks, the same salmon that feed the bears whose pawing aerates the soil that . . .

We know now that this is true, but interconnection is anathema to a consumer notion of the world, where each of us is useful precisely to the degree that we consider ourselves the center of everything. We believe that pleasure comes from being big, outsized, immortal; now our zealots imagine genetically engineering us for greater greatness. But the testimony of the rest of creation is that there's something to be said for fitting in.

And because of that, the natural world offers us a way to think about dying, the chief craziness for the only species that can anticipate its own demise. If one is a small part of something large, if that something goes on forever, and if it is full of beauty and meaning, then dying seems less shocking. Which undermines about half the reason for being a dutiful consumer, for holding aging forever at bay. Six months from now, on the shortest night of the year, this field will be under two feet of snow. Most of what I can see will be dead or dormant. And six months after that it will be here again as it is tonight.

Advertising, hyperconsumerism, ultra-individualism—these are designed to make you crazy. Nature, like close-knit human community, is designed to help you stay sane. You needn't be in the wilderness to feel in balm: a park, a container garden on the patio, a pet dog, a night sky, a rainstorm will do. For free.

# · 5 ·

## Full Circle

—*Nature Conservancy,* Summer 2006

We stuck our canoes in the water at Round Lake—a name that tells you confoundingly little. There are Round lakes and Round ponds scattered across the Adirondack region; I can call to mind half a dozen without even looking at a map. There's so unbelievably much water here that it must have exceeded the imaginative reserves of the early settlers. With few Indian names to draw on (Native Americans used the central Adirondacks as a summer hunting ground, not a permanent settlement), the first European arrivals were left to their own devices for designating roughly three thousand lakes and ponds and countless rivers and streams. Hence Round. Also Clear. Also Mud. Also Fish.

But our trip, more precisely, began at the end of Round Lake at an old rock dam, started in 1892, that was designed to raise the level of the water in the spring so that lumbermen could flush a winter's worth of logs down to the mill. The dam (which has made the lake anything but round) does in fact tell you something about this place: though very wild, the land we'd be traveling for the rest of the week isn't wilderness. People have used it, and in some cases used it hard, since the late nineteenth century. Perhaps you could say it's in recovery now; perhaps that's what this trip was really celebrating.

I was joined in my journey by the Frenette brothers, Jim and Bill. For me, the chance to paddle with the Frenettes was as sweet as the chance to paddle the newly conserved lands that would make our route possible. At ages seventy-six and seventy-eight, respectively, Jim (former head of the land zoning commission) and Bill (a former trustee of the Nature Conservancy's Adirondack chapter) are nearly as much landmarks of this place as the mountains circling the lakes. After a lifetime of hunting, fishing, hiking, skiing, snowshoeing, dog sledding, and otherwise reconnoitering this landscape, they were the best possible guides. Except for one thing: they kept disappearing over the horizon, their effortless tandem paddling pulling them steadily away from me in my solo boat.

We set out at noon, on a perfect high-summer day, big fair-weather clouds in a blue sky, a small wind at our backs as we went from Round Lake on to Little Tupper (named for being smaller than Tupper Lake, which was named for the surveyor who'd first mapped it). Little Tupper was long the summer home of the Whitneys, as in, for instance, Manhattan's Whitney Museum. A few years ago the state finally managed to persuade the family matriarch to sell the lake so it could be added to the nearly 3 million acres of the Adirondack Forest Preserve lands—lands within Adirondack Park that were designated "forever wild" by the New York legislature in 1885. The remainder of the 6-million-acre park is private land, including small hamlets, timberlands, farms, homes, and camps.

And loons. We were halfway down the lake when we noticed a collection of eleven large birds a little to our left. They looked like loons, but none of us had ever before seen them gather in such flotillas, except sometimes right before they migrate. They didn't leave us guessing for long—they broke out into a cacophony of unmistakable tremolos and trills and stern laughter, the loon music that would inhabit our dreams each night of this journey. With their benediction at our backs, we paddled past the peninsula where a Whitney hunting camp, Camp Bliss, had been removed and the land allowed to return to forest, and then chased a decorous great blue heron down a short stream into Rock Pond (I can think of half a dozen Rock ponds, too), where we spent the night.

A clear night with the moon just past full, a heavy dew to shake from our tents, a rising sun as we paddled across Rock Pond, and an osprey to watch over us as we made our way. "That nest was there in 1960," said Bill. "Right on the same branch. How about that." Almost too good to be true, which also could be said of the day's start: we'd paddled only twenty minutes when the time came to get out, pack gear, and start the first of many portages. In the Adirondacks we call them "carries," but never mind—they're the same the world over, the sweaty toll extracted for the right to skim these lakes, these highways of the forest. This carry began with a series of epic mudholes. I nearly lost a sandal in the very first and had to stick my arm in well past the shoulder to pull it out, affording me a neat layer of Adirondack sunscreen. Fortunately, Bill and Jim were (as usual) out of sight up ahead, sparing me the indignity of an audience.

The rhythm lasted most of the day: short paddles across small ponds, long carries between them, and occasional stops for landmarks, like the spot near Touhey Falls where in the early 1930s one logging baron had built a railroad to get his logs out. The tracks were gone now, but the level grade remained, a reminder that though we were the only people out in these wild tracts, we were accompanied by ghosts of a busier day. Ghosts who were doubtless giggling as we humped the canoes along the last hard carry of the day, and then settled with some relief into the waters of Shingle Shanty Brook, a glorious meander that doubled back on itself in infinite and hypnotic variations. Exploring the brook, barely a paddle's width across in many places, was like meandering the hallways of a vast country estate: around one corner, and another, and another, never sure what treasure would be revealed next. Cardinal flowers, in this case; great scarlet banks of them.

And then finally, as the sun was losing its sweaty power, out we came from the reeds into the sweeping shallow bay at the end of Lake Lila, a beloved queen of Adirondack waters. Lila Vanderbilt was the wife of the man who owned these lands once—another nineteenth-century baron, this one named William Seward Webb. In 1978 the Conservancy bought the lake and surrounding forests and transferred them to the state. Lila has been a favorite of paddlers ever since. We pulled tired into a campsite along a sandy beach, and swam, and waited. Waited because we knew that Todd Dunham of the Conservancy staff was even now paddling in to join us. Waited because we suspected he might be bringing beer.

As it turned out, we were right: Saranac Ale, one of the finer local brews. And he brought stories, too—in particular, the story of how the Conservancy had come to purchase the 26,500 acres at either end of our trip, the land that made this extended journey possible. "Seven or eight years ago, International Paper did an analysis of what it was costing them to pay taxes on the bodies of water where they couldn't grow any trees," Dunham said. "Even with leasing lands to hunting camps, the taxes on waterfront property were so huge that they couldn't cover their costs." The company brought together a variety of Adirondack interests, including the Conservancy, to discuss the prospects for the lakes, but real action waited until a real estate agent found a buyer for Round Lake, the eight-hundred-acre gem where we'd begun our journey. "Their buyer was ready to meet IP's price," Dunham added. "But when they were a month from closing, the company said to us, 'If you can match this price, you can buy it.'

"It wasn't cheap," said Dunham. "But when was the last time someone sold an eight-hundred-acre lake around here? So we started throwing all sorts of various pieces on the table. Would you sell us this, and this and this? By the end, we were up to 26,500 acres." The land was protected less with an eye to particular rare species (indeed, much of the acreage had been heavily and repeatedly logged) than with the knowledge that it would consolidate some 195,000 acres of protected land around it—including the Five Ponds Wilderness, one of the Adirondacks' largest wilderness areas. That it would also round out the great canoe routes of the area was a bonus. "We got one tour of the property in an IP pickup truck, but that was enough to help us realize the recreational possibilities," says Dunham. That helped interest the state of New York, which is in the process of purchasing some of the land from the Conservancy for inclusion in the Adirondack Forest Preserve.

Anywhere else in the eastern United States, 26,500 acres would be a huge land purchase. In the Adirondacks, the deal will add less than 1 percent to the total protected land in Adirondack Park. Which raises the question: is it as urgent to buy land here as in other places? There's no perfect answer to that query, but here's why I think so: there's almost no other place in the country, and certainly nowhere else in the East, where the chance exists to complete, not begin, the cycle of protection. Elsewhere it's crucial scraps and remnants and odd corners that get bought in a mad scramble to save them ahead of the developers. But here, because of the century-old state commitment to wilderness, those scraps and corners are rounding out a whole, allowing us to imagine what a truly conserved landscape looks like. In many places we have no choice but to save fragments of the old tunes, allowing us to imagine what once they sounded like and what they might sound like again some day in the distant future. In the Adirondacks, as in Alaska, you can hear the symphony as it was meant to be played.

Philosophical reflection ceased at 8:30 the next morning, which was the hour we finished our paddle across Lake Lila and plunged into the woods. This was the carry we'd been talking about since we began—relatively short, but absolutely trackless, save for a few pieces of flagging along a route that Jim had explored a few weeks before.

It was here that my canoe really came into its sweet own. Built by Adirondack craftsman Pete Hornbeck, it's a high-tech knockoff of a cedar-strip design built in the nineteenth century for an early Adirondack explorer. It paddles beautifully on open lake, and even better in narrow channels, but you really bless its builder when you come to a carry like this one. That's because it weighs about fourteen pounds. You can put on your pack and sling the boat over your shoulder like a giant handbag, then negotiate fallen trees, moss-slicked rocks, crowding alders, scraping spruces. It took us twenty minutes, and suddenly we popped out into the sunshine at Harrington Pond, another long, flowing, marshy land, this one rich in purple pickerel weed.

We hauled the canoes out of the water once more half an hour later, this time on a railroad track, the one that was used for generations by freight and passenger trains running north from Utica into the heart of the mountains. Jim and Bill were soon telling stories. "I can remember watching the train stop at Dr. Webb's private depot," said Bill. "We'd scratch the frost off the windows and watch the people getting down, the staff with lanterns there to greet them. It was real pretty." Their grandfather had been an engineer on the railroad. In fact, in 1908, when a great fire ignited by sparks hitting logging slash had swept through the area, he'd backed the train down these tracks into the tiny town of Sabattis to rescue the encircled inhabitants. Now, shielded from the hot sun by the boats on our heads, we just trudged slowly along.

After crossing diminutive Clear Pond, we spent the night in a grove of hemlocks on a little peninsula jutting into Bog Lake. I swam for a while, and then wandered off along the old logging roads on the only kind of biological survey for which I am well qualified: I found not only blueberries, not only lush and heavy raspberries, but even a few bushes of early, perfectly ripe blackberries.

At sunrise the next morning, we set off on our final day's paddle, out the marshy outlet of Bog Lake and on to Lows Lake, another long, narrow, well-loved sheet of Adirondack water. It had been the center of Augustus Low's nineteenth-century empire. At one time, insisted Bill, the maple trees in this vast sugarbush had produced more syrup than the entire state of Vermont. "And it would win all the medals at their state fair, too, till they made a rule that the entries had to come from Vermont."

The longer we paddled, the longer I listened to the stories of the Frenettes, and the more I saw the old rail tracks and the scars of the logging fires and the remnants of the nineteenth-century baronial camps, the more I understood why these purchases seem so vital to me. The Adirondacks are perhaps the world's greatest experiment in ecological recovery, a place hard used a century ago and now slowly reverting, slowly proving that where humanity backs off, nature rebounds. And these parcels are paradigmatic: few places in the Adirondacks have been worked as many ways, have had as much timber and game and beauty wrung out of them. And now all of that hard use is slowly ceasing.

I tried my theory out on Jim. "Yeah, I guess," he said. "It's like an old man that works hard all his life, and then when he's done he gets to sit still and relax." And then he winked and tossed his canoe up on his shoulders and trotted off across the next carry.

# · II ·

# THE
# CHANGING PLANET

# · 6 ·

## The End of Nature:
## The Greenhouse Experiment

—*The New Yorker*, September 11, 1989

Svante Arrhenius took his doctorate at the University of Uppsala in 1884. His thesis earned him the lowest possible grade short of outright failure. Nineteen years later, the same thesis, which was on the conductivity of solutions, earned him a Nobel Prize. He later explained the initial poor reception: "I came to my professor, Cleve, whom I admired very much, and I said, 'I have a new theory of electrical conductivity as a cause of chemical reactions.' He said, 'This is very interesting,' and then he said, 'Good-bye.' He explained to me later that he knew very well that there are so many different theories formed, and that they are almost all certain to be wrong, for after a short time they disappeared; and therefore, by using the statistical manner of forming his ideas, he concluded that my theory also would not exist long."

Arrhenius's understanding of electrolytic conduction was not his only shrug-provoking new idea. As he surveyed the first few decades of the Industrial Revolution, he realized that man was burning coal at an unprecedented rate—"evaporating our coal mines into the air." Scientists already knew that carbon dioxide, a by-product of fossil-fuel combustion, trapped solar infrared radiation that would otherwise have been reflected back to space. The French polymath Jean-Baptiste-Joseph Fourier had speculated about the effect nearly a century before, and had even used the hothouse metaphor. But it was Arrhenius, employing measurements of infrared radiation from the full moon, who did the first calculations of the possible effects of man's stepped-up production of carbon dioxide. The average global temperature, he concluded, would rise as much as nine degrees Fahrenheit if the amount of carbon dioxide in the air doubled from its preindustrial level; that is, heat waves in mid-American latitudes would run as high as a hundred and thirty degrees, the seas would rise several meters, crops would wither in the fields.

This idea floated in obscurity for a very long time. Now and then, a scientist took it up—the British physicist G. S. Callendar speculated in the 1930s that rising carbon-dioxide levels could account for the warming of North America and northern Europe which meteorologists had begun to observe in the 1880s. But that warming seemed to be replaced by a decline, beginning in the 1940s; in any case, we were too busy creating better living through petroleum to be bothered with such long-term speculation. And the few scientists who did consider the matter concluded that the oceans, which hold much more carbon dioxide than the atmosphere, would soak up any excess that man churned out—that the oceans were an infinite sink down which to pour the problem.

Then, in 1957, two scientists at the Scripps Institution of Oceanography, in California, Roger Revelle and Hans Suess, published a paper in the journal *Tellus* on this question of the oceans. What they found may turn out to be the single most important limit in an age of limits. They found that the conventional wisdom was wrong: the upper layer of the oceans, where the air and sea meet and transact their business, would absorb less than half of the excess carbon dioxide produced by man. "A rather small change in the amount of free carbon dioxide dissolved in seawater corresponds to a relatively large change in the pressure of carbon dioxide at which the oceans and atmosphere are at equilibrium," they wrote. That is to say, most of the carbon dioxide being pumped into the air by millions of smokestacks, furnaces, and car exhausts would stay in the air, where, presumably, it would gradually warm the planet. "Human beings are now carrying out a large-scale geophysical experiment of a kind that could not have happened in the past nor be repeated in the future," they concluded, adding, with the morbid dispassion of true scientists, that this experiment, "if adequately documented, may yield a far-reaching insight into the processes of weather and climate." While there are other parts to this story—the depletion of the ozone, acid rain, genetic engineering—the story of the end of nature centers on this greenhouse experiment, with what will happen to the weather.

·  ·  ·

When we drill into an oil field, we tap into a vast reservoir of organic matter—the fossilized remains of aquatic algae. We unbury it. When we burn oil—or coal, or methane (natural gas)—we release its carbon into the atmosphere in the form of carbon dioxide. This is not pollution in the conventional sense. Carbon monoxide is pollution—an unnecessary by-product; a clean-burning engine releases less of it. But when it comes to carbon dioxide a clean-burning engine is no better than a motor in a Model T. It will emit about five and a half pounds of carbon in the form of carbon dioxide for every gallon of gasoline it consumes. In the course of about a hundred years, our various engines and industries have released a very large portion of the carbon buried over the last five hundred million years. It is as if someone had scrimped and saved his entire life and then spent everything on one fantastic week's debauch. In this, if in nothing else, wrote the great biologist A. J. Lotka, "the present is an eminently atypical epoch." We are living on our capital, as we began to realize during the oil crises of the 1970s. But it is more than waste, more than a binge. We are spending that capital in such a way as to alter the atmosphere.

There has always been, at least since the start of life, a certain amount of carbon dioxide in the atmosphere, and it has always trapped a certain amount of the sun's radiation to warm the earth. If there were no atmospheric carbon dioxide, our world might resemble Mars: it would probably be so cold as to be lifeless. A little greenhouse effect is a good thing—life thrives in its warmth. The question is: how much? On Venus, the atmosphere is 97 percent carbon dioxide. As a result, it traps infrared radiation a hundred times as efficiently as the earth's atmosphere, and keeps the planet a toasty seven hundred degrees warmer than the earth. The earth's atmosphere is mostly nitrogen and oxygen; it is only about .035 percent carbon dioxide, which is hardly more than a trace. The worries about the greenhouse effect are worries about raising that figure to .055 or .06 percent, which is not very much. But enough, it turns out, to make everything different.

In 1957, when Revelle and Suess wrote their paper, no one even knew for certain whether carbon dioxide was increasing. The Scripps Institution hired a young researcher, Charles Keeling, and he set up monitoring stations at the South Pole and on the side of Mauna Loa, in Hawaii, eleven thousand feet above the Pacific. His data soon confirmed their hypothesis: more and more carbon dioxide was entering the atmosphere. When the first readings were taken, in 1958, the atmosphere at Mauna Loa contained about 315 parts per million of carbon dioxide. Subsequent readings showed that each year the amount increased, and at a steadily growing rate. Initially, the annual increase was about seven-tenths of a part per million; in recent years, the rate has doubled, to one and a half parts per million. Admittedly, one and a half parts per million sounds absurdly small. But scientists, by drilling holes in glaciers and testing the air trapped in ancient ice, have calculated that the carbon-dioxide level in the atmosphere prior to the Industrial Revolution was about 280 parts per million, and that this was as high a level as had been recorded in the past hundred and forty thousand years. Since carbon dioxide at a very low level largely determines the climate, carbon dioxide at double that very low level, small as it is in absolute terms, could have an enormous effect.

And the annual increase seems nearly certain to go higher. The essential facts are demographic and economic, not chemical. The world's population has more than tripled in this century, and is expected to double, and perhaps triple again, before reaching a plateau in the next century. Moreover, the tripled population has not contented itself with using only three times the resources. In the last hundred years, industrial production has grown fiftyfold. Four-fifths of that growth has come since 1950, almost all of it based on fossil fuels. In the next half century, a United Nations commission predicts, the planet's $13 trillion economy will grow five to ten times larger.

These facts are almost as stubborn as the chemistry of infrared absorption. They mean that the world will use more energy—2 to 3 percent more a year, by most estimates. And the largest increases may come in the use of coal—which is bad news, since coal spews more carbon dioxide into the atmosphere than any other fuel. China, which has the world's largest hard-coal reserves and recently passed the Soviet Union as the world's largest coal producer, has plans to almost double coal consumption by the year 2000. A model devised by the World Resources Institute predicts that if energy use and other contributions to carbon-dioxide levels continue to grow very quickly, the amount of atmospheric carbon dioxide will have doubled from its pre–Industrial Revolution level by about 2040; if they grow somewhat more slowly, as most estimates have it, the amount will double by about 2070. And, unfortunately, the solutions are neither obvious nor easy. Installing some kind of scrubber on a power-plant smokestack to get rid of the carbon dioxide might seem an obvious fix, except that a system that removed 90 percent of the carbon dioxide would reduce the effective capacity of the plant by half. One often-heard suggestion is to use more nuclear power. But, because so much of our energy is consumed by automobiles and the like, even if we mustered the political will and the economic resources to quickly replace each of our nonnuclear electric plants with nuclear ones our carbon-dioxide output would fall by only about 30 percent.

. . .

I took a day's hike last fall, following the creek that runs by my home in the Adirondacks to the place where it crosses the main county road. It's a distance of maybe nine miles as the car flies, but rivers are far less efficient, and endlessly follow time-wasting, uneconomical meanders. The creek cuts some fancy figures, and so I was able to feel a bit exploratory—a budget Bob Marshall. In a strict sense, it wasn't much of an adventure. I stopped at the store for a liverwurst sandwich at lunchtime, the path was generally downhill, the temperature stuck at an equable fifty-five degrees, and since it was the week before the hunting season opened I didn't have to sing as I walked. It isn't Yosemite, this small valley, but its beauties are absorbing, and one can say, with John Muir on his mountaintop, "Up here all the world's prizes seem as nothing."

And so what if it isn't nature primeval? One of my neighbors has left several kitchen chairs along his stretch of the bank, spaced at fifty-yard intervals, for comfort in fishing. At one old homestead, a stone chimney stands at each end of a foundation now filled by a graceful birch. Near the one real waterfall, a lot of rusty pipe and collapsed concrete testifies to the mill that once stood there. But these aren't disturbing sights; they're almost comforting—reminders of the way that nature has endured and outlived and with dignity reclaimed so many schemes and disruptions of man. (A mile or so off the creek, there's a mine where a hundred and fifty years ago a visionary tried to extract pigment for paint and pack it out by mule and sledge. He rebuilt after a fire; finally, an avalanche convinced him. The path in is faint now, but his chimney, too, still stands, a small Angkor Wat of free enterprise.) Large sections of the area were once farmed; but the growing season is not much more than a hundred days in a good year, and the limits established by that higher authority were stronger than the (powerful) attempts of individual men to circumvent them, and so the farms returned to forest, with only a dump of ancient bottles or a section of stone wall as a memorial. These ruins are humbling sights, reminders of the negotiations with nature which have established the world as we know it.

Changing socks in front of the waterfall, I thought back to the spring of 1987, when a record snowfall melted in only a dozen or so warm April days. A little to the south, a swollen stream washed out a highway bridge, closing the New York Thruway for months. The creek became a river, and the waterfall, normally one of those diaphanous-veil affairs, turned into a cataract. It filled me with awe to stand there then, on the shaking ground, and think, This is what nature is capable of. But as I sat there this time, and thought about the dry summer we'd just come through, there was nothing awe-inspiring or instructive, or even lulling, in the fall of the water. It suddenly seemed less like a waterfall than like a spillway to accommodate the overflow of a reservoir. That didn't decrease its beauty, but it changed its meaning. It has begun, or will soon begin, to rain and snow when the chemicals we've injected into the atmosphere add up to rain or snow—when they make it hot enough over some tropical sea to form a cloud and send it this way. In one sense, I will have no more control over this process than I ever did. But the waterfall seemed different, and lonelier. Instead of a world where rain had an independent and mysterious existence, I was living in a world where rain was becoming a subset of human activity: a phenomenon like smog or commerce or the noise from the skidder towing logs on the nearby road—all things over which I had no control, either. The rain bore a brand: it was a steer, not a deer. And that was where the loneliness came from. There's nothing here except us.

At the same time that I felt lonely, though, I also felt crowded—without privacy. We go to the woods in part to escape. But now there is nothing except us, and so there is no escaping other people.

As I walked in the autumn woods, I saw a lot of sick trees. With the conifers, I suspected acid rain. (At least I have the luxury of only suspecting; in too many places, they know.) And so who walked with me in the woods? Well, there were the presidents of the Midwestern utilities, who kept explaining why they had to burn coal to make electricity (cheaper, fiduciary responsibility, no *proof* it kills trees), and then there were the congressmen, who couldn't bring themselves to do anything about it (personally favor, but politics the art of compromise, very busy with the war on drugs), and before long the whole human race had arrived to explain its aspirations. We like to drive, it said, air-conditioning is a necessity nowadays, let's go to the mall. Of course, the person I was fleeing most fearfully was myself, for I drive, and I'm burning a collapsed barn behind my house next week because it is much the cheapest way to deal with it, and I live on about four hundred times the money that Thoreau conclusively proved was enough, so I've done my share to take this independent, eternal world and turn it into a science-fair project.

Our local shopping mall has a club of people who go "mall-walking" every day. They circle the shopping center en masse— Caldor to Sears to J. C. Penney, circuit after circuit, with an occasional break to shop. This seems less absurd to me now than it did at first. I like to walk in the outdoors not solely because the air is cleaner but also because outdoors we venture into a sphere larger than we are. Mall-walking involves too many other people, and too many purely human sights, ever to be more than good-natured exercise. But now, out in the wild, the sunshine on one's shoulders is a reminder that man has cracked the ozone, that, thanks to us, the atmosphere absorbs where once it released. The greenhouse effect is a more apt name than those who coined it can have imagined. The carbon dioxide and the other trace gases act like the panes of glass of a greenhouse—the analogy is accurate. But it's more than that. We have built a greenhouse—a human creation—where once there bloomed a sweet and wild garden.

# · 7 ·

## Not So Fast

—*The New York Times Magazine*, July 23, 1995

Here's a short chemistry lesson. Grasp it and you will grasp the reason the environmental era has barely begun; perhaps you will grasp the history of the next fifty years.

Put a gallon of gasoline in the tank of your car and go out for a drive. Assuming your engine's well tuned, burning that gallon of petroleum should put about half a pound of carbon in the form of carbon monoxide—CO—into the air. A generation ago that number was closer to one pound; by decade's end, as new technologies clean the exhaust, it should drop to barely a tenth of a pound. The steady decrease in carbon monoxide emissions, as well as in those of nitrous oxide and particulates, is the reason the air is clearer and safer now in Los Angeles than it was a generation ago.

On the same drive, however, that gallon of gas will also transmute itself into almost five and a half pounds of carbon in the form of carbon dioxide—$CO_2$. Long considered proof that gas was burning cleanly, invisible and odorless carbon dioxide is the inevitable by-product of fossil fuel consumption. It doesn't matter if your car's old or new; there's no filter you can stick on the exhaust to reduce carbon dioxide production. And if the wide international consensus of scientists is correct, this carbon dioxide is now warming the planet more quickly and to higher temperatures than ever in human history.

CO versus $CO_2$. One damn oxygen atom, and all the difference in the world.

If you focus on carbon monoxide, then you can count yourself among the currently fashionable environmental optimists. Pollution, from their perspective, is an unfortunate by-product of an essentially sound system. Since smog and its many analogues (river pollution, acid rain, crowded landfills) are precisely the sorts of things that can be tamed with filters and scrubbers, or with small changes in human behavior like recycling, the optimists are in some ways right. Though Congress is even now gutting the laws that have begun to clean America, and though there are plenty of poor and minority communities that never began to get cleaned in the first place, the technology exists to diminish smog, to purify drinking water. It's merely a matter of finding the will to pay for it—there's no reason for rivers to catch fire. (And every poll suggests that the will is there, that after a quarter-century of hard-fought environmental campaigns the American people are far more convinced than their congressmen that the environment is worth cleaning up.) So if carbon monoxide turns out to be the real issue, then it's just a systems problem. Environmentalism is a success story, and the world we die in will resemble the one we were born into, albeit with more computers.

That's the conventional wisdom of the moment, best expressed by Gregg Easterbrook in his book *A Moment on the Earth*. And yet there are those of us who are not soothed—who grow more worried with each passing month, and not simply by the fact of a Republican Congress. Those in this second camp tend to be focused on problems like widespread extinction, growing populations, dying fisheries, and dwindling wilderness—signals, like the ever-expanding cloud of carbon dioxide, indicating that our societies and their appetites have simply grown too large. Signals still all but ignored.

Since the environmental movement began, all these crises have been lumped together. The same people who worried about clean air worried about recycling and species extinction, about dirty rivers and the press of population. All these causes are important—now more than ever as the right attempts to undermine environmental protection—but acting as if they were all essentially the same crisis carries risks as well as benefits. While it's certainly easier to focus on things like smog, which people see around them every day, the logic of focusing on the most visible pollution cuts both ways. Such a narrowly pragmatic vision is potentially paralyzing precisely because you can clean urban air, you can return fish to the Great Lakes, you can recycle enough to keep landfills from overflowing.

Unfortunately, you can do all these quite vital things without having any real effect on the more systemic troubles. The progress we've made in solving environmental problems is deceptive: we're making no progress at all on the deeper problems, because they do not spring from the same sources. One set stems from a defect in the car; the other set comes from the very existence of the car. And in an odd way, solving the first kind of problem makes the deeper ones ever more intractable—if visible air pollution starts to decline, then the push for better mass transit dwindles, and with it the chances of cutting the invisible carbon dioxide.

The environmental movement, in other words, has reached a diagnostic crisis. To use a medical analogy: the world has presented itself, complaining of chest pains. After three decades of examination, there are still those who insist it's indigestion and want to prescribe some Bromo. Others say arteriosclerosis, which means our most basic behaviors must change. Most people—not just CEOs—badly want to find out that our problems are not related to our lifestyles. Change frightens us: we've come to believe, for instance, that our well-being is lashed to constant economic growth. "It's the economy, stupid."

And yet the basic laws of chemistry may soon demand that we give up such fixations. The Intergovernmental Panel on Climate Change, a group of scientists assembled by the United Nations, has calculated that an immediate 60 percent reduction in fossil fuel use is necessary to stabilize global climate. This could not happen in a world that closely resembles ours. Addicted to growth, busily spreading our vision of the good life around the globe, we are sprinting in the opposite direction. The growth in our economies and populations wipes out our incremental gains in energy efficiency: from 1983 to 1993, despite a tremendous push toward efficiency by power companies, Americans increased their per capita power usage by more than 22 percent. Electric utilities offered rebates for installing compact fluorescent bulbs, and, indeed, between 1986 and 1991 the typical household added one such light. But as Andrew Rudin pointed out in *Public Power* magazine, the typical household also added more than seven incandescent lamps.

Since the greenhouse effect and other consequences of our civilization's basic momentum have yet to hit us full-on, no mass movement has developed to challenge that momentum. "We are in an unusual predicament as a global civilization," Al Gore said when I interviewed him early in his vice presidency. "The maximum that is politically feasible, even the maximum that is politically imaginable right now, still falls short of the minimum that is scientifically and ecologically necessary." And that was before Newt Gingrich.

But this state of affairs may not last. According to the most accurate computer models of global climate, for instance, increased global temperatures may be obvious to the man in the street by decade's end. For all the right-wing bluster about taming the environmental movement, for all the happy-talk books about our ecological triumphs, it will take only a hot summer or two, a string of crop failures or some similar catastrophe to bring these issues center stage once more. A spate of recent studies has begun to make clear that an average temperature increase of only a few degrees hides tremendous heat waves, droughts, and storms; the insurance industry has actually begun to worry publicly about the greenhouse effect and the losses it will cause.

If and when such stresses really show themselves, though, we will need an environmental movement that understands what is happening—that understands that more recycling is not the main answer, that is willing to advocate the unpopular and the disturbing. Partly this means a stepped-up political campaign—continual pressure on governments around the world to sign and fulfill treaties, share renewable technologies, and pass steep new taxes on the use of fossil fuels and other polluters. Already a small segment of the environmental movement has begun to focus on such issues.

But remember the numbers. A 60 percent reduction in fossil fuel use? Even under the most hopeful technological scenarios, it won't happen if we're simultaneously doubling or tripling our economies. More money makes reducing smog easier, because you can afford to build better cars; more money makes dealing with the greenhouse effect harder, because you can afford to buy more cars. So the sweet dream that we'll all grow rich enough to turn green is simply that—a dream, and one that will turn into a nightmare if we try to follow it.

We face tough choices. The most pragmatic realism, rooted in the molecular structure of carbon dioxide, demands electric cars. It also demands nothing less than heresy: an all-out drive for deep thrift, for self-restraint, for smaller families. Brute objectivity requires new ideas about what constitutes sufficiency: smaller homes, more food grown locally, repair instead of replacement. Environmental visionaries have always talked about simplicity and community, but now atmospheric chemists are starting to say the same things. Not for esthetic and moral reasons, but for eminently practical ones. The world can't support a population of five and a half billion people living like middle-class Americans, much less the eight or nine billion that will soon share the planet with us. That's the crux of the issue—that and the fact that as long as we go on living the way we do everyone else will want to as well. We need China to stop burning so much fossil fuel—the developing world now produces as much carbon dioxide as the developed— but China will pay no attention until we start cutting back too.

Clearly, it's as immoral as it is impractical for us to demand that underdeveloped countries remain underdeveloped—those countries passionately want to develop. But it's terrifying to imagine Asians owning cars in the same numbers as we do. The only way out of this dilemma is to rethink what we mean by "development"—and to do it here first. We've exported our passion for democracy, our devotion to human rights. But that's not all we've exported. More than a billion humans, one in five of us, watch *Baywatch* every week. If the good life whose pictures we flash around the world doesn't change, then all the treaties on earth won't do the job. We need bicycles and we need buses, and we need to make them seem as marvelous as Miatas.

Rush Limbaugh has it right when he denounces environmentalists as a threat to current ways of life. The systemic environmentalism he fears has one question to ask: "How much is enough?" How much convenience, how many people, how much money? It's a question that won't go away. It's a question with a time limit, too: either we make these changes soon, or it won't be worth the bother.

# · 8 ·

## Maybe We Should Call It
## Something Scarier

*—The Boston Globe,* October 26, 1997

Maybe the problem is with the name. "Global warming" just doesn't sound that bad.

That's the only explanation I can think of for how unworried we are by the onset of the greenhouse effect.

The halfhearted set of measures announced by President Clinton aren't really designed to "combat" global warming; they're designed, eventually, to slow it down a tad. Under his plan, by 2010 or thereabouts we will try to return to emitting no more carbon dioxide than we emitted in 1990—which was exactly the same promise President Bush made in Rio in 1992, except that Bush was ambitious enough to promise he'd do it by 2000. Even the Japanese, completely dependent on imported fuel, have called for tougher measures.

Contrast that nonchalance with the flurry of activity and interest surrounding that other weather menace, El Niño. We have national conferences, emergency plans, T-shirts, weathermen pointing transfixed at a map of the Pacific, showing the pool of warm water sneaking up on the California coast; we have contractors working around the clock to fix people's roofs, all before the first drop of torrential rain hits the subdivisions of Greater Los Angeles. It's enough to make Noah look like a carefree slacker.

And yet what is El Niño? It's a weather phenomenon that begins off the coast of South America with the appearance of warmer-than-expected water. It changes weather patterns in several parts of the globe for a year or two, and then switches, becoming a La Niña, a pool of cooler-than-expected water.

In other words, El Niño is like a temporary junior version of global warming: a small-scale greenhouse effect. If it worries you, then consider that within fifty years we will have a permanent, planetwide El Niño that does all the same things, just forever.

Already, in fact, we are seeing far more severe disruptions of the planet's climate than El Niño threatens. Warmer air means more evaporation and hence more rainfall—already, global warming has increased severe storms across our continent by 20 percent. Warmer air means changes in the seasons—already, global warming has moved winter around, bringing spring a week earlier to the northern hemisphere. New studies show widespread permafrost melting across the Arctic and rapid glacial melting everywhere from Montana to Patagonia. Global warming means nothing less than the most fundamental alteration of the planet's systems since the last ice age; El Niño is just a thirty-second trailer before the main feature, a feature that lasts into eternity, or at least until the next big asteroid slams into the earth.

And yet it doesn't bother us much, at least not compared with the possibility of economic disruption that effective controls might mean. Administration economists hand around reports showing that taxing carbon enough to reduce its emissions might reduce GNP 1 percent or 3 percent, as if that was a danger comparable to changing the planet's basic functioning. Even environmentalists don't give the White House enough grief to balance the lobbying from carmakers and utilities and coal miners.

So here's my plan. Let's give global warming a new, scarier name. *El Piquante Grande*, perhaps? Or *La Chaleur Enorme*. Do those sound malevolent enough? How about Hell on Earth? Maybe then it will start to sink in.

# · 9 ·

# Warming Up to Kyoto

*—Audubon,* March/April 1998

Perhaps the most famous spot in all of Kyoto's 1,800 shrines and temples is the Zen rock garden called Ryoanji. It's only ten by thirty meters—a bed of raked stone with fifteen rocks large and small, dotted in clusters—but it draws thousands of visitors a day. The masters say that if you look at it long enough you can see nothingness—or the entire world.

I went there in December, on the final morning of the Kyoto negotiations on global warming. It seemed the right place for a meditative interlude, for the treaty that emerged from those talks, a mix of triumphs and complications, shares some of the garden's Zen qualities. Stare into the document long enough, and much about the world becomes clear. First and foremost, of course, is the fact that we moderns are wedded to fossil fuel. In some sense, being modern means that you are a machine for burning coal and gas and oil with every action of your daily life. And so a strike at those fuels is a strike at the routines, large and small, of our lives and our economies. It is an assault on our very identity.

The question that everyone asked as the conference concluded—

Will this new treaty prevent global warming?—is the wrong question. For one thing, we've already pumped enough carbon into the atmosphere to guarantee us major trouble. But more important, this enormous gathering was simply the first step in a political process that will last beyond any of our lifetimes—a process likely to define the next century, just as the battle with totalitarianism helped define this one. So what's important to figure out from Kyoto is the lay of the land, the obstacles that politics and economics will toss up to thwart real change, and the infant forces that might overcome those obstacles. What Kyoto offers is a crude and diagrammatic map of the future.

The most prominent feature of that map, the range that first draws your eye, is the fact that the United States is not quite ready to consider *any* big changes. That unwillingness colored every hour of the talks. In name this was an international conference—you could tell because they translated every speech into seven languages, and speakers from countries you've barely heard of (Niue?) rattled on for hours, and every so often you'd find yourself waiting in line behind someone Clad in Colorful Native Garb. In fact, however, it was mostly a meeting of Americans, a fight between Yanks. Other countries sent a delegate or two or three, a handful of reporters, perhaps a representative of a small ecology organization. But from the United States came Vice President Al Gore; nine environmental groups; a legion of suppliants from the oil-and-auto lobby, marshaled by the ambiguously named Global Climate Coalition; the second-in-command at the AFL-CIO, who'd come to complain that coal miners might lose their jobs; and a raft of the world's top-flight climate scientists. And as if that weren't enough, there was also a huge contingent from Congress. Everywhere around the media room, TV lights were fastened on one American or another—Senators Joe Lieberman and John Kerry calling for a treaty, Senator Chuck Hagel denouncing the idea. Robert Byrd, the senator from Appalachian coal, didn't actually make the trip, but he faxed in regular ripostes from the States, which were duly distributed to every reporter. The world would have saved a lot of carbon if they'd held the meeting in Chicago.

In some ways, the entire tortured negotiation resulted from our intransigence. On the first major sticking point—how deeply to cut emissions—most of the industrialized world agreed on the major reductions for carbon dioxide, methane, and nitrous oxide proposed by the European Union. The recalcitrants were organized chiefly by the United States. (It's hard to imagine Australia, say, disrupting the talks without the cover we provided.) And on the second major brouhaha—whether or not the developing countries should be required to participate—it was only our peculiar brand of attack politics that got in the way. No one else seriously thought that nations like India, whose residents use a tenth per capita as much fuel as we do, should have to start cutting their consumption right away. But in an effort to wreck the whole process, the oil lobby had spent millions of dollars on ads insisting that they should, and under that pressure our Senate had voted 95–0 that it would ratify no treaty without the "meaningful participation" of "key developing countries." Day after day reporters asked delegates from every nation how they thought this or that provision would play in the U.S. Congress. Finally one day, the Tanzanian spokesman for the poor nations looked up and said, "I think the compromise needs to be between Democrats and Republicans, not developing countries and Republicans."

Some small part of the focus on America reflects our uniquely vigorous and divided politics. (No one would pay any attention to the opposition in parliamentary Britain, for instance, since it is powerless.) But one suspects it has a deeper meaning—that as the nation most deeply versed in consumerism, we're uniquely resistant to any kind of sacrifice or inconvenience. We've spent the decade rolling in money, our unemployment rate is microscopic, and still we won't budge. For the first time in history, last November saw more Americans buy light trucks than cars. Don't mess with my Navigator, damn it. In our ubiquitous language of addiction, we may be powerless over oil, but we haven't hit bottom yet. We're resolutely modern; even our environmental groups spoke constantly of how changes in energy technology would unleash yet another burst of material prosperity.

If the United States' immaturity is the first essential fact of the modern world, the second is the chasm between the rich nations of the North and the poor countries of the South. That immense gulf now taints every international discussion with as much poison as the split between East and West did during the Cold War, and it makes clear why this would be a tough battle even without the oil lobbyists.

Halfway through the Kyoto conference, for instance, New Zealand pushed a proposal demanding that the developing countries commit to their own timetables for limiting emissions. It was as if the Kiwis had lobbed a grenade into the vast meeting hall. Delegate after delegate from the developing world rose, pointing angrily to the obvious truth that most carbon dioxide came from the rich nations, which had burned vast amounts of fossil fuel to arrive at their enviable state. Why should poor countries limit their emissions just as their economies were taking off? "In the developed world only two people ride in a car, and yet you want us to give up riding on a bus," said the Chinese spokesman. (He obviously hadn't visited the States recently; it's the rare sport-utility vehicle that carries more than a single body.) Five nights later, in the confused and bizarre final session, the poor nations succeeded in eliminating even a provision that would have allowed *voluntary* commitments on their part. Their suspicion ran deep, and not without reason: if the U.S. Congress won't support a nickel tax on a gallon of gas, why should Chinese politicians do anything to slow their people's climb to incomes a twentieth the size of ours? They are determined to make their way to modernity, and who can blame them? It's our incredibly persuasive consumerism, after all, that now shapes desires the world around.

Unfortunately, though, the Earth's atmosphere cares very little for justice. Developing countries will be the worst losers if the temperature climbs. Vast swaths of China, Bangladesh, and Egypt will disappear underwater. (Indeed, the developing countries that inhabit low-lying islands, like Nauru or Samoa, find their very survival at stake; their speeches from the floor were the grimmest of all the words at Kyoto.) Depending on their mood, even the most demagogic of the Third Worlders realized their predicament, and so said they'd forgo fossil fuels in exchange for the money and technology to develop in other ways. There's no inherent reason this shouldn't happen. China, for instance, is currently building its telecommunications network around cellular phones, leapfrogging our whole system of poles and wires. You can imagine the same thing happening with solar collectors and hydrogen fuel cells, whole villages going overnight from dung fires to photovoltaics. But using those technologies would have to be cheaper than tapping China's vast coal reserves, and that will be the case only if the West chips in. If the U.S. Congress is ever going to ratify the treaty, it's clear that China and India and Brazil and the other big developing countries will need to agree to emissions cuts; before Asia and Latin America agree to emission cuts, however, Congress may need to agree to what amounts to a vast new foreign aid project. That's the Mexican standoff that now dominates all deliberations about the planet's climate.

Beyond the clotted politics of privilege and poverty, however, there were tantalizing signs of another worldview emerging. The very fact of this conference represented an admission of sorts—the first teensy-tiny glimmer of unwilling recognition by the leaders of the species that our human enterprise may have grown about as large as it can grow.

Almost everyone involved would have denied it; even the environmentalists, as I have said, spoke in the old language of economic growth. But it was clear that some nations came to the talks determined to make real progress, particularly the Europeans.

Their governments are increasingly influenced by the Green parties, and their populations are now stable or shrinking—a signal perhaps that endless growth is not the imperative it once was in parts of the Old World.

And in parts of the New World, too. The most impressive speech at the conference went all but unnoticed, because it came just before Al Gore's speech instructing American negotiators to show "increased flexibility," which allowed the whole conference to continue. In the long run, though, I think that the words of José Figueres, president of Costa Rica, will carry more weight. Unlike the Americans and the Chinese, who see global warming as a bump in the highway, he called for "a future which will not be a continuation of the past," for "an age characterized not by the quantity of growth but by the quality of human development."

And he didn't just call for it; he's bet his country on it. By 2010 Costa Rica plans to generate all its electricity from renewable sources; it's running large-scale experiments with electric bicycles and electric scooters. A gas tax directly supports the planting of trees; the country then "sells" its carbon-storage capacity to U.S. or European utilities looking to offset their own emissions.

In Costa Rica, in other words, they are trying to build a subtly different world. Fossil fuel has been the fuel of choice for hyperpowered expansion; solar collectors and windmills may well underwrite an equal prosperity, but it will feel different. Figueres offered a glimpse of what can only be called a postmodern future, one that might appeal to both pollution-choked Beijing and prosperity-glutted Boston. And he offered a solution that might help both to get there. The rich nations need to send resources, as efficiently as possible through technology transfer and schemes like leasing Costa Rica forests, to the poor nations. And the poor nations need to see how stupid it is to say that simply because we've polluted the planet, they should be allowed to as well. Neither North nor South, Figueres said, can be "full of the emotions of the past." In so saying he touched the heart of this debate.

The rock garden at Ryoanji has one peculiar feature. From any spot along the wooden veranda that overlooks the garden, you can see fourteen of the fifteen stones, but one is always hidden. If you shift your spot the hidden rock may come into view, but another will disappear.

Kyoto laid bare most of the landscape of the climate issue, but there was—and will be for many years to come—at least one hidden rock. The mystery that remains is how the atmosphere will react to the insults we've already offered it, and to those we will inevitably offer in the years to come. One afternoon, while the conference limped along with still more debate over precisely how much the Americans and Europeans should cut their emissions in the next decade, I dropped in on a panel of scientists who were holding a symposium in a side room. The panelists, organized by the small but impressive U.S. environmental group Ozone Action, sounded, in a curious way, less urgent than the negotiators. Not because they were less concerned—in fact, one after another they stressed the enormity of the problem and the real possibility of unpleasant surprises from the global climate. But precisely because they understood the scale of the predicament, they were focused beyond the next ten years.

The thermal inertia of the oceans, the long residence time of carbon in the atmosphere, the lag between emissions and warming—these were the recurring themes of the session. And therefore, in the words of climate guru Robert Watson, environment director at the World Bank, we need to "structurally decarbonize" the economy so that by the new century's middle or end fossil fuels will have all but disappeared. The way to judge any agreement, the panelists said, was on whether it sent the right signals, whether it created a set of financial, political, and social incentives for business and industry in the next decade to choose renewable power sources—or at least natural gas—over coal and oil. The underlying hope is that even a modest agreement on emissions may finally shake new technologies—hybrid cars, hydrogen fuel cells—off the shelves and onto the streets.

That's one reason the scientists worried about the series of loopholes that nations, especially the United States, kept inserting into the treaty. Since on the one hand the Clinton administration wanted an agreement, and since on the other hand it had ruled out any gas tax, the job of figuring out how we'll cut back is enormous. So our negotiators larded the text with plans for "emissions trading"—whereby we could purchase credits for carbon that Russia would have emitted had its economy not tanked in the post-Soviet era—and for counting "sinks"—forests, essentially—against our emission targets. It's not that either of those is necessarily a terrible idea on its face; the Russians could certainly use the foreign aid, and forests do absorb carbon dioxide. Besides, we do need ways to reward developing nations such as Costa Rica for protecting their forests.

But if we're able to buy our way out of our cuts, or calculate our way out of them with our vast forests, then we won't make the changes necessary to blunt the momentum of our fuel use. As U.S. negotiator Stuart Eizenstat acknowledged in his final press briefing, the Americans appeared to have conceded a lot of ground—they'd come saying they supported stabilizing U.S. emissions at 1990s levels by 2010, and they'd gone away agreeing to cut them 7 percent. But once all the loopholes had been figured in, he said quite frankly, our commitment was at best a reduction of a percent or two.

On the face of it, that doesn't sound like enough change to really send a signal. But the calculations need to go a little deeper. In an odd way, the job of environmentalists has been made easier by Bill Clinton's abject failure to honor the commitments George Bush made at the 1992 Earth Summit, in Rio de Janeiro, Brazil. There we promised to cut emissions to 1990 levels by the year 2000; instead we've gone on an unprecedented binge. Our fuel use shot up 3.5 percent last year, the biggest annual increase on record. By 2000 we'll be burning 15 percent more fossil fuel than we did in 1990, and thus spewing out nearly 15 percent more greenhouse gases—which, added to our Kyoto commitment, means our real reduction target will be 22 percent over ten years.

And that's a cut large enough to explain the slumped shoulders of William O'Keefe, chairman of the Global Climate Coalition, better known as the world oil-and-auto lobby. He looked almost physically stunned by the deal. "It's in free fall now." Gore had sold out the president's position of stabilizing emissions when he directed his team to reach a deal. "It was like holding up a sign that said: 'Pigs—$10 or Less,'" said O'Keefe. By no means had he or his band of oilmen and utility execs given up; they were heading home eager to fight on friendlier ground. But there was a strong sense that the tide had turned; for all their money and power, the oil companies and the coal barons were now on the defensive. If the enviros had not exactly triumphed, the powers that be had lost, if only for the moment.

. . .

How long that moment lasts will depend, more than anything, on the weather. There's now the precarious framework of a process in place, a framework that could crumble if the U.S. Senate or the Chinese overlords decide they can't afford it. But another nasty summer, another spasm of storms, another round of reports about increased precipitation and changing seasons, another few years of rising sea levels—those might be enough to cement this new politics into place. They would force home the realization that what we risk is a permanent, planetwide El Niño—an eternal recalibration of the planet that for so long has supported us generously.

It's entirely possible that we've waited too long to prevent that. Word came during the Kyoto conference that 1997 would set a new record for the highest average global temperature, inching out 1995. The changes already under way are immense. But at least now we've engaged the fight, given ourselves the noble if perhaps quixotic task of forging a new future somewhere out past modernity.

# · 10 ·

## Of Caribou and Carbon

*—Arctic Refuge* (Milkweed Editions), 2001

I know as much about caribou as your average resident of the northeast United States, which is to say not overly much. In my mind they are sort of like the moose, except perennially attending some vast convention. So while I am entirely in favor of them, and their babies, you will have to browse elsewhere for a lyrical account of what it is like to be immersed in a sea of them, with their great rhythmic breathing (or whatever) opening up a clear channel to God. I want to concentrate on the entirely prosaic and unlyrical question of whether or not, caribou aside, it makes sense to drill for oil in the Arctic.

In fact, let's grant, just for a moment, every possible argument to the Exxons of the world. Let's say that beneath the Arctic National Wildlife Refuge there are vast pools of oil (though the mainstream geologists tell us otherwise). Let's say that those vast pools of oil could be sucked to the surface without damaging the environment (the testimony of every other large-scale oil project on earth to the contrary). Let's even wave our wand and say you could transport it back to the world's gas stations and power plants without it leaking from your pipeline or spilling from your ship. What then? Now is it a good idea?

Well, consider. Oil is a hydrocarbon. In the form of, say, gasoline, it weighs about eight pounds a gallon. When you burn that gasoline, slightly more than five pounds of carbon in the form of carbon dioxide enter the atmosphere. (Makes no difference how well tuned your engine is—carbon dioxide release is an inevitable by-product of fossil fuel combustion.) The molecular structure of that carbon dioxide traps heat near the planet that would otherwise radiate back out to space. It warms the planet. How much does it warm the planet? The Intergovernmental Panel on Climate Change, a UN body comprising the world's climatologists, released its set of predictions in January 2000 in Shanghai. By century's end, it said, the world's temperature will likely have increased about five degrees Fahrenheit, with a worst-case scenario of ten or eleven degrees. That's a lot. That's hotter than it was when the dinosaurs were wandering around and keeling over and being converted into petroleum.

And so what? Well, so far we've warmed the world a degree and a half by burning fossil fuels. Nine of the ten warmest years on record occurred in the last decade. As a result, the planet is already starting to unravel. Storms are growing more frequent and more intense, and both drought and flood more common. Sea levels are starting an inexorable rise. And northward, in the area of the Arctic National Wildlife Refuge, the physics of the planet makes the warming even more dramatic. Already, Arctic ice is 40 percent thinner than it was in 1960. An area twice the size of Massachusetts melts permanently each year. Already the permafrost in many places is turning to soup. Already native peoples are reporting that it is impossible to hunt in the ways and places they have long used. Already polar bears in northern Canada are 20 percent scrawnier than just a few years ago—there's no longer enough pack ice to reliably support their long-standing hobby of hunting seals. Already the computer models are starting to issue dire hints of what happens to global ocean currents when you melt all that Arctic ice and change the salinity of the northern seas.

Already, in other words, we've gone a long way toward wrecking ecosystems the world over, and in the far north in particular. And this damage will only get worse unless we leave that carbon in the ground, trapped down there below the surface where it can do no damage. Right now it's benign, lying in its ancient vault, but the minute it's pumped up and put in gas tanks or turbines, it turns deeply dangerous. The oil spill may not happen in ANWR, but it will definitely happen in the atmosphere. Think of the caribou as security guards trying to prevent the theft of a deadly poison.

We need to leave a lot of other carbon in the ground too, of course—in coal mines the world over, and in oil fields from the North Sea to the Niger Delta, from the Gulf of Arabia to the Gulf of Mexico. That's hard for us to hear. We've grown to like a steady supply of incredibly cheap fossil fuel. But we need to make the transition—quickly—to an entirely different way of powering our world. We need solar and wind power, we need hydrogen fuel cells, and we need them fast. We need cars that make sense (and buses and bikes) instead of Navigators and Explorers and the other military vehicles that carry us back and forth to the Shop & Save.

We need an all-out all-in effort—we need willpower.

And the place to start that effort is clear. It's in northern Alaska, on the last possible edge of the continent, where we can finally say no. We don't need this. It's not good for us. Eventually we're going to make this switch. Everyone knows it, even Exxon. Physics and chemistry mandate it, much as Congress and OPEC may resist. The only question is when we'll finally get around to it, and what will be left when we do. I vote for now, and I vote for caribou.

# Year One

—*Sierra*, January/February 2006

Pictures like these never quite fade. The iconic images of Hurricane Katrina—the sodden Superdome with its peeling roof, the corpses floating in the street, the hapless crowds waiting for help that wouldn't come—were enough to nudge the September 11 snapshots from the center of our brains. They were also enough to move the national debate back in the direction of domestic politics: to poverty, race, and whether a functioning government is worth paying for.

But it was another set of pictures—less seen but just as eerie—that foreshadowed the rest of the century. These were satellite images released in late September by the scientists charged with keeping track of ice in the Arctic. What they showed was simple: more water, less ice—20 percent less than the historical average. As climate change pushes polar temperatures higher, each summer's melt takes a bigger toll—and by last year, the scientists were saying, it seemed to have become a self-reinforcing process. That is, there was less white ice to reflect sunlight out to space and more blue water to absorb the heat, water that in turn melted more ice. "This will be four Septembers in a row that we've seen a downward trend," Mark Serreze, a scientist at the National Snow and Ice Data Center, told Britain's *Independent* newspaper. "The feeling is we are reaching a tipping point or threshold beyond which sea ice will not recover."

By itself, of course, the extent of Arctic ice affects relatively few of us. But it's not a singular case; it's a highly visible manifestation of the chaos we've let loose on the planet's physical systems. The waterlogged horror in the Gulf of Mexico was another. Katrina was not an isolated natural disaster but an obvious sign of a future far less predictable than the past.

No single hurricane is the result of global warming. But a month before Katrina hit, Massachusetts Institute of Technology hurricane specialist Kerry Emmanuel published a landmark paper in the British science magazine *Nature* showing that in the past half century tropical storms have been lasting 60 percent longer and spinning winds 50 percent more powerful. Two weeks after Katrina struck, *Science* published another paper, by a Georgia Institute of Technology team, demonstrating that Category 4 and 5 hurricanes have become twice as likely in recent decades. The cause: the ever-warmer tropical seas on which they thrive. Katrina, a Category 1 storm when it crossed Florida, roared to monster size in the abnormally hot waters of the Gulf. Within a day, a million people were homeless. That's far too many, we soon found out, for the federal government to cope with. And it's just the beginning.

More than a decade ago, environmental researcher Norman Myers began adding up the number of humans at risk of losing their homes to global warming. In coastal China, India, Bangladesh, the tiny island states of the Pacific and Indian Oceans, the Nile delta, Mozambique, and other areas, he predicted that 150 million people could become "environmental refugees" by 2050, displaced by rising waters. That's more than the total number of political refugees sent scurrying by the bloody century we've just endured. Or, put another way, it's 150 Katrinas, most of them in places without Superdomes, buses, or the odd $200 billion to make repairs.

The bulk of those refugees will be in countries where nobody emits much carbon. (Global warming is man-made, but that doesn't mean it's made by all men.) The United Nations can hardly calculate Bangladesh's emissions—the country uses so little fossil fuel that it's a rounding error. Even China, with its booming economy, consumes only about an eighth as much energy per capita as the United States does. Its car-to-person ratio, though growing fast, is the same as ours was in 1912. Meanwhile, the 4 percent of the world's population living in the United States produces 25 percent of the planet's carbon dioxide.

Now the bill is coming due, with cruel poetic justice for some. Katrina cast up ironies like so much flotsam and jetsam. The storm, for instance, wreaked particular vengeance on Mississippi, a state governed by Haley Barbour, who in an earlier incarnation as a GOP power broker and energy lobbyist helped persuade President George W. Bush to renege on his promise to treat carbon dioxide as a pollutant. Thanks to Barbour and the other lobbyists-turned-administrators who throng the White House, the federal government has done exactly nothing to slow the progress of climate change. Today we're emitting 20 percent more carbon than we were in 1990, when scientists were first issuing their prescient warnings.

More ironies: The sky-high gasoline prices that followed Katrina actually reduced the amount of energy Americans used, at least for a few weeks, something that hadn't happened since the Carter administration. And the scores of Explorers and Navigators running out of gas on Houston freeways as their owners fled Hurricane Rita may have marked the beginning of the end of the SUV era.

Of course, it's too late to prevent global warming. So far we've raised the temperature of the planet by about one degree, globally averaged, and that's been enough to set the poles to melting and the winds to roaring. Even if, right now, we started doing all that we could to overhaul our energy economy, we'd probably still be stuck with a couple more degrees of warming, and the world would change more profoundly than at any time in human history.

But hope of progress in Washington is nil. The criminally lazy energy bill signed by Bush a few weeks before Katrina struck enshrined our current approach to energy, which, at its essence, can be summed up as "more": more drilling, more refining, more combustion, and more handouts to the oil and gas industry. Growing numbers of state and local governments have begun to act, and their efforts hold promise for the future. In the meantime, what do we have to look forward to? The computer modelers tell us that the mid-case estimate—not the worst-case but the most likely scenario for the rest of the century—is in the range of another five degrees of warming. That would make the planet hotter than it has been through all of human history.

· · ·

All of this will take time to sink in. We're not used to the idea that the earth is shifting beneath us. For ten thousand years of human civilization, we've relied on the planet's basic physical stability. Sure, there have been hurricanes and droughts and volcanoes and tsunamis, but averaged out, it's been a remarkably stable run. Unfortunately, stability is a thing of the past.

We will soon learn, for example, that what we've been calling "global warming" is better thought of as excess energy trapped in the atmosphere, which will express itself in every possible way. Like the Bush administration's energy bill, these manifestations will also be about "more": more evaporation in arid lands and then more flooding when it eventually rains; more wind as air pressure rises from warmer areas; more extreme heat waves like the one that killed tens of thousands of Europeans in 2003 or the one that cut North American grain yields by a third in 1988; more ecological disruption as summers lengthen, winters shorten, and sea levels rise; more disease as mosquitoes spread to once-cool climes; and even more nonlinear surprises like the possible shutdown of the Gulf Stream.

Katrina revealed deep helplessness among our rulers. Part of it stemmed from cronyism and incompetence, part from the sheer overwhelming force of the blow. We will slowly recover, but even the United States has only so many hundreds of billions to spare. New Orleans will be rebuilt—this time. But what if hurricanes like Katrina go from being once-in-a-century storms to once-in-a-decade-or-two storms? How many times will we rebuild?

A final picture that haunts me is one I first saw as a young man: the photograph taken by the early Apollo astronauts from outer space that showed our blue and white orb against the endless black background of the universe. The picture that, for a moment, illuminated the essential borderlessness of our planet, and helped launch the environmental movement.

What haunts me is that the picture is no longer accurate. It's like a college yearbook photo of a man now middle-aged. In the few decades since it was taken, we've changed the earth in profound ways. Much of that northern ice has turned to water. The deserts have grown. And now parts of the Gulf Coast have sunk beneath the sea. It's a new, less friendly world, and it needs its own numbering system. So let Katrina mark Year One of our new calendar, the start of an age in which the physical world has flipped from sure and secure to volatile and unhinged.

# · III ·

# CONSUMED

# · 12 ·

## What's On: 11:30 A.M.

—*The New Yorker,* March 9, 1992

*I Dream of Jeannie* (the one where she gets tomorrow's newspapers, complete with racing results) has just come on. I'm watching 1965. According to CNN, a statue of Philo Farnsworth was unveiled yesterday in the Capitol Rotunda. As a sixteen-year-old high school student in Provo, Utah, Philo described to his physics teacher the idea for what he called an "image dissector," or camera tube. Five years later, in 1927, he used the device to transmit a picture—appropriately, a picture of a dollar sign. That's the outside edge of the history of television; at most, it's sixty-five. In truth, though, television as we know it was postponed by the Second World War, and it wasn't until 1946 or 1947 that people started buying sets in any real numbers. That is to say, the television we would recognize stretches back about forty-five years. But because of TV's power, and, even more, its limits, those forty-five years make up most of our sense of the world—at least, if we were born in these years. We know the period stunningly well; it has a nuanced, subtle familiarity, unlike anything else in human experience.

This is a most curious distortion of our sense of time. We don't know the past forty-five years so well just because they're so recent; if that were the case, we'd have a gradual tailing off in our knowledge, with the sixties much less vivid than the seventies. We know those years because we watch them constantly, again and again. The history—social, cultural, musical, economic, political—of the last forty-five years appears every day a thousand times on our screens, and more and more frequently as the days go by. You could spend an entire day hopping from channel to channel and never leave sixties sitcoms. And they are not mere filler. Cable channels like Nickelodeon have discovered that large numbers of people will watch the past's network fare over and over; in a row the channels run *Dobie Gillis*, *Bewitched*, *Green Acres*, *The Donna Reed Show*, *Rowan and Martin's Laugh-In*, *My Three Sons*, *The Patty Duke Show*, and *Make Room for Daddy*, then go back to *Dobie Gillis* for the next installment. The networks understand this appeal, too: as the *Rolling Stone* critic Jay Martel noted, in 1990 they ran a movie called *Gunsmoke: The Last Apache*, and also *Return to Green Acres*; updates of *Candid Camera*, *Dark Shadows*, *Lassie*, and *To Tell the Truth*; and a program called *The Brady Brides*. Lisa Kennedy pointed out in the *Village Voice* that on the new Fox network almost every show "refers knowingly to some other point in TV history: *Totally Hidden Video* to *Candid Camera*, *21 Jump Street* to *The Mod Squad*, *The Simpsons* to the Charlie Brown specials." Advertisers are hip as well: Coca-Cola resurrected its classic hilltop commercials, and Mr. Peanut shills once more for Planters. We are happily trapped in a familiar museum, condemned to know in unbelievable detail the attitudes and styles of this one period. What happened before will always seem strange and dreamlike.

To understand the depth of that absorption, look at the old cartoons that still run. A whole series without main characters dates from the late thirties and early forties; the cartoons are small, exquisitely animated operas, and are shown regularly in the preschool and home-from-school slots. They are among the only punctures in this closed system—when they were made, there wasn't TV, or just barely was, and so their content had to come from before television. There's one cartoon of a bookshelf, for instance, with Little Women coming to life on a book jacket and swooning over Frank Sinatra. Mother Goose appears, too, and Kim. The wolf from Little Red Riding Hood chases Daffy Duck until a cop steps off the cover of the *Police Gazette* to arrest him; the judge from the magazine *Judge*, which ceased publication during the Depression, delivers the verdict, and the wolf falls into Dante's *Inferno*. In a Merrie Melodies short called *Goofy Groceries*, the cow on a can of condensed milk croons to the bull on a tobacco tin. A stick of Wiggly Gum turns into Little Egypt, the stripper, while the navy beans rush to rescue the cancan (tomato) dancers from the Animal Crackers ape. I have no idea what kids make of this—I imagine that most of it goes over their heads, as when Porky Pig, in the French Foreign Legion, goes off to a Legion convention in Boston to hear an address by General Delivery, or when Popeye goes to the jungle in a faithful Stanley-and-Livingstone reenactment ("Dr. Bluto, I presume"). The crackle of reference after reference, all of which are from the world before television, and many of which go over my head, too, makes these shows hypnotically different from the fare of just a decade or two later. By then, Wilma is saying to Fred and Betty and Barney, "Let's have our kind of fun tonight. Let's just stay home, curl up in front of the TV, and make some popcorn." Stone Age life is utterly familiar—that's the joke.

TV can't go back before the turn of the century, obviously. To TV, that is a black hole that can't be illuminated, because there is no film. It's all prehistory, cave paintings, to be explored only occasionally, in a costume drama. But because it is a costume drama it doesn't seem *real*, and we have a deep and intuitive sense of the "real": real is when you have a picture of it, even if it's a soap opera. But it needs to be a good, crisp picture. The newsreel images from the cusp of the TV age look a little distorted. In the 1930s and '40s, did boxers really fall differently when they were punched? Because the early cameras filmed at slower speeds, the herky-jerkiness, the sudden, fast drop to the canvas make the fight films seem odd, dated, the way that crowds seem to move through the streets too fast in Chaplin films. We instantly recognize these images as outside television—as archival. Even after the camera was working smoothly, it took a while for nonactors to learn to look natural. One documentary on A&E showed newsreel footage of Eisenhower inaugurating the Echo 1 satellite: he spoke *at* the microphone, like someone ordering from a Burger King drive-through. "It gives me great personal satisfaction to participate in this communications experiment," he said, unconvincingly. In another documentary that day, J.F.K. appeared. He was, of course, a vastly different man, but that was only part of it; more important, appearing on TV was no longer a historic event. Speaking to a banquet audience, he said, "I am the man who accompanied Jacqueline Kennedy to Paris," and then he grinned his broad grin. The distance between that moment and the present is as nothing.

And after that time nothing looks "old." Not Fred MacMurray lecturing his boys, not the Dick Van Dyke living room with the famous ottoman. The Mary who lived in that house was an emblem of a very different time from that of the Mary who worked with Ted and Murray and Lou, but both are utterly and equally accessible to us—neither looks "off." They don't clash. Time within the TV period is fluid, usable—we can all deconstruct and reassemble it as if we were a nation of Ph.D. candidates. Consider the strange case of Martha Quinn, who was one of the original VJs a decade ago on MTV. Then she was hip, up-to-the-minute. All the other original VJs have long since been replaced by much younger kids, but Martha is still there, and she has swung back through time. Here she is in a crushed-velvet gown, like something from a chic Haight-Ashbury thrift store. "The other day, I heard on the radio—the radio station played the entire album of *Sergeant Pepper's*," she's saying, in her appealingly goofy, straight-haired way. "And I was completely blown away. I was thinking, What if it was back in 1967, and this is when, like, 'The Letter' by the Box Tops was out, or Lulu's 'To Sir with Love'? These were the albums that were on the charts. And all of a sudden Paul McCartney's whole concept of *Sergeant Pepper's Lonely Hearts Club Band*! . . . Absolutely incredibly mind-blowing. And the man who came up with the *concept* of the *idea* of it being a band, Sergeant Pepper, is Paul McCartney. We have Paul McCartney coming up." And, sure enough, after some commercials here came Paul McCartney, equal parts cute Beatle and "serious musician" and venerated star, singing his new single.

You don't have to have been there physically to achieve this kind of fluency. The next song, "Put the Message in the Box," was by a group called World Party, whose members looked as if they might have been in fourth grade when Jefferson Airplane sang "White Rabbit." And yet they'd painstakingly made their video appear as if it had emerged in, say, May of 1969. There's a guy in an old hat with the brim pinned back looking as if he'd stepped off the cover of a Paul Revere and the Raiders album. A Hindu deity flashes up on the screen. The lead singer has those big, pillowlike headphones around his neck. Wait—the picture is revolving! Every detail is right, down to the wide, colorfully embroidered guitar strap. Other hot groups on MTV that day included Wilson Phillips, kiddos of Mamas, Papas, and Beach Boys; and Nelson, the sons of the rock-and-roll-but-especially-TV star Ricky Nelson. The *grandsons* of Ozzie and Harriet.

Our sense of time within these television years is so acute that we can make all sorts of jokes from it. One ad features a man from a marketing concept called the '70s Preservation Society, offering an album called *Those Fabulous '70s*, with songs like the Partridge Family's "I Think I Love You," and the Bay City Rollers' "Saturday Night," and Paper Lace's "The Night Chicago Died" and "Billy, Don't Be a Hero." Time-Life, a kind of cataloguing service for the images of this era, sells a sounds-of-the-seventies set, one volume per year. Or you can buy uncut versions of the great

*Beverly Hillbillies* episodes, or expand your *Looney Tunes Library*. This is our cultural patrimony. Ira Gallen, the host of a public-access cable program that takes "an affectionate glance at the television programs and commercials of the fifties and sixties," told the *New York Times* recently, "I'll be turning forty next month, and those of us on the brink belong to the first generation able to look back to a blatantly documented childhood. Everything we ate, drank, wore, touched, was seen on television and is there for all time." There, every day, at every turn, TV life is being lived in exhaustive detail by people who weren't alive when it happened the first time.

TV endlessly refers to itself, thereby adding to the strange sense that you are pickling in its juices. The most fanatic environmentalist doesn't recycle with half the relish of television producers. Even the mistakes made on TV are lovingly collected. Turn on HA!, the "humor" network (it later merged with the Comedy Channel to become Comedy Central), and you see a rerun of *TV's Bloopers and Practical Jokes*—that is, a rerun of a collection of old, old clips introduced by Dick Clark and Ed McMahon, who themselves have been here forever. What funny film they've got! Look—Willard Scott has lost his hairpiece! Then they show some "sexy foreign commercials," made under "regulations a lot more relaxed," Dick explains as he introduces a reel of salacious Italian ads. Advertisements stay as monuments in our minds. On the *Today* show, three jingle writers have appeared to sing their hits, like "Good time, great taste of McDonald's," or "Can't beat the real thing," or "All aboard Amtrak," or "Listen to the heartbeat of America." On *Top Card*, on the Nashville Network, contestants need to know if Carly Simon's "Anticipation" was the song for Hunt's or Heinz ketchup, and to recognize the Marlboro theme song, which hasn't been played for two decades—not since Congress outlawed televised cigarette commercials. Even when the question's not about TV, we assume that it must be. On a forgettable program called *Win, Lose or Draw*, a celebrity is trying to illustrate the phrase "Father, Son, and Holy Ghost," but all that the contestant can think of is the name of the clergyman on the old sitcom *Happy Days*.

The talk shows, of course, are mostly about TV, and the news has the same internal preoccupations. All day, it reported that Kelsey Grammer (Dr. Crane on *Cheers*) had missed a court-ordered drug-rehabilitation date. But there he was on *Cheers*, drinking beer! Nearly every newscast also reported in great detail on the suicide the previous day of a dwarf actor named David Rappaport, who had appeared often on *L.A. Law*. On *L.A. Law* itself, ruthless Ros resigned from the firm. The show ended, the news came on, and there was Diana Muldaur, the actress who played Ros, giving a long interview about her role: "She horrifies me, to be honest with you. Every time I would read a script, I would just say, 'Oh, she's not going to do that. It's just too horrible.' " It was like watching a post-game interview with an athlete.

There are all sorts of comedy on television—whole networks are devoted to stand-up routines—and an awful lot of jokes refer to TV, the great common reference. Here's a brilliant impression of the Six Million Dollar Man. Then there's the theme from *Hawaii Five-O* on a kazoo. There's even one comic on *An Evening at the Improv* whose shtick consists of impersonating a TV, switching constantly from one channel to the next. Layers of reference pile up on each other like the ruins of successive cities: to promote its reruns of *Dobie Gillis*, Nickelodeon uses the slogan "Man, it's, like, Gilligan in a goatee."

But this staggering absorption in TV culture comes at a price. History is weirdly foreshortened; for instance, all anniversaries from the TV period are marked with great care and attention—at least, if whatever happened was captured on film. This was the day before the twentieth anniversary of Kent State, so every station was gearing up its coverage—digging out the shaky film clips of the Guardsmen and the students facing each other across the practice field, and the footage of Walter Cronkite delivering the news, and expert after expert agreeing that this incident, seen immediately all across America, "brought the war home." However, nothing that happened *before* television is covered in any detail. The brightness surrounding the last forty-five years blinds us to everything that preceded it—and forty-five years is a very short time, even to an individual. Bob Hope, for instance, came on the J. C. Penney shopping channel to hawk his new book. We know Bob Hope from years of specials, from footage of him entertaining the troops. But he is an old man. He's talking about the Second World War, and tells a joke about how F.D.R. trained his dog Fala on the *Chicago Tribune*. The interviewer brays—convulses—but, until Bob explains, it's hard to believe he knows anything about Colonel McCormack's feud with Roosevelt; Bob might as well be telling Thomas Aquinas jokes.

There are shows that become part of the oversoul. Take *The Brady Bunch*, whose theme song is as widely known as the national anthem, and whose example is invoked over and over. A Showtime program on divorce, for instance, presents a bewildered kid saying, "We were like a very hip *Brady Bunch*." In Chicago, and then in Manhattan, crowds jam a theater each week to see a different *Brady Bunch* episode performed live. The Lifetime network, on one of its talk shows, convened a summit of sitcom moms. All kinds of women were there—the mom from *One Day at a Time*, and the woman Fred MacMurray finally married during the 1969–70 season of *My Three Sons*, and Mrs. Jefferson, and Molly Dodd's mother, and even the actress who played Lily Munster. But they all deferred to Florence Henderson, Mrs. Brady, who talked about how every parent strives for a union like that between the Bradys, and said that psychiatrists used tapes of the show in counselling couples—a job that may have grown more interesting after the revelation (on *Geraldo*) that the actor playing the eldest son, Greg, had dated Florence Henderson during the filming of the show. A survey of twenty-one-to-twenty-five-year-olds, commissioned by MTV, revealed that their favorite program was *The Brady Bunch,* which ended its original run when they were three-to-seven-year-olds. "I think it gave people hope that there was a family like that," Florence Henderson said. An utterly *normal* family—their "gimmick" was *not* being a rock band or interracial or robots. Ostensibly, they were two separate families—three guys and three gals ("with hair of gold like their mother's")—that had come together. But this never caused any tension in the show. Almost nothing ever caused tension; it was just kids being kids and parents being parents. A professor from the State University of New York said, "My students know *The Brady Bunch* better than their own parents' birthdates."

That is, they know a life where no work is done—usually not even by the maid—because there are appliances in every corner. They know a life where everything happens in a big and isolated suburban home. Where parents are mostly pals, where money flows in, where food just appears. We can make fun of it, laugh at it, deconstruct it, but all of us who grew up with it, which is to say nearly everyone born since it went on the air, are affected by it. Very few of us can afford to live like the Bradys; even the *hope* of such a lifestyle, which once seemed an obvious promise of the future, is fading as the middle class shrinks, and as having just one or two children requires both parents to work. And, even if individuals can afford that lifestyle, it's also become clear that the planet probably can't—that the world, were it composed of a billion Brady Bunches, would buckle under the environmental strain. We may recognize, almost instinctively, those problems. The absurd excess of the eighties, the painful slowdown of the nineties—many of us are left wondering if there isn't some other path. But *The Brady Bunch* and all its imitators are what we know in our hearts. And so the search for something different—something more sustainable and maybe less sterile—never gets under way, because we *know* what normal is.

# · 13 ·

## Out There in the
## Middle of the Buzz

—*Forbes ASAP*, December 2, 1996

Out on a recent hike, I stopped for lunch at the edge of a high mountain pond. I could see another solitary hiker on the other side of the water, stretched out on a shelving rock about a hundred yards away. And I could hear him talking (sound carries extremely well across water; never negotiate a deal in a canoe). "It's so beautiful up here," he was saying. "It's so peaceful. What's happening with you?"

What I couldn't figure out was who he was talking to. Until I pulled out my binoculars and saw, of course, that he had a cell phone. For a moment I felt vastly superior—and then I reflected a bit. It's true I wouldn't carry a phone with me up a mountain. But I had carried my world with me nonetheless, marched right up there with my eyes fixed on the same vague middle distance that you see when you drive. My mind was abuzz with images, opinions; my mind was its own Bloomberg box, happily chattering away with a thousand dispatches an hour.

We live in the middle of the Buzz. Those billions of microprocessors that have spawned like springtime frogs in the last quarter century are constantly sending us information, data, images. Our minds marinate in it, till we're worried when it shuts off. What do you do first when you walk into an empty hotel room? Savor the silence? Or turn on the TV? And even when we get away from the machines for a while—even when we leave the phone at home—the Buzz comes with us. Quiet, solitude, calm: these are no longer automatic parts of the human experience. You have to fight as hard for them as a farm boy had to fight for novelty and thrill a century ago. How many minutes can you watch a sunset before your mind grows hungry for some faster diversion? How long can you stare up into the night sky?

This constant whispering in our ears, this constant dancing in front of our eyes—that's how technology changes us, weaning us away from ourselves. How can you figure out what you really want when someone's always talking to you, when there's always another home page to click through? When you can't warm yourself by a mountain lake without checking in at home? Electronic communication, for the first time, makes culture ubiquitous. Almost nobody read books five hours a day, or went to the theater every night. We live in the first moment when humans receive more of their information secondhand than first; instead of relying primarily on contact with nature and with each other, we rely primarily on the prechewed, on someone else's experience. Our life is, quite literally, mediated.

Maybe that's a good thing; maybe it's the direction in which we need to evolve on an ever more crowded planet. But I think it may be breeding a kind of desperation in us, too, a frantic, reactive nervousness. That low, rumbling broadcast that comes constantly from ourselves, the broadcast that tells us who we are, what we want from life—that broadcast is jammed by all the other noise around us, the lush static of our electronic age. We look for solitude in our (expensively silent) cars, but first the radio, then the phone, then the computer and the fax intrude. We look for peace in the mountains, but we drag the world along on a tether.

To quote Thoreau is to risk rejection as a romantic. But here goes. "Let us spend one day as deliberately as Nature, and not be thrown off the track by every nutshell and mosquito's wing that falls on the rails," he writes. Now that we've built a technosphere to amplify the sound of every nutshell and to broadcast high-quality pictures of each mosquito's wing, it's even better advice, albeit harder than ever to follow. Solitude, silence, darkness—these are the rarest commodities after a half century of electronics. The incredible economics of the information age mean that almost anyone can afford a large-screen television, a 28.8 modem. But how many can afford peace and quiet?

# · 14 ·

## Covetousness

—*Outside,* June 1997

At a recent mammoth outdoor-equipment show, I stopped by a seminar in which a merchandising specialist was advising shopkeepers how to paint and light their outlets for maximum sales; he also pitched a machine that pumped certain pleasing scents into the retail air. Anyway, the crucial place in any store, according to this man, was the Zone of Decision. That was the place about three feet back from the shelf where the customer takes a backpack and turns it over in his hands and wonders if he might, you know, appear somewhat Himalayan if he purchased it. And look at all those ice-ax loops. Why, a person could carry four ice axes simultaneously! The expert warned that the Zone of Decision is often improperly lighted, causing the merchandise to look less desirable (flatter, almost real) than it does on the shelf or in the mind's eye, hence depressing sales. The solution? Halogen bulbs. And blast some of that pine smell over this way.

It is true that I am a Methodist Sunday-school teacher theoretically immune to covetousness of all sorts, and that as an environmental writer I'm quite aware that if we all continue to buy immense amounts of things we will wreck the planet, requiring us to wear SPF 300 sunscreen and grow webbed feet. I own a crummy car, no television, a wood-burning stove, and extremely virtuous if somewhat abrasive toilet paper. On the other hand, I'm a sucker in the Zone of Decision.

Why, I'll say to myself, this pair of hiking boots weighs a full two ounces less than the pair I currently own. Lifting two ounces at a time in the course of taking, oh, eight million steps would waste enough energy to raise the level of the Nile six inches. I'll take them. I've got a six-person, four-season tent, but do I have a four-person, six-season tent? I do now. Why, this field guide is covered in Gore-Tex! Maybe they have one covered in Activent for summer reading! Maybe I could have my whole body dipped in liquid Gore-Tex! Perhaps if I drank Gore-Tex, I would never sweat again!

Whenever I am pinned down in the Zone of Decision, I try to recall my Uncle Ernie. A couple of years ago we hiked the Wonderland Trail, a hundred miles or so around Mount Rainier. Uncle Ernie was seventy-five at the time, and he was retracing a journey he'd first taken sixty years earlier. Not only that, he was retracing it with what must have been the same pack. It was called a Trapper Nelson, and it came with canvas shoulder straps, a wood frame, and no hip belt. He was outfitted more or less like that Ice Man they found in the Alps, though Uncle Ernie did have some matches he'd dipped in wax instead of a live ember in a little grass bag. Somehow my uncle made it, and quite cheerfully too.

So now when I stand in the Zone of Decision, overawed by a sleeping pad with a sticky cover or a stove that burns not only unleaded gas but also fermenting yak dung, I try to imagine what Uncle Ernie would do. And then, after I break down and buy the thing anyway, I tell myself that when I'm seventy-five it will look really cool, in a retro kind of way.

# · 15 ·

## The Cuba Diet

*—Harper's Magazine,* April 2005

The pictures hanging in Havana's Museum of the Revolution document the rise (or, depending on your perspective, the fall) of Cuba in the years after Castro's revolt, in 1959. On my visit there last summer, I walked through gallery after gallery, gazing upon the stock images of socialist glory: "anti-imperialist volunteers" fighting in Angola, Cuban boxers winning Olympic medals, five patients at a time undergoing eye surgery using a "method created by Soviet academician Fyodorov." Mostly, though, I saw pictures of farm equipment. "Manual operation is replaced by mechanized processes," read the caption under a picture of some heavy Marxist metal cruising a vast field. Another caption boasted that by 1990, seven bulk sugar terminals had been built, each with a shipping capacity of 75,000 tons a day. In true Soviet style, the Cubans were demonstrating a deeply held (and to our eyes now almost kitschy) socialist belief that salvation lay in the size of harvests, in the number of tractors, and in the glorious heroic machinery that would straighten the tired backs of an oppressed peasantry—and so I learned that day that within thirty years of the people's uprising, the sugarcane industry alone employed 2,850 sugarcane lifting machines, 12,278 tractors, 29,857 carts, and 4,277 combines.

Such was communism. But then I turned a corner and the pictures changed. The sharply focused shots of combines and Olympians now were muddied, as if Cubans had forgotten how to print photos or, as was more likely the case, had run short of darkroom chemicals. I had reached the gallery of the "Special Period." That is to say, I had reached the point in Cuban history where everything came undone. With the sudden collapse of the Soviet Union, Cuba fell off a cliff of its own. All those carts and combines had been the products of an insane "economics" underwritten by the Eastern bloc for ideological purposes. Castro spent three decades growing sugar and shipping it to Russia and East Germany, both of which paid a price well above the world level, and both of which sent the ships back to Havana filled with wheat, rice, and more tractors. When all that disappeared, literally almost overnight, Cuba had nowhere to turn. The United States, Cuba's closest neighbor, enforced a strict trade embargo (which it strengthened in 1992, and again in 1996) and Cuba had next to no foreign exchange with anyone else—certainly the new Russia no longer wanted to pay a premium on Cuban sugar for the simple glory of supporting a tropical version of its Leninist past.

In other words, Cuba became an island. Not just a real island, surrounded by water, but something much rarer: an island outside the international economic system, a moon base whose supply ships had suddenly stopped coming. There were other deeply isolated places on the planet—North Korea, say, or Burma—but not many. And so most observers waited impatiently for the country to collapse. No island is an island, after all, not in a global world. The *New York Times* ran a story in its Sunday magazine titled "The Last Days of Castro's Cuba"; in its editorial column, the paper opined that "the Cuban dictator has painted himself into his own corner. Fidel Castro's reign deserves to end in home-grown failure." Without oil, even public transportation shut down—for many, going to work meant a two-hour bike trip. Television shut off early in the evening to save electricity; movie theaters went dark. People tried to improvise their ways around shortages. "For drinking glasses we'd get beer bottles and cut the necks off with wire," one professor told me. "We didn't have razor blades, till someone in the city came up with a way to resharpen old ones."

But it's hard to improvise food. So much of what Cubans had eaten had come straight from Eastern Europe, and most of the rest was grown industrial-style on big state farms. All those combines needed fuel and spare parts, and all those big rows of grain and vegetables needed pesticides and fertilizer—none of which were available. In 1989, according to the United Nations Food and Agriculture Organization, the average Cuban was eating 3,000 calories per day. Four years later that figure had fallen to 1,900. It was as if they suddenly had to skip one meal a day, every day, week after month after year. The host of one cooking show on the shortened TV schedule urged Cubans to fry up "steaks" made from grapefruit peels covered in bread crumbs. "I lost twenty pounds myself," said Fernando Funes, a government agronomist.

Now, just by looking across the table, I saw that Fernando Funes had since gained the twenty pounds back. In fact, he had a little paunch, as do many Cuban men of a certain age. What happened was simple, if unexpected. Cuba had learned to stop exporting sugar and instead started growing its own food again, growing it on small private farms and thousands of pocket-sized urban market gardens—and, lacking chemicals and fertilizers, much of that food became de facto organic. Somehow, the combination worked. Cubans have as much food as they did before the Soviet Union collapsed. They're still short of meat, and the milk supply remains a real problem, but their caloric intake has returned to normal—they've gotten that meal back.

In so doing they have created what may be the world's largest working model of a semi-sustainable agriculture, one that doesn't rely nearly as heavily as the rest of the world does on oil, on chemicals, on shipping vast quantities of food back and forth. They import some of their food from abroad—a certain amount of rice from Vietnam, even some apples and beef and such from the United States. But mostly they grow their own, and with less ecological disruption than in most places. In recent years organic farmers have visited the island in increasing numbers and celebrated its accomplishment. As early as 1999 the Swedish parliament awarded the Organic Farming Group its Right Livelihood Award, often styled the "alternative Nobel," and Peter Rosset, the former executive director of the American advocacy group Food First, heralded the "potentially enormous implications" of Cuba's new agricultural system.

The island's success may not carry any larger lesson. Cuban agriculture isn't economically competitive with the industrial farming exemplified by a massive food producer across the Caribbean, mostly because it is highly labor-intensive. Moreover, Cuba is a one-party police state filled with political prisons, which may have some slight effect on its ability to mobilize its people— in any case, hardly an "advantage" one would want to emulate elsewhere.

There's always at least the possibility, however, that larger sections of the world might be in for "Special Periods" of their own. Climate change, or the end of cheap oil, or the depletion of irrigation water, or the chaos of really widespread terrorism, or some other malign force might begin to make us pay more attention to the absolute bottom-line question of how we get our dinner (a question that only a very few people, for a very short period of time, have ever been able to ignore). No one's predicting a collapse like the one Cuba endured—probably no modern economy has ever undergone such a shock. But if things got gradually harder? After all, our planet is an island, too. It's somehow useful to know that someone has already run the experiment.

· · ·

Villa Alamar was a planned community built outside Havana at the height of the Soviet glory days; its crumbling, precast-concrete apartments would look at home (though less mildewed) in Ljubljana or Omsk. Even the names there speak of the past: a central square, for instance, is called Parque Hanoi. But right next to the Parque Hanoi is the Vivero Organopónico Alamar.

*Organopónico* is the Cuban term for any urban garden. (It seems that before the special period began, the country had a few demonstration hydroponic gardens, much bragged about in official propaganda and quickly abandoned when the crisis hit. The high-tech-sounding name stuck, however, recycled to reflect the new, humbler reality.) There are thousands of *organopónicos* in Cuba, more than two hundred in the Havana area alone, but the Vivero Organopónico Alamar is especially beautiful: a few acres of vegetables attached to a shady yard packed with potted plants for sale, birds in wicker cages, a cafeteria, and a small market where a steady line of local people come to buy tomatoes, lettuce, oregano, potatoes—twenty-five crops were listed on the blackboard the day I visited—for their supper. Sixty-four people farm this tiny spread. Their chief is Miguel Salcines López, a tall, middle-aged, intense, and quite delightful man.

"This land was slated for a hospital and sports complex," he said, leading me quickly through his tiny empire. "But when the food crisis came, the government decided this was more important," and they let Salcines begin his cooperative. "I was an agronomic engineer before that," he said. "I was fat, a functionary. I was a bureaucrat." Now he is not. Most of his farm is what we would call organic—indeed, Salcines showed off a pyramidal mini-greenhouse in which he raises seedlings, in the belief that its shape "focuses energy." Magnets on his irrigation lines, he believes, help "reduce the surface tension" of the water—give him a ponytail and he'd fit right in at the Marin farmers' market. Taking a more traditional organic approach, Salcines has also planted basil and marigolds at the row ends to attract beneficial insects, and he rotates sweet potato through the rows every few plantings to cleanse the soil; he's even got neem trees to supply natural pesticides. But Salcines is not obsessive even about organicity. Like gardeners everywhere, he has trouble with potato bugs, and he doesn't hesitate to use man-made pesticide to fight them. He doesn't use artificial fertilizer, both because it is expensive and because he doesn't need it—indeed, the garden makes money selling its own compost, produced with the help of millions of worms ("California Reds") in a long series of shaded trenches.

While we ate rice and beans and salad and a little chicken, Salcines laid out the finances of his cooperative farm. For the last six months, he said, the government demanded that the *organopónico* produce 835,000 pesos' worth of food. They actually produced more than a million pesos' worth. Writing quickly on a piece of scrap paper, Salcines predicted that the profit for the whole year would be 393,000 pesos. Half of that he would reinvest in enlarging the farm; the rest would go into a profit-sharing plan. It's not an immense sum when divided among sixty-four workers—about $150—but for Cuban workers this is considered a good job indeed. A blackboard above the lunch line reminded employees what their monthly share of the profit would be: depending on how long they'd been at the farm, and how well they produced, they would get 291 pesos this month, almost doubling their base salary. The people worked hard, and if they didn't their colleagues didn't tolerate them.

What is happening at the Vivero Organopónico Alamar certainly isn't unfettered capitalism, but it's not exactly collective farming either. Mostly it's incredibly productive—sixty-four people earn a reasonable living on this small site, and the surrounding neighbors get an awful lot of their diet from its carefully tended rows. You see the same kind of production all over the city—every formerly vacant lot in Havana seems to be a small farm. The city grew 300,000 tons of food last year, nearly its entire vegetable supply and more than a token amount of its rice and meat, said

Egidio Páez Medina, who oversees the *organopónicos* from a small office on a highway at the edge of town. "Tens of thousands of people are employed. And they get good money, as much as a thousand pesos a month. When I'm done with this job I'm going to start farming myself—my pay will double." On average, Páez said, each square meter of urban farm produces five kilograms of food a year. That's a lot. (And it's not just cabbage and spinach; each farm also seems to have at least one row of spearmint, an essential ingredient for the mojito.)

So Cuba—happy healthy miracle. Of course, Human Rights Watch, in its most recent report, notes that the government "restricts nearly all avenues of political dissent," "severely curtails basic rights to free expression," and that "the government's intolerance of dissenting voices intensified considerably in 2003." It's as if you went to Whole Foods and noticed a guy over by the soymilk with a truncheon. Cuba is a weird political system all its own, one that's been headed by the same guy for forty-five years. And the nature of that system, and that guy, had something to do with the way the country responded to its crisis.

For one thing, Castro's Cuba was so rigidly (and unproductively) socialist that simply by slightly loosening the screws on free enterprise it was able to liberate all kinds of pent-up energy. Philip Peters, a Cuba analyst at the conservative Lexington Institute, has documented how the country redistributed as much as two thirds of state lands to cooperatives and individual farmers and, as with the *organopónico* in Alamar, let them sell their surplus above a certain quota. There's no obvious name for this system. It's a lot like sharecropping, and it shares certain key features with, say, serfdom, not to mention high feudalism. It is not free in any of the ways we use the word—who the hell wants to say thank you to the government for "allowing" you to sell your "surplus"? But it's also different from monolithic state communism.

In 1995, as the program geared up, the markets were selling 390 million pounds of produce; sales volume tripled in the next three years. Now the markets bustle, stacked deep with shiny heaps of bananas and dried beans, mangoes and tomatoes. But the prices, though they've dropped over the years, are still beyond the reach of the poorest Cubans. And the government, which still sells every citizen a basic monthly food ration for just a few pesos, has also tried to reregulate some of the trade at the farmers' markets, fearing they were creating a two-tier system. "It's not reform like you've seen in China, where they're devolving a lot of economic decision making out to the private sector," Peters said. "They made a decision to graft some market mechanisms onto what remains a fairly statist model. It could work better. But it has worked."

. . .

Fidel Castro, as even his fiercest opponents would admit, has almost from the day he took power spent lavishly on the country's educational system. Cuba's ratio of teachers to students is akin to Sweden's; people who want to go to college go to college. Which turns out to be important, because farming, especially organic farming, especially when you're not used to doing it, is no simple task. You don't just tear down the fence around the vacant lot and hand someone a hoe, quoting him some Maoist couplet about the inevitable victory of the worker. The soil's no good at first, the bugs can't wait to attack. You need information to make a go of it. To a very large extent, the rise of Cuba's semi-organic agriculture is almost as much an invention of science and technology as the high-input tractor farming it replaced, which is another thing that makes this story so odd.

"I came to Havana at the time of the revolution, in 1960, to start university," said Fernando Funes, who now leads the national Pasture and Forage Research Unit. "We went from eighteen thousand university students before the revolution to two hundred thousand after, and a big proportion were in agricultural careers. People specialized in soil fertility, or they specialized in pesticides. They were very specialized. Probably too specialized. But yields were going up." Yields were going up because of the wildly high-input farming. In the town of Nuevo Gerona, for instance, there is a statue of a cow named White Udder, descended from a line of Canadian Holsteins. In the early 1980s she was the most productive cow on the face of the earth, giving 110 liters of milk a day, 27,000 liters in a single lactation. Guinness certified her geysers of milk. Fidel journeyed out to the countryside to lovingly stroke her hide. She was a paragon of scientific management, with a carefully controlled diet of grain concentrates. Most of that grain, however, came from abroad ("this is too hot to be good grain country," Funes said). White Udder was a kept woman. To anyone with a ledger book her copious flow was entirely uneconomic, a testimony to the kinky economics of farm subsidies.

"In that old system, it took ten or fifteen or twenty units of energy to produce one unit of food energy," Funes said. "At first we didn't care so much about economics—we had to produce no matter what." Even in the salad days of Soviet-backed agriculture, however, some of the local agronomists were beginning to think the whole system was slightly insane. "We were realizing just how inefficient it was. So a few of us were looking for other ways. In cattle we began to look at things like using legumes to fix nitrogen in the pasture so we could cut down on fertilizer," Funes said. And Cuba was inefficient in more than its use of energy. Out at the Agrarian University of Havana on the city's outskirts, agriculture professor Nilda Pérez Consuegra remembers how a few of her colleagues began as early as the 1970s to notice that the massive "calendar spraying" of pesticides was breeding insect resistance. They began working on developing strains of bacteria and experimenting with raising beneficial insects.

They could do nothing to forestall the collapse of the early 1990s, though. White Udder's descendants simply died in the fields, unable to survive on the tropical grasses that had once sustained the native cattle. "We lost tens of thousands of animals. And even if they survived, they couldn't produce anything like the same kind of milk once there was no more grain—seven or eight liters a day if we were lucky," Funes said. Fairly quickly, however, the agricultural scientists began fanning out around the country to help organize a recovery. They worked without much in the way of resources, but they found ways.

. . .

One afternoon, near an *organopónico* in central Havana, I knocked on the door of a small two-room office, the local Center for Reproduction of Entomophages and Entomopathogens. There are 280 such offices spread around the country, each manned by one or two agronomists. Here, Jorge Padrón, a heavyset and earnest fellow, was working with an ancient Soviet refrigerator and autoclave (the writing on the gauges was in Cyrillic) and perhaps three hundred glass beakers with cotton gauze stoppers. Farmers and backyard gardeners from around the district would bring him sick plants, and he'd look at them under the microscope and tell them what to do. Perhaps he'd hand them a test tube full of a *trichoderma* fungus, which he'd grown on a medium of residue from sugarcane processing, and tell them to germinate the seed in a dilute solution; maybe he'd pull a vial of some natural bacteria— *Verticillium lecanii* or *Beauveria bassiana*—from a rusty coffee can. "It is easier to use chemicals. You see some trouble in your tomatoes, and chemicals take care of it right away," he said. Over the long run, though, thinking about the whole system yields real benefits. "Our work is really about preparing the fields so plants will be stronger. But it works." It is the reverse, that is, of the Green Revolution that spread across the globe in the 1960s, an industrialization of the food system that relied on irrigation, oil (for both shipping and fertilization), and the massive application of chemicals to counter every problem.

The localized application of research practiced in Cuba has fallen by the wayside in countries where corporate agriculture holds sway. I remember visiting a man in New Hampshire who was raising organic apples for his cider mill. Apples are host to a wide variety of pests and blights, and if you want advice about what chemical to spray on them, the local agricultural extension agent has one pamphlet after another with the answers, at least in part, because pesticide companies like Monsanto fund huge amounts of the research that goes on at the land-grant universities. But no one could tell my poor orchardist anything about how to organically control the pests on his apples, even though there must have been a huge body of such knowledge once upon a time, and he ended up relying on a beautifully illustrated volume published in the 1890s. In Cuba, however, all the equivalents of Texas A&M or the University of Nebraska are filled with students looking at antagonist fungi, lion-ant production for sweet potato weevil control, how to intercrop tomatoes and sesame to control the tobacco whitefly, how much yield grows when you mix green beans and cassava in the same rows (60 percent), what happens to plantain production when you cut back on the fertilizer and substitute a natural bacterium called *A. chroococcum* (it stays the same), how much you can reduce fertilizer on potatoes if you grow a rotation of jack beans to fix nitrogen (75 percent), and on and on and on. "At first we had all kinds of problems," said a Japanese-Cuban organoponicist named Olga Oye Gómez, who grows two acres of specialty crops that Cubans are only now starting to eat: broccoli, cauliflower, and the like. "We lost lots of harvests. But the engineers came and showed us the right biopesticides. Every year we get a little better."

Not every problem requires a Ph.D. I visited Olga's farm in midsummer, when her rows were under siege from slugs, a problem for which the Cuban solution is the same as in my own New England tomato patch: a saucer full of beer. In fact, since the pressure is always on to reduce the use of expensive techniques, there's a premium on old-fashioned answers. Consider the question of how you plow a field when the tractor that you used to use requires oil you can't afford and spare parts you can't obtain.

Cuba—which in the 1980s had more tractors per hectare than California, according to Nilda Pérez—suddenly found itself relying on the very oxen it once had scorned as emblems of its peasant past. There were perhaps fifty thousand teams of the animals left in Cuba in 1990, and maybe that many farmers who still knew how to use them. "None of the large state farms or even the mechanized cooperatives had the necessary infrastructure to incorporate animal traction," wrote Arcadio Ríos, of the Agricultural Mechanization Research Institute, in a volume titled *Sustainable Agriculture and Resistance.* "Pasture and feed production did not exist on site; and at first there were problems of feed transportation." Veterinarians were not up on their oxen therapy.

But that changed. Ríos's institute developed a new multi-plow for plowing, harrowing, ridging, and tilling, specially designed not "to invert the topsoil layer" and decrease fertility. Harness shops were set up to start producing reins and yokes, and the number of blacksmith shops quintupled. The ministry of agriculture stopped slaughtering oxen for food, and "essentially all the bulls in good physical condition were selected and delivered to cooperative and state farms." Oxen demonstrations were held across the country. (The socialist love of exact statistics has not waned, so it can be said that in 1997 alone, 2,344 oxen events took place, drawing 64,279 participants.) By the millennium there were 400,000 oxen teams plying the country's fields. And one big result, according to a score of Ph.D. theses, is a dramatic reduction in soil compaction, as hooves replaced tires. "Across the country we see dry soils turning healthier, loamier," Professor Pérez said. Soon an ambitious young Cuban will be able to get a master's degree in oxen management.

· · ·

One question is: how resilient is the new Cuban agriculture? Despite ever tougher restrictions on U.S. travel and remittances from relatives, the country has managed to patch together a pretty robust tourist industry in recent years: Havana's private restaurants fill nightly with Canadians and Germans. The government's investment in the pharmaceutical industry appears to be paying off, too, and now people who are fed by ox teams are producing genetically engineered medicines at some of the world's more advanced labs. Foreign exchange is beginning to flow once more; already many of the bicycles in the streets have been replaced by buses and motorbikes and Renaults. Cuba is still the most unconsumer place I've ever been—there's even less to buy than in the old Soviet Union—but sooner or later Castro will die. What then?

Most of the farmers and agronomists I interviewed professed conviction that the agricultural changes ran so deep they would never be eroded. Pérez, however, did allow that there were a lot of younger oxen drivers who yearned to return to the cockpits of big tractors, and according to news reports some of the country's genetic engineers are trying to clone White Udder herself from leftover tissue. If Cuba simply opens to the world economy—if Castro gets his professed wish and the U.S. embargo simply disappears, replaced by a free-trade regime—it's very hard to see how the sustainable farming would survive for long. We use pesticides and fertilizers because they make for incredibly cheap food. None of that dipping the seedling roots in some *bacillus* solution, or creeping along the tomato rows looking for aphids, or taking the oxen off to be shoed. Our industrial agriculture—at least as heavily subsidized by Washington as Cuba's farming once was subsidized by Moscow—simply overwhelms its neighbors. For instance, consider Mexico and corn. Not long ago the journalist Michael Pollan told the story of what happened when NAFTA opened that country's markets to a flood of cheap, heavily subsidized U.S. maize: the price fell by half, and 1.3 million small farmers were put out of business, forced to sell their land to larger, more corporate farms that could hope to compete by mechanizing (and lobbying for subsidies of their own). A study by the Carnegie Endowment for International Peace enumerated the environmental costs: fertilizer runoff suffocating the Sea of Cortéz, water shortages getting worse as large-scale irrigation booms. Genetically modified corn varieties from the United States are contaminating the original strains of the crop, which began in southern Mexico.

Cuba already buys a certain amount of food from the United States, under an exemption from the embargo passed during the Clinton administration. So far, though, the buying is mostly strategic, spread around the country in an effort to build political support for a total end to the embargo. No one ever accused the Cubans of being dumb, said Peters of the Lexington Institute. "They know the congressional district that every apple, every chicken leg, every grain of wheat, comes from." But that trickle, in a free-trading, post-Castro Cuba, would likely become, as in Mexico and virtually every other country on earth, a torrent, and one that would wash away much of the country's agricultural experiment.

· · ·

You can also ask the question in reverse, though: does the Cuban experiment mean anything for the rest of the world? An agronomist would call the country's farming "low-input," the reverse of the Green Revolution model, with its reliance on irrigation, oil, and chemistry. If we're running out of water in lots of places (the water table beneath China and India's grain-growing plains is reportedly dropping by meters every year), and if the oil and natural gas used to make fertilizer and run our megafarms are changing the climate (or running out), and if the pesticides are poisoning farmers and killing other organisms, and if everything at the Stop & Shop has traveled across a continent to get there and tastes pretty much like crap, might there be some real future for low-input farming for the rest of us? Or are its yields simply too low? Would we all starve without the supermarket and the corporate farm?

It's not a question academics have devoted a great deal of attention to—who would pay to sponsor the research? And some clearly think the question isn't even worth raising. Dennis Avery, director of global-food issues at the conservative Hudson Institute, compared Cuba with China during the Great Leap Forward: "Instead of building fertilizer factories, Mao told farmers to go get leaves and branches from the hillsides to mulch the rice paddies. It produced the worst soil erosion China has seen." Raising the planet's crops organically would mean "you'd need the manure from seven or eight billion cattle; you'd lose most of the world's wildlife because you'd have to clear all the forests."

But strict organic agriculture isn't what the Cubans practice (remember those pesticides for the potato bugs). "If you're going to grow irrigated rice, you'll almost always need some fertilizer," said Jules Pretty, a professor at the University of Essex's Department of Biological Sciences, who has looked at sustainable agriculture in fields around the world. "The problem is being judicious and careful." It's very clear, he added, "that Cuba is not an anomaly. All around the world small-scale successes are being scaled up to regional level." Farmers in northeast Thailand, for instance, suffered when their rice markets disappeared in the Asian financial crisis of the late 1990s. "They'd borrowed money to invest in 'modern agriculture,' but they couldn't get the price they needed. A movement emerged, farmers saying, 'Maybe we should just concentrate on local markets, and not grow for Bangkok, not for other countries.' They've started using a wide range of sustainability approaches—polyculture, tree crops and agroforestry, fish ponds. One hundred and fifty thousand farmers have made the shift in the last three years."

Almost certainly, he said, such schemes are as productive as the monocultures they replaced. "Rice production goes down, but the production of all sorts of other things, like leafy vegetables, goes up." And simply cutting way down on the costs of pesticides turns many bankrupt peasants solvent. "The farmer field schools began in Indonesia, with rice growers showing one another how to manage their paddies to look after beneficial insects," just the kinds of predators the Cubans were growing in their low-tech labs. "There's been a huge decrease in costs and not much of a change in yields."

And what about the heartlands of industrial agriculture, the U.S. plains, for instance? "So much depends on how you measure efficiency," Pretty said. "You don't get something for nothing." Cheap fertilizer and pesticide displace more expensive labor and knowledge—that's why 219 American farms have gone under every day for the last fifty years and yet we're producing ever more grain and a loaf of bread might as well be free. On the other hand, there are those bereft Midwest counties. And the plumes of pesticide poison spreading through groundwater. And the dead zone in the Gulf of Mexico into which the tide of nitrogen washes each planting season. And the cloud of carbon dioxide that puffs out from the top of the fertilizer factories. If you took those things seriously, you might decide that having one percent of your population farming was not such a wondrous feat after all.

· · ·

The American model of agriculture is pretty much what people mean when they talk about the Green Revolution: high-yielding crop varieties, planted in large monocultures, bathed in the nurturing flow of petrochemicals, often supported by government subsidy, designed to offer low-priced food in sufficient quantity to feed billions. Despite its friendly moniker, many environmentalists and development activists around the planet have grown to despair just about everything the Green Revolution stands for. Like Pretty, they propose a lowercase greener counterrevolution: endlessly diverse, employing the insights of ecology instead of the brute force of chemistry, designed to feed people but also keep them on the land. And they have some allies even in the rich countries—that's who fills the stalls at the farmers' markets blooming across North America.

But those farmers' markets are still a minuscule leaf on the giant stalk of corporate agribusiness, and it's not clear that, for all the paeans to the savor of a local tomato, they'll ever amount to much more. Such efforts are easily co-opted—when organic produce started to take off, for instance, industrial growers soon took over much of the business, planting endless monoculture rows of organic lettuce that in every respect, save the lack of pesticides, mirrored all the flaws of conventional agriculture. (By some calculations, the average bite of organic food at your supermarket has traveled even farther than the 1,500-mile journey taken by the average bite of conventional produce.) That is to say, in a world where we're eager for the lowest possible price, it's extremely difficult to do anything unconventional on a scale large enough to matter.

And it might be just as hard in Cuba were Cuba free. I mean, would Salcines be able to pay sixty-four people to man his farm or would he have to replace most of them with chemicals? If he didn't, would his customers pay higher prices for his produce or would they prefer lower-cost lettuce arriving from California's Imperial Valley? Would he be able to hold on to his land or would there be some more profitable use for it? For that matter, would many people want to work on his farm if they had a real range of options? In a free political system, would the power of, say, pesticide suppliers endanger the government subsidy for producing predatory insects in local labs? Would Cuba not, in a matter of several growing seasons, look a lot like the rest of the world? Does an *organopónico* depend on a fixed ballot?

There's clearly something inherently destructive about an authoritarian society—it's soul-destroying, if nothing else. Although many of the Cubans I met were in some sense proud of having stood up to the Yanquis for four decades, Cuba was not an overwhelmingly happy place. Weary, I'd say. Waiting for a more normal place in the world. And poor, much too poor. Is it also possible, though, that there's something inherently destructive about a globalized free-market society—that the eternal race for efficiency, when raised to a planetary scale, damages the environment, and perhaps the community, and perhaps even the taste of a carrot? Is it possible that markets, at least for food, may work better when they're smaller and more isolated? The next few decades may be about answering that question. It's already been engaged in Europe, where people are really debating subsidies for small farmers, and whether or not they want the next, genetically modified, stage of the Green Revolution, and how much it's worth paying for Slow Food. It's been engaged in parts of the Third World, where in India peasants threw out the country's most aggressive free-marketeers in the last election, sensing that the shape of their lives was under assault. Not everyone is happy with the set of possibilities that the multinational corporate world provides. People are beginning to feel around for other choices. The world isn't going to look like Cuba—Cuba won't look like Cuba once Cubans have some say in the matter. But it may not necessarily look like Nebraska either.

· · ·

"The choices are about values," Pretty said. Which is true, at least for us, at least for the moment. And when the choices are about values, we generally pick the easiest and cheapest way, the one that requires thinking the least. Inertia is our value above all others. Inertia was the one option the Cubans didn't have; they needed that meal a day back, and given that Castro was unwilling to let loose the reins, they had a limited number of choices about how to get it. "In some ways the special period was a gift to us," said Funes, the forage expert, the guy who lost twenty pounds, the guy who went from thinking about White Udder to thinking about oxen teams. "It made it easier because we had no choice. Or we did, but the choice was will we cry or will we work. There was a strong desire to lie down and cry, but we decided to do things instead."

# · 16 ·

## A Grand Experiment

*—Gourmet,* July 2005

From before the first frost until after the salad greens had finally poked their heads above the warming soil, most of my food for seven months came from within a couple dozen miles of my house. For a few things, I traveled to the corners of this watershed, which covers the northwest third of Vermont and a narrower fringe along the New York shore of Lake Champlain. (I did make what might be called the Marco Polo exception—I considered fair game anything your average thirteenth-century explorer might have brought back from distant lands. So pepper and turmeric, and even the odd knob of ginger, stayed in the larder.) Eating like this is precisely how almost every human being ate until very recently, and how most people in the world still do eat today. But in contemporary America, where the average bite of food travels 1,500 miles before it reaches your lips, it was an odd exercise. Local and seasonal may have become watchwords of much new cooking, but I wanted to see what was really possible, especially in these northern climes. I know that eating close to home represents the history of American farming—but I sense it may have a future, too. The number of farms around Burlington, Vermont's chief city, has grown 19 percent in the past decade. Most of them are small, growing food for local consumers instead of commodities for export; the same trend is starting to show up nationwide. Something's happening, and I wanted to see exactly what.

I'm writing this, so you know I survived. But, in fact, I survived in style—it was the best eating winter of my life. Here's my report.

. . .

September—The farmers' market in Middlebury, Vermont, is in absolute fever bloom: sweet, sweet corn; big, ripe tomatoes; bunches of basil; melons. This is the bounty of our short but intense summer, when the heat of the long days combines with the moisture of these eastern uplands to produce almost anything you could want. It's the great eating moment of the year.

But I'm wandering the market trying to keep the image of midwinter in mind—the short, bitter days of January, when the snow is drifted high against the house and the woodstove is cranking. I'm used to getting the winter's wood in, but not to putting the winter's food by. In our world, it's always summer somewhere, and so we count on the same produce year-round. But that takes its toll: on the environment, from endless trucking and flying and shipping; on local farmers, who can't compete with the equatorial bounty and hence sell their fields for condos; and most of all, perhaps, on taste. There's nothing that tastes like a June strawberry; whereas a January supermarket strawberry tastes like . . . nothing.

All of which explains why I'm bargaining for canning tomatoes, the Romas with perhaps a few blemishes. Though mostly I want to spend the winter buying what's available, I'll put up a certain amount. My friend Amy Trubek volunteers to help—a food anthropologist, she's the head of the Vermont Fresh Network, which partners farmers with chefs; she and her husband, Brad Koehler, one of the chefs at (and general manager of) Middlebury College's renowned dining halls, also own a small orchard and a big vegetable garden, not to mention a capacious freezer. "A lot of people associate canning with their grandmother, hostage in the kitchen for six weeks," she said. "But, hey, this is the twenty-first century. We can freeze, we can cure, we can Cryovac—we can do all this a hundred different ways." An afternoon's work, with the Red Sox beginning their stretch drive on the radio, and I've got enough tomato sauce frozen in Ziplocs to last me through the winter.

• • •

October—Fall lingers on (and the Red Sox, too). I'm already regarding the leaf lettuce in our local food co-op with a kind of nostalgia, knowing it's about to disappear from my life. And I'm regarding two small bins in the co-op's bulk section as my lifeline. They're filled with local flour, fifty-nine cents a pound. Once upon a time, the Champlain Valley was the nation's granary—but that was back before the Erie Canal opened the way west and vast rivers of grain began rolling back from the deep topsoil of the Plains. Grain farming all but disappeared from the region; the most basic component of the American diet had to be imported from Nebraska.

But there's always an oddball, and, in this case, his name is Ben Gleason, who came to Vermont, as did many others, as a part of the back-to-the-land movement of the 1970s. He found an old farm in the Addison County town of Bridport and began to plant it in a rotation of organic hard red winter wheat. Last year, for instance, he grew thirty tons on twenty-eight acres, perfectly respectable even by Midwest standards, and he ground all of it with the small, noisy machine in the shed next to his house. He only does whole-wheat flour—white would require another machine, and anyway, as he points out, it's not nearly as good for you. In any event, his is delicious—making pancakes flavorful enough to stand up to the Grade B maple syrup that's the only kind we buy. (Grade A, Fancy—it's for tourists. The closer to tar, the better.)

"There's maybe four or five hundred acres altogether that's planted in wheat around the area," said Samuel Sherman, who owns Champlain Valley Milling, in Westport, New York. Mostly he grinds wheat that arrives by train car from the west, but he'd love to see more local product. "We can sell it in a minute," he said. The proof is just down the lakeshore, in the town of Crown Point, where a young baker named Yannig Tanguy makes artisanal bread—fougasse, baguette, Swabian rye—entirely with local wheat that he grinds himself, sometimes three hundred pounds in a day. Crown Point is a poor town next to an aging paper mill—and yet the door to the little bakery keeps popping open constantly. Here's someone who wants to reserve ten loaves for an elementary school dinner the next week; here's a woman to buy a cookie and say thanks for letting her park in the tiny lot during church that morning. "It's not like I'm trying to invent anything with local food," said Tanguy. "It all obviously worked for a long time. That we're here today is proof that it worked. And it can work again."

. . .

November—The traditional Thanksgiving dinner is also the traditional local foods dinner in this part of the world. Which makes sense, since the Pilgrims weren't in any position to import much food—they just hunkered down with the beige cuisine that begins to predominate as the summer becomes mere memory. (On Cape Cod, cranberries provide a flash of deep color; here, we have beets, which make a ruby slaw.) The kind of self-sufficient all-around farm with which the colonists covered the continent has essentially disappeared, at least outside of Amish country. Even the tiny growers in this valley specialize in order to stay afloat—I can show you a potato farmer in the hills above Rutland with fifty varieties on his three acres, or a bison wrangler on the lakeshore, or an emu rancher. Some of America's original community-supported agriculture farms (CSAs) are in this area, and none produce vegetables more glorious than those from Golden Russet Farm, in Shoreham, where Will and Judy Stevens are busy threshing dried beans when I stop by one afternoon to pick up some squash. If you pay them a few hundred dollars in the winter, they'll keep you supplied with a weekly bin of vegetables throughout the growing season and deep into the fall. But even Will and Judy go to the store for their milk.

Not so Mark and Kristin Kimball, the young proprietors of Essex Farm, on the New York side of the lake. If you want to join their CSA, you pay more like a few thousand dollars. But when you stop by on Friday afternoons for your pickup, it's not just vegetables: they have a few milking cows, so there's milk and cheese and butter; they have a small herd of grass-fed cattle, so there are steaks and burgers; the snorting tribe of pigs behind the barn provides bacon and lard; there are chickens and turkeys. Except for paper towels and dental floss, you'd never have to set foot in a store again—think Laura Ingalls Wilder, complete with a team of big Belgians. "There's nothing inherent about modern ways that I don't support," Mark insisted. "It just so happens that working with horses is—not better than working with tractors, but more fun. It's a more dynamic relationship. You can understand an engine. You'll never understand a horse."

You can't leave the farm without Mark loading your trunk full of food—"Do you have room for another chicken in there?"—and all of it tastes of the place. As you bump down the driveway, a look in the rearview mirror reveals Mark juggling carrots and grinning. "Occasionally I feel like I'm doing some work," he said. "But usually it feels more like entertainment for myself."

Is this realistic? Could you feed Manhattan in this fashion? You could not—every place is different. (And Manhattan is lucky to have New Jersey right next door, with some of the best truck-farming soil and weather anywhere on earth.) But you could feed Essex, New York, this way—Mark figures the fifty acres they're farming can support ten families, a reminder of just how fertile the earth is in the right hands.

· · ·

December—Here's what I'm missing: not grapefruit, not chocolate. Oats. And their absence helps illustrate what's happened to

American agriculture, and what would be required to change it a little bit.

Once upon a time, oats were everywhere—people grew them for their horses, and for themselves. But oats aren't easy to deal with. They have a hull that needs removing, and they need to be steamed, and dried, and rolled. You can do that more efficiently on an enormous scale in places like Saskatoon, Saskatchewan, where a single mill can turn out more than half a million pounds of oat products a day. For the moment, this centralization works. But that may change if the price of oil (the lifeblood of industrial agriculture) continues to climb, or as the climate continues to shift, or if global politics deteriorates. Even now, stubborn people keep trying to rebuild smaller-scale food networks, but it's hard going against the tide of cheap goods flowing in. A few years ago, for instance, a Vermonter named Andrew Leinoff decided to go into oats—he and his friend Eric Allen found some old equipment and started experimenting. But after a few years of struggling they gave up, and a little bitterly. The state's Agency of Agriculture talks a good game—a public service ad on the radio urges Vermonters to buy 10 percent of their food from within the state—but in the opinion of many small farmers, it spends most of its time and money propping up the state's slowly withering dairy industry, not supporting the pioneers trying to build what comes next.

They sold their equipment across the border in Quebec, to an organic miller named Michel Gaudreau, who does everything from hulling spelt to pearling barley. And Gaudreau found a farmer in the province's Eastern Townships, Alex Brand, whose family had been growing oats for many years. I tracked him down, delighted to find that Brand's Fellgarth Farm was right on the edge of my Champlain watershed. But shipping a bag of oats across the border was going to be hard work—it might, they warned, require a trip to Customs. Happily, Brand had an American distributor—Joe

Angello, in New York's Columbia County. By the time all was said and done, my "local" oats had traveled on a truck from Canada to the lower Hudson Valley, and then back to Vermont in a UPS sack. Not precisely an ecological triumph. On the other hand, they were delicious—plump, if oats can be plump. So now it's pancakes only every other morning.

. . .

January—Truth be told, my eleven-year-old daughter has used the words icky and disgusting on several occasions, always in connection with root vegetables. Not potatoes, not carrots—but turnips, and parsnips, and rutabagas. It is a little hard to imagine how people got through winter on the contents of their root cellars alone.

Which is why I'm glad for the Ziplocs full of raspberries and blueberries my wife froze in the summer. And why I'm glad for the high-tech apple warehouse just down the road in Shoreham. Here's the thing about apples: the best ones rot pretty fast. Sure, those brick-hard Red Delicious and Granny Smiths can be picked in New Zealand or South Africa or China or Washington and flown and trucked halfway around the world and sit on a shelf at the supermarket for a week and still look like an apple. (Taste is another story—they've been bred for immortality, and immortality alone.) But the great apples of the Northeast—your Cortland, your Empire, your Northern Spy, and, above all, your McIntosh—are softer, more ephemeral. For generations, people solved that problem by converting them to cider—hard cider, fermented for freezerless storage. That's what most of those apple trees around New England were planted for. But there's another solution if, like Barney Hodges, you have a storage shed where you can pump in nitrogen. "We push the oxygen level down from its normal twenty percent to just under three percent. The apple's respiration is slowed to the point where the ripening process is nearly halted," he explained. Every few weeks he cracks open another room in the warehouse, and it's as if you're back in September—the apples in his Sunrise Orchard bags head out to nearby supermarkets, where he frets that they won't be kept cool.

Apples help illustrate another point, too: in the years ahead, *local* may be a more important word than *organic* in figuring out how to eat. In fact, a British study published this winter found that buying food from close to home prevented twice as much environmental damage as buying organic food from a distance.

Now, the best solution might be local and organic; most of the food I've been eating this winter falls into that category. But apples aren't easy—an orchard is a monoculture, prey to a bewildering variety of insects and blights. And very few consumers, even at the natural foods co-op, will pick up a Macoun or a Paula Red if it's clear that some other creature has taken the first nibble, so almost all the area growers do a little spraying. "How little spray can I get away with, and still produce fruit that people will buy?" asked Bill Suhr, who runs Champlain Orchards, down the road just above the Ticonderoga ferry dock. His saving grace is the cider press that's clanking away as we talk: he can take the risk of using fewer chemicals because if the apples aren't perfect, he can always turn them into cider. Absolutely delicious cider, too—I've been drinking well north of two gallons a week, and I'm not sure I'll ever go back to orange juice. And each batch, because it draws on a slightly different mix of varieties, tastes a little different: tartest in early fall, sweetest and most complex at the height of the harvest, but always tangy and deep. It may not be organic, but it's neighborly, which is good enough for me.

· · ·

February—By now an agreeable routine has set in: pancakes or oatmeal or eggs in the morning, soup and a cheese sandwich for lunch. (I could eat a different Vermont cheese every day of the winter, but I usually opt for a hunk off the Orb Weaver farmstead round.) And for dinner, some creature that until quite recently was clucking, mooing, baaing, or otherwise signaling its pleasure at the local grass and hay it was turning into protein. Also potatoes. And something from the freezer—it's a chest-type, and in a dark corner, so you basically just stick a hand in and see what vegetable comes out.

And, oh, did I mention beer? Otter Creek Brewing, a quarter mile down the road from my daughter's school, makes a stellar wit bier, a Belgian style that is naturally cloudy with raw organic wheat from Ben Gleason's farm. It's normally sold in the summer, but I hoarded some for my winter drinking. "We'd love to use local barley for the rest of our beers," said Morgan Wolaver, the brewery's owner. But that would mean someone building a malting plant to serve not just Otter Creek but the state's seven other microbreweries. Perhaps right next to the oat mill . . .

· · ·

March—I can see spring in the distance—there are still feet of snow in the woods, but the sun is September strong, and it won't be long before down in the valley someone is planting lettuce.

But there's one last place I must describe, both because it's provided many of my calories and because it embodies the idea of a small-scale farmer making a decent living growing great food. Jack and Anne Lazor bought Butterworks Farm, in the state's Northeast Kingdom, in the mid-'70s, after a stint of working at Old Sturbridge Village, in Massachusetts: dressed in nineteenth-century costumes, they milked cows by hand and talked to the tourists. As it turns out, they weren't actors—they were real farmers. Slowly they've grown their business into one of the state's premier organic dairies: their yogurt is nearly a million-dollar business. I've been living off their dried beans, too, and their cornmeal. It's great fun, then, to sit in their kitchen eating bacon and eggs and watch Anne mix up some salve for the teats of her cows, and listen to them describe their life. The talk's a mix of technical detail (they milk Jerseys, not the more common Holsteins, which means less milk but higher protein, so their yogurt needs no pectin to stay firm) and rural philosophy. "We have such a 'take' mentality," Jack said. "It's part of our psyche, because we came to this verdant land as Europeans and were able to exploit it for so long."

But here the exploitation feels more like collaboration. We stroll over to his solar barn, where the hundred cows in the herd loiter patiently, mulling over the events of the day. "That's Morel, that's Phooey, that's Vetch, that's Clover, that's Jewel . . ." It's very calm in here, no sound but cud being chewed, and it's warm out of the late winter wind. Jack, who's a talker, explained how Vermont could market itself as the Sustainable State, and how he's hoping to sell *masa harina* for making tortillas next year, and so forth. I sort of listen, but mostly I just absorb the sheer pleasure of the scene—that this place works, that I've been connected to it all winter long, that it will be here, with any luck, for the rest of my life.

Look—eating this way has come at a cost. Not in health or in money (if anything, I've spent less than I usually would, since I haven't bought a speck of processed food), but in time. I've had to think about every meal, instead of cruising through the world on autopilot, ingesting random calories. I've had to pay attention. But the payoff for that cost has been immense, a web of connections I'd never have known about otherwise. Sure, I'm looking forward to the occasional banana, the odd pint of Guinness stout. But I think this winter has permanently altered the way I eat. In more ways than one, it's left a good taste in my mouth.

# · 17 ·

## The Great Leap

—*Harper's Magazine,* December 2005

On the flight from Newark to Beijing, I read the following small item in the *China Daily*:

> According to media reports, several air conditioner installers have fallen to their deaths in the last couple of days in Beijing alone.
>
> As the sweltering summer heat sweeps the country, sales of air conditioning units are booming. This has naturally led to strong demand for installation services.
>
> The spurt in installation service demand has left many firms understaffed, so some are temporarily recruiting untrained installers to cash in. . . . [Some] even refuse to provide safety belts to installers in order to save costs.

The article—evoking as it did a hazy urban sky filled with plummeting air-conditioner installers—coincided perfectly with my mental image of China, so I tore it out and filed it away. I'd done the same thing a hundred times before, creating for myself a carefully imagined China full of smog-blackened cities where people wore gas masks against the clouds of coal smoke; savagely Dickensian factories where young women were paid slave wages; a heedless and rapidly expanding consumer class hell-bent on buying cars and appliances with no regard for the environmental costs of their consumption. I wanted to see it for myself, to indulge in the kind of disaster tourism that makes one gaze agape at the sheer can't-take-your-eyes-off spectacle of it all, like the visitors who flocked to Niagara to watch boats filled with zoo animals wash over the falls. And then come home with head-shaking cautionary tales about what this combination of heedless growth and ecological unconcern meant for the future of the world. That was the plan, anyhow.

The "watch out for China" narrative offers something to every American. Liberals can be repulsed by China's destruction of the environment and conservatives can portend the rising hegemony of the East. Americans from across the political spectrum can frown upon China's dismal disregard for personal freedom—jails filled with Falun Gong devotees, always Tiananmen hovering in the background. The problem with actually reporting about a place, however, is that you start collecting stories, and they never quite fit. It's not that any of these angles are *wrong*—there are countless well-documented stories of nightmarish factory conditions, human rights violations, local corruption, and environmental folly—but even taken together they don't come close to adding up to China. And they allow us to ignore what might be most crucial about the emerging nation: the ways it is starting to resemble our own.

·  ·  ·

On my third day in China, still slightly jet-lagged, I piled into a VW Jetta driven by a Beijing software designer named Wen Jie and headed for the "Rongcheng Industry Zone" about one hundred miles southwest of Beijing—one of hundreds of such zones spread along China's coastline. We took an empty new highway out of the city. That highway joined another, and another, till finally we exited the toll-road system altogether and plunged into Third World rural chaos: overloaded trucks, flocks of sheep wandering across the street, a landscape scarred by tiny brickworks whose owners had mined out the top few feet of much of the surrounding landscape. And, covering every other bit of available land, the underlying green order of corn and rice fields, punctuated at irregular intervals by men and women, straw-hatted, backs bent, hoeing under the hot sun.

The Rongcheng Industry Zone turned out to be less grand than it sounded—a rural district with a higher density of factories and (another) brand-new highway, this one leading directly to Tianjin, the largest man-made port in China. We stopped at the Hebei Rongcheng LeJia shower-curtain factory to pick up its owner, Bao Jijun, who wanted to show us his and some of his friends' operations.

Now, given what I'm going to say, it matters how I came across Bao. I had avoided registering as a reporter with the Chinese government, and so I was spared a tour of some showpiece installation. On the other hand, the owner of any dark satanic mill or prison-slave-labor operation was surely bright enough to keep an American with a notepad away. In fact, I found Bao in as random a way as I could imagine: a friend in Vermont, where I live, introduced me to Wen (the software designer), who in turn introduced me to Bao, a kind of shirtsleeve cousin, who'd been making shower curtains since 2002.

Before showing me his factory, Bao wanted us to visit the Hua Xin Li Dress Co., Ltd., which was by Chinese standards a venerable firm. It had opened its doors in 1987, right around the time that Deng Xiaoping had begun to allow any such enterprise. From a home factory with five or six employees, it had grown into a medium-sized enterprise with several hundred workers. " 'First Quality and Prestige Supreme' is our aim," says the company's brochure; on the day we visited they were churning out slightly garish yellow dress shirts for the Eastern European market. The factory was three stories tall, and on each floor young women and a few young men in white company T-shirts sat, four abreast, in front of new sewing machines imported from Japan. It was a hot day, but big fans moved plenty of air around. There was a busy hum, but not a din. The women worked fast, especially the button-sewers at the end of the room, but not frantically. A large red banner hung over the middle of each room reading, in Chinese, "The Customer Is God and the Market Decides Everything."

What "the market" had decided was that these women would earn about 10,000 yuan a year ($.50 an hour). Two thirds of them commuted from the surrounding villages. The rest came from the provinces and lived behind the factory, in a dormitory with a water pump and a clothesline out in the courtyard. I cannot tell you if this was a hard life or even an acceptable life, but later, as we drove away from the factory, we did pass field after field of those men and women with bent-over backs.

After our tour of the Hua Xin Li Dress Co., Ltd., we got back in the Jetta and headed down the road to the Gold Pioneer Cow shirt factory, where in similar (although smaller) rooms young women and some men were sewing track suits for Germans, black vests for hotel waiters, and—under the Tact Squad label—dark blue uniforms for American cops. Gold Pioneer Cow also makes men's suits for the Chinese market. "In China, the requirement is that if you get married you need to have a wedding suit," the owner explained happily.

And then, at the end of a dusty road, we returned to the shower-curtain plant. Bao Jijun is in his early forties, tall, lean, and vigorous. He'd started his business three years before in a Beijing apartment with his wife and two other workers; within six months he was renting space at another factory; within a year he had leased this place. Now he had a hundred employees. We wandered through the workrooms, watching kids—almost everyone was between eighteen and twenty-two, as if the place were some kind of shower-curtain college—smooth long bolts of polyester onto huge tables, sew hems and grommets, fold the finished curtains into plastic bags, pack them into cartons. It's hard to imagine a much simpler product than a shower curtain.

Because of the summer heat, everyone worked from 7:30 to 11:30 and then again from 3:00 to 7:00. We'd been there for only a few minutes, in fact, when all labor ceased and everyone poured down the stairs into the cafeteria for lunch. Rice, green beans, eggplant stew, some kind of stuffed dumpling, and a big bowl of soup: 1.7 yuan, or about 20 cents. While people ate, we wandered into one of the dormitory rooms for girls (the boys were off a separate hall). Each room had four bunk beds, one of which was for storing suitcases and clothes. The others were for sleeping, six girls to a room. There were stuffed animals, posters of boy bands, stacks of comic books, little bottles of cosmetics. One desk to share, one ceiling fan. Next to the dormitory was a lounge with a giant TV and twenty or thirty battered chairs; the room next door had a Ping-Pong table. "Any of my workers who can beat me," Bao said, "gets a bottle of beer."

Virtually all of Bao's employees come from the province where he grew up, a couple hundred miles to the south. He let me interview as many as I wanted, with Wen acting as interpreter. He was especially pleased with my first pick, Du Peitang, a nervous twenty-year-old with a goofy grin and very bright eyes. His father had died and his mother had remarried and moved away, so he'd grown up with his grandparents. His first job had been as a guard at an oil company in Shandong province, but it paid only a few hundred yuan a month and there was no room or board. One of his relatives introduced him to Bao, who had the reputation of being nice to his workers, so he'd come to work, earning about 1,000 yuan a month. From that salary, he'd been able to save 12,000 yuan in a little less than two years—a pretty big stake. In another year or two, he said, he'd have enough to build a small house back home and get married. For fun, Du said, he played Ping-Pong and watched TV—a good plan, because, as Bao pointed out, buying a single Coke every night would come near to halving Du's savings.

The next worker I talked to was Liu Xia, eighteen years old, a lovely young woman nervous as hell about talking to a strange American who inexplicably and impertinently wanted to know about her life. "There are four people in my home. My parents, my elder brother, and me. My parents aren't healthy. They do farm work, but my father has a bad knee, so my mother carries most of the load. I really wanted to help her. And my brother could go to college, but it would cost a lot. He is in the Shandong University of Science and Technology, studying mechanical engineering." In fact, it turns out, he had graduated just a week before, thanks to her earnings here at the curtain factory. I asked her if she had a stuffed animal on her bed like everyone else. Her eyes filled ominously. She likes them very much, she said, but she has to save all her earnings for her future.

I could tell stories about this one factory for a long time. It was hot the night before we came, for instance, and so everyone had slept on the roof, and Bao had told them the old Chinese story about the spinning girl and the cowboy and the creation of the Milky Way. But I'll desist—for all I know, I'd stumbled into the one decent factory in all of China. After all, Chinese workers reportedly lose forty thousand arms, hands, and fingers to industrial accidents every year.

For his part, Bao says he thinks he's in the seventieth or eightieth percentile of factories, judging by working conditions. One reason his factory is decent is because he's a good guy. Another is that he sells some of his shower curtains to Ikea. The company sends an inspector, unannounced, several times a year to check on the living spaces and the number of toilets and so on, and slowly these inspectors have been checking off the improvements. "It adds to the cost, but I appreciate it. I regard the requirements as help to reach the level of a factory in a developed country," Bao said with a kind of Rotarian pride.

Depending on the model, Bao can make a shower curtain for about 21 yuan. He can sell one for about 24 yuan. When you buy a similar shower curtain in an American big-box store it retails for about $30, or about 240 yuan. But Bao doesn't do much business directly with American-owned retailers. When a pair of buyers from the States came to visit a few months earlier, they had told him they could sell millions of curtains. But he would somehow have to drive the price down to 18 yuan. Which would mean, say, getting rid of the Ping-Pong table, or adding a few hours to the workday, or doubling the price of the soup.*

· · ·

Seeing the sheer volume of industrious labor in those few factories began my education. But it was only toward the end of my four-week visit, in the city of Yiwu, that I really began to understand not only the scale of China's manufacturing enterprise but the force of the momentum behind it.

I'd taken a packed and sweltering train from Shanghai to Yiwu, which despite being home to more than a million people didn't even appear in my nine-hundred-page tourist guide to China. Yiwu is home to the International Trade City, where you can see sights every bit as awesome as the terracotta warriors of Xian or even the Great Wall. The place is only two-fifths complete, but the two huge buildings already standing—they each look like the Empire State Building laid on its side and mated with a fleet of aircraft carriers—demonstrate the unavoidable truth that anything that can be made can be made cheaper in China.

Take, for instance, the "Suitcases and Bags, Including School Bags" section of the International Trade City. There are about eight hundred ten by twelve stalls, each representing a different

---

*Ikea's slogan, which in the modern economy almost passes as humane, is "Low Price, But Not at Any Price."

factory, each showing its wares to buyers in the hope they'll order lots of ten or twenty or thirty thousand. There are stalls with
duffel bags, change purses, wallets of every kind. Fanny packs,
metal lunch boxes, jewelry cases. It's a kind of headquarters of
dubious English: "I dream of being the best basketballer in the
town." "Durable Performance Based on the 58's 123–45 Vintage
Spirit." "My grandfather has white hairlike snow." I stared for a
long time at a backpack that said "All Things Grow with Love"
before I figured out that it looked weird because it was grammat-
ically correct.

"Suitcases and Bags, Including School Bags," took up only half
a floor. The story above was entirely devoted to "Hardware Tools
and Fittings," which is another way of saying pretty much everything on earth: knife blocks, car jacks, chaise longues, surge pro-
tectors, lint rollers, jumper cables, carabiners, bike pumps, rubber
bands, cheese graters. One stall had thousands of those Lance
Armstrong "Livestrong" bracelets in a rainbow of colors. Lucky
rabbit's feet, singing birthday cards, nail clippers, safety pins,
ratchet sets, thigh exercisers, bathroom scales, toilet-bowl deodor-
izers, plaid wheelchairs, feather dusters, meat-pounding mallets.
Dozens of models of magnetic patriotic ribbons for the backs of
American cars ("Freedom Is Not Free"). Pruning shears, putty
knives, carafes, egg cups, cake-decorating nozzles, depilatory machines, giant martini glasses, immersion heating coils, disposable
cameras, hip flasks, sake sets, mortar and pestles, cereal dispensers
(like you see on the buffet at the Motel 6), rolling pins, exit signs,
sander belts, key rings, rubber gloves.

In the "Regular Toys" section of Building 1 there are hundreds
of stalls offering variations on those weird squishy rubber balls:
skull-shaped balls whose eyes pop out when you squeeze, "yucky
maggot balls." Not to mention boogie boards, plastic hand grenades,
squeaky mallets, bow-and-arrow sets, toy pianos, "small chef"
ovens. After twenty minutes of walking you emerge into the
"Electric Toys" section. ("Does thinking the son and daughter

become the scientist? Then start growing from the electronic toy bricks! Train pilot! Look for the Bill Gates!") And then the "Inflatable Toys" section, and then, biggest of all, the "Fabric Plush Toys." The next floor is divided between artificial flowers and hair ornaments—you suddenly realize that there are 3 billion women on this planet, many of whom would probably be happy to have ribbons in their hair. And above that, miles of kitsch—the "Tourism Crafts" section, which could stock every gift shop on earth, with light-up Virgin Marys, "African" carvings, novelty bottle openers, refrigerator magnets by the millions. And on the top floor, the stalls that bring the world Christmas. Groves of artificial trees blinking with LEDs, squads of Santas playing electric guitars and riding exercycles and spinning hula hoops. Tinsel tinsel tinsel.

. . .

Once I'd been to Yiwu, sights I'd seen earlier made more sense. Chunming, for instance, was a tiny rural town in the hills of Sichuan. We'd spent the night before in Chengdu, the provincial capital, which is larger than New York City. Chunming was an hour's drive away, but it was the usual world apart. Most of the men worked up the hill at a makeshift coal mine, trying to avoid the cave-ins and explosions that maim a hundred miners a week around the country. The place was pretty bleak.

With my translator, a young environmental journalist named Zhao Ang, I wandered up to the first house we came to. The place was actually pretty big, a series of interlinked and crumbling courtyards. It had belonged to the local landlord until 1949, when it was expropriated in the wake of the Communist victory and given to seven or eight families to share. A few pigs slept in the room next to the kitchen. There was one girl we could talk to here, Zhao Lintao (no relation). She was twelve years old, and proudly spoke the English she'd learned in the overcrowded village school. When we asked her about her life, though, she was soon in tears: her mother had gone to the city to work in a factory and never returned, abandoning her and her sister to her father, who beat them regularly because they were not boys. The government was taking care of her school fees until ninth grade, but after that there would be no more money. Her sister had already given up and dropped out.

Multiply that story by half a billion and you will begin to understand why the biggest migration in the history of the planet is under way in China, why there are always more bodies to sit behind those sewing machines. Tens of millions of people leave desperately poor farms every year to work at the factories that feed Yiwu. By one estimate the country needs to add an urban infrastructure equivalent to Houston every month just to keep pace. More than a hundred cities in China have populations that top a million. And even so, the countryside still bulges.

What struck me about China, in fact, was not so much the teeming cities as that teeming countryside. China has a third of the planet's farmers and one fourteenth of its farmland. In places, the average farm plot is a sixth of an acre—smaller than many American houses. About 800 million people, roughly 65 percent of China's population, are crowded onto those tiny farms. And on average they are earning one third the income of city dwellers. It is easy to see why the United Nations predicts that by 2030, 60 percent of Chinese will live in the cities. With a massive effort, that number might be held down to 50 percent. But since about 1 percent of Americans currently work as farmers, down from 39 percent a century ago, we should be able to understand this tide.

Not that the path to the city is easy. The gulf between urban and rural Chinese is as profound as the racial gulfs that plague our own country. Here, for instance, is a small item that appeared one day in the section of the *China Daily* that runs down comical stories from around the country, tales like "Widowed Swan Finds

Love During Treatment" or "Princely Sum Offered for Return of Umbrella" or "Man Dislocates Chin in Laughing Incident."

## MIGRANT WORKERS TOLD TO
## ZIP UP IN ZHENGZHOU

Migrant workers are fresh out of luck if nature calls and they're anywhere near one public toilet in Zhengzhou, Henan province. . . .

The female guard of the toilet is on a campaign to keep migrant workers from using her lavatory.

She's even been known to yank anyone suspected of being a migrant labourer out of the restroom no matter what state of undress they're in.

The toilet's management said the practice was to keep the facilities clean.

But it means a long trek to relieve themselves for workers at a construction site near the toilet, as the only other spot they can squat in is wasteland 500 metres away.

A teacher I met in Beijing said he had been appalled at the discrimination he faced when he moved to the city from his village in Inner Mongolia ten years ago. He joined a guerrilla-theater troupe that performed at factory gates and construction sites. One of their most popular plays was the tale of a girl from the country who came to the city and crossed the road in front of a bus, forcing it to slam on its brakes. "Someone in the bus had a cake and it smashed and the man was angry," the teacher said. "The bus driver said the girl was at fault. So the people taking the bus dragged her into the bus and yelled and screamed at her. She got very scared and jumped out the bus window and died."

The teacher, who taught the children of other new arrivals, and who was scared to give his name, said he and his colleagues thought calling those new arrivals "peasants" was "impolite"—he proposed "the people who come to the city for a job" or "the workers" or "new citizens"—but many such new arrivals will never become citizens of Shanghai or Beijing or anywhere other than the villages from which they came. Internal migration being such a major factor in Chinese politics, moving officially requires new papers, and those papers are hard to come by. It was considered a sign of great progress, in fact, when China's premier, Wen Jiabao, went on TV to announce that contractors would no longer be allowed to get away with their usual fraud—turning workers away from construction sites without their last month's pay, a scam that costs workers billions of yuan annually.

If you wanted to slow down the tide of people, you'd need to do something to raise rural incomes. And there are people trying. Ren Xuping, for instance, who lives about an hour outside of Chengdu, in the village-turned-city of Dayi. He was a poor peasant in 1987 when Heifer International, the Arkansas-based rural-development charity, gave him forty-eight rabbits and some instruction on how to breed them. "At first I didn't really believe it was something free," he said. "It was like some pie dropping down from heaven." Within a few years, aided by the well-known reproductive success of bunnies, he was a millionaire. But Ren was a particular kind of millionaire, one who'd become obsessed with Heifer's credo of passing on the wealth. He'd soon delivered up the requisite one hundred animals for other farmers to use, but that was barely the beginning: he has since built a training school that, according to Heifer, has trained some 300,000 would-be rabbit farmers.

I spent an afternoon with Ren deep in the Chinese countryside, visiting poor farmers with new consignments of Heifer rabbits. The man can talk for a very long time (over stewed rabbit, spicy sautéed rabbit, deep-fried rabbit) about the advantages of bunnies. (They eat mostly grass, for instance, which can be harvested from recovering eroded hillsides. And every part of them can be used: Ren was opening a factory to make clothing and stuffed animals from rabbit fur.) But he was even more passionate about what rabbit income might mean for poor farmers. "You can make ten thousand yuan a year after two or three years," he said. "This can resolve the problem of supporting the old people and educating the children." The trick, he said, in full power-of-positive-thinking mode, "is to make a family become positive instead of passive. They can say, 'Oh, I live in a remote area, I'm illiterate, I'm poor.' That's a passive attitude, and it can be changed through things like Heifer. You want to make them become a bigger farmer, then an enterpriser. The key is they have to have a dream for the future, develop a mission. In so many cases, they don't have a dream, they just live day to day."

But the truth is, programs like Heifer's will help only so much. The push of the crowded countryside and the pull of urban opportunity are simply too strong. One sweaty night, I drove with Wen out beyond Beijing's fifth ring road, past a huge new condo development with its own McDonald's, and into a totally different world—a once-rural village now surrounded by city, soon to be swallowed up itself, but for the moment serving as home to tens of thousands of migrant families. At the north end of town, down a dark alley, we came to the home of Cao Zhonglong, fifty-seven years old, who came from Jiangxi province in 1987. "Our village didn't have enough food," he said. *"There was not any meat, not any alcohol."*

Cao's cousin had started a construction team, and so Cao went to work peddling a tricycle full of materials around job sites. Before long he'd learned ceramic tiling, then plastering and painting. He went into business on his own. He, his wife, and their three daughters shared a tiny room, one third of which was occupied by a tinier store. They slept in one bed. Throughout the night, people would stop in to buy beer from the cooler. And yet Cao was not a poor man. He'd saved enough to build two homes back in his village, one two stories tall and the other three. His mother lived in one, and he rented the other.

In Beijing, Cao had only enough money to live in a slum. But if he lived in his house in the countryside he'd have no way to make money. In any case, he had other things to accomplish in the city. His second daughter had, the spring before, graduated from university. She was now working for a joint-venture pharmaceutical company, at a starting salary of 2,400 yuan a month. I asked him if when she was born it had occurred to him she might someday go to university. He just looked at me and laughed.

We drove to Cao's first daughter's hut, a few slums away. She lives there with her husband, Wang Zhihua, who is also from the countryside, and who makes his money enclosing Beijing apartment balconies with glass. "I go to the apartment buildings," he said, "and I note the units where the balconies aren't yet enclosed, and I send them letters." With the money he's saving he plans to move back to the capital city of Jiangxi and start some business safer than fooling around on unenclosed balconies. In the meantime, he's putting his brother through college. The brother, who happened to be visiting the day I was there, speaks excellent English, even though he'd met only one other foreigner in his life. He's getting his degree in electronic-information-systems engineering and plans to start an Internet company.

· · ·

I'd been in Beijing just a few days when I was invited to the monthly meeting of the Environmental Journalists Salon. I went with an American environmentalist, Randy Kritkausky, whose small nonprofit organization, ECOLOGIA, had helped launch the salon five years before. More than eighty people jammed into a hot and sweaty conference room off the main newsroom of the *China Youth Daily*.

Which was impressive: in the still tightly controlled political environment, this group was not precisely dissident, but some of its members skated closer to the edge than most Chinese would want to go. One of the day's presenters, for instance, was a retired teacher, Yun Jianli, who'd traveled from Hubei province in the south to rouse among these writers interest in the problems of the Han River.

She showed photos of her brigade of activists walking more than a hundred miles along the water—which was gruesomely polluted by effluvia flowing from a hundred small factories—and of campaigners waving a huge green flag with "Save Our River" written in Chinese. She had a lot of pictures of herself at huge meetings, shouting into a megaphone, and of a riverside village of 300 people, 110 of whom she said had cancer. "We complain to the provincial officials, but we get no response," she said. Watching her was almost exactly like watching Lois Gibbs talk about Love Canal two decades ago.

Yun was typical of the kind of environmental activists who have arisen in China in the last few years. Chinese activists tend to focus on pollution in particular rivers and particular cities, as opposed to the more global concerns that increasingly worry Western environmentalists. By some accounts, there may be seventy thousand protests a year in China, many of them over particular factories spewing out toxins. While I was there, Howard French wrote a remarkable story in the *New York Times* about a crowd of fifteen thousand who rioted to close a pharmaceutical plant at Xin-chang. They said the plant had poisoned waterways for miles downstream.

The Chinese authorities, who value stability above all else, are attempting to respond. The Communist Party, for instance, under the influence of European environmentalists, has pledged its commitment to what it calls a "circular economy." In, say, Denmark this would mean organizing industrial parks such that a power company, a drug plant, a wallboard producer, and an oil refinery would be located near one another so that they could use one another's wastes as raw materials. In China it's so far meant a large number of conferences and pledges and confident announcements—pilot projects to turn sulphur slag into fertilizer, promises that, say, Guangdong province would, since round numbers are big in China, "introduce standard clean production systems to one hundred industrial enterprises, turn one hundred heavy polluting enterprises into more clean and efficient operations and promote one hundred types of new clean production skills and techniques." Given that there are millions of plants across China, it's hard to tell what any of this means, though the World Bank is ready to start spending and the restaurant next to the best hotel in Guiyang has an impressive list of German beers for the Teutonic experts who are arriving to dispense advice.

As it happened, I later visited a village near Guiyang devoted to another oddly green enterprise: organic peaches, each one individually wrapped in brown paper, while still on the branch, to prevent insects from causing trouble. China actually has a pretty good market for organic food, in part because consumers have good reason to worry about food safety. In one supermarket, I watched women wait in line for organic pork and saw mountains of eggs with individual "no harm" stickers. Demand is high enough to have blunted some of the momentum toward factory farming.

But the peaches, while delicious, were only half the story. Every house in the village had a biogas digester, a pit where manure and green waste rotted and gave off methane that in turn heated the wok and warmed the shower. (I even saw rice cookers converted to use the biogas.) According to local officials, 40 percent of the 400,000 farm families in the Guiyang metro area will have biogas pits of their own within the next five years. That would be a good thing. Meanwhile, the small cement operations that squat beneath the limestone hills are slowly being closed down and consolidated, the better to control their emissions. That will be a good thing, too. And the local head of the Circular Economy office is signing contracts, buying (German) pollution-control equipment, training factory managers.

· · ·

Such progress, however, is on the surface. Forget pollution for a minute—the bigger problem is that almost every natural system in China shows the effects of thousands of years of hard use and, especially, of the last half century of ideologically inspired misuse.

To get a sense of the burden the Chinese face, I got in a Chinese-made SUV one day in Beijing with Zhao Ang and a telecom programmer, Zhang Junfeng, who volunteers with a local environmental group that is monitoring the capital's water supply. Our goal was to follow the Chao River, the main source of Beijing's chief reservoir, as far upriver as we could. It was a trip none of us had taken before, and revealing in—well, in a hundred ways.

Each village we passed—and the villages essentially ran together without end—had one building with a long blackboard nailed to a wall. The blackboards turned out to contain the town records—the corn-planting schedule, the electricity fees. And a list of each of the recent births: name, date, whether it was the first or the second child for the couple in question, and whether it was legal or not. (Under certain circumstances, rural families can have two kids.)

Although the lowlands were covered in corn (and when you walked the rows you discovered that they were carefully interplanted with potatoes, something that doesn't happen on a tractor-planted Iowa industrial farm), the hills were essentially bare—without trees, eroding, a mess. In 1958, the Great Helmsman declared the Great Leap Forward. The people were to stop raising crops and start making steel in their backyards. Making steel required heat, which required wood, which required deforestation, and since not making steel would have been a bad idea, the hills were soon bare. The chaos of the Cultural Revolution led to a lot of tree-cutting too, and even the recovery from Mao took its toll—in 1979, when the "household responsibility system" was inaugurated and authorities divided communal land into individual plots, some people were afraid their neighbors would cut down "their" trees and so they axed them first.

Grasslands disappeared like forests. With newly prosperous urban markets for meat, the number of livestock swelled. American environmentalist Lester Brown, a longtime student of China, says that there are 339 million goats and sheep in the country, compared with 7 million in the United States. "I've been in areas where the farmers have to put human clothes on their mohair goats to keep them from grazing one another," he told me.

"There's nothing to eat." Without roots to hold the soil, much of the countryside has simply turned to sand. Deserts advance by hundreds of miles annually, and the dust storms of April and May are now a recognized Beijing season, just like spring and fall. Think Dust Bowl circa 1934—only in Pennsylvania and New Jersey, and with no vacant California left for the refugees.

The government has responded with tree-planting campaigns. On my way up to the Chao River, I was confronted with a grand vista—hundreds of brown hills that seemed to have broken out in a kind of acne. As I got closer, I saw that each white spot was in fact a small semicircular niche, maybe three feet round and two feet high, built of carefully stacked whitewashed stones—they were planters for trees, designed to catch water and nurture individual seedlings. I could see hundreds of thousands of them, the work of almost unimaginable man-hours. Pile all the rocks in one place and you'd have the pyramids.

When it comes to trees and erosion, the government seems also to have replaced the classic Communist sloganeering with stuff that sounds like it was written by bureaucratic Greenpeacers. One huge billboard I saw said, "Carefully operate the policy of the central government on forest management." Carved in ten-foot-tall chalk letters on one mountainside: "Keep the sand here and the water clean to make our area wealthy and serve Beijing!" The point, I guess, is that they've noticed they have a problem.

Which is not to say that they're necessarily solving it. Just as the Great Leap Forward produced great heaps of utterly useless pig iron, Maoist-style tree planting has its critics. I'd earlier watched a Powerpoint presentation by Jiang Gaoming of the Chinese Academy of Sciences demonstrating that in one project after another three out of four trees had perished. "It's a foolish policy," Jiang had said. "It emphasizes construction, not protection." On the other hand, Jiang's solution to the dust storms was to speed up the migration to the cities so there'd be fewer peasants out grazing their stock on fragile soil.

Certainly all the activity had yet to make much difference to the Chao River, which was dry in spots and a narrow, sudsy channel across a wide, empty bed in others. We drove through one small town where farmers had hung a banner across the road: "For our children, give us back our clean water. Stop the gold mine!" Soon after was the mine itself. Farmers had clearly rioted there the day before, barricading the entrance with paving stones and splashing paint across the walls.

Still, the farther up the winding river we ventured the greener things got. We were climbing now—five, six, seven thousand feet up. The road was petering out, into rutted dirt and then into tracks, and then—well, at some point Zhao and I got out to walk while Zhang looked for some way to get through. We reached a village so remote that I was rewarded with a shriek from a small girl unused to tall white guys wandering around. We talked with an old man smoking a handmade pipe. Seven years ago, he said, the sand was very bad in this valley. Then the government paid them 4,000 yuan to fence a lot of it off from the animals. The grass had come back within a year or two, he said—and indeed now it was a sea of grass, worked entirely by men on horseback.

It's questionable, though, whether such changes will make any real difference to the encroaching desertification. Although the country's south is saturated, always trying to fend off flood, China's north is simply parched. As the flow of the Chao and other rivers has been siphoned off by the cities growing alongside them, Beijing has been drawing more and more of its own water from an underground aquifer—half or more of the water it uses comes from underground, and as a result the water table is sinking by meters every year. "Some northern cities will simply be out of water in eight or ten years," Ma Jun, author of *China's Water Crisis*, the one great environmental book China has yet produced, told me over lunch in Beijing one day. The earth subsides into sinkholes in dozens of places every year now, and fissures yards wide suddenly appear like earthquake faults. *National Geographic* recently came for a look and decided the country was committing "ecological suicide." To deal with the crisis, China's leaders have dusted off a plan that Mao dreamed up in 1952: construct eight hundred-mile-long canals to carry water from the south to the north. That's an almost unimaginable idea, roughly comparable to putting Lake Superior in an aqueduct in order to let Phoenix keep watering its lawns. But it's a sign of the depth of the challenge that environmentalists like Ma cross their fingers and hope for the best. "People in the north have been using water in a crazy way for the last fifty years because they knew it would someday flow from the Yangtze," he said. "Now the time has come for the promise to be realized."

But the problem, he quickly added, is that the extra water will probably just be used to fuel a new round of rapid growth. One of the million reasons the Chao has run dry is that Beijing has thirteen ski slopes in the surrounding mountains, all of them relying on man-made snow. And they've just opened a fourteenth, this one entirely indoors.

· · ·

When we'd reached the headwaters of the Chao, we crossed a few valleys and drove back to Beijing along the equally dry White River—another of the city's main tributaries. But this time we were more interested in power than in water. Along the way we passed one new high-tension line after another. These massive, still-shiny steel towers crossed the mountains in the same lovely undulating ripples as the Great Wall; indeed we hiked to one ruined section of the wall to get a better look at the power lines, which represent an engineering feat on the same heroic/insane scale. In 2004, China added fifty gigawatts of generating capacity to its electric grid. In 2005, it will have added another sixty-five gigawatts. You can do the math any number of ways—they're adding two New Englands to their electric system annually, or half of India, or a Brazil. No power grid on earth has ever grown anywhere near that fast. Almost all of the new power comes from coal, which China has in cheap abundance; party officials have announced ambitious plans to build two nuclear reactors every year until 2020, but even if they manage to pull it off, only about 4 percent of their electricity will come from atomic reactors. Essentially, China is going to burn coal—it will have passed the 2-billion-ton mark this year. And even with that utterly unprecedented growth in supply, the country is stretched to the breaking point—twenty-four of thirty-one provinces had power shortages in 2004. "In some provinces plants operate only three or four days a week," said Yang Fuqiang, the Beijing-based vice president of the Energy Foundation. "You get five or six or seven percent loss in local GDP." In late July 2005 the Beijing authorities announced that the 4,689 local factories "will arrange week-long summer vacations for their employees in the coming four weeks" to save power, and then offset the holidays by "adopting a temporary six-day week schedule in the coming fall."

The explanation for this surge is relatively simple, and it has everything to do with those farmers streaming into the city: Yang, hunched over his computer in a Beijing office where the thermostat is turned to eighty-two to save energy, says the best guess is that more than 20 million people come to the cities every year. There they make enough money to start consuming power—in the city people get, say, small refrigerators or even air conditioners. And they get jobs making shower curtains and spatulas and suitcases, which also take some energy. And building even simple concrete huts for them requires all sorts of resources—5 percent of China's fuel may go to producing cement alone. China makes more steel than any nation on earth—not primitively, à la Mao, in the back yard, but it still takes energy.

Oh, and cars. Ten years ago there weren't any. "Driver" was an *occupation*—you took party officials around in a big black sedan. Today, China is the world's number-three car market. Demand is surging—vehicle sales grew 10 percent in the first half of 2005—and automakers expect to sell 5.6 million vehicles by year's end. Visiting the big car markets in Beijing is like going to a ball game in the United States—you park blocks away at a gas station where attendants wave you in; sidewalk vendors sell Cokes to the gawkers. (And teams of young men with big wooden clubs roam the car lot, looking for criminals.) It's a fascinating place to drive, because almost everyone is a tyro. The traffic patterns are unlike anywhere else in the world—people weave in and out constantly, merging from side streets without stopping—but crashes are relatively uncommon because speeds are low. Five years ago, you suddenly realize, these people were riding bikes.

Again, it's not as if the Chinese haven't noticed there are big problems that come with this kind of growth. By some estimates, 8 or 10 percent of the country's GDP is wasted dealing with pollution and the health effects it causes. In an interview of rare candor, Pan Yue, the country's deputy environment minister, told *Der Spiegel* that the country's economic "miracle will end soon because the environment can no longer keep pace. Five of the ten most polluted cities worldwide are in China; acid rain is falling on one third of our territory; half of the water in China's seven largest rivers is completely useless." But *without* that level of growth, there'd be no way to absorb the endless influx from the countryside. How are you going to keep people down on their sixth of an acre once they've heard that city dwellers *eat meat*?

Only with a level of repression that the post-Mao Chinese probably wouldn't tolerate, a level of repression that would shake the country's power structure. (And if that power structure fell, the democracy that replaced it would have many virtues, but controlling migration wouldn't be one of them.) That's why the country is busy building cars—because auto making, road building, tire patching, bumper fixing, and gas pumping are ways to build an economy. What's good for Shanghai Automotive, or so the thinking goes, is good for China.

*And so the country is trying to muddle through.* On the one hand, it must keep growing fast enough to absorb all that restless labor—the newspapers are already full of reports about college graduates unable to find jobs, and then there are those people pushed out of work in the vast and useless state heavy industries. And on the other hand, it must keep resource and energy use enough in check that China doesn't simply crash and burn. The official goal is to quadruple the size of the economy by 2020 while only doubling energy use—a target that's probably unattainable due to the huge growth in electric generation in the last couple of years. But devoted teams of Western planners arrive regularly with new schemes. Yang Fuqiang, whose Energy Foundation is funded primarily by the Hewlett and Packard fortunes, has managed to assemble an advisory council that includes twelve of the country's most senior officials. A vice premier comes to council meetings, listening carefully as plans are outlined for new building codes that would make apartments 50 percent more efficient than in the past, or price reforms that would end energy subsidies for heavy industry, or appliance standards—by 2030, according to Yang, "better household appliances alone would mean thirty fewer coal-fired power plants."

And the government has adopted most of these schemes, at least on paper. It has pledged to provide 10 percent of the power with renewable resources in the next fifteen years—windmills are being built left and right, which is more than America can say. And some of what the Chinese are doing Americans couldn't even begin to imagine. In Shanghai, for instance, if you want a new car you not only have to go buy it, you have to bid for a license plate—in an effort to control the growth in autos, the city allows only about six thousand new plates a month, and in the June 2005 auction they went for more than $4,000 apiece. Not only that, but they've built a remarkably good subway system, designed to persuade people to hold off buying cars. "Look, if you have a cheap, low-end metro, then the people who need to wear business clothes to the office simply won't take it," Ma Jun said. "And those are exactly the people with enough money to buy a car." The Shanghai metro has plasma screens on every car, delivering a continuous English lesson; the weekend I was riding the metro the screens were endlessly explaining the phrase "home field."

. . .

In 1997, when the world was negotiating the Kyoto Protocol, the U.S. Senate, by a vote of 95–0, passed a resolution that forbade any American involvement in a pact that limited American emissions— "unless the protocol or other agreement also mandates new specific scheduled commitments to limit or reduce greenhouse gas emissions for Developing Country Parties within the same compliance period." Although the resolution didn't cite China in particular, the testimony made it clear that China (and to a lesser extent India) was the nation everyone had in mind. Kyoto would give them a "free pass." Their economy would be allowed an "advantage" if the Chinese didn't sign on. It's an argument still in circulation— John Kerry, who voted for the original resolution, said during the 2004 presidential campaign that he thought Kyoto should be renegotiated to make the Chinese start reducing their energy use. More than any other argument, this idea of "fairness" has derailed American participation in the only international attempt to do *anything* about the biggest environmental problem our species has yet faced.

It used to be said that the point of travel was to see your own home more clearly. So let's look. When you're standing in Shanghai, at the city's urban-planning exhibition, admiring the basketball-court-sized model of the city's future plan, with every skyscraper and apartment complex carefully detailed, you just viscerally *know* that there are two countries that really count right now. You just viscerally *know* that this is the story that will define the future. China and the United States are now the world's biggest consumers of raw material, and of food, and of energy. *Are they therefore morally equivalent?*

That's not just a rhetorical question—it's a deeply practical one. And answering yes has a certain straightforward appeal. Sometime in the next few years, China will pass the United States as the largest carbon emitter in the world—already it produces 16 percent of the world's carbon dioxide compared with America's 25 percent. That is, they are now joining us in the task of undermining the planet's physics and chemistry.

The longer I looked, however, the less alike the two nations seemed. Take cars, for instance. Cars *define* America—their proliferation is the single physical item that makes our continent's civilization unique. We have nearly the same number of cars as we have people. In China the number of automobiles is growing fast. But if the Chinese sell 6 million cars this year, that will be 11 million fewer than the United States—in a population more than four times as large.

In fact, the size of China's population queers every discussion of numbers. If you're interested in global warming, it doesn't make moral sense to divide up the atmosphere by *nations*—if it did, then there'd be nothing wrong with Luxembourg producing as much waste as America. If you think about it for even a minute, the only unit that works is *people*—Zhao Ang, my translator, has as much right to the sky as I do, which is to say as much right to a car or a big house. And measuring by people, when China passes the United States as the world's largest carbon emitter the average *Chinese* will still be producing only a quarter as much carbon as the average American. And of course it goes deeper than that—the reason the atmosphere is filled to the danger point with carbon is because *we've* already been filling it for two centuries, burning coal and oil to get rich while the Chinese have been staying poor. As Ma Jun—a daring environmentalist who's taken big risks to write his books—told me one day, "Nearly eighty percent of the carbon dioxide has come from two hundred years of the industrial world. Let's be realistic. Those historic burdens have to be shouldered by those countries that have enjoyed the benefits." In any just scheme, it's not morally required of the Chinese to help solve global warming, any more than it's your kids' responsibility to work out the problems in your marriage.

This does not mean that the Chinese *should* burn all their coal. (After all, they'll have to deal with a wrecked world, just like your kids will have to deal with a broken home.) What it means is that we face an actual tragedy. The world, as it turns out, cannot afford two countries behaving like the United States. It lacks the atmosphere (and it also may lack the resources, as the scramble for control over oil in the summer of 2005 makes clear. We can't let the Chinese buy Unocal, because we need its reserves for us). And the reason it's an actual tragedy is because, right now, a rapidly growing China is actually accomplishing some measurable good with its growth. People are enjoying some meat, sending their brothers to school, heating their huts. Whereas we're burning nine times as much energy per capita so that we can: air-condition game rooms and mow half-acre lots, drive SUVs on every errand, eat tomatoes flown in from Chile. I understand that our country has people living in poverty, some of whom are now losing their jobs to Chinese competition, but that's simply our shame—we have all the money on earth, and we haven't figured out how to spread it around. China has hundreds of millions of people too poor to have clean water, and they sense that a few decades of burning coal might do something about that.

Which is why it seems intuitively obvious when you're in China that the goal of the twenty-first century must somehow be to simultaneously develop the economies of the poorest parts of the world and *undevelop* those of the rich—to transfer enough technology and wealth that we're able to meet somewhere in the middle, with us using less energy so that they can use more, and eating less meat so that they can eat more. (Indeed, baby steps toward such transfers of technology and wealth are enshrined in the Kyoto formula.)

One name for this kind of statistical mean is "Europe" or "Japan," whose citizens use half the energy of Americans. (And indeed the Chinese would almost certainly be willing to head in that direction. While I was there, for instance, they adopted new mileage standards for cars based on European standards—their showrooms are filling fast with tiny cars, like the Chery QQ, that come with 0.8-liter engines.) But try to imagine the political possibilities in America of taking Chinese aspirations seriously—of acknowledging that there isn't room for two of us to behave in this way, and that we don't own the rights to our lifestyle simply because we got there first. The current president's father announced, on his way to the parley in Rio that gave rise to the Kyoto treaty, that "the American way of life is not up for negotiation." That's what defines a tragedy.

· · ·

Here's another way to say it. On my last night in Shanghai, after about a month of touring the country, I ended up strolling the Bund, the strip of old European banking houses that faces the Huangpu River. On the other bank, in the Pudong District that China has made its great urban showpiece, huge towers rose in neon splendor—the Jinmao Tower, with the highest hotel on earth taking up its top thirty-four floors; the Oriental Pearl TV tower, its great kitschy globes glowing pink against the sky; the Aurora building, with its vast outdoor TV screen showing ad after ad. The vista was a little less grand than usual—the temperature had topped ninety-five degrees that day, so the government had decreed a power cut—but it was still enough to draw tens of thousands of spectators, content just to stand there in the dark and look. Many, perhaps most, were new arrivals from the countryside, in shabbier clothes and with ruddier faces than the city folk; they posed for pictures along the railing with the promise of the country glowing behind them.

I don't think in the end it's a real promise—I'm not sure China can escape the horrible environmental contradictions of its own growth (the soil is subsiding even in Pudong as Shanghai overpumps groundwater). I'm not sure globalization makes sense for the globe even if it makes sense for China (in fact, I'm almost sure it doesn't— that ninety-five-degree day was not unique; both China and the planet were suffering through the hottest year on record while I was there). I'm not sure that if the Chinese someday got as rich as we are they'd be any happier than us. That's why meeting in the middle makes so much sense. But in moral terms I am completely sure that that vista across the Huangpu River is filled with a kind of hope for the people who nightly drink it in, and that that hope is, for now, essentially innocent.

The only neon spectacle I've ever seen that compares is Vegas, with its pyramids and dancing waters. But what is Vegas? It's the search for some kind of new stimulus for the jaded. Some thicker meat and pricier alcohol, for people who've been packing away meat and alcohol for decades. Some attempt to figure out what more might mean when you've already had too much. Whatever else it is, China's not like that at all.

# · 18 ·

## Pie in the Sky

—*Orion Magazine*, March/April 2006

Question: should anyone who requires a "revolutionary new laser technology system" in order to figure out if they're parking in the right spot inside their own garage really be allowed behind the wheel in the first place? Compared with the other tasks of a driver—making right-hand turns, making left-hand turns, deciphering the red-amber-green vernacular of a stoplight—safely positioning your auto within the confines of your own garage seems like a fairly straightforward task, the kind of thing that might not require a laser. But you'd be surprised how useful lasers can be. The Hairmax Laser Comb, for instance, used only fifteen minutes a day, three times a week, results in noticeably thicker locks and tresses. And not just lasers. Ions are also surprisingly useful—confusingly, negative ions. A lamp made of salt crystal mined from the Himalayas emits them, aiding you in the fight against "dust mites" and also "depression."

If there's any piece of writing that defines our culture, I submit it's the SkyMall catalogue, available in the seatback pocket of every airplane in North America. To browse its pages is to understand the essential secret of American consumer life: we've officially run out not only of things that we need, but even of things that we might plausibly desire. But we in the airline traveling class still have a few problems to solve in our lives. Judging from the joys on offer, our particular worries at the moment might be categorized as follows:

*I'm overworked and overtired.* In which case, I need a $4,000 massaging recliner with voice control, synthetic leather ("softer, more plush than leather"), and thirty-three airbags—a machine that "pampers your body and soothes your soul." And if perchance I drift off to sleep, "the peaceful progression wake-up clock" will rouse me with infinite care. "Thirty minutes before wake-up time, the light glows softly, brightening over the next half hour, while faint aromatherapy scents release into the air. Fifteen minutes before wake-up, the clock generates one of six soft nature sounds." In case that isn't quite enough, I might want to back it up with the "sensory assault alarm clock," whose large, wired vibrating pad placed under the mattress shakes you awake in time to turn off the clock before it emits a ninety-five-decibel alarm and starts flashing a strobe light.

*I have an immense supply of trousers,* and hence require the closet organizer trouser rack to keep twenty pairs of slacks neatly hung and readily accessible. The five-eighths-inch-diameter birch dowels "reduce creasing of even fine fabrics," and "nylon washers between the dowels ensure smooth swing motion."

*I distrust my neighbors and my government,* and so would benefit from a giant-capacity mailbox that holds up to two weeks of mail (catalogues, presumably). "Don't bother a neighbor to get your mail, and don't tell the post office you'll be away."

*I am extremely, extremely clean.* I'm therefore thankful that my toothbrush has been ultraviolety cleansed overnight to remove the "millions of germs" that would otherwise accumulate, and my room is protected against "airborne bacteria, viruses, and germs" by a Germ Guardian machine, "proven by a Harvard researcher," which "takes ultraviolet C energy and multiplies its germ-killing power in our exclusive Intensifier Chamber." Also, I have another very similar-looking machine "now with exclusive Ozoneguard" in case any ozone is nearby. And a soap dispenser with infrared sensor technology for my shower, a "no-touch approach that dramatically reduces the chance of spreading germs."

*I have way too many watches,* and therefore might benefit from a $300 case that will shake them all with "intermittent timers and directional controls" to mimic the action of a human wrist and hence keep them fully wound at all times.

*I have plugged in so many things that the planet has warmed considerably, reducing the chances that my children will experience a natural winter.* So I have purchased a "weatherproof light projection box that rests on your front lawn and transforms the entire facade of your house into an illuminated snowscape. The box creates the illusion of gently falling snow flurries by directing a bright white beam onto a rotating mirrorball." Flake size and fall rate are, pleasingly, adjustable. I have opted also to purchase an "exclusive heavy duty vinyl snow castle" that will "set up almost anywhere in just minutes with the included electric pump." A real snow castle would, SkyMall notes, "take hours to build and require lots of snow," but this version "encourages children to use their imaginations while having fun."

*I have an enormous number of remote controls,* and hence need caddies to store them, small "buddy lights" to illuminate them, and locator devices to find them when I have mislaid them.

*I may be devolving.* Though for eons my ancestors have grilled meat over flames, I am no longer very clear on the concept and so would like a digital barbecue fork that I can stick into my burger or steak and receive a readout indicating whether it is currently rare, medium, or well done. Also, it would help a lot to have all the lights already strung on my artificial Christmas tree, and the difficult task of marinating would be much easier if I had a $199.95 marinating machine. Frankly, I've lately found grilled cheese sandwiches more trouble than I want, but with my dishwasher-safe Toastabag I can simply place a slice of cheese between two slices of bread and pop it in my toaster. (Depressing the toaster lever still requires my thoughtful attention, as does chewing the resulting treat.)

There are a few problems SkyMall can't solve (the lack of community that comes when you live in a giant stuff-filled house marooned on its half-acre lot, the lack of security that comes when your country is spending its money on remote-control golf balls instead of, say, health care and retirement savings). And there's always the vexing question of what the people who are making these items think about the people who will buy them. (When I was in a shower-curtain factory in rural China last year, the very nice people sewing the curtains told me that they'd never actually encountered a shower curtain outside the factory. If that's true for a shower curtain, one wonders what their fellow workers make of the traveling wine trolley, the pop-up hot-dog cooker, the hand-held paper shredder with wood-grain plastic handle.)

But this kind of talk sounds tired, clichéd, left over from the '60s. Everyone knows that the most important thing we can do is grow the economy. When you buy the Designated Driver, a faux golf club that you store in your bag to dispense forty-eight ounces of cold beverages, then you grow the economy. No doubt about it. Also, the Vintage Express Aging Accelerator that ages your bottle of wine ten years in ten seconds by surrounding it with "extremely powerful Neodymium magnets to replicate the Earth's magnetic field." Only a real jerk or a Christian or something would point out that there might possibly be items in this world that it would make more sense to spend our money on. (Insecticide-impregnated bed nets to stop the spread of malaria run about five dollars. If only they came in self-erecting pastel versions that would also rouse you out of bed with gentle nature sounds.)

# · 19 ·

# Hype vs. Hope

—*Mother Jones*, November/December 2006

Ten percent of a two-year-old's nouns are brand names; by the time an American child heads to school, he or she can recognize hundreds of logos. Disney is now putting its cartoon characters on fresh fruit, arguing (perhaps correctly) that it's the only way to get kids to eat it. If that's the world we're born into, is it any wonder we want corporations to solve our biggest problems as well? Isn't it a parent's job to protect us? And besides, who else has the capital and the power to do what needs to be done in the face of a crisis like global warming?

Any sign that corporations might be willing to take on the job is greeted with an enthusiasm that borders on delusion. When John Browne, the head of British Petroleum, gave a speech in 1997 admitting that global warming exists, and announcing that business must respond "to the reality and the concerns of the world in which you operate," people began calling him the "Sun King." The head of California's Environmental Protection Agency ventured that "this bold move will set the world stage for other companies to emulate." BP commissioned green roofs for its filling stations, along with a whole slew of ads touting its vision for a world "beyond petroleum." And there is every reason to think Lord Browne was sincere—he'd studied the problem, knew it was big, and was willing to buck the rest of the industry in saying so.

Browne was not the only executive thinking aloud about how corporations relate to the rest of the world. His comments came as the debate over "corporate social responsibility," long a preoccupation for people in fuzzy sweaters, was about to explode into mainstream business culture. The movement has now spawned a booming industry in consultants and conferences; just this summer the World Business Council on Sustainable Development issued a manifesto titled "From Challenge to Opportunity," filled with pictures of baking deserts and disease-stricken peasants, but also with promises to "seek greater synergy between our goals and those of the society we serve." BP signed on, and so did everyone from Adidas to Procter & Gamble.

Which is nice. The question is, what does it amount to?

Take BP. In 2004, its revenues from solar power were almost $400 million; its total revenues, almost entirely from hydrocarbons, were $285 billion. In other words, the company has gone beyond petroleum to the tune of about one-sixth of 1 percent of sales. And the news gets worse from there. The leak disaster that led to the sudden shutdown of BP's Alaska pipeline in the summer of 2006 turns out not to have been sudden at all. Back in 1992, when a whistle-blower raised concerns about corrosion in the pipeline, BP responded with a corporate crackdown that a federal judge said was "reminiscent of Nazi Germany." Elsewhere, the *Wall Street Journal* reported that federal regulators were investigating whether BP tried to influence crude-oil prices using information about its Oklahoma pipelines and storage tanks; in a separate probe, investigators were trying to figure out if BP gamed gasoline prices on the New York Mercantile Exchange. Meanwhile, the company's top American executive was cochairman of the George W. Bush reelection campaign in Alaska. Not very far beyond petroleum, that.

There is no question that entrepreneurs with a social bent can do enormous good—especially until they decide to go public or sell out to a larger corporation. And they can do well at the same time, connecting with a reasonably large block of motivated consumers. If I need paper towels, they're damn well going to come from Seventh Generation. I would probably wear Patagonia jackets even if they weren't so incredibly warm.

But these tend to be one-off deals. Ben and Jerry didn't seem to change the way Häagen and Dazs viewed the world. Somehow, Bounty has been willing to leave the thoughtful paper towel market to Seventh Generation. For several decades now, environmentalists have been citing the work of Ray Anderson and Interface, and it's a great example—but why is there still only one Ray Anderson?

Often the difficulty is built right into a company's business model. It makes scant difference whether Wal-Mart starts stocking organic food or not, because the real problem is the imperative to ship products all over the world, sell them in vast, downtown-destroying complexes, and push prices so low that neither workers nor responsible suppliers can prosper. (In fact, Wal-Mart's decision to sell organic food will almost certainly mean the final consolidation of the industry into the hands of a few huge growers that ship their produce across thousands of miles—not to mention that the people ringing up the organic groceries will still make below-poverty wages and taxpayers will still be footing the bill for their health care. There's something gross about buying a healthy carrot from a sick company.)

By the same token, though, business models can propel companies forward even if the CEOs couldn't care less about the planet: Dow and DuPont have cut their carbon emissions by upward of 50 percent this decade, simply because their managers started to pay attention to energy costs and figured out that efficiency went straight to the bottom line.

"Will business save the world?" turns out to be the wrong question. The right question is "How can we structure the world so that businesses play their part in saving it?" And the answer to that, inevitably, is politics.

Some of it is the politics of public awareness. It's no accident that Vermont and Oregon are hotbeds of do-good capitalism; in these places attitudes have shifted so that conscience pays. Many of us have worked like crazy to get people excited about, say, hybrid cars—and, aided by rising oil prices, the propaganda has begun to succeed.

But mostly we need politics of a more straightforward, and entirely unglamorous, variety. If you want energy companies to rearrange their portfolios so that way more money goes to renewables and way less to hydrocarbons, the best way forward is not to appeal to the CEO's conscience—it's to pass laws to push him in the right direction. This is what has happened in Europe, where regulators told car manufacturers last August to cut vehicles' greenhouse emissions by 25 percent—or else. "The car industry should be aware that we are watching the situation very closely," one official told reporters, adding that the EU "will not hesitate to replace the carrot with the stick." There's nothing particularly European about that logic—witness the efforts in the United States of a few bold state attorneys general, who in the face of federal inaction have begun to sue major carbon emitters on their own. They may not win—but the threat of liability has already gotten big polluters to talk about offering voluntary carbon cuts in exchange for legal immunity. In an August 2006 report, the investor activist group Ceres quoted a Goldman Sachs analysis that put possible global warming liability on the same scale as the fallout from asbestos. That kind of information will grab a CEO's attention in a hurry.

Helping corporations do the right thing through regulation—which, it should be noted, also levels the playing field so that a greenish BP doesn't have to worry about a dirty ExxonMobil—is not exactly a new idea. It's more or less what we used to do, in the long period from Teddy Roosevelt and the trustbusters on to about the 1980s.

One reason for the shift is the enormous political power of corporations, which they use almost exclusively to boost their own profits. But in a way, you can't blame them for that. The strange part is how little opposition the corporate agenda meets anymore—how many of us have accepted the ideological argument that as long as we leave commerce alone, it will somehow, magically, solve all our problems. We could compel Big Oil to take its windfall profits and build windmills; instead we stand quietly by, as if unfettered plunder were the obvious and necessary course.

Explaining this mystery may bring us back to where we started. In the childlike enchantment we've lived under since the Reagan era, we've wanted very much to believe that someone else, some wavy-haired CEO, would do the hard, adult work of problem solving. In fact, corporations are the infants of our society—they know very little except how to grow (though they're very good at that), and they howl when you set limits. Socializing them is the work of politics. It's about time we took it up again.

# (Tod) Murphy's Law

—*Yankee,* September/October 2007

How local is the Farmers Diner? The first thing you see when you walk in the door of this Quechee, Vermont, restaurant is a jukebox, glinting like any diner jukebox. Some Willie Nelson, some John Cougar Mellencamp. But half the albums are by Vermonters. Phish, sure. But it's Grace Potter and the Nocturnals who get the most play. And they're just the start.

You'll find the Starline Rhythm Boys (singing "The Tavern Parking Lot") and Banjo Dan and the Mid-Nite Plowboys ("The Cider Song"). And Patti Casey, of course. Never heard of Patti Casey? Your loss, but that's the point. In an economy where music comes from L.A. or Nashville, she's from *here*.

Turn left, and head for the restored 1946 Worcester diner car. The menu, at first glance, looks like any diner menu. Hash and eggs. Liver and onions. Bacon cheeseburger. Pancakes. At diner prices—$4 for a grilled cheese, home fries for $1.75. But look a little closer: almost every item comes with a modest biography. The blue cheese comes from Jasper Hill Farm in Greensboro, Vermont. The yogurt is from Butterworks Farm up in Westfield, which also supplies wheat flour for the pancakes. The Swiss cheese comes from Walpole, New Hampshire, across the Connecticut River. The sauerkraut? Wellspring Farm in Marshfield. In an economy where diner food rolls up on an eighteen-wheeler from the factory farms of the South and Midwest, your Farmers Diner patty melt is like the music on the jukebox: it comes from *here*.

And, it comes with an attitude. One page of the menu is given over to Kentucky farmer and writer Wendell Berry's magnificent poem "Manifesto: The Mad Farmer Liberation Front": "So, friends, every day do something / that won't compute . . ." Another is taken up by Thomas Jefferson's 1803 letter calling for a conversion of the nation's "charitable" institutions into "schools of agriculture" so our citizens may "increase the productions of the nation instead of consuming them."

And, this may be the only diner in the world with a mission statement: "to increase the economic vitality of local agrarian communities." The bumper sticker above the counter says it even more plainly: "Think Globally—Act Neighborly."

In other words, this is one cool place. The Farmers Diner is to, say, Denny's as John Coltrane is to Kenny G. But it's not all glory. For one thing, this is the second incarnation of the Farmers Diner; the first one, some forty miles up the highway in the much grittier town of Barre, failed. And thus far, founder Tod Murphy's vision of Farmers Diners across New England, each supporting local growers and suppliers, is only that—a vision that has yet to prove its mettle in the rough-and-tumble of the food economy. The Farmers Diner is cool—but it's complicated.

It started, as most such ventures do, with a simple epiphany. Murphy had spent the early years of his career in the coffee industry: first in Seattle as a barista at one of the early Starbucks outlets—where he got to watch the start of the greatest entrepreneurial success in the food-and-beverage industry since McDonald's—and then in New York as an executive at a copycat chain of coffee shops opening across the Northeast.

Ten years ago, he took his winnings from that gig and, like many before him, moved north to Vermont. He bought a small farm in Washington, near the center of the state, and stocked it with sheep and cattle. They were grass-fed. The meat was delicious, but it was almost unsalable: chefs at high-end restaurants wanted cases of top round but had no interest in the rest of the animal.

Even when he did find customers, Murphy was competing with a price set by commodity meat producers on the vast feedlots of the Midwest. The question that started reverberating in his brain went like this: "How do you create a company that will take food off the farmer's hands in the easiest way for him, and set it in front of the customers in the easiest way for them, and do it at a price point everyone can live with?"

In fact, it's pretty much the same question that the entire local-food movement, now burgeoning across New England, is asking: can we figure out how to make a living for growers close to home while selling food at a price that people can afford?

Farmers are exploring dozens of different schemes. Some are small: growing specialty produce or meat for white-tablecloth restaurants. Others sound great but are somewhat out of the mainstream: for example, CSA (community-supported agriculture) programs, whereby customers pay the farmer a few hundred bucks in early winter; the farmer uses the money to plant a crop; and then the vegetables are divided every week among the shareholders.

More and more people are trying more and more approaches, and the successes keep mounting. Farmers' markets are the fastest-growing part of the region's food economy, and Vermont's largest city, Burlington, harvests almost a tenth of its fresh food from the 120 acres of river-bottom farmland in its Intervale area.

Still, most New Englanders eat most of their meals at a distance: the average bite of food travels more than 1,500 miles to reach our lips. It's cheap for the moment, but if you're concerned about energy (it takes thirty-six calories of fossil fuel to haul one calorie of lettuce back East from California), or about sprawl or about taste, it's a shame.

Murphy set out more publicly than anyone to reverse the trend: to make local food a reality for people who weren't yuppies or hippies or teensy-tiny-baby-vegetable gourmets. He would make the French fry local. The Farmers Diner, he announced, would buy most of its food from within fifty miles of the kitchen door.

When the Barre restaurant opened in the summer of 2002, it drew all kinds of attention. Food writers from around the country came to eat, and they wrote glowing reviews. It didn't hurt that Murphy is genial, and country handsome. ("Dealing with customers fits my Aquarian personality," he said. "You don't have to make a long-term commitment, but you do get to converse.")

Tailing him for a day as he made the rounds of his suppliers showed the promise of the idea. You could start the morning in Strafford, say, at Rock Bottom Farm, where Earl Ransom's cows were producing organic milk and cream on the land where he was born. ("I had to educate people that cream isn't necessarily white," Murphy recalled. "When the cows went out to pasture in the spring, the half-and-half changed color noticeably, and the waitresses were afraid people would freak.") Then you could drop by the farm's Strafford Organic Creamery, which was processing Rock Bottom's dairy products, providing along the way the basic ingredients for that famous diner staple the milk shake. Utterly delicious ice cream, too.

Or you could go up the road to Thistle Hill Farm in Pomfret, where John and Janine Putnam were making a Gruyère-like cheese called Tarentaise, which they could have sold for $21 a pound in New York. "I totally subscribe to the idea of local," said Janine. "The people around here *should* eat our cheese." So it was neat that Murphy was using some of it in his ploughman's lunch—a truly delectable ploughman's lunch.

But the Barre operation had problems, and they could be summed up this way: too small. The diner itself had only sixty seats, and the kitchen was considerably smaller than any of the home kitchens you see in a magazine photo shoot. It was a cramped and greasy alcove, with no room for the machinery that might have made it more efficient. So French fries meant a guy cutting potatoes with a knife, which meant high costs, which meant that one day in the summer of 2005, Murphy put a sign on the door saying that he was shutting down for a month. A month turned into a year, and plenty of people thought Murphy was finished.

But it's hard to keep a good idea down. Early last fall, the Farmers Diner reopened, half a mile east of Quechee Gorge on Route 4. It's a different world from downtown Barre, where the diner sat next to an Aubuchon hardware store. Here it's in a rusticated, tourist-cutesy strip mall, complete with a toy locomotive that kids can ride in an endless circle. Whereas there used to be cops at the counter, here you'll more likely find vacationers, which means you can charge a little more. Not a lot—but a burger might run you $8.50, not $6.50.

It's bigger, too—there are 120 seats, plus room for 40 more people outside in the summertime. And the kitchen is much roomier. Now there's a machine that can take a sack of Vermont potatoes and turn them into a pile of French fries in just minutes. And that frees the cooks to do other things—like produce the homemade English muffins that have become the restaurant's new calling card.

Still, says Murphy, the diner remains too small to really make economic sense. What it needs are siblings: two or three more scattered around the state that he can serve from a central commissary kitchen in Quechee. The machine could be making French fries for all of the outlets, and the ad budget could be spread across three rooms full of munching patrons.

And, more to the point, the money that investors have put up to build these diners might come back with some profit attached. Plenty of communities across the state might welcome the idea: a Farmers Diner in Middlebury, in St. Johnsbury, in Bennington.

But of course this is the line of thinking that led to McDonald's. Once upon a time, it was a single restaurant, too, with a small machine to cut French fries. But the more restaurants the company opened, the higher the returns, so it just kept growing. Now the chain's manufacturing plants peel, slice, and freeze 2 million pounds of spuds a day. If you follow the logic of economies of scale, that's where you end up—as far from local food as it's possible to be.

Which is why, Murphy says, he's got different ideas for expansion. The business model calls for growth by regions—"pods," he calls them. Already, he says, investors in the Boston area are keen to open outlets there. Maybe they'd have five or six, served by their own central commissary kitchen. Probably they'd serve some different things: clam rolls, maybe.

In fact, if Murphy's scheme really works, there might be Farmers Diners across the country someday—each one buying food from farmers in a close radius around the city, creating new opportunities for local farmers, and serving local tastes. You'd get the economies of scale that come from standardization: Murphy can wax poetic about "modular buildout," or about the fact that the walk-in refrigerator at every Crab House restaurant in America is laid out in exactly the same way, so that managers can move easily from one to the next. But you'd still be local.

Even if Murphy can get the scale right for *his* operation, though, it's not clear he can make it mesh with the scale of the local farmers he set out to try to help. Consider, for instance, the pig.

When the first Farmers Diner opened in Barre, it needed bacon—you can't have a diner without bacon. The problem was that no one was producing pork commercially in Vermont. Fifty years ago, sure—every farm had a few hogs growing fat on leftover milk from the dairy herd. But as agriculture became a commodity business—as dairy producers concentrated on cows, and pork producers on pigs—that changed. Vermont dairies became fewer in number and much, much bigger, and in other parts of the nation the same thing happened with hogs.

According to Brian Halweil in his book *Eat Here,* for instance, there's a hog farm in Utah with 1.5 million pigs. That's absurd—they produce more solid waste each day than the entire city of Los Angeles. It's also cheap—so cheap that it sets the psychological price for a pound of bacon pretty low.

So when Murphy wanted to buy pigs for his bacon and sausage business, a Diner sideline called Vermont Smoke and Cure, he approached a few farmers to see whether they were interested. One was Maple Wind Farm, a breeder in Huntington raising fifty hogs a year, mostly to sell at farmers' markets. They're fed on grass and organic grains—the pork tastes absolutely incredible—and they fetch good money.

"We get $7.50 a pound for bacon at the farmers' market, and $8.50 a pound for pork chops," said Beth Whiting, who runs the farm with her husband, Bruce Hennessey. So when Murphy asked them if they could raise him some pigs at eighty-nine cents a pound, "we had to bury our laughter."

And yet, eighty-nine cents a pound is more than upscale national pork producer Niman Ranch pays its contract pig farmers.

In essence, it's a Goldilocks problem: somehow Murphy has to find just the right size. What his operation really requires is not huge commodity producers or small, incredibly wonderful gourmet farms.

"What I need are 1950s-size farms," he said. Not a million hogs, but not fifty, either—maybe three or four hundred, say. Not organic operations necessarily, just family farms. Precisely, in other words, the kinds of farms that have almost all gone out of business in recent decades.

Murphy can still find vegetable growers to fit his needs; he's found someone to plant five acres of cucumbers this season, for instance, enough to fill his pickle needs. But to help rebuild the supply of meat and chicken farmers, he's launching a nonprofit foundation. Named for a character in one of Wendell Berry's novels, the Jack Beecham Foundation will help growers with business plans and marketing strategies.

If all goes according to plan, it will let small farmers grow just big enough to make it in the food economy Murphy is trying to create.

All this to make a smoked-turkey club. Or, to read from today's specials menu, some poached Vermont eggs with Cabot cheddar cream sauce. Or some maple-butternut squash. Or some Cortland apple cobbler topped with local granola, and a scoop of that Strafford ice cream. With some Grace Potter wailing from the jukebox.

For change back from a ten-dollar bill, it doesn't get much sweeter than this. It *should* work.

# · IV ·

# COMMUNITIES

# · 21 ·

# Job and Matthew

—*Communion* (Anchor Books), 1996

Through no precise fault of the pleasant suburban church where I was raised, I reached college in the year 1978 unaware that the Bible contained material that might shake me up. That is, I knew that the Gospels commanded compassion toward the poor, the hungry, the naked—but that was my politics anyway, for other reasons. (Good reasons, like the example of my parents, and mixed reasons, like a yearning for the sexy sixties.) I knew I was supposed to turn the other cheek, but so what—it would never have occurred to me to hit someone other than my brother anyhow. I was a good kid.

My leftism grew more righteous in college, but still there was something pro forma about it. Being white, male, straight, and of impeccably middle-class background, I could not realistically claim to be a victim of anything. (Not for lack of trying—in one short but loony phase I convinced myself that I was Irish-American and wore black armbands when Bobby Sands and his IRA companions starved themselves to death.) Mostly, I supported everyone else—marched in Take Back the Night marches, signed petitions for minority centers and Hispanic studies, conspicuously sat at dinner with gays and lesbians during gay and lesbian week. But I couldn't even claim the pleasure of enlightenment, as I was not a bigot or a chauvinist or a homophobe to begin with. I was, as I say, a good kid.

In those early years of the 1980s, with Reaganism ascendant and Lech Walesa busily proving to anyone who had not yet figured it out that communism was a stinking corpse, the only promising strain of "leftism" seemed to emanate from Latin America. And it was less the Sandinistas that fascinated me than the liberation theologians, who seemed to be issuing a coherent and genuinely popular response to the poverty and violence around them, a response perhaps not automatically fated to become a tyranny of its own. I can recall hearing for the first time about this "new" theology (in fact it was already a decade old but it had been slow, because it involved religion, to penetrate college reading lists). I haunted the library of the divinity school, where I'd never been before, trying to find the one title someone had written out for me: *Christology at the Crossroads*, by a Jesuit priest named Jon Sobrino. After several trips I finally found it on the shelf and grabbed it—only to find it dense going. I had no idea what Christology was, for example. (The liberation theologians piled the technical language of the left atop the technical language of the theologians, and most of it was translated from the Spanish to boot.) I kept reading, however, for I knew there was something vital beneath the jargon—it was during this period, after all, that Oscar Romero, archbishop of El Salvador, was assassinated for enunciating these complex ideas in the simplest terms. I can remember sitting in a leather chair in the library sounding out Gutierrez and Segundo, Boff and Cardenal, Miranda and Miguez-Bonino with a rising thrill, a feeling that this world of Christianity, to which I had at least a slight connection, was on a cutting edge sharper than any other around.

And yet it was still somehow removed from me. I believed that the Church should, in Gutierrez's key phrase, have "a preferential option for the poor." I believed that the poor should remake the

Church and then the society to serve their needs. The poor, I read again and again, have to take charge of their own destiny. Praxis— that was one of the keys. I had no argument. But I was not poor. Not rich, certainly—by the standards of my college, halfway to shabby. But not poor, no more than I was gay or black. It seemed still as if a rooting interest was all I could muster. And part of me wished for something more.

. . .

The year I graduated school I left for Manhattan, where I found work writing magazine stories. At some point, for some reason, I decided I was actually going to read the Bible. (I am aware that this sounds absurd, that I should have read it long before I started digging into Latin American Christology. But I am well educated in a modern way, which is to say far more comfortable with commentary than text.) To slow myself down so I'd actually *read* it, I decided to copy it out word for word in a notebook, beginning with the Gospels. And as I crawled along through Matthew, a chapter a day from my previously uncracked Comfirmation Bible, a blend of excitement and dread grew in me. This was addressed to me after all—amid the encouragement of the oppressed and scourging of the truly wicked, there was plenty aimed at the decent-but-complacent. That comes as revelation to no one else, of course, but it was the more powerful to me for coming late.

One story in particular startled me. It seemed to be my story, as if Jesus was one of those stage psychics who can pick people out of a crowd. First told in Matthew 19, it's not a parable, just an incident from Jesus' life. A man approaches him while he is preaching in Judea and says, "Teacher, what good deed must I do to have eternal life?" And Jesus answers him—a little dismissively, or so it sounds—"Why do you ask me about what is good? One there is who is good. If you would enter life, keep the commandments." The man asks, "Which?" And Jesus—curtly still—says, "you shall not kill, you shall not commit adultery, you shall not steal, you shall not bear false witness, honor your father and mother, and love your neighbor as yourself." Not that old list again—you can almost hear the young man's impatience. And mine too—clearly I was never going to murder anyone, and I didn't lie more than anyone else, and since no one I knew was married, adultery was not a great temptation. I was on good terms with my parents (which was enough of a rarity to make me feel virtuous). And I loved my neighbor, or at least said I did. I wanted off the sidelines. I wanted a real challenge.

So too with the man questioning Christ. "All these I have observed; what do I still lack?" Jesus—and you can feel the pause, feel the turn to look him straight in the eye—says this: "If you would be perfect, go, sell what you possess, and give to the poor, and you will have treasure in heaven; and come follow me." And, says Matthew, "when the young man heard this he went away sorrowful, for he had great possessions."

"If you would be perfect." Well, yes, that was one crux of it. I was yearning for some sort of moral heroism, and if I did not in fact have great possessions, I realized that my privileged life and connections and opportunities were a kind of capital, included in what Jesus was describing—I had been to Harvard, after all, and I was working at the *New Yorker*. It wasn't the "treasure in heaven" that interested me, since then and now I had only a mild interest in heaven. Instead, as usual, my attraction was for a mix of good reasons and bad. I am certain that the idea of renunciation appealed to my vanity. But perhaps I also glimpsed the possibility of a kind of *intensity* of life once one was free of the insulation from the world provided by money and belongings. That insulation had surrounded me always—an American suburb is a device for turning money into a kind of armor against experience: the experience of other kinds of people, of nature, of one's body. Maybe this was early-onset midlife crisis: the strong sense that there was something *more* and that the path to it lay through *less*. I had no idea quite how to go about it. Join a monastery? But I wasn't a Catholic, and anyway intense quiet did not yet appeal to me. Join the Peace Corps? But I couldn't actually *do* anything useful to anyone except write "Talk of the Town" stories. Still, I knew there were things I could have done.

But "went away sorrowful"—that was the other crux, the perfect description for my inability to take such a leap. Not "went away angry," or "went away scornful," but went away sorrowful, more than half-convinced the message was right, and yet unable to act on it. Exactly why I am not sure. It was early in the Reagan age, and Manhattan's streets were filling with homeless people—as a reporter I lived for a while as a homeless man, and then I helped start a small homeless shelter in the basement of my church, and frankly the fact of homelessness scared me. My profession seemed particularly economically insecure—my father, also a writer, had lost a magazine job when I was in high school, and I could still remember the fear when, for a while, he could find no other work. In retrospect my worries were exaggerated—but I was twenty-one, twenty-two, twenty-three at the time. What did I know?

The compromise that I reached, without thinking about it as such, was a strange one: I lived extremely frugally, and put the money I earned in the bank. In so doing I preserved both the option to do something heroic at a later date (only dimly sensing that the diving board would just get higher and higher with each extra dollar), and also the right to feel superior to my yuppie peers. When I say frugal, I mean frugal. One day, burglars broke into the sublet that I was sharing with a friend. They found him asleep, tied him up, and robbed thousands of dollars' worth of his belongings. From me they took two cardboard boxes. They dumped my small record collection out of one and used it to haul away David's computer. They dumped my dirty clothes from the other and carried out his VCR.

· · ·

A few years later I quit my job and moved to the wild and distant Adirondack Mountains, and some of these concerns began to fade.

Poverty is intense here, but it is not confrontational; no one begs, there are no spokesmen. And, too, I had met and married a wonderful woman; helping to care for a family on the precarious earnings of a freelance writer made me thankful for the money I'd saved in the city.

Most of all, though, I had finally found a cause in which to immerse myself. It did not take me long to fall in love with the natural world, a world more real and engaging than any I had known before. I bushwhacked up mountains, skied lakes at midnight by the light of the moon, tracked coyote and deer across the ridges. And as quickly as my love for wild places grew, so too did my sense of their peril. My environmentalism began locally, fighting the constant threats to all the places where I hiked and canoed and lay out under the stars. It soon grew to encompass the globe, as I realized that the very climate of these remote Adirondacks was being changed by the habits of our species.

Such realization depressed me, of course: the title of my first book, *The End of Nature*, testifies to that despair. But this passion also allowed, finally, my full participation. Environmental change threatened me as much as any other human on the planet: white skin offered no special protection against the ultraviolet pouring in through the hole in the ozone layer. What's more, the greatest threat was not to humans at all, but to the rest of creation. And there seemed nothing paternalistic or patronizing about going to bat for bats, or wolves or hemlocks or salamanders.

I'd started going to the one local church almost as soon as I'd moved here, a tiny Methodist congregation with maybe twenty souls on a Sunday morning. The minister when I arrived was a recently released jailhouse convert, a Holy Roller who, as it turned out, soon returned to state custody after embezzling from one of his old lady parishioners. Though he was succeeded by a more congenial cleric, it was probably fortunate that I had begun to find my church in the woods and mountains, in a minor-key version of the religious ecstasy that marked, say, John Muir's first summer in the Sierras.

I might have turned into a full-fledged pagan had not my wife happened to give me a copy of Stephen Mitchell's translation of the book of Job from the Hebrew Bible. (The only way I've ever been able to understand the Holy Spirit is as that force which, out of all the books in the world, puts a particular volume in your hand at a particular time.) It shocked me at least as much as my first encounters with liberation theology: I sensed once more that the Bible had a great deal to say on subjects close to my heart, that it went beyond mere radicalism to roots.

The story of Job is, of course, familiar—a righteous man is felled by misfortune, reduced to living on a dungheap at the edge of town, his body a mass of oozing sores. In legend he is renowned for his patience, but in practice he is anything but. He rejects the counsel of his friends, who push the conventional wisdom that he must have sinned unwittingly and now is being punished. Instead he demands an interview with God, demands an explanation for his suffering. He gets the interview, but the explanation is not what he expects. Appearing in a whirlwind, God tells him zip about justice or righteousness or the meaning of suffering. Instead God taunts Job with his unimportance. ("Were you there when I planned the earth? . . . If you shout commands to the thunderclouds will they rush off to do your bidding? If you clap for the bolts of lightning will they come and say 'Here we are'? . . . Have you seen where the snow is stored?") Job is being shown the limits of his human-centered logic; his affliction has nothing to do with his sins, because *man is not at the center of all things.*

> *Who cuts a path for the thunderstorm*
> *and carves a road for the rain—*
> *to water the desolate wasteland,*
> *the land where no man lives;*
> *to make the wilderness blossom*
> *and cover the desert with grass?*

For me, living on the edge of the wilderness, this matched the new-found feelings flooding my senses: the glory of a true night sky, the loud piping of a life-filled marsh, the flight of a hawk. "Do you teach the vulture to soar and build his nest in the clouds," God asks Job. "He makes his home on the mountaintop, on the unap-proachable crag. He sits and scans for prey; from far off his eyes can spot it; his little ones drink its blood. Where the unburied are, he is." I saw turkey vultures every day now, circling over carrion; this was the world I was coming to know, to relax into.

And the message of Job also meshed neatly with the ideas along the cutting edge of environmentalism: the "deep ecologists" and the "biocentrists" who were arguing convincingly that our entire ecological crisis stems from philosophical roots, from turning everything around us into "raw materials" and "resources" for us to use as we pleased. In a way, it was all a great relief: a worldview that went well beyond ethics and even morality. And this, of course, is one of the great cries against environmentalists; in my case, I deserved it.

For the only problem with God's message to Job was that it seemed to be less true with each passing year. The more I learned about the greenhouse effect, for instance, the more I realized that God's unanswerable taunts to Job were suddenly—in my lifetime—turning into the empty boasts of an old geezer. "Were you there . . . when I closed in [the sea] with barriers and set its boundaries, saying 'Here you may come but no farther; here shall your proud waves break.' " Job has to stand in humble silence, but not us. By pumping clouds of carbon dioxide into the atmosphere—clouds that rise from every car and furnace and factory—we are raising the temperature of the planet and hence its sea level. Collectively, the five and a half billion of us are large enough to take the measure of this bragging deity. Thunderstorms "R" Us too, and hurricanes; we are busy cre-ating our own Leviathans and Behemoths with our genetic engineer-ing, even as we wipe out the ones with which we shared the planet of our birth.

So I could read Job as a vision of what had been before history, and as a partial description of what remaining wilderness now resembled, and as a glorious picture of what the world might look like once again in the deep future. But this struggle requires more than vision; it demands, of course, that we acknowledge and deal with five and a half billion human beings. It demands that we deal with the wealth driving environmental destruction, and with the myth of the rich world that someday everyone else will be like us. There isn't atmosphere enough for them to be like us—so it demands, painfully, that we deal with ourselves.

Consider the following fact, tucked away in a recent paper by a Syracuse University research team led by Professor Charles Hall. "One way to view the relationship between economic activity and environmental impact is that each time a person spends a U.S. dollar approximately 3000–4000 kilocalories of energy (about 15 Joules, or the equivalent of one half liter of oil) is extracted from the earth and burned to produce the goods or services purchased by that dollar." Every time a liter of oil is burned, pounds of carbon dioxide waft into the atmosphere, increasing the amount of the sun's heat trapped near the earth.

In other words, our possessions are linked directly to the destruction of the planet: along with the size of human populations, and the efficiency of their consumption, the amount that they consume determines how much fuel is burned, how many forests chainsawed, how many marshes drained and hillsides mined. Spending twenty dollars on a book requires that ten liters of oil go up in smoke.

In other words, I'd come full circle, led myself back to the same place though from another direction. If we are to know the vision offered Job, the vision of an intact world where we are not at the center of things but instead a part of a functioning and glorious planet, then the advice of Jesus to the rich young man is a crucial prerequisite. We need to cease consuming at anything like our current rate, for our consumption drives the planet's deterioration.

And, having ceased, we need to share with the rest of the world, now struggling to emulate our ways. For in a world where the average citizen of the First World has fifty-nine times the income of the average citizen of the Third World, it is no use denying our wealth, and no use denying its attraction.

The second time I crashed into this story, the collision shook me even harder. My mind had long since ceased dwelling on the advice to the rich young ruler; I thought I had escaped it. But now I was back to it, and from a very different angle. Christ's admonition echoed and anticipated, of course, the advice of a thousand other saints and cranks and gurus. Always for them the advice had been aesthetic, moral, personal, spiritual. And always, as in my case, it had gone too against the grain of the culture for more than a noble few to follow. Now it seemed to be converging with the very practical advice of scientists, of men clutching satellite data and computer printouts as they too made the case for simplicity and community and other religious joys.

This confluence makes it no easier to follow the injunction, and indeed I have taken but the first baby steps in that direction; I doubt my will to go very far down that road. But I do not doubt it is the right road, for reasons of nature and of social justice and of fulfillment. I reread the various Gospel accounts of the incident as I wrote this essay, and saw that although they are remarkably similar, Mark adds one clause. When the rich young man badgers him about what to do beyond keeping the commandments, Jesus softens; the man's zeal seems to touch him. "And Jesus looking upon him loved him," and said to him, change your life in the most fundamental ways. It is that tenderness that charges this story, that turns its seeming sternness upside down. It is that tenderness that makes it attractive, even seductive, not repellent. It is that tenderness that keeps it ever in my mind.

I read my words and think they must seem bizarrely literal—as if, having left the Bible mostly unread as a child, I now can read it only with a childish simplicity. I am not a fundamentalist, obviously. But the things that worry me—food and shelter for people who lack them, the gaseous composition of the atmosphere, a right life—seem to me fundamental. They seem literal. This story haunts me; may it always.

# State Fair

*—DoubleTake,* Fall 1996

"This woman lives with no head. Her fingernails grow. The hair on her arms and legs grows out after a period of time. Some say she is the most amazing scientific discovery of the twentieth century."

Down the midway from the headless woman, inside the swine barn, a judge explains his choice in the class of January-born boars of the Duroc breed: "I just admire that animal for his overall thickness."

The cooking contests are under way—cash prizes for the best salad made "with at least one half cup of Kraft mayonnaise."

In the Horticulture Building, three judges pull apart bales of hay, searching for the forage with the cleanest smell, best leaf retention, and fewest weeds. ("Hey—what's this? A leaf of fleabane?")

In the 4-H Building, kids display projects on growing beetles from mealworms: "Mealworm beetles are clean pets that need little maintenance."

The New York State Fair draws upward of 850,000 people a year, several of whom come from New York City. "I think we had a couple from Brooklyn sign in at the guest relations booth," said fair director Wayne Gallagher. The rest are from the vast upstate, which, with 8.3 million acres in farmland, trails only Wisconsin and California among dairy states. It is second in calves slaughtered, apples picked, wine bottled, and beets grown for processing, and third in grapes, tart cherries, and Italian cheese. It leads all comers in corn silage, acreage in cabbage (much of it grown for kraut), and creamed cottage cheese, and ranks third in flowers and bedding plants, fourth in green beans, cauliflower, and ice cream, fifth in celery and green peas, sixth in lettuce and ice milk, tenth in carrots, eleventh in clover and grass hay, and twelfth in potatoes.

And its state fair, while not the biggest, is the most venerable. The state legislature voted in 1841 to authorize eight thousand dollars for a fair promoting "agriculture and household manufacturing in the state," and every year since, save for the world wars, it has been drawing speakers like Daniel Webster, Henry Clay, and Stephen Douglas, pickpockets from around the nation, and curiosities like Big John Lawes, who at seven foot five inches tall and five foot ten inches wide compared to "Other Fat Men" as the Washington Monument compared to "Other Structures of Its Class in Height," and to whose booth clergy and doctors were granted free admission.

Anything that recurs so regularly involves the past and the future more than the present. The state fair, more than any other institution, has stood for progress—uplift, improvement, betterment, ascent. Once, this was the shiniest week of an otherwise muddy year—the acme of scientific advancement, the definition of modernity. Now, of course, it is the odor of nostalgia that combines with the scent of manure and fried dough in the air along the midway.

. . .

Most visitors to the fair ignored the vast animal barns and headed right for the Ferris wheels—only one pen really drew crowds, a stall where a purebred Chester White sow lay nursing ten week-old piglets. And even there, when the hog stood up for a moment and rooted around, snorting at her offspring, people immediately started saying things like "Where's the guy who runs this? They shouldn't be letting that big pig in there with those little ones." And "She must be having PMS if she's acting like that."

Despite the mountains of cottage cheese and corn silage, there are only a fifth as many farms in New York now as there were in 1900, and they cover half the acreage. As farm life began to wither here, with it went the necessary props, the support systems. Grange Hall, for instance, which was once one of the liveliest corners of the fair, now seems all but moribund—a dusty display case listing the achievements of the Grange ends in 1890 with the Sherman Antitrust Act.

Over in the agricultural museum, a corner is dedicated to re-creating the "Wired Woodshed" of WSYR radio personality Robert "Deacon" Doubleday, who died in 1971. His well-loved programs included the daily "RFD Time," and "Sunday Morning after Chores," which always included marvelous doggerel, delivered in a voice like Paul Harvey's but without the halt.

> *The old rustic rail fence, rickracking its way,*
> *Crisscrossing the meadow and climbing the brae,*
> *It's crowded with cedars and oak trees and pine*
> *And tangled with bittersweet and blackberry vines. . . .*
> *Nestled beneath the long tall grass heaps*
> *In dry mossy beds the soft brown hare sleeps*
> *And deer find the shelter its mazy form makes,*
> *Streams mirror its lattice and snow fills its breaks.*
> *The landscape is lovelier—but fading from view*
> *Is the old rustic fence that the countryside knew.*

When the RFDeacon, "your only hired man in the great Northeast wired for sight and sound," signed off his final broadcast swinging on his imaginary barnyard gate and urging his listeners, as always, to "grab it and slam it and I'll see you in the morning," he was not replaced.

. . .

Over in Center of Progress building, meanwhile, lifestyle improvement seems to have stalled. In 1903, cars appeared for the first time. In 1916, the state police impressed everyone with a brand-new "herringbone" parking arrangement, "which allowed each driver to depart at any time without being blocked by other vehicles." But in recent years, the one certifiably new invention in the whole building was a snowplow that fit onto the front of any foreign-made car, allowing you to clear six or eight inches of snow from your driveway. ("I got a guy with kidney failure and he couldn't run his snowblower—he got one," said the inventor.) Otherwise, it was the Multigrater, the Combi-Chef, the washable lint brush, the Gel-Filled Headache Mask, the air freshener bearing the logo of your favorite NFL team, and KM, a botanical substance that increases your energy level by oxygenating your blood. ("It contains a whole new substance," explained the salesman. "They can't explain what it is, but it gives you vigor. It's used by professional athletes including Reggie White and some of his friends. It contains angelica root. It does phenomenal things for different people in different ways.") Also there's Klipette, an advanced nostril groomer. "Do Not Pull Out Nose Hairs by the Root!" warns its maker. "It Can Cause Fatal Infection."

They've given up demonstrating atomic power in the Industrial Building, the ballistic missile is no longer displayed in Empire Court, and the local utility's House of Tomorrow, a cramped ranchstyle with all-electric baseboard heat, has been turned into the public relations office.

. . .

Several generations of suburban life, however, have been insufficient to breed out a certain impulse to look at blood. Nothing else can explain the most singular tradition at the fair, the live veterinary surgery performed four times daily in an amphitheater at one end of the horse barn. Ten minutes before the program is to begin on the first day of the fair, a hundred and fifty folks have already gathered on the hard wooden bleachers, and when the white-coated master of ceremonies asks "Did any of you see this as a child and now you're bring your own children?" several hands go up. The show begins with a video about an Irish setter named Robin who is going to be spayed; the soundtrack is dense with medicalese ("as the vein is occluded by the assistant, you will notice the return blood flow distends the vein, insuring the placement of the catheter atraumatically"), which is clearly designed to show that you're not in the presence of mere horse doctors. Pretty soon, Robin flops over, out like a light, and the video goes off. A door at the back of the operating theater opens, and the live patient—an eleven-month-old beagle named Buddy—is wheeled on. "It's a little warm today," says the presiding vet. "If you feel a little bit queasy, a little extra warm, then stay put, let someone know, and we will help you down from your seat." Buddy is on his back, a tube in his mouth, his limbs strapped to the operating table. A cameraman is relaying a live close-up of his genitals on a large-screen TV in case anyone can't see quite clearly, and another vet is narrating. "The incision is right in front of the midline. Now he's holding the testicle, kind of pushing it up and the testicle will . . . just . . . pop . . . out! And here . . . comes . . . testicle . . . number . . . Two!" A great bloody scar fills the giant TV screen as people file out past a display of six pickled cat uteruses, two pickled dog uteruses, a grub larva removed from a kitten, and rusty fetal-head forceps once used on livestock. "We will give a straight answer to any question," boasted Dr. Robert Fuess, who began doing fair surgery twenty-two years ago. "Usually some one of us slips and we go into vet language and talk about a bitch and someone gets upset. Well, 'bitch' is a perfectly normal word. Do people ever get queasy? Sure they do. Most of the gals wear shorts or slacks, thank God, because when they pass out, we carry them outside and put their butt on the ground and prop their feet up against the barn."

. . .

What else stays the same? The ladies' garden clubs, for one. Their "floral interpretation" competition glides serenely on—one recent contest featured themes like "Columbus Sailed the Ocean Blue" and "Indian Powwow." Only "Age of Invention," with one arrangement planted in a hubcap, and another (a tribute to Velcro) composed of burrs, suggested the approaching millennium. Men's garden clubs were also represented. "The ladies are more into crafts," said Henry Smith of the Syracuse club. "My wife has an eagle on the wall made from—I don't know what you'd call them. When you pull a pine cone apart. With us men, it's more a 'Let's get out there and dig in the dirt' kind of thing."

The 4–H clubs seem resistant to unnecessary innovations as well. Their building at the fair was decorated with all sorts of official banners from 4–H headquarters designed to prove that 4–H was something different these days. "4–H is more than dairy goats—It's developing time-management and record-keeping skills," declared one banner with slightly Leninist overenthusiasm. "4–H is more than arts and crafts—it's learning to recycle materials to create innovative and useful items for home and environment."

But the long hall of displays belied the trendiness. Set up by region, allowing the visitor to savor New York's ancient county names (Chautauqua, Chenango, Oswego, Tioga, Oneida, Cayuga, Otsego, Cattaraugus), the booths were still featuring the old standards: science fair projects about the best conditions for yeast to rise, and newly sewn jumpers and tunics, and tremendous collections of beetles on pins in glass cases. Several Orleans County youth displayed an expansive collection of dried beans (Indian wild goose beans, case knife pole beans, pencil pod black beans, and slenderettes, thousand-to-ones, county churches, Hutterite soups, Vermont cranberries), while Niagara's young decorated notepaper with potato stamps, and the Herkimer club outlined the "Seven Steps of Baking a Cake." One young man had repeated the classic investigation where you train a bird to come to a particular cup for food and then switch cups to see if you can confuse it. "Nope, not tricked," his summary reported. "A chickadee still came back."

At one end of the 4–H Building, a crowd gathered to watch ducklings slide down a ramp into a pool of water—a display that shows up in pictures from the fairs of the 1930s and 1940s. A hundred feet down the hall, at the public speaking area, one youth after another delivered carefully prepared speeches. A pleasant girl in a homemade dress gave her talk on AIDS—it was impassioned but seemed somehow secondhand in the surroundings ("Remember to clean your needles!" she said perkily). She was followed by an Onondaga County boy lecturing on tractor safety in words that sounded like the product of hard experience. Fasten your safety belt, he warned, unless your tractor has no cab, in which case you don't want to be pinned underneath. Many accidents occur because of loose clothing around the power take-off shaft (he demonstrated with a small doll, who was caught in a model he'd built of a take-off shaft and whirled mercilessly). Don't check for leaks in the hydraulic system with your bare hands—the fluid is under two thousand pounds of pressure and a pinhole leak could penetrate your skin.

· · ·

Early one morning in the beef cattle barn, the grand champion 4–H steers and hogs are auctioned off to various buyers, and it is clear that for many of the children pride mixes with sadness at the thought of selling the animals they've worked so hard to raise. Elaine Cooper is standing next to Michelangelo, a steer she named for a Teenage Mutant Ninja Turtle and that she's been tending for seventeen months. "The first time I sold one I was in tears. Right now I'm not so sad, but I will be later when he's gone." She's brushing him over and over again so he'll look his best in the auction ring—"I wouldn't eat a steak from him," she said.

Brian Gale, a twelve-year-old from Erie County, stands nearby with his grand champion hog, all 226 pounds, that he's just sold at $2.50 a pound. "This one is called Crybaby because he squeals a lot." At first Brian admits to being a little sad, but quickly catches himself, saying, "Not much. I got more at home I like." Crybaby goes to Russ Mitchell, director of meat merchandising for sixty-four upstate P & C supermarkets. "These will be in the butcher store by the end of next week," he said. "We'll put the ribbons up next to the meat counter. But no pictures—that might be a little too close a connection. The very first time it can be a little hard for these kids to sell. But they know what they're raising them for—they're farm kids. Some of the kids probably name the animals, but personally I hate to get a bill with a name on it."

. . .

One or two other items are eternal as well. "Our biggest task? That's probably making sure the barns get cleaned out," said Bill Quinn, codirector of the agricultural portion of the fair. "Come by tonight and you'll really see the manure flying." Asked what had changed the most at the fair over his fifty years, cattle superintendent Dr. Henry Slack did not mention the genetically improved cows with their double yields, or the collapse of the family farm. He said, "We're much better at taking care of manure now than we used to be." Indeed, by nine that night the final Holsteins had been ponderously loaded onto trucks and four or five snowplows were racing around the aisles, pushing the hay and manure into great piles and then out the door. Men followed with brooms, sweeping every last scrap from the concrete floors.

Only two cows were left in the barn, standing calmly in their stalls near the milking parlor. They were Elsie and her calf Beauregarde, flagcattle of the Borden Dairy empire, who had stood patiently by the entrance to the Dairy Products Building throughout the fair, absorbing the pats of an endless stream of children. Tonight, as the barn emptied out, they chewed quietly, permitting themselves only an occasional lonely moo.

# · 23 ·

# If You Build It, Will They Change?

—*Toward the Livable City* (Milkweed Editions), 2003

Here's the event, now three decades past, that started Curitiba in a new direction: the city's mayor, Jaime Lerner, decided not to proceed with a plan to reduce congestion in the southern Brazilian city by routing a new freeway through the historic center of the town. Instead, he announced that the maze of streets at the city center would be closed to cars altogether, creating a pedestrian plaza. This was the early 1970s. Except maybe for the old quarter of Munich, there was hardly a pedestrian mall anywhere on urban planet earth. So it was a brave thing for the mayor of a provincial Brazilian city to decide that he would defy the town's business leaders and install one—literally do it over a single weekend, marshaling every city employee down to schoolteachers for the task of ripping up concrete and putting in cobblestones. When shopkeepers arrived on Monday to open their stores, they were outraged to find all the parking gone. Outraged until about midday, when it became clear that throngs of people were strolling the streets, stopping in to shop. By late afternoon, merchants in surrounding streets were demanding that their streets be ripped up too. The next weekend, when the local automobile club descended on the downtown to "retake" the street for cars, they found no police, no barricades. Instead, the Department of Public Works had unrolled half a mile of newsprint down the plaza and set out pots of paint. Hundreds of children were crouched there, drawing pictures. The drivers turned around and went home.

Changing the face of a city is a matter of blueprints, of dollars, of cubic feet of concrete, of cranes and bulldozers. Changing the heart of a city is more difficult, and more important—there's no simple way to bulldoze attitudes, to pour old feelings into plywood forms and let them harden in better shapes. And so Curitiba is an interesting story. Not because it has succeeded entirely, but because it has tried. Made a conscious effort to transform not only the shape of the city, and then through that physical transformation to reshape its citizens. To *unalienate* people. Not through propaganda, not through intimidation. Through respect.

Consider first the slum dwellers, the inhabitants of that rickety ring of *barrios* and *favelas* that circle every Latin American city. Go to Rio and, if you dare, wander the endless shantytowns, worlds to themselves, existing beyond the effective rule of law, even the effective reach of, say, the post office. You can meet fifth-generation residents—five generations of living next to open sewers, amid piles of trash.

Curitiba had always been relatively prosperous, mostly free of such spectacles. But in the 1980s, as agribusiness forced more and more peasants off the fertile land of its home state of Parana, the edges of the city began to swell with poor folk. The shacks started going up, and in the course of a few months, the health department noted an alarming rise in rat-borne diseases like leptospirosis. What to do?

The traditional answers, elsewhere in the hemisphere, have been to ignore the slums or to bulldoze them. Lerner and his team decided instead to try to incorporate their residents into the city, no easy task. Their initial problem, and initial opportunity, was the trash choking the alleys. There was no way to get garbage trucks down those narrow corridors, so they came up with an alternative. Signs went up all over the area, telling residents that if they carried a sack of trash to the nearest paved road at, say, 10 A.M. on Tuesday, they would receive a sack of food in return. It took almost no time to clean up the shantytowns; residents got calories they badly needed; food for the program came from the remaining farms around the city, stabilizing what was left of smaller-scale local agriculture. It was a problem solved, and the lines of people clutching their sacks of trash were a moving sight.

But the city didn't stop with that. Soon it was distributing bus tokens, too, and whenever a big concert—Julio Iglesias, say—came to the municipal concert hall, some percentage of the tickets were handed out along the garbage lines. "We have to have communication with the people of the slums," says Hitoshi Nakamura, one of Lerner's longtime assistants. "If we don't, if they start to feel like *favelados* [slum dwellers], then they will go against the city. Before they feel like *favelados* we must get there and implant these programs. If we give them attention, they don't feel abandoned. They feel like citizens."

In certain ways, though, the poor are easy—they have desperate needs that you can meet. The middle class, the well off, are in some ways harder. Their needs are less pressing, subtler; their choices are more varied. As in the United States, so around the world: increasingly, people with any options have left behind the public realm and found themselves private schools, private transportation, private enclaves with private guards posted at the private gate. Private *attitudes*. Luring them back into the life of the city requires at least as much creativity.

In Curitiba that meant things like the downtown shopping plaza. But it also meant a system of public parks that now provides more green space per inhabitant than any city on earth.

The money for that green necklace came from an unlikely source. When the federal government offered money for flood control, most Brazilian cities followed the example of the developed countries and "channelized" their rivers in concrete pipes, made them disappear from the center city. Curitiba took the cash and bought land, a series of parks along each of the rivers as they came into town, parks that featured lakes at their centers. When the rivers rose in the stream, the lakes in the parks simply expanded; for a few weeks, the jogging track or the bike path might have to be rerouted. But the rest of the year you had a park, a place for municipal bike rental stands, for outdoor restaurants, for city-owned skateboard parks and go-kart ramps. For the municipal Creativity Center, a former glue factory that now hosted a ceramics studio and a darkroom. For the city's very own remote-control airplane range. Did it work? Well, property values around each of the parks soared, enough that the increased tax collections paid for the improvements and then some. Did it work? So well that the biggest problem was how to cut all the thousands of acres of lawn the city now owned. And the solution, typically Curitiban, was to find a displaced shepherd newly arrived in one of the *favelas* and give him a truck and a municipal sheep flock, which makes its way from one park to the next, trimming and fertilizing.

The car, of course, is the ultimate symbol of the private worlds we now inhabit—our own transportation to take us exactly where we want exactly when we want, no questions asked, no concessions to anyone else's schedule, anyone else's taste in radio stations. Our own sheet-metal universe. This religion has spread outward from America to anywhere else where people are sufficiently wealthy. (And with some baroque variations. A few hundred miles north of Curitiba, in São Paulo, street crime makes even driving too dangerous for the very rich, and so a fleet of private helicopters buzzes the city at all hours.) Wrenching people from their cars may be the hardest of all public policy projects, one we've essentially abandoned in North America.

But Lerner had a different vision, of a city that moved primarily on public wheels. Bus wheels, because subways were far too expensive. He built a pretty good bus system, but the growth in car traffic kept up, and so he stopped to reevaluate. He took a lawn chair and set it up next to the bus stop by city hall, and for several days he simply watched to see what slowed buses down, made them maddeningly lurching creatures. It was the wait while people walked up the stairs, put in their coins, and made their way to the back of the bus, he decided. And so he sketched a new kind of bus stop, one that was built all over the city within a few years. It was a glass tube, elevated a few feet above the sidewalk. You walk up a stair, put your fare in the box, and wait for the bus to come. When it does, the doors open as they would on a subway; twenty people a second can climb on or off. When you've built a bus like that, you can make it long. Curitiba's double-hinged "speedybuses" can hold four hundred people. They can't be expected to snake through traffic, though—instead, they move on dedicated bus lanes and special bus-only streets, carrying traffic as fast as the New York express subways. But at a hundredth the cost. On busy routes at rush hour a bus pulls in every sixty seconds. Unlike New Yorkers, grimly peering out through scratched Plexiglas windows as the bus makes its halting way up, say, the East Side of Manhattan, Curitibanos can connect almost anywhere, whizzing through their city. The bus *serves* you—you feel in control of the city, not a victim of the tie-ups and bottlenecks and every-day-repeated traffic jams that mark every American town I know.

Does it work? Everyone takes the bus. Even with low fares, it pays for itself without tax subsidies. The fare box even pays for capital costs, for new buses and stations. Does it work? People in Curitiba use a quarter less fossil fuel, on average, than other urban Brazilians. That's a big number. Not enough to stop global warming, but remember, that savings comes before you install any fancy new engines or invent hydrogen fuel cells or whatever. It comes just from changing behavior. Does it work? At first some people detested all the bus lanes. It made driving more difficult. But when Lerner left office because of term limits, his approval rating was 92 percent.

But does it *really* work? Have any of these changes really changed *people*? Or maybe *change* is the wrong word. Has it managed to bring out the part of their nature, the part of all our natures, that likes the public world, the world of parks and plazas and barrooms and theaters, that likes to rub shoulders with the rest of the city? Change like that is essential if we're ever to deal with the core environmental and social questions we face. And change like that is harder to gauge. You need to leave statistics behind, try to get deeper.

The last time I was in Curitiba, I made it a point to talk with several writers who had lived there most of their lives, who had peopled their novels and poems with Curitibanos. The city, they agreed, represented an interesting test case. Populated largely by the descendants of European immigrants, it has always been a pretty stiff place. The rest of Brazil walks with a sway, but Curitibanos always stayed pretty much to the straight and narrow. "*Carnaval* is never much of a success here," said novelist Cristovao Tezza. "It's sort of something forced on us." Valencio Xavier, another writer, said that "when someone invites you to visit him in his house, you know he wasn't born here."

Lerner's reforms didn't change that character completely. "In some ways we remain spectators of the town," said Tezza. "I went to a rock show in the old part of town. It was an amazing spectacle— lights, lasers, stroboscopes. But people were just standing and watching. They didn't know if it was okay to dance." Still, they agreed, much was different. "Before in Curitiba things had always happened within four walls," said Xavier. "Lerner obliged us to walk. He had these street fairs; he made parks. Before we were like oysters that crack open just a little bit to get the world passing by. Now we are opening up."

"Look," said Lerner. "I know it's the right of people to live where they want. If you want to live in a condominium of wealthy people, that's okay." And in fact there are gated communities in Curitiba, a few. But government doesn't have to let everything inevitably slide in that direction. "You can also offer an option for people who want to live more . . . gregariously," he said. It's not a word many American politicians would employ. But it's the word that best defines a city worth living in.

Life is far from perfect in Curitiba. Too many of its residents are still poor. Lerner has run into trouble with leftists since he became governor of the surrounding state—he hasn't helped the landless, they claim. The antiglobalization campaigners don't like the fact that the city's success rests in part on the large corporations that have flocked there, lured by the good civic services, the safe streets. Too many of the reforms have been top-down, not democratic. Some residents say the stories about Curitiba's success are in great measure hype. It's not paradise.

But if you want paradise, you'd better look on a different planet. Curitiba offers what Lerner calls a "point of reference" for a world where urban too often means despair—even in places far richer than southern Brazil. For me, here's the "point of reference" from which to judge Curitiba:

When the mayor had sketched out his new scheme for bus stops, and city planners were getting set to build them, the first question was what material to use. The natural answer was glass—it is beautiful, and easy to clean, and durable: the glass in the windows of your home may have been there a century, and it works just as well as it did the day it was installed. But the public works commissioner wasn't so sure. The obvious drawback to glass is that you can chuck a rock through it. Maybe they should go with Plexiglas, he said, just to be safe.

No, said Jaime Lerner. "We have respected the people of the city, and they will respect the city in return." Glass it was. And the last time I was there, the shelters remained just as they'd been the day they were built. Gleaming. Uncracked. And busy.

# · 24 ·

## High Fidelity

—*Christian Century*, March 23, 2004

I live in the north country mountains, where winter begins in late October and gives up, some years, in early May. That means you come to church half the year in boots—heavy boots, in case you get stuck in a snowbank on the way. Which means, in turn, that the carpet on the floor better be some shade of brown.

Two or three times in my years there I've vacuumed the church. (Not very often, because we tend to divide up jobs along Traditional Gender Lines. Men make sure the furnace is turned up, change the storm windows, lift heavy things, paint, put away folding chairs, shovel the stairs. Women do everything else.) The first time I vacuumed I was merrily buzzing away between the pews, listening to the random click-clack of sand disappearing up the hose, when all of a sudden the noise trebled—click-click-click, like a Geiger counter in a uranium mine.

At that moment I was vacuuming beneath the third pew right along the center aisle. Right where Frank and Jean have been sitting every single Sunday that I can remember. I believe that Frank and Jean began attending our congregation the Sunday after the Council of Nicea. Each time they claim the same spot.

I kept vacuuming, hoovering up the same steady background level of sand, until I reached the sixth pew, against the right wall, where Velda and Don sit each Sunday—each Sunday they possibly can, that is, as both of them have been as much in the hospital as out lately. Again my Geiger counter went off. I decided that instead of radioactivity, it was measuring something else. Fidelity.

"Spirituality" is our watchword at the moment, of course. And rightly so. But Woody Allen had a point when he said that 90 percent of life consists in just showing up.

Consider what it means to belong to the same rural Methodist church for sixty or seventy years. Because Methodist central command insists on changing preachers about as frequently as Sheraton changes sheets, and because small, poor, rural congregations serve as practice ground for the rawest seminary graduates, anyone sitting in the pews for a decade or two sees a head-spinning mix of styles, theologies, and talents.

When I first arrived, the incumbent pastor was a jailhouse convert—the holy roller with a pinkie ring who returned whence he had come after embezzling a widow's insurance. Since then we've had wonderful people in the pulpit—some conservatives, some progressives. Some of them illustrated their sermons with examples taken from some preacher's helper that must have been published in 1921 because the anecdotes all involved World War I. We've taken communion by every method short of scuba diving into a tank of wine. We had one truly great preacher. She was young, smart, funny, full of love, able to talk to young and old, able to afflict the few of us who were comfortable while simultaneously comforting the many afflicted. And she hadn't been there a month before we were, all of us, worried sick about what it was going to be like when, inevitably, she would have to leave. Though none of us would have traded her years for anything, in certain ways it was the hardest passage of all.

Through it all Don and Velda and Frank and Jean never wavered. They might not have liked some new theological twist or liturgical gambit, but they didn't complain very much. (Not even when every other pastor would reinstitute the Greeting of the Neighbors, or the Passing of the Peace, or whatever they called it—a practice that makes less sense when the same fifteen people are there every week, and you've greeted them when you came in, and you're going to greet them again at coffee hour.) And they kept doing the fairly awesome amount of labor even a poor small church requires if it is to keep going.

It's easy to say that all this doesn't add up to a daring relationship with God, that it's Mary and Martha come to life, that routine can suck the meaning out of something as bracing as the gospel. But those of us who've claimed this place were attracted by the sheer dogged devotion of the regulars.

My generation has been good at many things, but tenacity—faithfulness—is not one of them. Sometimes, in fact, we simply want too much. Like marriages that complete us, fulfill us in every way, make us whole, instead of marriages where, on most days, it's enough to be living faithfully together, adding another increment of quotidian devotion, giving each other the benefit of the doubt. Or like religious *experiences*, instead of the experience of being religious. I have no real sense of what it might have felt like to inhabit the medieval world, when the church was simply the air one breathed, the environment in which one lived. Or rather, what sense of that world I have comes from watching people like Frank and Jean and Don and Velda.

One spring day some years ago, when Don and I had finished taking down the storm windows, we decided to climb up into the steeple on a rickety ladder so that we could take in the view across our small town. We could see the house where he'd grown up, and the graveyard where many generations of his ancestors were buried. And while we were up there Don showed me something else—the place he had carved his initials, and Velda's. Sometime in the 1920s, when they were in grade school.

# · 25 ·

## The Christian Paradox

—*Harper's Magazine,* August 2005

Only 40 percent of Americans can name more than four of the Ten Commandments, and a scant half can cite any of the four authors of the Gospels. Twelve percent believe Joan of Arc was Noah's wife. This failure to recall the specifics of our Christian heritage may be further evidence of our nation's educational decline, but it probably doesn't matter all that much in spiritual or political terms. Here is a statistic that does matter: three quarters of Americans believe the Bible teaches that "God helps those who help themselves." That is, three out of four Americans believe that this uber-American idea, a notion at the core of our current individualist politics and culture, which was in fact uttered by Ben Franklin, actually appears in Holy Scripture. The thing is, not only is Franklin's wisdom not biblical; it's counterbiblical. Few ideas could be further from the gospel message, with its radical summons to love of neighbor. On this essential matter, most Americans—most American *Christians*—are simply wrong, as if 75 percent of American scientists believed that Newton proved gravity causes apples to fly up.

Asking Christians what Christ taught isn't a trick. When we

say we are a Christian nation—and, overwhelmingly, we do—it means something. People who go to church absorb lessons there and make real decisions based on those lessons; increasingly, these lessons inform their politics. (One poll found that 11 percent of U.S. churchgoers were urged by their clergy to vote in a particular way in the 2004 election, up from 6 percent in 2000.) When George Bush says that Jesus Christ is his favorite philosopher, he may or may not be sincere, but he is reflecting the sincere beliefs of the vast majority of Americans.

And therein is the paradox. America is simultaneously the most professedly Christian of the developed nations and the least Christian in its behavior. That paradox—more important, perhaps, than the much touted ability of French women to stay thin on a diet of chocolate and cheese—illuminates the hollow at the core of our boastful, careening culture.

· · ·

Ours is among the most spiritually homogenous rich nations on earth. Depending on which poll you look at and how the question is asked, somewhere around 85 percent of us call ourselves Christian. Israel, by way of comparison, is 77 percent Jewish. It is true that a smaller number of Americans—about 75 percent—claim they actually pray to God on a daily basis, and only 33 percent say they manage to get to church every week. Still, even if that 85 percent overstates actual practice, it clearly represents aspiration. In fact, there is nothing else that unites more than four fifths of America. Every other statistic one can cite about American behavior is essentially also a measure of the behavior of professed Christians. That's what America is: a place saturated in Christian identity.

But is it *Christian*? This is not a matter of angels dancing on the heads of pins. Christ was pretty specific about what he had in mind for his followers. What if we chose some simple criterion—say, giving aid to the poorest people—as a reasonable proxy for Christian behavior? After all, in the days before his crucifixion, when

Jesus summed up his message for his disciples, he said the way you could tell the righteous from the damned was by whether they'd fed the hungry, slaked the thirsty, clothed the naked, welcomed the stranger, and visited the prisoner. What would we find then?

In 2004, as a share of our economy, we ranked second to last, after Italy, among developed countries in government foreign aid. Per capita we each provide fifteen cents a day in official development assistance to poor countries. And it's not because we were giving to private charities for relief work instead. Such funding increases our average daily donation by just six pennies, to twenty-one cents. It's also not because Americans were too busy taking care of their own; nearly 18 percent of American children lived in poverty (compared with, say, 8 percent in Sweden). In fact, by pretty much any measure of caring for the least among us you want to propose—childhood nutrition, infant mortality, access to preschool—we come in nearly last among the rich nations, and often by a wide margin. The point is not just that (as everyone already knows) the American nation trails badly in all these categories; it's that the overwhelmingly *Christian* American nation trails badly in all these categories, categories to which Jesus paid particular attention. And it's not as if the numbers are getting better: the U.S. Department of Agriculture reported last year that the number of households that were "food insecure with hunger" had climbed more than 26 percent between 1999 and 2003.

This Christian nation also tends to make personal, as opposed to political, choices that the Bible would seem to frown upon. Despite the Sixth Commandment, we are, of course, the most violent rich nation on earth, with a murder rate four or five times that of our European peers. We have prison populations greater by a factor of six or seven than other rich nations (which at least should give us plenty of opportunity for visiting the prisoners). Having been told to turn the other cheek, we're the only Western democracy left that executes its citizens, mostly in those states where Christianity is theoretically strongest. Despite Jesus' strong declarations against divorce, our marriages break up at a rate—just over half—that compares poorly with the European Union's average of about four in ten. That average may be held down by the fact that Europeans marry less frequently, and by countries, like Italy, where divorce is difficult; still, compare our success with, say, that of the godless Dutch, whose divorce rate is just over 37 percent. Teenage pregnancy? We're at the top of the charts. Personal self-discipline—like, say, keeping your weight under control? Buying on credit? Running government deficits? Do you need to ask?

· · ·

Are Americans hypocrites? Of course they are. But most people (me, for instance) are hypocrites. The more troubling explanation for this disconnect between belief and action, I think, is that most Americans—which means most believers—have replaced the Christianity of the Bible, with its call for deep sharing and personal sacrifice, with a competing creed.

In fact, there may be several competing creeds. For many Christians, deciphering a few passages of the Bible to figure out the schedule for the End Times has become a central task. You can log on to RaptureReady.com for a taste of how some of these believers view the world—at this writing the Rapture Index had declined three points to 152 because, despite an increase in the number of U.S. pagans, "Wal-Mart is falling behind in its plan to bar code all products with radio tags." Other End-Timers are more interested in forcing the issue—they're convinced that the way to coax the Lord back to earth is to "Christianize" our nation and then the world. Consider House Majority Leader Tom DeLay. At church one day he listened as the pastor, urging his flock to support the administration, declared that "the war between America and Iraq is the gateway to the Apocalypse." DeLay rose to speak, not only to the congregation but to 225 Christian TV and radio stations. "Ladies and gentlemen," he said, "what has been spoken here tonight is the truth of God."

On Sundays children played with church-distributed Xboxes, and many congregants had signed up for a twice-weekly aerobics class called Firm Believers. A list of bestsellers compiled monthly by the Christian Booksellers Association illuminates the creed. It includes texts like *Your Best Life Now* by Joel Osteen—pastor of a church so mega it recently leased a sixteen-thousand-seat sports arena in Houston for its services—which even the normally tolerant *Publishers Weekly* dismissed as "a treatise on how to get God to serve the demands of self-centered individuals." Nearly as high is Beth Moore, with her *Believing God*—"Beth asks the tough questions concerning the fruit of our Christian lives," such as "are we living as fully as we can?" Other titles include *Humor for a Woman's Heart*, a collection of "humorous writings" designed to "lift a life above the stresses and strains of the day"; *The Five Love Languages*, in which Dr. Gary Chapman helps you figure out if you're speaking in the same emotional dialect as your significant other; and Karol Ladd's *The Power of a Positive Woman*. Ladd is the co-founder of USA Sonshine Girls—the "Son" in Sonshine, of course, is the son of God—and she is unremittingly upbeat in presenting her five-part plan for creating a life with "more calm, less stress."

Not that any of this is so bad in itself. We do have stressful lives, humor *does* help, and you *should* pay attention to your own needs. Comfortable suburbanites watch their parents die, their kids implode. Clearly I need help with being positive. And I have no doubt that such texts have turned people into better parents, better spouses, better bosses. It's just that these authors, in presenting their perfectly sensible advice, somehow manage to ignore Jesus' radical and demanding focus on others. It may, in fact, be true that "God helps those who help themselves," both financially and emotionally. (Certainly fortune does.) But if so it's still a subsidiary, secondary truth, more Franklinity than Christianity. You could eliminate the scriptural references in most of these bestsellers and they would still make or not make the same amount of sense. *Chicken Soup for the Zoroastrian Soul*. It is a perfect mirror of the secular bestseller lists, indeed of the secular culture, with its American fixation on self-improvement, on self-esteem. On self. These similarities make it difficult (although not impossible) for the televangelists to posit themselves as embattled figures in a "culture war"—they offer too uncanny a reflection of the dominant culture, a culture of unrelenting self-obsession.

. . .

Who am I to criticize someone else's religion? After all, if there is anything Americans agree on, it's that we should tolerate everyone else's religious expression. As a *Newsweek* writer put it some years ago at the end of his cover story on apocalyptic visions and the Book of Revelation, "Who's to say that John's mythic battle between Christ and Antichrist is not a valid insight into what the history of humankind is all about?" (Not *Newsweek*, that's for sure; their religious covers are guaranteed big sellers.) To that I can only answer that I'm a . . . Christian.

Not a professional one; I'm an environmental writer mostly. I've never progressed further in the church hierarchy than Sunday school teacher at my backwoods Methodist church. But I've spent most of my Sunday mornings in a pew. I grew up in church youth groups and stayed active most of my adult life—started homeless shelters in church basements, served soup at the church food pantry, climbed to the top of the rickety ladder to put the star on the church Christmas tree. My work has been, at times, influenced by all that—I've written extensively about the Book of Job, which is to me the first great piece of nature writing in the Western tradition, and about the overlaps between Christianity and environmentalism. In fact, I imagine I'm one of a fairly small number of writers who have had cover stories in both the *Christian Century*, the magazine of liberal mainline Protestantism, and *Christianity Today*, which Billy Graham founded, not to mention articles in *Sojourners*, the magazine of the progressive evangelical community cofounded by Jim Wallis.

Indeed, it was my work with religious environmentalists that first got me thinking along the lines of this essay. We were trying to get politicians to understand why the Bible actually mandated protecting the world around us (Noah: the first Green), work that I think is true and vital. But one day it occurred to me that the parts of the world where people actually had cut dramatically back on their carbon emissions, actually did live voluntarily in smaller homes and take public transit, were the same countries where people were giving aid to the poor and making sure everyone had health care—countries like Norway and Sweden, where religion was relatively unimportant. How could that be? For Christians there should be something at least a little scary in the notion that, absent the magical answers of religion, people might just get around to solving their problems and strengthening their communities in more straightforward ways.

But for me, in any event, the European success is less interesting than the American failure. Because we're not going to be like them. Maybe we'd be better off if we abandoned religion for secular rationality, but we're not going to; for the foreseeable future this will be a "Christian" nation. The question is, what kind of Christian nation?

. . .

The tendencies I have been describing—toward an apocalyptic End Times faith, toward a comfort-the-comfortable, personal-empowerment faith—veil the actual, and remarkable, message of the Gospels. When one of the Pharisees asked Jesus what the core of the law was, Jesus replied:

> You shall love the Lord your God with all your heart, and with all your soul, and with all your mind. This is the greatest and first commandment. And a second is like it, You shall love your neighbor as yourself. On these two commandments hang all the law and the prophets.

Love your neighbor as yourself: although its rhetorical power has been dimmed by repetition, that is a radical notion, perhaps the most radical notion possible. Especially since Jesus, in all his teachings, made it very clear who the neighbor you were supposed to love was: the poor person, the sick person, the naked person, the hungry person. The last shall be made first; turn the other cheek; a rich person aiming for heaven is like a camel trying to walk through the eye of a needle. On and on and on—a call for nothing less than a radical, voluntary, and effective reordering of power relationships, based on the principle of love.

I confess, even as I write these words, to a feeling close to embarrassment. Because in public we tend not to talk about such things—my theory of what Jesus mostly meant seems like it should be left in church, or confined to some religious publication. But remember the overwhelming connection between America and Christianity; what Jesus meant is the most deeply potent political, cultural, social question. To ignore it, or leave it to the bullies and the salesmen of the televangelist sects, means to walk away from a central battle over American identity. At the moment, the idea of Jesus has been hijacked by people with a series of causes that do not reflect his teachings. The Bible is a long book, and even the Gospels have plenty in them, some of it seemingly contradictory and hard to puzzle out. But love your neighbor as yourself—not do unto others as you would have them do unto you, but *love your neighbor as yourself*—will suffice as a gloss. There is no disputing the centrality of this message, nor is there any disputing how easy it is to ignore that message. Because it is so counterintuitive, Christians have had to keep repeating it to themselves right from the start. Consider Paul, for instance, instructing the church at Galatea: "For the whole law is summed up in a single commandment," he wrote. " 'You shall love your neighbor as yourself.' "

American churches, by and large, have done a pretty good job of loving the neighbor in the next pew. A pastor can spend all Sunday talking about the Rapture Index, but if his congregation is thriving you can be assured he's spending the other six days visiting people in the hospital, counseling couples, and sitting up with grieving widows. All this human connection is important. But if the theology makes it harder to love the neighbor a little farther away—particularly the poor and the weak—then it's a problem. And the dominant theologies of the moment do just that. They undercut Jesus, muffle his hard words, deaden his call, and in the end silence him. In fact, the soft-focus consumer gospel of the suburban megachurches is a perfect match for emergent conservative economic notions about personal responsibility instead of collective action. Privatize Social Security? Keep health care for people who can afford it? File those under "God helps those who help themselves."

Take Alabama as an example. In 2002, Bob Riley was elected governor of the state, where 90 percent of residents identify themselves as Christians. Riley could safely be called a conservative—right-wing majordomo Grover Norquist gave him a Friend of the Taxpayer Award every year he was in Congress, where he'd never voted for a tax increase. But when he took over Alabama, he found himself administering a tax code that dated to 1901. The richest Alabamians paid 3 percent of their income in taxes, and the poorest paid up to 12 percent; income taxes kicked in if a family of four made $4,600 (even in Mississippi the threshold was $19,000), while out-of-state timber companies paid $1.25 an acre in property taxes. Alabama was forty-eighth in total state and local taxes, and the largest proportion of that income came from sales tax—a super-regressive tax that in some counties reached into double digits. So Riley proposed a tax hike, partly to dig the state out of a fiscal crisis and partly to put more money into the state's school system, routinely ranked near the worst in the nation. He argued that it was Christian duty to look after the poor more carefully.

Had the new law passed, the owner of a $250,000 home in Montgomery would have paid $1,432 in property taxes—we're not talking Sweden here. But it didn't pass. It was crushed by a factor of two to one. Sixty-eight percent of the state voted against it—meaning, of course, something like 68 percent of the Christians who voted. The opposition was led, in fact, not just by the state's wealthiest interests but also by the Christian Coalition of Alabama. "You'll find most Alabamians have got a charitable heart," said John Giles, the group's president. "They just don't want it coming out of their pockets." On its Web site, the group argued that taxing the rich at a higher rate than the poor "results in punishing success" and that "when an individual works for their income, that money belongs to the individual." You might as well just cite chapter and verse from *Poor Richard's Almanack*. And whatever the ideology, the results are clear. "I'm tired of Alabama being first in things that are bad," said Governor Riley, "and last in things that are good."

· · ·

A rich man came to Jesus one day and asked what he should do to get into heaven. Jesus did not say he should invest, spend, and let the benefits trickle down; he said sell what you have, give the money to the poor, and follow me. Few plainer words have been spoken. And yet, for some reason, the Christian Coalition of America—founded in 1989 in order to "preserve, protect and defend the Judeo-Christian values that made this the greatest country in history"—proclaimed last year that its top legislative priority would be "making permanent President Bush's 2001 federal tax cuts."

Similarly, a furor erupted last spring when it emerged that a Colorado jury had consulted the Bible before sentencing a killer to death. Experts debated whether the (Christian) jurors should have used an outside authority in their deliberations, and of course the Christian right saw it as one more sign of a secular society devaluing religion. But a more interesting question would have been why the jurors fixated on Leviticus 24, with its call for an eye for an eye and a tooth for a tooth. They had somehow missed Jesus' explicit refutation in the New Testament: "You have heard that it was said, 'an eye for an eye and a tooth for a tooth.' But I say to you, Do not resist an evildoer. But if anyone strikes you on the right cheek, turn the other also."

And on and on. The power of the Christian right rests largely in the fact that they boldly claim religious authority, and by their very boldness convince the rest of us that they must know what they're talking about. They're like the guy who gives you directions with such loud confidence that you drive on even though the road appears to be turning into a faint, rutted track. But their theology is appealing for another reason too: it coincides with what we want to believe. How nice it would be if Jesus had declared that our income was ours to keep, instead of insisting that we had to share. How satisfying it would be if we were supposed to hate our enemies. Religious conservatives will always have a comparatively easy sell.

But straight is the path and narrow is the way. The gospel is too radical for any culture larger than the Amish to ever come close to realizing; in demanding a departure from selfishness it conflicts with all our current desires. Even the first time around, judging by the reaction, the Gospels were pretty unwelcome news to an awful lot of people. There is not going to be a modern-day return to the church of the early believers, holding all things in common—that's not what I'm talking about. Taking seriously the actual message of Jesus, though, should serve at least to moderate the greed and violence that mark this culture. It's hard to imagine a con much more audacious than making Christ the front man for a program of tax cuts for the rich or war in Iraq. If some modest part of the 85 percent of us who are Christians woke up to that fact, then the world might change.

It is possible, I think. Yes, the mainline Protestant churches that supported civil rights and opposed the war in Vietnam are mostly locked in a dreary decline as their congregations dwindle and their elders argue endlessly about gay clergy and same-sex unions. And the Catholic Church, for most of its American history a sturdy exponent of a "love your neighbor" theology, has been weakened, too, its hierarchy increasingly motivated by a single-issue focus on abortion. Plenty of vital congregations are doing great good works—they're the ones that have nurtured me—but they aren't where the challenge will arise; they've grown shy about talking about Jesus, more comfortable with the language of sociology and politics. More and more it's Bible-quoting Christians, like Wallis's *Sojourners* movement and that Baptist seminary graduate Bill Moyers, who are carrying the fight.

The best selling of all Christian books in recent years, Rick Warren's *The Purpose-Driven Life*, illustrates the possibilities. It has all the hallmarks of self-absorption (in one five-page chapter, I counted sixty-five uses of the word "you"), but it also makes a powerful case that we're made for mission. What that mission is never becomes clear, but the thirst for it is real. And there's no great need for Warren to state that purpose anyhow. For Christians, the plainspoken message of the Gospels is clear enough. If you have any doubts, read the Sermon on the Mount.

Admittedly, this is hope against hope; more likely the money changers and power brokers will remain ascendant in our "spiritual" life. Since the days of Constantine, emperors and rich men have sought to co-opt the teachings of Jesus. As in so many areas of our increasingly market-tested lives, the co-opters—the TV men, the politicians, the Christian "interest groups"—have found a way to make each of us complicit in that travesty, too. They have invited us to subvert the church of Jesus even as we celebrate it. With their help we have made golden calves of ourselves—become a nation of terrified, self-obsessed idols. It works, and it may well keep working for a long time to come. When Americans hunger for selfless love and are fed only love of self, they will remain hungry, and too often hungry people just come back for more of the same.

· 26 ·

# Will Evangelicals Help Save the Earth?

—*OnEarth*, Fall 2006

In the beginning (say, the Reagan era), all was darkness. To liberal American Christians, the environment was largely a luxury item, well down on the list below war and poverty. "I remember one Catholic bishop asking me, 'How come there aren't any people on those Sierra Club calendars?'" says one of the few religious conservatives of that era. To conservative Christians, *environmentalism* was a dirty word—it stank of paganism, of interference with the free market, of the sixties. Meanwhile, many environmentalists were more secular than the American norm, and often infected with the notion spread by the historian Lynn White in his famous 1967 essay, "The Historical Roots of Our Ecological Crisis," that Christianity lay at the root of ecological devastation. Everyone, in short, was scared of everyone else.

But there were a few lights starting to shine in that gloom. Calvin DeWitt carried one lantern. A mild-mannered midwesterner with a Ph.D. in zoology, he helped in 1979 to found the Au Sable Institute in northern Michigan. The institute devotes itself to organizing field courses and conferences that teach ecology, always stressing the Christian notion of stewardship, the idea that, as it says in Genesis, we are to "dress and keep" the fertile earth. To understand what a religious environmental worldview might look like, consider this from one of DeWitt's early statements: "Creation itself is a complex functioning whole of people, plants, animals, natural systems, physical processes, social structures, and more, all of which are sustained by God's love and ordered by God's wisdom. Thus, Au Sable brings together the full range of disciplines—from chemistry to economics to marine biology to theology—that we need if we are to be good stewards of God's household." That doesn't sound too frightening, right?

In DeWitt's Reformed Church tradition, God has left us two books to read. First, the book of creation, "in which each creature is as a letter of text leading us to know God's divinity and everlasting power." And second, the Bible. It's easy to see how environmentalism connects with the first of these, but it's taken longer to understand its relevance to the second.

"When we started, for the first two or three or four years almost everything we were dealing with was an Old Testament text, from the Hebrew Bible," said DeWitt. That makes sense. Since the Old Testament starts at the beginning, it almost has to deal with questions about the relationship between people and land. There's Noah, the first radical green, saving a breeding pair of everything; there are the Jewish laws mandating a Sabbath for the land every seventh year; there's the soliloquy at the end of the book of Job, which is both God's longest speech in the whole Bible and the first and best piece of nature writing in the Western tradition.

But the sparer, more compressed text of the Gospels and Epistles had never been read with an eye to its ecological meaning—in large part because it wasn't necessary. Medieval Christians, say, weren't living in a time of planetary peril. But now that we were, people started finding passages like this from Colossians: Jesus "is the image of the invisible God, the first-born of all creation; for in him all things were created, in heaven and on earth . . . all things were created before him and through him." It may not sound exactly like an Audubon Society mailer, but the insistence on this world as well as the next was important in helping many pastors open up to environmental thinking. Or this, from Revelation, describing the final judgment, when the time would come for rewarding the servants and prophets and "for destroying the destroyers of the earth." (That's a little scarier to secular ears, but if you've ever sung Handel's *Messiah*, the "trumpet shall sound" stuff echoes the same passage.) The point is, once people started looking, the Scriptures started speaking.

Something else happened too: the emergence of climate change as the key question for the environmental movement. On the one hand, confronting global warming made everything harder—environmental groups suddenly found themselves contending with the main engine of our economy. But for many religious environmentalists, heightening the stakes may have made progress easier—this was a cosmological question, one about the ultimate fate of our species, our planet, God's creation. Unlike, say, clean drinking water, where simple, practical wisdom was enough to offer you an answer, global warming almost demanded a theological response. In that sense, it was like the dawn of the nuclear age. "The magnitude, the comprehensiveness, the totality of the challenge it represents to God's creation on earth, the profoundly intergenerational nature of the damage that was being done—it became the central axis," said Paul Gorman.

Gorman is a story in himself. A former speechwriter for Eugene McCarthy, in 1993 he cofounded the National Religious Partnership for the Environment, which, with generous amounts of foundation money, set out to build environmental support among American Jews, Catholics, mainline Protestants (like Methodists and Lutherans), and evangelical Christians. Crucially, it was willing to go slowly enough to build a solid foundation. "It's not going to be the environmental movement at prayer," said Gorman, "not about providing more shock troops for the embattled American greens. We have to see the inescapable, thrilling, renewing religious dimension of this challenge." A thousand Sunday school curriculums and special liturgies and summer camps later, Gorman's effort is bearing real fruit. In 2001, for instance, America's Catholic bishops issued a pastoral statement on the environment, one that fits the question into their long-standing theology of "prudence" and relates it to their centuries of work against hunger and poverty around the world. "If you measure [the change] against the speed with which religious life integrates fundamental new perspectives, then historically it's been kind of brisk," said Gorman.

. . .

On occasion, the religious environmental movement flared into public view. At the turn of the century, for instance, while spending a year as a fellow at Harvard Divinity School, I helped organize a series of demonstrations outside SUV dealerships in Boston. Before one demonstration with a bunch of mainline clerics, Dan Smith, then the associate pastor of the Hancock United Church of Christ in Lexington, Massachusetts, where I'd grown up, and I painted a banner that said "WWJD: What Would Jesus Drive?" The initials were borrowed from evangelical circles, where they stood for What Would Jesus Do and usually referred to questions of sex or drugs. But we liked the emphasis on personal responsibility—and we guessed that the newspapers might like it too. Guessed correctly, as it turned out, for the sign was splashed across the front pages and Web sites the next day. Within a matter of months, it wound up back in more conservative circles, where the Evangelical Environmental Network, of which DeWitt was a founder, used the slogan as part of a multistate advertising campaign. Most of the time, though, the progress has been slower, steadier, and less visible. The Evangelical Climate Initiative document, for instance, grew out of a very private retreat for select leaders at a Christian conference center on the Maryland shore, a gathering that included many of the evangelical movement's luminaries, most of whom had not been deeply involved in environmental issues. The opening remarks came from Sir John Houghton, an English physicist and climate expert who had served as chairman of the scientific assessment team for the Intergovernmental Panel on Climate Change (IPCC), the group that definitively broke the news that humans were indeed heating the planet. Sir John was also a lifelong British evangelical (on a continent where Christians are less politically polarized) and a friend of John Stott, another Brit and a beloved elder statesman in evangelical circles. Sir John also could point to his collaborations with business leaders in Europe, like John Browne, chairman of British Petroleum, who were far more open to acknowledging global warming than were their American counterparts at companies like ExxonMobil.

"When John Houghton speaks, he speaks with both biblical authority and scientific authority," said DeWitt. "The critic, the detractor, the naysayer has to deal with a person who is both the scientist and the evangelical scholar in one and the same person. As an evangelical, Bible-believing, God-fearing Christian as well as a scientist, he'd made sure that the IPCC reports were absolutely the best and most truthfully stated documents ever produced in science." And, he added, "it helps that he's got a British accent."

By the conference's close, the participants had made a covenant to address the issue, and then spent months gathering signatures. When it was eventually released, some leaders of the Christian right, like Jerry Falwell, Pat Robertson, and James Dobson, demanded that it be retracted. Climate science was unsettled, they said. Speaking anonymously, one conservative Christian lobbyist scoffed to a reporter, "Is God really going to let the earth burn up?" The National Association of Evangelicals, the umbrella group for the entire movement, feared a split and stayed officially neutral. But the bulk of the eighty-six signers (who included seminary presidents, charity directors, and prominent pastors like Rick Warren, the author of *The Purpose-Driven Life*) held strong, some of them quietly relishing the chance to say that their movement was larger than high-profile televangelists and not necessarily a steady date of the

GOP. "The grace of it!" said Gorman. "I think you could say this is one of the first significant events of the post-Bush era."

It's had legs, too. In the spring of 2006 the *New Republic* reported that in Pennsylvania the incumbent Republican senator Rick Santorum had come under religious fire for his stand on climate change. At a panel on the subject, a biology professor at Messiah College in Grantham, Pennsylvania, "tore into the senator, accusing him of selling out the environment to business interests." In the words of Richard Cizik, the chief lobbyist for evangelical causes in Washington, "there's going to be a lot of political reconsideration on this in the coming year. The old fault lines are no more."

Other evangelicals are less political, but at least as subversive. A former emergency room doctor named Matthew Sleeth, for instance, quit his job to preach the green gospel and says the reaction has been far greater than he could have guessed. His book *Serve God, Save the Planet* was published in the spring, and he had been traveling to churches ever since. Everywhere his message is the same: God asks us to surrender some of our earth-wrecking wealth. "Bible-believing Christians have confused the kingdom of heaven with capitalism and consumerism," Sleeth said. He's not attracted to electoral politics. Instead he's been downsizing his life—putting up the clothesline, selling his stuff, buying a Prius. (He writes his books on a lifetime supply of old computer paper he rescued from a Dumpster.) The ecological battles ahead of us compare to the greatest battles in American history, he says, and his models include people like the abolitionist John Brown, who practiced exactly what he preached, sharing his farm with freed slaves. "There's a longing for a spiritual life in this country," he said, over and over. "A great hunger for something more than capitalism."

· · ·

It's far from clear, however, that faith communities will take this fight as far as it needs to go. Simply breaking ranks with the George W. Bush administration on this issue took enormous courage for evangelical leaders. So if some legislator offers any kind of deal to "fix" the problem of global warming, it may win all-too-easy endorsement. Some kind of Kyoto-lite measure, like the one proposed by Senators John McCain and Joe Lieberman, might pass the Congress in the next few years. If it does, the bar has been set so low that environmentalists of all stripes, but especially those out on a limb like the evangelicals, might well sign on, even though the steadily worsening scientific findings make it very clear that bold and rapid action is required. Here's John Houghton, speaking hard words to Americans: "You've got to cut your own greenhouse gas emissions, on the fastest time scale you can possibly do. You've got to help China and India develop in ways that are environmentally friendly and don't emit too much, but allow them to develop at the same time." Those are precisely the fights—over scale, speed, and international equity—that will bedevil whatever steps we take to fight global warming, and it's not clear that the faithful are really girded for the fight. "Will this groundswell have the real moral edge to keep the pressure on over the long haul?" asks Gorman, and he doesn't answer his own question.

If the answer is going to be yes, a couple of things may need to happen. One, the mainline Protestant denominations will have to step up to the plate. They long ago passed all the proper resolutions decrying the destruction of creation, and certain congregations have launched interesting initiatives. (An upstart group called Episcopal Power and Light, for instance, pioneered the practice of supplying congregations with green power.) But not many mainline Protestants have stepped far outside their comfort zones—in part because the denominations themselves are dwindling in number and beset by internal divisions over questions like the ordination of gay clergy. Still, there are increasing hints of future activism: planning for possible widespread nonviolent civil disobedience to draw attention to global warming, for instance, was widely discussed at a recent National Council of Churches meeting in storm-wrecked

New Orleans. Protests at Ford headquarters? Blocking the entrance to the EPA? Sitting on the tracks of coal trains? Whatever the strategy, it will play better on TV if there are some clerical collars near the front.

The critique from all quarters will need to get sharper too. Calvin DeWitt pulls no punches: "We've spiritualized the devil," he said. "But when Exxon is funding think tanks to basically confuse the lessons that we're getting from this great book of creation, that's devilish work. We find ourselves praying to God to protect us from the wiles of the devil, but we can't see him when he's staring us in the face."

Much of the uncertainty about the future of such efforts stems from this: Christianity in America has grown very comfortable with the hyperindividualism of our consumer lives. In one recent poll, three-quarters of Christians said they thought the phrase "God helps those who help themselves" came from the Bible, when in fact it derives from Aesop via Ben Franklin and expresses almost the exact opposite of the Gospel injunction to "love your neighbor as yourself." Said DeWitt, "By accommodating to a new philosophy about how society works, we've flipped Matthew 6:33 on its head. Instead of 'Seek ye first the kingdom of God and all the rest shall be added unto you,' we're looking out for number one." Which makes it a lot harder for politicians to start talking about carbon taxes or other measures that might actually start to bring our emissions under control.

Still, there are continuing signs of progress—what Christians might call evidence of the Holy Spirit at work. In August 2006, after the hottest early summer on record in the United States, even Pat Robertson announced his conversion—people were heating the planet, he said, and something needed to be done. In the end, it's clear that this battle is not only for the preservation of creation. In certain ways, it offers the chance for American Christianity to rescue itself from the smothering embrace of a culture fixated on economic growth, on individual abundance. A new chance to emerge as the countercultural force that the Gospels clearly envisioned. And also a chance to heal at least a few of the splits in American Christianity. Fighting over creation versus evolution, for instance, seems a little less crucial in an era when de-creation has become the real challenge.

## · V ·

# HEROES

made their presence felt, but their number is too small and their careers are too varied to provide much in the way of models.

David Garrow's *Bearing the Cross: Martin Luther King, Jr. and the Southern Christian Leadership Conference* demonstrates just how harrowing the demand for unceasing creativity can be. The King who emerges in this splendidly detailed new life owns a nearly inhuman strength. And yet much of the book shows him in despair, unsure how to keep his movement (which depended on public interest, not electoral power) from fizzling. King had one tremendous insight: that his message—the dignity of black men and women—could be embodied in the means of its delivery, nonviolent struggle. But that realization, though it gave him the possibility of success, did not remove the endless problems of strategy, tactics, personality, and morality which he faced from the Montgomery bus boycott until his death in Memphis. What mattered most—public accommodations or voting rights or economic progress? Was it time to take the movement North? Which injunctions should be violated? Which Southern city—Albany or St. Augustine or Birmingham or Selma—would best dramatize the struggle? Was Jesse Jackson operating too independently in Chicago? Why was the Southern Christian Leadership Conference staff so inefficient? Often a single decision had elements of the moral, the tactical, and the personal. King knew that his conscience demanded he speak out against America's involvement in Vietnam, for instance, but he also knew that speaking out would complicate his civil rights work, infuriate many of his allies, and give comfort to his enemies. Quite often, too, decisions had to be made on the fly. SCLC staffers spent countless hours preparing and squabbling over extravagant campaigns that never got off the ground—campaigns that until now have received scant attention. Other plans of theirs bogged them down in all manner of sinkholes; a chapter describing the effort to desegregate and de-slum the Chicago neighborhoods, for example, makes it clear that King and his colleagues badly overestimated their power to force economic change. The campaigns that did work often started spontaneously, or through the work of other groups, and King was called in only after the foundations, crooked or straight, had been laid.

Again and again, though, as if by some magical force, King managed to say and do the right thing, to create the necessary confrontation, to write the perfect sermon. Garrow's book lacks an adequate description of that mysterious force, just as it lacks any overt conclusions about the less mystical aspects of King's public life. Instead, Garrow spent many years collecting documents under the Freedom of Information Act, interviewing King's surviving friends and colleagues, living with the records of the determinedly unorganized SCLC, and fashioning it all into a careful, sober, readable account. He is relentlessly chronological; at first, this seems to lead to endless repetition, but then one remembers that most lives, even most fascinating lives, are endlessly repetitive. The real-time feel of this volume will give those who follow King as rebels an idea of what to expect, and allows the rest of us to draw some informed conclusions about a life that has too often been shrouded in clouds of adoration.

The most striking of those conclusions, as I've already suggested, may be that King's life was almost unimaginably difficult. Not his early life but his public life—the life that began when, as a twenty-six-year-old preacher, he was persuaded to lead the ministerial alliance coordinating the Montgomery bus boycott. Many people have said in retrospect that "the time was ripe" for racial progress in the late fifties and early sixties. Garrow reminds us that King had to fight hard—*hard*—and that his obvious enemies, the diehard segregationists, were in some ways the least of his problems. Their viciousness—the four little black girls killed in the Birmingham Sunday school bombing; Chaney and Schwerner and Goodman buried in a cattle-pond dam near Philadelphia, in central Mississippi; Viola Liuzzo shot driving to Montgomery to help transport marchers; Medgar Evers killed on his lawn—must never be downplayed. But in a curious sense the Wallaces and the Ross Barnetts

and the White Citizens Councils were the honorable opponents—
the opposition that King and his followers had signed on to fight.

A worse enemy, in a way, both for its invisibility and for its implacability, was the federal government—especially the Federal Bureau of Investigation. Garrow, in 1981's *The F.B.I. and Martin Luther King, Jr.* detailed the campaign of harassment; here he fits it into the stream of King's life to show how it devastated King psychologically. The FBI tapped his phones for many years, because J. Edgar Hoover wanted proof that he was linked to international communism and that he went to bed with women to whom he was not married. Hoover had mixed success with the first smear (King did rely on several former or inactive communists, but they did not manipulate him) and great luck with the second. He kept tapes of King's assignations, and an agent—the assistant director of the FBI, William Sullivan—sent King a copy of some of the recordings along with an anonymous note urging him to commit suicide. "King," it said, "there is only one thing left for you to do. You know what this is. . . . You are done. There is but one way out for you. You better take it before your filthy abnormal fraudulent self is bared to the nation."

Suicide must have seemed an attractive proposition at times. Garrow makes a convincing case that living with the steady fear of what Hoover's revelations would do to him and to his cause darkened the last years of King's life. And it wasn't as if the course of the public struggle provided constant cheer. In hindsight, it may seem a time of rapid and almost smooth progress, but the short bursts of real action around the Freedom Rides, Selma, and Birmingham came before and after long periods that left plenty of room for despair. The behavior of many of those who considered themselves his allies disappointed King enormously (and helps give the lie to the notion that the civil rights movement was an inevitability). We think of Walter Mondale, for instance, as a good liberal. He was a good liberal in 1964, too, when, as Garrow reminds us, he helped lead the behind-the-scenes battle to make sure that the

Mississippi Freedom Democratic Party delegation was not seated at the national convention in place of the segregationist regulars. Again and again, King was way out in front, and half the fire he weathered came from his rear. Two days after he gave a sermon at Riverside Church outlining his opposition to our participation in Vietnam, the *Washington Post* solemnly and patronizingly explained that he "had done a grave injury to those who are his natural allies [and] an even graver injury to himself. Many who have listened to him with respect will never again accord him the same confidence." In the last month of his life, after violence marred a Memphis march that King had not even organized, the *New York Times* called it a "powerful embarrassment" to him and warned that he ought to call off his Poor People's Campaign for fear of further disruptions. Fellow civil rights leaders, of course, were forever damning him, publicly and privately, as too rash (Roy Wilkins, of the National Association for the Advancement of Colored People) or too tame (the Student Nonviolent Coordinating Committee, the Panthers, Malcolm X).

King had himself to contend with as well. He caused those around him and (more to the point of this story) himself great pain—both spiritual and practical—by his dalliances and infidelities. Yet one senses from Garrow's book that though the fear of Hoover's revelations cost him sleepless nights a sense of guilt did not. He recognized that he was a sinner, and that he was not the man people thought he was; but he also seemed to believe, quite sincerely, that God forgave sinners. "There is a schizophrenia . . . within all of us," he once told his Atlanta congregation. "There are times when all of us know somehow that there is a Mr. Hyde and a Dr. Jekyll in us." Still, "God does not judge us by the separate incidents or the separate mistakes that we make, but by the total bent of our lives." The world needn't think that he was a saint, he said. "I want you to know this morning that I am a sinner like all of God's children, but I want to be a good man, and I want to hear a voice saying to me one day, 'I take you in and I bless you because you tried. It was well that it was within thy heart.'" It takes monumental faith to believe that much in God's mercy, but King probably came as close as anyone to possessing it. Nonetheless, on top of his public troubles his own weakness must have grieved him.

So how, in the face of all this, was he able to go on? In answer, Garrow makes extensive use of an early incident in King's life as a rebel. One Friday night about eight weeks into the Montgomery boycott, a day after his first arrest, King returned home late from an organizing meeting. The phone rang, and an anonymous caller—not the first, and certainly not the last—said, "Nigger, we are tired of you and your mess now. And if you aren't out of this town in three days we're going to blow your brains out and blow up your house." All his doubts, King later said, came suddenly to the fore when the caller hung up—he thought about his wife, and his newborn daughter, Yolanda, and the people he was leading into far from metaphorical battle. He prayed—prayed out loud at his kitchen table: "Lord, I'm down here trying to do what's right. I think I'm right. I think the cause we represent is right. But Lord, I must confess I'm weak now. I'm faltering. I'm losing my courage. And I can't let people see me like this because if they see me weak and losing my courage, they'll begin to get weak." At that moment, King said, "it seemed . . . I could hear an inner voice saying to me, 'Martin Luther, stand up for righteousness. Stand up for justice. Stand up for truth. And lo I will be with you, even until the end of the world' . . . I heard the voice of Jesus saying still to fight on. He promised never to leave me, never to leave me alone. No never alone. No never alone. He promised never to leave me, never to leave me alone." Three days later, his house was bombed, but King took it calmly: "My religious experience a few nights before had given me the strength to face it."

Over and over, Garrow returns to that dramatic visitation in the Montgomery kitchen in an attempt to explain what kept King going through the struggles within the movement, the setbacks in Georgia and Florida, the sick frothings of the FBI, and premonitions of his approaching death. After a wilier-than-usual sheriff—Laurie Pritchett, of Albany, Georgia—prevented overt violence against protesters, robbing them of publicity and sympathy and dealing a real blow to the tactical prestige of nonviolence, King, though despondent, knew he had the responsibility to continue: "He had known ever since that Friday night in the kitchen in Montgomery that it could not be shirked." As King grew increasingly to symbolize the entire movement, and to be held accountable by the press and the public for any of its failings, "the revelation in the kitchen seven years earlier . . . fundamentally eased his acceptance of that responsibility, for the tangible experience of a transforming faith is a profoundly strengthening and liberating event." After the SCLC foray into Chicago in 1966—a debacle that produced only a wishy-washy accord with local realtors—King told his Atlanta congregation that he would continue even if it meant dying, "because I heard a voice saying 'Do something for others.'" It was, Garrow writes, "the voice he had heard in the kitchen in Montgomery ten years earlier, the voice that gave him the stamina to carry on when others were . . . falling victim to the angry sentiments of 'black power,' or castigating the Chicago settlement as a 'sellout.' Even when times were bad—and it was hard to remember when events had been more frustrating and debilitating than over the past three months—that voice sustained him. He was profoundly uncertain of what would come next, terribly vulnerable to doubts about where he and the movement were headed, but still he had the strength to go forward."

· · ·

Something crucial happened in that kitchen, of that there can be no doubt. But Garrow has perhaps overplayed the importance of this one incident. Or, rather, he has used it as convenient shorthand that removed the need to delve very deeply into King's religious thought. For King had faith, surely, but that faith had *content*—content that stretched well beyond the bounds of his own life. Another recent, and thick, book, *A Testament of Hope: The Essential Writings of Martin Luther King, Jr.*, edited by James M. Washington, makes it clear that the ideas embedded in his faith mattered as much as its personal experience. (This should not surprise us. Millions of Americans believe sincerely that they have a "personal relationship" with God, and that He is sustaining them in time of trouble, but that personal relationship doesn't necessarily lead them to do any of the things Martin Luther King did.) *A Testament of Hope* collects parts of five books by King, all the famous sermons and addresses, and a sampling of his many essays on nonviolence. It is startling to see how often King returns to the same few quotations and passages, especially for his thundering perorations—the parts of his speeches he knew would stay ringing in the ears of his hearers. Simply because it is typical, I will quote at some length from the end of a fairly obscure speech he delivered before the Fellowship of the Concerned, an interracial Atlanta group, in November of 1961. He spoke of the sufferings of the Freedom Riders earlier that year, and then said:

> There is something in this student movement which says to us, that we shall overcome. Before the victory is won some may have to get scarred up, but we shall overcome. Before the victory of brotherhood is achieved, some will maybe face physical death, but we shall overcome. Before the victory is won, some will lose jobs, some will be called communists, and reds, merely because they believe in brotherhood, some will be dismissed as dangerous rabble-rousers and agitators merely because they're standing up for what is right, but we shall overcome. That is the basis of this movement, and as I like to say, there is something in this universe that justifies Carlyle in saying that no lie can live forever. We shall overcome because there is something in this universe which justifies William Cullen Bryant in saying truth crushed to earth shall rise again. We shall overcome because there is something in this universe that

justifies James Russell Lowell in saying, truth forever on the scaffold, wrong forever on the throne. Yet that scaffold sways the future, and behind the dim unknown, standeth God within the shadow, keeping watch above His own.

It is almost a shame that King's most famous words—the "I Have a Dream" speech delivered in Washington—were so eloquent, for the absolute confidence of the conclusion cited above is even more standard than the merely optimistic "dream" of that mighty sermon. Over and over again, he quotes Bryant; in many of his speeches, he gives the concluding lines from Lowell's powerful hymn "Once to Every Man and Nation" (a product of the abolition era). At the end of the bloody march from Selma, on the steps of the building that was once the capitol of the Confederacy and is now the capitol of the State of Alabama, he ended a short, punching speech in this fashion:

> I know that you are asking today, "How long will it take?" I come to say to you this afternoon, however difficult the moment, however frustrating the hour, it will not be long, because truth pressed to earth will rise again.
>
> How long? Not long, because no lie can live forever.
>
> How long? Not long, because you still reap what you sow.
>
> How long? Not long, because the arm of the moral universe is long but it bends toward justice.
>
> How long? Not long, 'cause mine eyes have seen the glory of the coming of the Lord, trampling out the vintage where the grapes of wrath are stored. He has loosed the fateful lightning of his terrible swift sword. His truth is marching on.
>
> He has sounded forth the trumpets that shall never call retreat. He is lifting up the hearts of man before His judgment seat. Oh, be swift, my soul, to answer Him. Be jubilant, my feet. Our God is marching on.

And the night before his assassination, at a time of exhaustion and despair, he finished his speech at the Mason Temple in Memphis with the now famous words "He's allowed me to go up to the mountain. And I've looked over. And I've seen the promised land. I may not get there with you. But I want you to know tonight, that we as a people will get to the promised land. And I'm happy tonight. I'm not worried about anything. I'm not fearing any man. Mine eyes have seen the glory of the coming of the Lord."

Did he actually believe such things, or was it wishing—mere moral support for his flock in an hour of trouble? I think he did believe them, and strongly. He knew that his ideas were controversial. If he knew that Thomas Carlyle had said no lie can live forever, he also knew that Carlyle's contemporary, friend, and intellectual foe John Stuart Mill had written, "It is a piece of idle sentimentality that truth, merely as truth, has any inherent power denied to error, of prevailing against the dungeon and the stake." And he certainly knew that many Americans not only did not share his optimism but looked at the modern world with ever more skepticism and doubt. There are, I think, serious sources for his serious belief. One set of reasons had to do with America: the country's democratic heritage and rhetoric, he thought, gave him a lever to pry open its institutions and "bring into full realization the American dream." More important was his one great strategic idea: he placed enormous trust in active, nonviolent resistance to evil. His experience in Montgomery and his pilgrimage to "the land of Gandhi" solidified early in his public career his belief in the tactic he had begun to think about in theological school (and had been exposed to all his life in the Gospels). But his belief in nonviolence was not purely practical—and in this he differed from many of the student militants, who used nonviolence, at least for a time, because it seemed to work in an American context, but who did not commit their lives to it or urge it upon their brothers in the decolonizing Third World. At some level, his faith in nonviolence came out of his faith in the universe.

And the reason for his faith in the universe—his almost anachronistic assurance that good would triumph—can be understood only by examining his understanding of God. He talked less specifically about this before secular America than from the pulpits of his Montgomery and Atlanta churches, before the black congregations that would be sympathetic to his argument and his language. A few of these sermons are gathered in *A Testament of Hope*, and give some idea of the content of this huge faith. Speaking one Sunday on a text in Jude ("Now unto him that is able to keep you from falling"), he outlined his belief in an omnipotent God. Against the rising belief in man, amidst the replacement of the church by the laboratory and of the prophet by the scientist, "the ringing testimony of the Christian faith is that God is able." Evil lives in the world, and "the Hitlers and the Mussolinis have their day, and for a period they may wield great power, spreading themselves like a green bay tree, but soon they are cut down like the grass and wither as the green herb." For God "has placed within the very structure of this universe certain absolute moral laws. We can neither defy them nor break them. If we disobey them, they will break us." As an example of this, King says that God gives one the "interior resources" to confront the difficulties of life, and cites specifically his visitation in the Montgomery kitchen. In another sermon, entitled "Antidotes for Fear," he recommends courage and love but, above all, faith. "Religion," he says, "endows us with the conviction that we are not alone in this vast, uncertain universe. Beneath and above the shifting sands of time, the uncertainties that darken our days, the vicissitudes that cloud our nights, is a wise and loving God. This universe is not a tragic expression of meaningless chaos but a marvelous display of orderly cosmos."

· · ·

One cannot fault Garrow for ignoring the substance of King's beliefs. His intention was not to write an intellectual biography—if he had tried, he would only have muddied the splendid stream of his detailed scholarship—and there is little that is tremendously new in King's view of the world. For a preacher of King's background at that time, it was a conventional view—and yet there were other conventional views, and other notes to sound, and King chose over and over to stress this one. To understand how he could do what he did without understanding how he saw the universe is impossible: his confidence gave him the ability to stand up under attacks that would have crippled men who thought differently, who believed that the battle they fought was a personal slog against hopeless odds. He did grow depressed and despondent, did eat constantly, did turn to casual sex as a "form of anxiety reduction" and a solace, and yet when he stood at the rostrum or took up the pen, when he concentrated all his dispersed private energies into his pure public self, he *always* concluded that "deep down within there is something in the very structure of the cosmos that will ultimately bring about the fulfillment and the triumph of that which is right." "And this," he would add, "is the only thing that can keep one going in difficult periods." This King, though not as accessible to the biographer, is at least as real as the private, doubting King.

It is hard to trace much more deeply the sources of King's belief in an ultimately just universe. He was not a theologian, except in the theology of praxis, but if it was in some way a simple belief (much like his belief in justice, equality, and liberation) that does not diminish its power in his life. The rest of us, who may not share such a belief a priori, and, indeed, may think the world to be just the opposite sort of place, should probably not demand proofs that his faith was correct—the meaning of faith, of course, is that the question of correctness cannot be objectively answered. But as citizens of a divided America, in the chill shadow of the events at Howard Beach, New York, in December 1986, we need to ask if, in a limited historical period, his optimism was justified. The experience of virtually all of our lives in residentially and economically divided cities and towns might lead us to refute his hope; the persistence of racism should perhaps convince us that there is some ineradicable malign force at work in the universe. We live in a country, and a world, with vast and increasing gaps between the fed and the hungry: what does that mean? But it is worth remembering that when Martin Luther King Jr. began the modern phase of the civil rights movement in Montgomery his audience included the children of people who had been slaves. And we should remember, too, that when the bus boycott began it did not even challenge segregation but merely asked for the right to sit in the back of the bus unmolested, and not be forced to give up a seat to a white man if the bus was full. That was barely thirty years ago.

Yet there is no denying that progress has stalled since the late 1960s, just as it stalled after Reconstruction until the King era. Since King was killed in the late '60s, another question arises: how vital was King, as an individual, to the movement? Garrow, after 624 pages of tightly focused biography, appends a bizarre epilogue that runs just three-quarters of a page. It argues that, in the words of a civil rights colleague, "the movement made Martin rather than Martin making the movement." This is important, another civil rights worker is quoted as saying, because "if people think that it was Martin Luther King's movement then today they—young people—are more likely to say, 'Gosh, I wish we had a Martin Luther King here today to lead us.' If people knew how that movement started, then the question they would ask themselves is, 'What can I do?'" Garrow certainly has earned the right to try to summarize the meaning of King's life, but his book, which is wonderful for its concentration on King largely to the exclusion of an analysis of the rest of the movement, much less the society, gives no authority to these claims. They serve only to stifle an important debate about how social change happens. For it could be that Martin Luther King Jr. was absolutely necessary for the civil rights movement to develop in the time and shape it did, and that without him it might have taken different turns or made less progress (or, theoretically, more).

I don't have the answer to his question, either, but I would like to end by describing the march on Washington held several years ago, on the twentieth anniversary of the "I Have a Dream" speech. The day dawned hot and at noon was hotter, but hundreds of thousands of people gathered anyway around the reflecting pool in front of the Lincoln Memorial. A long procession of men and women spoke, one after another, on into the afternoon. They talked of legislation—of affirmative action, of enforcing the Voting Rights Act, and so on. These were good men and women who, living on past Memphis, had worked longer than King and at least as hard. But their speeches sounded a little hollow. There is in this rich nation no majority about to be argued into blessing the powerless with power and the hungry with food. Hearts need still to be converted. King had a method—nonviolent courage—for doing that, and he had the firm belief, through all his depressions, that it could be done. Perhaps without him that belief has faded, and with it the chance for conversion. Perhaps it would have faded anyway, even in his heart—perhaps the Poor People's Campaign would have collapsed, and his nonviolence would have crumpled against the invisible miseries of poverty. But perhaps not, for faith is contagious. Or maybe a stove is a better metaphor—a hot stove sending out heat to warm the cold around it. Faith is not necessarily a private matter. Its manifestations touch even those of us who cannot bring ourselves to share it. We may be made uneasy even by the discussion of faith as a political tool, but that does not mean King's speeches did not affect us for reasons beyond their content. In any event, late that afternoon, as the crowd began to filter out through the stands of trees on either side of the pool a tape of King's great sermon filled the space it had filled twenty years before. Then his words, and his presence, had inoculated people with hope and confidence. Now, as I looked around, many were weeping.

# The Desert Anarchist

—*The New York Review of Books*, August 18, 1988

Early in his first collection of essays, *Desert Solitaire*, Edward Abbey describes a scene from a summer he spent as the ranger at the then-deserted Arches National Monument in southern Utah, his nearest neighbor twenty miles distant across the sand and the slickrock. Wishing one evening to write a letter, Abbey went outside and hooked up the four-cylinder gas engine that served as his generator. "The engine sputters, gasps, catches fire, gains momentum, winds up into a roar, valves popping, rockers thumping, pistons hissing up and down inside their oiled jackets." The lights go on—indeed,

> the lights are so bright I can't see a thing and have to shade my eyes as I stumble toward the open door of the trailer. Nor can I hear anything but the clatter of the generator. I am shut off from the natural world and sealed up, encapsulated, in a box of artificial light and tyrannical noise. . . . I have exchanged a great and unbounded world for a small, comparatively meager one.

Abbey has spent most of his life in the boundless American desert, occasionally coming in to write. His novels and essay collections (six of each) have found a devoted, even fanatic audience in the western states, where he is the subject of critical studies and symposiums. Less well known in the East, Abbey was born on a hardscrabble Pennsylvania farm just before the Depression. He hitchhiked to the canyon country as a teenager, and vowed to return as soon as he was out of the service—the great stone sculptures, the naked drops, had knocked from his heart the "fuzzy hills" of his Appalachian boyhood.

Of his forty years in the Southwest, a great many have been spent alone—not alone in a room, or alone in a crowd, but all by himself a dozen miles from the last pavement, in a fire tower or ranger shack or bedroll spread by a pool of water. For many years, until the movie option payments on his novel *The Monkey Wrench Gang* began to support his modest way of life, he worked as a seasonal employee of the Park Service or the Forest Service—at Arches, at Organ Pipe Cactus National Monument, on the empty North Rim of the Grand Canyon, at the Petrified Forest. And when he had a few days or a few months off, he would take a vacation deeper into the wilderness—a long, foolhardy solo hike, perhaps, trudging 120 miles from one dwindling, briny waterhole to the next. All in all, I would wager, he has spent more time alone than all but a few thousand Americans of his generation.

. . .

America, of course, has always been open to voices of solitude and of nature. Abbey argues in an essay from his 1982 collection *Down the River* that only specialists still find interest in William Ellery Channing or Dr. Holmes, and Emerson is more espoused than read, but "in the ultimate democracy of time" Thoreau, who died a minor writer, has outlived his contemporaries. Abbey fills Thoreau's ecological niche, I suppose—besides cantankerousness they share obsessions with the natural world as against human culture, and also with the duty and the methods of resistance.

But the differences are as distinct as the landscapes that inspired the two men—actually, the landscapes probably account for many of the differences. Thoreau reveled in the profligate, fecund bounty of the Northeast—no need, he said, for a yard with "unfenced Nature reaching up to your very sills. A young forest growing up under your windows, and wild sumachs and blackberry vines breaking through into your cellar; sturdy pitch-pines rubbing and creaking against the shingles for want of room, their roots reaching quite under the house." Abbey chose to live in a region with much less rainfall and a higher mean temperature. The desert's main features—the canyons, mesas, buttes, reefs, spires—are the work of geologic time; even its stunted junipers are the slow, seemingly pointless (no saw-timber here) product of centuries. "Alone in the silence," he writes in *Desert Solitaire* of a hike to Rainbow Bridge,

> I understand for a moment the dread which many feel in the presence of primeval desert, the unconscious fear which compels them to tame, alter or destroy what they cannot understand, to reduce the wild and pre-human to human dimensions. Anything rather than confront directly the antehuman, that *other world* which frightens not through danger or hostility but in something far worse—its implacable indifference.

As a result, Abbey's thoughts echo those of the voice from the whirlwind, which asks Job if he knows why the rain falls in the wilderness, far from any human habitation. All creation is not for man, insist God and Abbey; the reasons for the desert, if reasons exist, are beyond our understanding. This thought injects a truly radical perspective into Abbey's nature writings—a perspective implicit in Thoreau, in John Muir, in Aldo Leopold, and in a hundred other unlikelier places, but a perspective still struggling to break into the culture.

· · ·

The anthropocentric model remains as central as the idea, before Copernicus, that the earth stood at the hub of the universe. It is a comforting notion, the absolute primacy of man, and any attempt to break from it must disquiet us. In one essay, Abbey describes hiking in with a search party to Grandview Point, 2,700 feet above the Colorado, to find a missing tourist. The man is discovered, dead, "limbs extended rigidly from a body bloated like a balloon." Although the buzzards "for some reason have not discovered him two other scavengers, ravens, rise heavily and awkwardly from the corpse as we approach." Eight men carry the body back to the road.

> Each man's death diminishes me? Not necessarily. Given this man's age, the inevitability and suitability of his death, and the essential nature of life on earth, there is in each of us the unspeakable conviction that we are well rid of him. His departure makes room for the living. Away with the old, in with the new. He is gone—we remain, others come. . . . A ruthless, brutal process—but clean and beautiful.

Perspective, though, differs from detachment. Abbey is firmly attached to the place he loves. He chose to live there because he found it so haunting and awesome. This attachment blazes again and again into anger, as he watches other people destroy what he adores. In one of his finest essays, "How It Was," from his 1971 collection, *Beyond the Wall*, he recollects a trip from Blanding to Green River across the Utah desert. With three friends, he drove a pickup truck over 180 miles of unpaved jeep track past piñon pine and juniper, through the streamside cottonwoods "attended by a few buzzing flies and the songs of canyon wren," across the Colorado on a cable ferry, and up a side canyon, North Wash, where they camped by the bank of a flash flood. "Today the old North Wash trail is partly submerged by the reservoir, the rest obliterated." Utah has run a paved highway through the region, bridging the canyons. The Colorado River lies a hundred feet beneath Lake Powell.

All of this, the engineers and politicians and bankers will tell you, makes the region easily accessible to everybody, no matter how fat, feeble or flaccid. That is a lie.

It is a lie. For those who go there now, smooth, comfortable, quick and easy, sliding through as slick as grease, will never be able to see what we saw. They will never feel what we felt. They will never know what we knew, or understand what we cannot forget.

Over and over again the same sequence recurs. The Arches National Monument has been paved, with plenty of parking space and Coke machines. The air above the Grand Canyon is filled with the never-ending drone of sightseeing helicopters. The deep vistas are closed in by the smog from the Phelps-Dodge copper smelter.

Abbey does not consider such developments the sad by-products of growth and progress, side effects to be ameliorated when possible and tolerated when not. He considers them—he speaks fairly crudely, on purpose—symptoms of the "madness," the "insanity," the "monster" that is Industrial Civilization. And here he begins to tread on dangerous ground. We Americans can deal with someone who contends that he looks forward to the buzzards picking clean his bones; but what about someone who says, as Abbey does, that we must "curtail our gluttonous appetite for things, ever more things, learn to moderate our needs."

· · ·

We don't worry, of course, that he threatens our standard of living. It is our peace of mind he disturbs, with the insidious idea that someone else might be leading a life with different means and ends, a fuller, more satisfying, life. (A life that, not coincidentally, does less harm to the planet.) Wouldn't *we* rather be floating down some canyon on a raft? Spending the night in Concord jail was not the most subversive thing Thoreau ever did; far worse was spending eight months living on $61.99 3/4. ("Poverty gave him all his wealth," wrote Van Wyck Brooks. "The leisure to spend a day, whenever he chose, walking twenty or thirty miles, or voyaging about the river in December, when the drops froze on his oars, pleased with the silvery chime of the icicles against the stem of his button-brushes.") Dangerous examples these, undercutting our consoling sense of the inevitability of our lives. For their power to disturb, they recall Muir's remark, after he climbed a pine tree in a gale to see what it would be like at the top: "Our own little journeys, away and back again, are only little more than tree-wavings— many of them not so much."

Abbey does not explicitly claim that the mass of us lead lives of quiet desperation, but he repeatedly advances examples that make the point. In his first book of essays, in 1968, he identified an enemy—"Industrial Tourism"—that he has been fighting ever since. Industrial Tourists, he explains,

> work hard. . . . They roll up incredible mileages on their odometers, rack up state after state in two-week transcontinental motor marathons . . . and endure patiently the most prolonged discomforts: the tedious traffic jams, the awful food of park cafeterias, . . . the nocturnal search for a place to sleep or camp, . . . the ever-proliferating Rules and Regulations, the fees and the bills and the service charges,

and so on.

> Look here, I want to say, for god-sake folks get out of them there machines. . . . Dig your toes in the hot sand, feel that

raw and rugged earth, split a couple of big toenails, draw blood! Why not? Jesus Christ, lady, roll that window down! You can't see the desert if you can't smell it. Dusty? Of course it's dusty—this is Utah!

Though it's obviously not his doing, in the two decades since Abbey wrote that passage, more people have begun to explore, to hike beyond the parking lot. At least his crankiness wasn't entirely eccentric.

• • •

He's had considerably more effect in spreading another idea, one that found in his writing its most eloquent expression—the idea of personal direct action to protect the environment. Vandalism, some might say, though Abbey would probably call it countervandalism. As early as his college days he was knocking over billboards. In *Desert Solitaire* he describes pulling up the survey stakes laid out by the crew planning the paved road through the Arches, forcing surveyors to do their work over—"a futile effort, in the long run, but it made me feel good." During the years that followed, working by night he poured sand or sugar in the fuel tanks of a "goodly number of earthmovers, ore trucks, front-end loaders and Caterpillar bull-dozers," anything that spent the days ripping up his desert.

Finally he wrote *The Monkey Wrench Gang*, an adventure story about a team of four people—Hayduke, a Vietnam vet; Seldom Seen, a jack Mormon outfitter; Doc Sarvis, a Tucson physician; and Bonnie Abbzug, Sarvis's girlfriend—who set out across the canyon country, doing their best to wreck bridge after mine after road, a spree of merry ecological sabotage. The book, while not as carefully written as his other novels, has much beer-drinking in it, as well as car chases and pickup chases and four-wheel-drive jeep chases through towering scenery, as angry developers and rednecks less enlightened than Abbey's rednecks pursue the quartet.

Abbey also provides a large supply of very American technical details about how to damage machinery ("Now we select our operating speed. We have five speeds forward, four in reverse. . . . Now we engage the flywheel clutch." The bulldozer lurches forward, over a cliff, never to build another road). Unlike his other books, *The Monkey Wrench Gang* sold half a million copies, and provided the ready-made legend for a radical environmental organization, Earth First!, that was formed a few years later, adopting Abbey as its patron saint.

Dave Foreman, who founded Earth First!, resigned as chief Washington lobbyist for the Wilderness Society in the late 1970s after becoming convinced that the mainstream environmental organizations were compromising too often, surrendering too much of the remaining American wilderness to miners, ranchers, and oil interests. Foreman, who organized the loosely knit and fast-growing group as a "tribe," and who speaks nostalgically of a return to a hunter-gatherer society, still spends most of his time arguing for increased wilderness tracts. But along with letter writing, civil disobedience, and guerrilla theater, Earth First! members engage in fairly wide-spread "ecotage." The group took as its emblem the monkey wrench, and as one of its chief slogans "Hayduke Lives!" (As indeed, at the book's end, he does.) They have dreamed up new techniques Abbey didn't consider (putting spikes in old-growth Douglas firs and redwoods to keep loggers from felling them, for instance) and they have refined others. *Ecodefense*, a handbook of sabotage tips culled from the advice column of the Earth First! journal, has already gone through two editions. But the soul of the enterprise is still *The Monkey Wrench Gang* and Abbey's blend of Thoreau and Ned Ludd.

· · ·

In his 1988 collection, *One Life at a Time, Please*, Abbey argues his view in three short pieces. The first, "Arizona: How Big Is Big

Enough?,"" asks if increasing the population of Tucson and Phoenix is really a laudable goal: "Where, when, and how is this spiraling process supposed to reach a rational end—a state of stability, sanity, and equilibrium? . . . Growth for the sake of growth is the ideology of the cancer cell." In "Eco-Defense," where he instructs readers on the proper size nails to use in spiking trees (60-penny) he argues in the simplest terms the right to resist—if an Englishman's home is his castle, "the American's home is his favorite forest, river, fishing stream, her favorite mountain or desert canyon, his favorite swamp or woods or lake." Finally, in three pages on anarchy—the most insistently political essay of his career, written for the *Earth First! Journal*—he predicts our civilization will not last a century more before an environmental crisis will force a return to a

> higher civilization: scattered human populations modest in number that live by fishing, hunting, food gathering, small-scale farming and ranching, that gather once a year in the ruins of abandoned cities for great festivals of moral, spiritual, artistic, and intellectual renewal, a people for whom the wilderness is not a playground but their natural native home.

His idiosyncratic anarchic vision exalts human dependence on the natural world at least as much as human freedom. Freedom, he implies, involves fitting back into our proper place, "remaining loyal to our basic animal nature."

One could argue with all this, of course. Monkey-wrenching costs time and money to people whose only crime is that they grew up to be loggers or surveyors. It bypasses, in the fashion of the Old West, the democratic process of discussion and compromise. It probably makes life harder for more conventional environmentalists. The saboteurs give traditional answers too—that it's the huge mining corporations and the powerful timber lobbyists that override democracy. Or that wilderness gone is gone forever, so the stakes are high. Or that a clearcut hillside is the real destruction, and a spike in a tree merely a "vaccination." Or that the radicals can act as Malcolm X to the Sierra Club's Martin Luther King Jr., making the mainstream conservationists look more reasonable. Or that conscience leaves them no choice. In any event, Earth First! members seem more and more inclined to protest peacefully, sitting down in the path of roads or camping high in trees slated for felling or hanging banners off the side of Mount Rushmore, rather than risk muddying their message with debates about "terrorism."

. . .

For even the most radical tactics mask the true extremism, which is in ends, not means. Virtually every act of a normal modern life argues with Abbey's premises. Most of us do not really believe that we need to fit back into nature, to dramatically temper our ambitions as individuals or as a species. Sometimes, amid the oil crisis of the 1970s, scientists or politicians would argue that we lived in an "age of limits," a very mild form of the radical ecological argument. Ronald Reagan successfully attacked this line of reasoning as the pitiful, whining surrender of men unwilling to push forward and seize their destiny—of men who didn't understand that it was morning in America. Of weak men, like Jimmy Carter. And Abbey—with his vision of a nomadic society, of Tucson buried under sand dunes over which "blue-eyed Navajo bedouin will herd their sheep and horses, following the river in winter, the mountains in summer"—goes farther than Jimmy Carter.

Abbey, though, has a natural advantage. His gruff pronouncements have an almost unfair power to persuade because they come from a leathery cowboy-without-cattle, a loner, and because they echo up from the canyons of the arid West, the landscape where our idea of ourselves has traditionally been formed. Hayduke is a sort of Henry David Wayne. And Abbey's argument is the argument of a confident man who poses a dare. Man's special gift is reason, as a bird's is flight. His highest calling, then, is to overcome his biological instinct to breed in great numbers and to extend his range of habitation—to use reason to do the one thing no other animal can do, that is, limit himself voluntarily. Not to build more dams and use more power and grow genetically "improved" mice, but to use less power and tear down dams and leave mice the way we found them.

Perhaps the premise is utterly wrong—the advantages of industrial civilization hardly need listing, and maybe man's happiness does lie in growing in numbers and in power, using his technical ability to stave off disaster. (The oil crisis, after all, went away.) Or perhaps the premise is half right, and Abbey and others like him will help move us toward a balance somewhere between the Santa Ana Freeway and the state of nature. But the ozone hole above the Antarctic widens each year and the global temperature climbs with each decade and a radical analysis becomes at least a little plausible.

. . .

The ultimate goal of the Monkey Wrench Gang is to destroy Glen Canyon Dam, which backs up the Colorado River into "Lake" Powell. Glen Canyon stands with Muir's drowned Hetch Hetchy atop the list of places mourned by American environmentalists. Smaller and more intimate than its downstream neighbor the Grand Canyon—but what, on earth, isn't?—Glen Canyon disappeared before all but a few thousand had the chance to float down it. Abbey was one of the lucky ones, making the trip while construction on the dam was in progress. Abbey called the canyon "paradise," and the descriptions of his trip in *Desert Solitaire* make the term sound technical, precise. From an anthropocentric point of view, the great concrete plug made a certain sense, providing light and power to the expanding Southwest, and helping to water the region even during drought. But Glen Canyon is the navel of Abbey's universe—its degradation stands for all human folly and arrogance, and its salvation would be the sign that man had turned the corner, begun the trek back toward his proper station. Abbey has not figured out in any systematic way what his ideal, ecologically sound world would look like. It is safe to say, though, that in it Glen Canyon would be a canyon again, not a dead reservoir.

When Earth First! formed, its initial major action was the symbolic destruction of the dam. Standing on top of the giant structure, members unfurled a black plastic crack that, filmed from a distance, looked astonishingly like the real thing. If the dam ever does go, Abbey once wrote,

> [It] will no doubt expose a drear and hideous scene: immense mud flats and whole plateaus of sodden garbage strewn with dead trees, sunken boats, the skeletons of long-forgotten, decomposing water-skiers. But to those who find the prospect too appalling, I say give nature a little time. In five years, at most in ten, the sun and wind and storms will cleanse and sterilize the repellent mess. The inevitable floods will soon remove all that does not belong within the canyons. Fresh green willow, box elder and redbud will reappear; and the ancient drowned cottonwoods (noble monuments to themselves) will be replaced by young of their own kind. . . . Within a generation—thirty years—I predict the river and canyons will bear a decent resemblance to their former selves. Within the lifetime of our children Glen Canyon and the living river, heart of the canyonlands, will be restored to us. The wilderness will again belong to God, the people and the wild things that call it home.

# · 29 ·

## Prophet in Kentucky

*—The New York Review of Books,* June 14, 1990

Earth Day provided the occasion for publishing dozens of environmental books, most of them along the lines of *Fifty Simple Things You Can Do to Save the Planet.* The hints these books contain—use Tupperware instead of plastic wrap, separate your bottles, put a brick in the toilet—are unexceptionable. But unfortunately, if scientists are at all correct about the magnitude of the perils we face, then the changes eventually demanded of us will not be so simple. If, for instance, the fossil fuel era must come rapidly to a close, then the changes required are likely to be far more dramatic and difficult.

That is why Wendell Berry's new collection of essays, *What Are People For?,* was probably the most important book published on Earth Day, even though it has very little to say about ozone depletion or global warming. (It is also, I feel sure, the best written.) *What Are People For?* continues Berry's quarter-century-old argument with the modern world:

> There is no longer any honest way to deny that a way of living that our leaders continue to praise is destroying all that our country is, and all the best that it means.

Berry is a poet and novelist as well as an essayist, but most of all he is a farmer. He believes that we face an agricultural crisis, and that it is a part of a moral, philosophical, and social crisis that demands that we change our lives.

· · ·

The first question—whether we can continue to farm the way we are currently farming—has been perhaps Berry's chief concern since his earliest books. He rarely writes more than a few paragraphs without mentioning the word "topsoil." Over and over he argues that farming done on too large a scale, and in too mechanized a fashion, inevitably degrades the layer of rich and fertile earth that is America's greatest single asset. Today's farmers, he maintains, can't produce a bushel of corn without sending a bushel of topsoil floating down the Mississippi. This sort of degradation, he argues, is nearly irreversible under the present system, because too few people are farming—the care and the highly localized skill needed to protect and nourish the soil is impossible when a single farmer, riding high in the cab of a modern tractor, must tend hundreds of acres. The overemphasis on production has also caused most of the economic crises that frequently ravage the Farm Belt. High production means high costs—for the petroleum-based fertilizers that provide much of the soil's fertility and for the equipment needed to manage so large an area—and this in turn means high debt and high vulnerability.

By contrast, Berry gives the examples of his own farm in the agriculturally marginal hill country of Kentucky and the farms of the Amish communities across the country. Jealous of his privacy, he tells us little in his essays about his own land; one gets a better sense of its day-to-day workings from his novels and poems. But he is frank about the mistakes he has made—the hillside he washed away with an ill-considered attempt to build a pond, for instance. It is clear from his writings that his farm is small, orderly, productive, and recovering its health after years of neglect by its former owners:

> *Growing weather; enough rain;*
> *the cow's udder tight with milk;*
> *the peach tree bent with its yield;*
> *honey golden in the white comb;*
> *the pastures deep in clover and grass,*
> *enough, and more than enough;*
>
> *the ground, new worked, moist*
> *and yielding underfoot, the feet*
> *comfortable in it as roots;*
>
> *the early garden; potatoes, onions,*
> *peas, lettuce, spinach, cabbage, carrots,*
> *radishes, marking their straight rows*
> *with green, before the trees are leafed.*

In his essays he writes somewhat more systematically about Amish agriculture, reporting on his visits to several farms in Indiana and elsewhere. Though "the Amish no doubt have their problems," he admires their communities and farms, seeing them as useful models. The Amish generally disdain both government subsidy and debt, and are therefore free to concentrate on a method of farming that has endured for many generations. Like Berry they use horses instead of tractors, and this automatically limits the size of their farms and ensures that the farmer pay closer attention to the subtleties of his particular fields, the peculiarities of its hills and gullies. Instead of relying heavily on oil-based fertilizer, the Amish practice strict crop rotations that employ legume crops to fix nitrogen in the soil. Their farms also tend to be far more diversified, with many small sources of food and what little cash income their self-sufficient lives require; not many Amish buy milk at the supermarket, a commonplace with America's big-time farmers. This kind of farming results in healthier soils with better cultivation of land, more water retention, and reduced erosion. It also results in somewhat lower yields per acre.

Are these old-fashioned practices just the aesthetic preferences of quaint religious folk and gentle plowing poets? The answer is obscured by the undeniable success of modern agriculture in growing food. Between 1950 and 1984, in large measure because of many of the practices Berry abhors, world grain harvests grew by two and one half times. That 3 percent annual increase outstripped the rate of population increase, and so per capita grain production rose by one third. With success of that sort, one could overlook a lot of disappearing topsoil.

But bad practices have a way of catching up with us. The 1990 edition of the Worldwatch Institute's invaluable *State of the World* report concentrates much of its attention on food supply, and the news is not encouraging. Between 1984 and 1989 overall world food production rose only 1 percent. This meant, of course, a decrease in per capita grain production, since the world's growing population requires 2 percent annual gain just to keep people eating at the same—in many cases inadequate—level. Though the Worldwatch Institute cautions that the five-year period is "too short to show a trend because weather fluctuations could be partly responsible," they cite three apparent reasons for the plateau. For one thing, the world is running out of new cropland— even the rapid rise in irrigated fields has peaked. For another, there have been few new technological advances comparable to the Green Revolution and the spread of fertilizers to boost yields in recent years, and none seem forthcoming. (Agricultural biotechnology, they assert, will have at most a very limited impact for many years.) And finally, exactly the sort of environmental degradation long predicted by tiresome cranks like Berry seems to be taking place.

Each year, researchers estimate, the world's fields shed 24 billion tons of topsoil, which means that in the 1980s alone the world has lost the equivalent of half of America's rich supply. (We've managed to cut American losses somewhat in recent years, but elsewhere there is little improvement.) This reduces yields, as does the salinization of irrigated fields: in a great many cases, fields were artificially irrigated without proper drainage. Over time they have become waterlogged, and as the water reaches the top few inches of soil it is evaporated out into the atmosphere, leaving behind a layer of salt. One fourth of the world's irrigated cropland may be affected to some degree, the Worldwatch Institute estimates.

As a result of such problems, the world's food supply is dangerously vulnerable to other possible risks. The prospect of hotter summers from the greenhouse effect, for instance, is a real and deeply troubling one. Nineteen eighty-eight was the hottest year since human beings began keeping records—it may not have been a result of the greenhouse effect, but it was a fair warning of what we may expect soon if scientists are correct in their predictions of global warming. In that year the American grain harvest fell by 27 percent, the Russian by 8 percent, and the Chinese by 2 percent. Severe famine was averted by the use of reserve stocks. Nineteen eighty-nine was a normal weather year, and higher grain prices led U.S. farmers to press more acreage into production. But the reserves were not built back up—"carryover stocks now amount to little more than pipeline supplies," the Worldwatch Institute says, because the world needs to feed 100 million more people annually.

· · ·

All of this would suggest that Berry may be a good prophet, all too correct about our capacity to sustain agriculture—that we may have reached that spot on the bell-shaped curve where we can no longer assume rapid advance in food supply, and indeed that it may decline, because we have been careless stewards of the land. The problem, of course, is that any rapid retreat to a saner but less productive method of agriculture might well mean famine in the nations that depend on America's surplus, in the same way that any quick cut in the use of fossil fuels might cripple the economy. If all American farmers started emulating the Amish tomorrow, Malthus could quickly be proved right. If they keep farming using present methods, Malthus may have to wait a few decades—or at least until the next extraordinarily hot summer.

But Berry's argument is not a purely or even chiefly scientific one: he is a moral critic. He has little patience with the American agricultural officials who boast that 95 percent of Americans have "been freed from the drudgery of preparing their own food," for he believes that more of us should be doing the physical work of providing for ourselves, and not just because it would make for more intensive and careful farming. He believes that there are other, less practical reasons why more of us should do physical labor. We should be working not solely in the fields—there's plenty of room in his world for, say, a good carpenter (though, better yet, the community carpentry of an Amish barn-raising) and even a part-time jurist, a part-time priest, a part-time legislator, a part-time writer. But, at least by implication, there is a good deal less need for the rest of us, the innumerable creators and fillers of the lesser human desires, the legions of middlemen, the tiers of executives. Such a view has a long pedigree, of course—Berry is a Jeffersonian. But Berry has two advantages Jefferson didn't have—one is the particular credibility that comes from having worked his own acres instead of handing them over to slaves, and the other is the in many ways deteriorated state of our society. Jefferson anticipated what would happen if the speculators and the manufacturers won out; Berry sees the results all around him.

Our great aim "to this day has been 'freedom from drudgery,' " Berry writes in his book of essays *The Hidden Wound*. "The great motive and selling point of industrialism has been 'less work'; our national goal, indeed, has been less work and we have succeeded." But this success, he contends, has been a great loss, the cause of both environmental and psychological woe. And indeed he can make even the grittiest field labor sound so appealing that one begins to wonder what kind of down payment is needed for a small Kentucky farm of one's own.

> I can say, for example, that the tobacco harvest in my own home county involves the hardest work that I have done in any quantity. . . . This work usually occurs at some time between the last part of August and the first part of October. Usually the weather is hot; usually we are in a hurry. The work is extremely demanding, and often, because of the weather, it has the character of an emergency. Because all of the work still must be done by hand, this event has maintained much of its old character; it is very much the sort of thing the agriculture experts have had in mind when they have talked about freeing people from drudgery. . . . But for me, and I think for most of the men and women who have been my companions in this work, it has not been drudgery. None of us would say that we take pleasure in all of it all of the time, but we do take pleasure in it, and sometimes the pleasure can be intense and clear. Many of my dearest memories come from these times of hardest work. . . . Neighbors work together; they are together all day every day for weeks. The quiet of the work is not interrupted by machine noises, and so there is much talk. There is the talk involved in the management of the work. There is incessant speculation about the weather. There is much laughter; because of the unrelenting difficulty of the work, everything funny or amusing is relished. . . . Ultimately, in the argument about work and how it should be done, one has only one's pleasure to offer.

Such an account provokes the same sharp pleasure we feel on reading, say, Tolstoy's account of Levin's day in the field, when he shared the peasant's food, "and talked to him about his family affairs, taking the keenest interest in them, and told him about his own affairs . . . and could not help smiling at the affection he felt for the old man." Levin learns to swing the scythe, and soon finds it moving almost without him, "as though by magic, without thinking of it, the work turned regular and precise by itself. These were the most blissful moments." But with Levin one can't help asking whether perhaps it's only the knowledge that he's working for a few days, by his own choice, that makes the work so inspiring. What if Levin had to go to the fields every day? Wouldn't we all want to flee from the rigors of farm life as our forebears did, and as people in the third world continue to do?

Berry answers this in two ways. First he says it was the ruinous economics of farming (an economics often promoted by government policy) combined with the seductive promises of the "modern," "advanced," consumer life that drew people off the land. This may or may not be true—it depends in part on how truly happy you think most urban and suburban dwellers are. But there is no quarreling with his second answer, which is the testimony of his own life.

· · ·

After beginning a conventional literary and academic career— teaching English at New York University, among other jobs— Berry returned, more than twenty years ago, to the Kentucky county of his youth and bought a farm. He has since brought in an annual harvest of hay, corn, tobacco, and books. I know of no other American writer who seems so happy with the conditions of his life, and whose delight does not seem at all false or forced; nor, to judge from his books, has it diminished with hard work or the years.

Hard work is not the point. Farmers work no harder than coal miners, and their lives are regulated by the sun so that they can't possibly keep working until ten at night, like Manhattan lawyers. But farming, almost uniquely, employs all the human skills, physical and mental:

On a good farm, because of weather and other so-called variables, neither the annual series of problems, nor any of the problems individually is ever quite the same two years running. The good farmer (like the artist, the quarterback, the statesman) must be master of many possible solutions, one of which he must choose under pressure and apply with skill in the right place at the right time.

But even the quarterback sits down on defense, and he doesn't need to sell season tickets. The good small farmer is both manager and employee, and so he is neither one nor the other; his life is not abstracted. I once edited a small daily paper, where I assigned and wrote stories, designed and pasted up pages, then helped to prepare the plates for the press and bundled the papers as they came clattering off the conveyor at four in the morning. It was immensely satisfying, in a way no job since has been. But even that work was pretty much by rote, with none of the calibration and risk taking demanded of a farmer.

· · ·

Good farming, the sort that doesn't simply involve mining the soil or rely on packaged "inputs," also requires enormous amounts of information, which must be passed along from one generation to the next. It requires continuity and, therefore, community:

> That is, a neighborhood of people who know each other, understand their mutual dependencies, and who place a proper value on good farming. In its cultural aspect, the community is an order of memories preserved consciously in instructions, songs, and stories, and both consciously and unconsciously in *ways*. A healthy culture holds preserving knowledge *in place* for a *long* time. That is, the essential wisdom accumulates in the community much as fertility builds in the soil.

The communities Berry describes—communities where people help one another at harvest and slaughter, where they do the big jobs like barn building and quilting and canning together—are precisely the sort of communities we seldom find in this country. True, Berry minimizes the trouble such small societies can cause—the unnecessary feuds, for instance, that derive from some forgotten insult three generations back, or the mean prejudices and claustrophobia that so many people move to the city to escape. But someplace like the Port William he describes in his novels is where many of us would like to live. In "It Wasn't Me," one of six stories in *The Wild Birds*, Wheeler Catlett explains to Elton Penn, a young farmer he has helped, why Penn is not obliged to him. "It's not accountable," he says,

> because we're dealing in goods and services that we didn't make, that can't exist at all except as gifts. Everything about a place that's different from its price is a gift. Everything about a man or woman that's different from their price is a gift. The life of a neighborhood is a gift. I know that if you bought a calf from Nathan Coulter you'd pay him for it, and that's right. But aside from that, you're friends and neighbors, you work together, so there's lots of giving and taking without a price—some that you don't remember, some that you never knew about. You don't send a bill. You don't, if you can help it, keep an account. Once the account is kept and the bill presented, the friendship ends, the neighborhood is finished. . . .

Berry's stories often are accounts of rural communities and the skills and mutual concerns to be found in them. People rally around. But the thought of rebuilding these communities, and the farms that supported them, is daunting, not least because most of the information they once depended on has died out. Three percent of the country's population now work on farms, and only a fraction of these people, by Berry's definition, farm well. Even if we wanted to join them, it seems unlikely that we could do so; the circle may be irreparably broken. There are, he writes, two muses:

> the Muse of Inspiration, who gives us inarticulate visions and desires, and the Muse of Realization, who returns again and again to say "it is yet more difficult than you thought."

It is this second muse that knows about cover crops and harnesses and when to plant. Berry makes it abundantly clear how hard farming is—even building a decent farm road that won't wash out requires "not only correct principles, skill, and industry, but a knowledge of local particulars and many years." Not only is there a dire shortage of good farmers, there is no longer even a "considerable number of people knowledgeable enough to look at the country and see that it is not properly cared for." Most of us can't tell oats from barley at ten paces. Our fathers won't tell us—they don't know either. And anyway there are far too many of us to go straight back to Jefferson's dream.

· · ·

The question is, does Berry's message have meaning for the majority of Americans who by choice or circumstance are not living on the land? I think it does—especially because, as I have said, we may be entering an era in which the world's environmental problems will demand dramatic changes in the way we live.

Although he is widely read by environmentalists, Berry's views are somewhat outside the mainstream of environmental thought, which as he says in *The Unsettling of America* has tended to be either "vacation-oriented or crisis-oriented." Those American environmentalists who have seen past the most obvious problems of controlling noxious industrial emissions have usually followed John Muir and concentrated on the wilderness—on our need both to preserve the wild and to rediscover the wild in ourselves. The most eloquent exponent of this idea in recent times—and Berry's only equal as an essayist of the real world—was Edward Abbey, the Southwestern desert anarchist who died in the spring of 1989. Berry appreciates and supports the case for the wilderness, and has always been a champion of Abbey's. ("A Few Words in Favor of Edward Abbey," in *What Are People For?*, is illuminating on both men. Berry remarks that an ability to laugh at himself was among Abbey's greatest gifts, adding that it is not among his.)

Berry is Abbey's ally in the fight against the "nature conquerors," the strip miners, copper smelters, old-growth loggers, and other black hats of our landscape. But Berry differs from those who think the best use of most land would be to leave it alone. He is a farmer—the sight of a meadow reverting to young birch and bramble does not fill him with rustic delight. He is closer in spirit to John Burroughs, the most popular of all American nature writers in his day. One summer a Catskill neighbor of Burroughs cleared a field. "Land whose slumbers had never been disturbed with the plough was soon knee-high with Hungarian grass," Burroughs wrote. "How one likes to see permanent betterment of the land like that!" Like Abbey, Berry wants to protect the wildcat and wolf, but he would also agree with what Burroughs said of the cow, "She is the cause of tranquil if not great thoughts in lookers-on, and that is enough." Since, as Berry writes, in the foreseeable future "we cannot hope—for reasons practical and humane we cannot wish—to preserve more than a small portion of the land in wilderness," we will have to decide how to use it. He argues, as I have said, that we should use it as personally as possible, and as responsibly.

· · ·

In some sense, the controversy over the wilderness is philosophical, not practical—there is, even at this late date, land enough in North America to increase tenfold our wilderness without infringing on any but the poorest farmland. Millions of acres of the arid

West, for instance, are disastrously overgrazed and yet produce only 3 percent of America's beef. But there is an important difference in emphasis, in the view of what man is. *What Are People For?* contains a remarkable essay, "Writer and Region," about Huckleberry Finn. In Huck's escape from Miss Watson and the "enclosure of conventional piety and propriety" Twain touches, of course, on an important part of our national character. But Huck's final decision at book's end to "light out for the Territory," his refusal to be adopted and "sivilized" by Tom's benign Aunt Sally, represents for Berry not only the flaw in the book but also "a flaw in our national character, a flaw in our history, and a flaw in much of our literature." Too much of our culture, he says, is suspended between the choices of stifling civilization or "an escape into some 'Territory' where we may remain free of adulthood and community obligation." Boyhood and bachelorhood have "remained our norms of 'liberation,'" creating a situation where the choices may seem to be narrowed to fishing all day or working in an investment bank—returning to a hunter-gatherer civilization or going on with the strip-mining of America. With this stunted perspective, "we have hardly begun to imagine the coming to responsibility that is the meaning, and the liberation, of growing up."

This almost fatherly message runs through almost everything Berry writes. His essays and poems are concerned with how to live with the land, but almost as often they are about how to live with others. He writes extensively about marriage, arguing that "people stay married for different reasons [from] those for which they get married," and that though it may begin as dreamy romance, marriage must deepen (not descend) into an "insistently practical union." In the ideal modern house, he says,

> the residers do not work. . . . According to the ideal, work should be done *away* from home. . . . In such a "home," a married couple are mates, sexually, legally, and socially,

but they are not helpmates; they do nothing useful either together or for each other.

Worked out in place and time and circumstance, however, love and devotion, as Berry writes about them, can become tangible; in "The Boundary," one of the short stories in *The Wild Birds,* he tells of an old man who thought of giving up his garden. His wife told him no, and she was right, for "after even so many years, he still needed to be bringing something to her."

· · ·

But before people can live in harmony with their communities, or their spouses, or their topsoil, they need to be at peace with themselves, and that is Berry's main concern. We need to live in real places, not in the generalized lobbies that modern houses often are. We need to be at home in our bodies, too—not in the "useless, weak" husks that we drag daily to the fluorescently cheerful "health club," but a body that each day knows the "elemental pleasures of eating and drinking and resting, of being dry while it is raining, of getting dry after getting wet, of getting warm against after getting cold, of cooling off after getting hot." Of being tired at sundown and at life's end feeling "a great weariness, . . . like the lesser weariness that comes with day's end—a weariness that had been earned and was therefore accepted."

The rigorous life, with some goal beside a higher "standard of living," Berry implies, need come not only through farming. The same forces that distort and maim our agriculture—fear of drudgery, the endless demand for more, and faster—also cause many other problems, both environmental and social, that we face. We drive or take a taxi when we should walk or ride a bike—if we were on foot we would not only emit less carbon dioxide, we'd be in closer touch with our communities, the way a farmer on a horse-drawn plow knows his field better than the pilot of a huge combine. And we would use the muscles that we must have been born with for some better reason than bouncing in front of a video. We would be out in the weather, and at day's end we'd be weary instead of tense.

There are a thousand other ways we could try to shift our lives to create a more sustainable world; but, as Berry makes clear, it would be foolish to underestimate how difficult this will be or how powerful are the habits and interests that must be overcome. As economic actors we, through our investments, require corporations to look ahead a quarter or a year at a time, to make for us as much money as possible, even if that means, to give the tiniest example from the most recent Exxon annual meeting, not building our oil tankers with double hulls. As consumers, even those of us who are well-to-do often demand the cheapest possible food, though this requires the most harmful farming, and the most comfortable cars and houses, though they may well be helping to create an uncomfortable planet.

As citizens we demand lower taxes, instead of devoting ourselves to figuring out how to share the world's greatest concentration of wealth with an increasingly poor nation and world. Suspicious of real change, and of more work and less luxury, we place our faith in frequent incantations about unceasing economic growth and technological expansion, even though our logic tells us they are as unlikely as endless growth in the food supply and our scientific instruments tell us they are starting to harm our planet as surely as poor farming erodes our soils.

Wherever we live, however we do so, we desperately need a prophet of responsibility; and although the days of the prophets seem past to many of us, Berry may be the closest to one we have. But, fortunately, he is also a poet of responsibility. He makes one believe that the good life may be not only harder than what we're used to but sweeter as well.

# 30

# Getting Warmer

—*Outside*, May 1993

If you care for metaphors, Helene Wilson might be night nurse for the planet. Once a month, the Columbia University research scientist leaves her second-floor cubbyhole and climbs five flights of stairs to a slightly larger office, where she hands her boss, Jim Hansen, earth's latest set of vital signs: temperature readings from more than two thousand stations on land and sea. Hansen, in this metaphor, is earth's attending physician, though he's really more of a pathologist. The worse the patient gets, the better it fits his bold diagnosis—should earth's fever break tomorrow, he'd look like a quack. And in fact the only hope for a cure may be a continued deterioration, a slide so alarming that it shocks the rest of us (currently metaphorical germs, but perhaps potential antibodies) into action, so that we as a species can swab our skin with the anesthetic called Fear and then plunge the hypodermic labeled Restraint into our meaty . . . Enough metaphor. The story itself is compelling enough.

For the last five years, Hansen, the middle-aged, middle-western, middle-tempered physicist who directs NASA's Goddard Institute for Space Studies from a cluttered office at 112th Street and Broadway in Manhattan, has been the point man in the most controversial, and probably the most important, scientific debate in the world. Until he testified before Congress in the summer of 1988, global warming had been a vague threat; after he announced his conclusion that man-made carbon dioxide was warming the atmosphere, "greenhouse effect" became a universal buzzword. More than any other piece of science—or, for that matter, propaganda—Hansen's simple declaration launched the world on the road that led to 1992's Rio summit and catapulted Al Gore's *Earth in the Balance* on to the bestseller lists.

Still, Hansen climbed out on a limb with his predictions, and competing scientists, bureaucrats, and even presidents have been trying to bring him down ever since. But as time went by, the branch grew somewhat stronger; the planet appeared to be backing up his predictions. The warmest year on record was 1990; the first half of 1991 was on the same track. Then Mount Pinatubo blew up that June.

It was the largest volcanic eruption of the century, and though it fouled up his temperature models, in a way it was a windfall for Hansen. The eruption injected huge amounts of sulfur dioxide gas into the atmosphere, allowing Hansen an opportunity to spot-check his computer model of climate. "We'd been looking for a nice, clean experiment, and nature provided one," he said. But good science doesn't always make good PR. Sulfur dioxide *cools* the atmosphere, temporarily masking the greenhouse effect. While this is not a fundamental challenge to the global warming theory (when the sulfuric acid disperses in a year or two, the warming should resume), Hansen knew that Pinatubo was going to confuse people. "But I thought I could minimize that confusion by publishing a prediction right away," he said—a prediction of how cold it would get in the coming eighteen months, a prediction that would make the cooling support the greenhouse theory. It was Hansen's first testable prediction and, of course, his first chance to utterly screw up and hand some of the momentum back to the skeptics.

"Remember Mary Lou Retton?" he said. "Remember when she was doing her routine and she had to come off the bars and land absolutely flat on her feet and get a ten to win the gold medal? When your predictions are wrong in science, it's not supposed to be devastating—the errors help you make refinements. But in this case I felt a little like Mary Lou Retton. I had to stick it."

If the actual temperature eventually mirrored his prediction—if the world's temperature fell about one degree Fahrenheit (just over half a degree Celsius) over the course of fifteen months—Hansen would land flat on his feet.

. . .

Hansen began his career studying Venus, not earth, focusing on that planet's clouds. He analyzed the polarization of sunlight reflected by Venus, concluding that its clouds had a refractive index varying between 1.46 in the ultraviolet spectrum and 1.43 in the infrared, which means, in case you didn't memorize your chemistry textbook, that they are composed of sulfuric acid. "I was really excited, completely happy, to be working on Venus," he says, and it is easy to imagine him at the NASA lunch table chatting merrily about the spherical droplets in the Venusian atmosphere. One day, though, a postdoc from Harvard arrived at Hansen's lab and asked for some help studying the effects of trace gases, such as methane, in earth's atmosphere. It was Hansen's introduction to terrestrial climatology, and he was soon hooked. All of a sudden Venus, a planet with a static atmosphere, unchanged over aeons, fascinated him less. "It's interesting to try and understand what's on another planet," he said. "But if our own planet is *changing*, that's even more interesting."

Since the Industrial Revolution, human beings have been pouring carbon dioxide and other gases into the atmosphere with abandon—any fossil-fuel combustion gives off carbon dioxide as a by-product. And carbon dioxide, because of its molecular structure, traps heat that would otherwise radiate back out to space. The amount of extra heat is not on its face enormous—each square meter of earth's surface will in effect receive the equivalent of four extra watts of solar power, or something like 2 percent more than the current total. That's enough, all other things being equal, to raise the temperature about two degrees Fahrenheit.

But earth is a complex planet, and all other things rarely are equal. The extra heat will set off a variety of feedbacks. Warm air holds more water vapor, for instance, and that should further warm the atmosphere. At the same time, the number of clouds may increase, which could moderate the warming. And so on almost infinitely—even Hansen's model, the product of many man-decades of labor, is crude in its computerized depiction of how all these forces will interact. As a result, the best anyone can do is offer a range of how much temperature will rise once carbon dioxide levels double. Researchers call this figure the sensitivity of the climate, and it is the grail of their profession. "If the sensitivity is one degree Fahrenheit," said Hansen, "we don't need to worry." But his work indicates that the number is somewhere between four degrees and seven.

Throughout the 1980s Hansen and other researchers worked to narrow the range of possible sensitivities, issuing one little-read report after another, each of which concluded that we were facing temperatures higher than earth had seen in hundreds of thousands of years. Slowly these reports began to draw some attention, most notably from a few environmentally minded members of Congress. As the end of the decade neared, according to Environmental Defense Fund scientist Michael Oppenheimer, "there was a pile of straw lying around waiting for someone to light it." The frighteningly hot summer of 1988 dried that straw to tinder—by the end of June, drought had stopped barge traffic on the Mississippi, and cornfields across the heartland were shriveling in hundred-degree heat. Then-Senator Tim Wirth of Colorado called a hearing of the Committee on Energy and Natural Resources, and his staff alerted the Washington press corps that it might produce some interesting news.

"I didn't realize what was going to happen," said Oppenheimer. "I was at my summer house on Block Island, and I really didn't want to go to Washington to testify because it was so damned hot." But he went anyway, and sat just down the witness table from Hansen, who, in an unassuming monotone, not only uttered his apocalyptic warning but also stated that, based on his reading of the temperature data from the past century, the heating had already begun. While he stressed that no one could say for certain that the 1988 heat wave was the product of global warming, Hansen said it was consistent with what his model showed would soon be happening. "It's time to stop waffling so much. It's time to say the earth is getting warmer," he told reporters after the testimony.

"Other researchers had been saying stuff like this in the bathroom at seminars," recalled Oppenheimer, "but he had the guts to do it out in public." In an hour's time Hansen had moved the problem from the theoretical to the immediate, from obscure journals straight to CNN.

The reaction among scientists began at once, and it still hasn't completely abated. "It was the normal scientific give and take, magnified about a hundred times because of the stakes," said one of Hansen's competitors. The only recent, comparable outburst was the flap that followed the announcement of cold fusion in 1989. While environmentalists rallied behind Hansen, his colleagues lined up to take potshots. Staid conferences turned into "get Hansen" sessions. It's unnerving to speak with Hansen's various critics and defenders and see how quickly they get down and dirty. Richard Lindzen, a professor of meteorology at MIT and a prominent greenhouse-theory skeptic, charged for instance that Hansen isn't even an expert in the field: "His background is in space," said Lindzen, theorizing that Hansen may be attempting to gain notoriety for his lab in order to keep NASA from merging it with a larger facility in Maryland. Then again, said George Woodwell, a biologist at the Woods Hole Research Center, in Massachusetts, who studies the effects of forests on the composition of the atmosphere, Lindzen himself has an agenda. In the fall of 1992, Woodwell dismissed Lindzen as "just someone trying to curry favor with a neoconservative administration that wants to deny the basic reality of the planet."

Perhaps more than his science or its political implications, it's Hansen's unusual ability to speak in climatological sound bites that annoys his colleagues, who are more comfortable with the endless hedging and uncertainty of cloistered research. "For all his shambling, gee-whiz, farm-boy manner," said Oppenheimer, "he's better than most scientists at understanding the part of his work policymakers and the public would be interested in." For instance, Hansen used his model not only to calculate global average temperatures but also to make specific predictions about specific places: that Dallas, say, which currently tops ninety degrees on nineteen days in an average summer, would see that figure rise to seventy-five days by the middle of the next century. And early in 1990 he stirred up an auditorium full of scientists by beginning a lecture with a wager. He challenged anyone in the room to a bet that one of the next three years would be the warmest on record. Only one of the ninety scientists took him up on it, betting $100; when 1990 cracked the old mark, Hansen collected. It was not a stunt, he insists—he simply wanted to show his confidence in certain calculations he had made about the thermal inertia of the oceans. "I was willing to give odds," said Hansen earnestly. But it would be his last bet. "My wife thought it was a bad example for young people, like Pete Rose."

As time passed, the furor died down a little, in part because Hansen stopped giving interviews and speeches. "Environmentalists say you have to do advocacy," he explained. "But I could easily spend one hundred percent of my time on the political aspect of all this. And the absence of the science is what makes it hard to convince the policymakers and the public. I had to keep reminding myself, 'It's the science, stupid.'" Meanwhile, as more and more scientists studied the phenomenon, a rough consensus began to emerge not so far removed from Hansen's calculations. The Intergovernmental Panel on Climate Change, a group of researchers assembled by the United Nations, estimated the climate's sensitivity to doubled carbon dioxide at about three to eight degrees Fahrenheit, slightly broader than Hansen's range and enough, in all likelihood, to raise oceans, parch continents, exterminate species, destroy vast forests.

There remain plenty of skeptics. Andrew Solow, an associate scientist at the Woods Hole Oceanographic Institution who has dissected the temperature record of the last century, said two and a half degrees Fahrenheit is his best guess, while Lindzen maintained that the actual number is negligible, about one degree or less. "In ten years we'll know a lot more about it and it won't seem a big deal," he contended. Still, according to Oppenheimer, five years after Hansen's testimony, "We're approaching zero on the number of scientists who argue that the world isn't going to warm noticeably."

The calculations remain tentative, however; the system that scientists are trying to understand and model is nothing less than an entire planet, from magma to plankton to rain forests to ice sheets to deep-ocean currents. Each phenomenon requires its own physics, and they must be linked together accurately, at a scale small enough to run on a computer but large enough to capture the world's complexity. Which is why an event like the Pinatubo eruption, twice as big as any since Krakatau, was so welcome: as the sulfuric acid dispersed around the planet, it offered a planetary test of at least some features of the model, allowing Hansen to make his one-degree prediction.

The early returns, however, didn't inspire much confidence in his predictive ability. Nine months after the eruption, scientists gathered in Hilo, Hawaii, to review the data. At that point, the graph of observed temperature versus his prediction looked bad— or perhaps good, if you feared the greenhouse effect more than you feared Jim Hansen's humiliation. In any event, earth was not cooling as predicted. Instead of admitting a basic flaw in his computer model, Hansen swallowed hard and said he thought it was only a matter of time, probably just a month or two, before the cooling would show up. He said, to be precise, "My guess is that this is probably a case where the model is right and the world is wrong."

For a comparable example of hubris, Oppenheimer suggested returning to Einstein. Informed that an experiment had finally confirmed his decade-old theory of relativity, Einstein remarked that had it been otherwise he "would have been sorry for the dear Lord, because the theory is correct." The difference is that Einstein made his boast after the data were in. Hansen said what he said when the results looked like they might bloody him.

· · ·

For all his residual confidence, the half-decade since he burst into the public eye has not been easy for Hansen. The scientific reaction to his remarks was bad enough, but it was mild compared with the behind-the-scenes political pressure. Because Hansen worked for the federal government, the ideologues of the Reagan and Bush administrations had easy access to him and his superiors. His bosses had tried to dissuade him from testifying at all in 1988, and as soon as he was done the White House was on the phone to his superiors, "very unhappy," Hansen said, "about my testimony." Meanwhile, his wife had been diagnosed with cancer, and later that summer his father died. "Taken altogether it had a very unscientific impact on me. I started to read because I was not able to sleep well. I didn't come from an intellectual background—my father was essentially a sharecropper—and I still never read, actually. But in the summer of 1988 I would wake up and start looking through various books. And I kept thinking about what was the right thing to do in these various situations. I read *The Grapes of Wrath* twice. There's this guy in the family who goes to California and ends up getting converted to the labor movement—just this farmer from Oklahoma who ends up on the wrong side of the authorities. He decides to do what he believes, and it leads him to a situation . . ." The sentence petered out, as if the "situation" is too painful to recall in detail. The next day, when we talked again, he had another book in mind. "*Pride and Prejudice*. It's by Jane Austen. This girl Elizabeth rejects this proposal by a guy whose name I can't remember who has a lot of wealth. He thought it was obvious she should jump at his proposal, but she told him to stick it in his ear. The point was, she was quite happy to stick to her principles, more happy doing that than compromising them."

If these sound like line readings for some Jimmy Stewart role, Hansen fits the part. He is shy, almost bland, but he's dogged, too, and seemingly oblivious to the go-along, get-along of politics. When he returned to Congress to testify in 1989, the Office of Management and Budget, which controls Goddard's funding, strong-armed him into watering down his testimony. Hansen went along with OMB, but later took his case to then-Senator Al Gore and blew the whistle on the Bush administration. Not long ago he had the NASA brass apoplectic at his relentless push for two small, cheap Climsat satellites to gather his data, a plan they feared might endanger their multibillion-dollar Earth Observing System.

If Hansen is part Mr. Smith, he's also at least half Mr. Spock. Considering that his research involves the most fundamental threat yet to the planet—the human alteration of its most basic physical systems—you would expect him to be motivated by a desire to save earth, to protect it for his grandchildren, to right the errant course of civilization before it steers off a cliff, to call us to our senses. "I wish I could say I was driven by concern for the planet when I do this work," he said as we walked along upper Broadway, "but that's not true. It's much more of a scientific curiosity." Shamelessly drilling for sentiment, I asked him how he thinks of the planet when he considers it as a whole. Does he see some image in his mind's eye? An ocean? A windy day? A fragile orb drifting lonely through the vastness of space? Hansen hemmed and hawed for a moment. "When I look at the planet, I really do look at it more as a very interesting physical experiment. Obviously the earth is a very wonderful physical system, but I look at it more as a scientist than in any emotional way."

He does not seem to be inventing this detachment to increase his credibility; it fits with his life, little of which is spent outdoors. "When I was a boy I used to take long walks, but that was because my dog liked it," he said. In the early 1980s, when political pressure reduced his funding, Hansen cut his workweek from sixty-seven hours (precision in all things) to the normal forty and found time to coach Little League and mow his lawn (with the mulching mower he bought because grass decomposing at the landfill creates methane, a greenhouse gas). But the funding reappeared, and he started spending every Sunday at the office again. After some prodding, he managed to recall one brief epiphany on Jones Beach, the Long Island strand bordered by parking lots and served hourly by public transit. "It was getting dark," he said. "There was a strong sea breeze coming in. It seemed very powerful, nature. And it seemed incredible that the small force due to this very tiny change in atmospheric composition, now about two watts per square meter, meant anything to those crashing waves."

But all my efforts couldn't keep Hansen on the beach for long; in a matter of seconds he switched back to science, his face relaxed, and he began to speak more quickly, more naturally. "It's remarkably exciting that you can investigate this phenomenon and come to a counterintuitive conclusion. You wouldn't think these perturbations would have the kinds of consequences that the analysis would lead you to believe. That's what's exciting. That's the excitement of science you'd like to share with young people."

By then we had reached Hansen's office again. The only pictures on the wall were a few dusty NASA stills of distant galaxies. Hansen was in his element—thumbing through phone-book-size binders of computer printouts, showing off his numbers on the northward transport of dry static energy, discussing the melting speed of methane clathrates with visiting researchers, coloring in new computer printouts with red markers to see the patterns of the future emerging before his eyes. "We're having a little trouble with the reflectivity of clouds along the equator," he said happily.

"It's as if there's a code he's trying to decipher," said Oppenheimer. "To do it he has to write the codebook first." So, when Helene Wilson climbs the stairs to Hansen's lab each month with the latest temperature map of the world, it's like a check of his understanding. It's like God saying, in both senses of the word, "You're getting warmer." By summer 1992, a year after the eruption, the data had begun to make Hansen feel better. By fall, he was grinning. At least for the moment, the world seemed to have decided that the model was right after all. It was finally cooling off in the wake of Pinatubo, pretty much exactly as predicted. To Hansen, even though it may chart the colossal danger we face as a planet, it was one of the sweeter sets of curves he'd ever seen.

"Now, it's not a home run yet," he cautioned. "The temperature still has to start coming back up the way we've said it will." And even if that happens, it will not convince some of his critics. "Hansen has pulled a fast one with this volcano," groused Lindzen. "It's a scam. It doesn't prove anything about the sensitivity of the climate long-term. Any model would show a result like this over a couple of years."

Hansen, too, said there's plenty of proof yet to be obtained. "The next big test is how the climate behaves in the late 1990s," he said. If his calculations are correct, by decade's end the global mean temperature will have surpassed 1990's record level, to the point where the average person will be able to notice changes in the frequency of hot spells. "We were beginning to notice before the volcano, I think," said Hansen. "And just a few tenths of a degree more will be evidence to the educated person." The precise effects of the changes are harder to predict, especially in the earlier phases of the warming. "The model suggests that it doesn't take much warming to begin having a noticeable effect on the hydrologic cycle," he said. "If we do get a few tenths of a degree above the 1990 levels, more water vapor in the air may mean increased floods in some places, more frequent and extreme dry spells elsewhere."

The inherent uncertainty of the warming calculations diminishes a little with each event, like Pinatubo or 1990's record temperature, that tends to confirm Hansen's thesis. The data are almost certainly strong enough to keep the politicians on track. In fact, the policy response is gathering powerful momentum: Oppenheimer sees the climate agreement in Rio as "a major breakthrough," and even though the vice president's plan to tax carbon emissions didn't make it into the White House's economic package, Gore's proximity to the Oval Office suggests that global warming will get executive attention.

Hansen and I had barely begun our interviews when a Toronto scientist arrived for lunch; he spent the meal describing that city's plans to retrofit every commercial, residential, and industrial structure in an effort to cut carbon dioxide emissions by one fourth. Hansen is much less zealous. He drives a Honda Civic, has installed a few compact fluorescent bulbs, has disconnected his basement refrigerator, and has planted some trees. "Against my better judgment," he said. "My wife twisted my arm into planting six white birches. We live in New Jersey, and that's already the southern edge of their climate zone. We've had tremendous trouble with pests, and I think that might be from those two warm summers." He's also backed the call of many moderate environmentalists for a "no regrets" policy, one that would mandate changes, like greatly increased energy efficiency, that would make sense even if global warming turns out not to be a catastrophe. To the argument that such a plan would wreak economic havoc, he answered, "That seems to me to be a wrong analysis. Germany and Japan don't seem to have destroyed their economies by becoming more efficient."

It is, however, amply clear that public policy on automobile mileage and air conditioner use is as far from Hansen's soul as the crash of ocean waves. His pleasure lies in finding answers. "It's pretty odd doing this work from high atop a Greek coffee shop," he said. "But you can see the sunsets from here—you can see the orange skies where the aerosols from Pinatubo are causing some coloration. You can see the Hudson if you crane your neck; it's saltwater here, of course, and it would be affected if the sea level rose. And you can see the buses and cars. You can see the phenomena forcing the system, and you can see the places where it will be impacted." And if you are smart enough and persistent enough, you can maybe figure out how they all fit together. "There's this song by Melanie," said Hansen, an extremely earnest, extremely white man. "If you put all the good times together end to end, it only adds up to like forty minutes in your life. But those are good times—like when you get to see what the world can do with your models."

# 31

# An Explosion of Green:
# The Bard of the Birdfeeder

*—The Atlantic*, April 1995

On August 18, 1587, Virginia Dare became the first child born to English parents in the New World. Her birthplace—on Roanoke Island, in what is now North Carolina—was Britain's first attempt at colonizing this continent, and was the site of the first recorded British murder of an Indian chief. Though Dare's band of settlers did not survive intact, Roanoke Island was the beginning of the historical process in which English-speaking Europeans settled and subdued North America over the next four centuries.

On September 14, 1987, four hundred years later, a team of biologists from the U.S. Fish and Wildlife Service office on Roanoke Island opened the gate of a pen and released a pair of red wolves wearing radio collars into the Alligator River National Wildlife Refuge. The animals disappeared into the woods perhaps half an hour's drive from the spot where Dare was born. Their species was the first ever to go extinct in the North American wild and then be reintroduced into the natural world from a remnant population in zoos. They were, as surely as Dare, pioneers.

The forces set in motion by European colonization had all but erased red wolves from the continent: settlers made wolves a symbol of the devil, placed bounties on their heads, organized state and federal predator-control programs, and farmed and developed their last few strongholds. The Roanoke Island biologists have watched and listened for the past eight years as the animals they released have reproduced and spread across the refuge's swampy, mosquito-infested 150,000 acres. As of this winter the biologists had counted sixty-one wild-born puppies. One wild-born female had borne four litters, and one of her pups had in turn given birth; a third generation of wild red wolves was howling in the night.

· · ·

Five hundred miles to the north, from his home on Nantucket, Peter Dunwiddie, a plant ecologist, studies core samples of swamps and bogs, looking at pollen under a microscope to figure out what was growing on Cape Cod and the neighboring Atlantic islands in the time before and after the Pilgrims debarked in nearby Plymouth. It's easy to spot the onset of European settlement in his pollen samples. "Literally in a matter of decades," he told me, "the forest was cleared. There's no more oak pollen, and all of a sudden lots of grass pollen. That persisted throughout much of the following couple of hundred years," as Europeans turned most of the area into a giant sheep pasture.

In the late 1800s, just as the agricultural economy was beginning to dwindle, local residents started taking photographs. In addition to his pollen samples, Dunwiddie has gathered a vast library of original pictures along with ones taken from the same places fifty or a hundred years later. "Here's Prospect Hill, on Martha's Vineyard, in 1916," he said to me, choosing one in which a stone wall marched up and over the top of a hill. "There's not a tree to be seen. The retake of the photo today is entirely of an oak forest—a mature oak forest. You can't see the stone wall; you can barely make out the contours of the hill at all, because of the forest."

The scenario—oak and pitch pine replace pasture—has repeated itself all over the area. "Sometimes we had to use a ladder and a pole to get the camera above the treetops just to take a picture," Dunwiddie said. In his bog cores "the pollen is beginning to resemble the pre-European." Coyotes, which in the 1970s crossed the Cape Cod canal and established themselves on the Cape, have recently managed the ocean crossing to the remote Elizabeth Islands. "They've very quickly decimated the feral sheep that were left out there," Dunwiddie said. "They're taking quite a toll on the deer population. The deer and the sheep had been browsing down the seedlings; there's likely to be a really dramatic spurt of growth."

. . .

Imagine the view from a satellite, Alan Duning writes in the 1994 edition of the Worldwatch Institute's *State of the World* report. A time-lapse film that showed you a thousand years each minute would reveal only the slightest changes in the earth's forests, which for millennium after millennium covered about a third of the planet's land surface. But in the film's last three seconds, he says—the years after 1950—the change "accelerates explosively."

> Vast tracts of forest vanish from Japan, the Philippines, and the mainland of Southeast Asia, from most of Central America and the horn of Africa, from western North America and eastern South America, from the Indian subcontinent and sub-Saharan Africa.... Southeast Asia resembles a dog with the mange. Malaysian Borneo is scalped. In the final fractions of a second, the clearing spreads to Siberia and the Canadian north. Forests disappear so suddenly from so many places that it looks like a plague of locusts has descended on the planet.

If you stared from space at eastern North America in the same three seconds, however, you'd see something different: a patch of green spreading like mold across bread, and spreading fast. In the early nineteenth century the cleric Timothy Dwight reported that the 240-mile journey from Boston to New York City passed through no more than twenty miles of forest. Surveying the changes wrought by farmers and loggers in New Hampshire, he wrote, "The forests are not only cut down, but there appears little reason to hope that they will ever grow again."

Less than two centuries later, despite great increases in the state's population, 90 percent of New Hampshire is covered by forest. Vermont was 35 percent woods in 1850 and is 80 percent today, and even Massachusetts, Connecticut, and Rhode Island have seen woodlands rebound to the point where they cover nearly three-fifths of southern New England. This process, which began as farmers abandoned the cold and rocky pastures of the East for the fertile fields of the Midwest, has not yet run its course. Forest cover in New York State, for instance, continued to grow by more than a million acres a decade through 1980. In sum, writes Douglas MacCleery, of the Forest Service, "the forest and farmland landscape of the Appalachians, as well as many other parts of the East and South, has come full circle. By the 1960s and 1970s, the pattern of forest, fields, and pastures was similar to that prior to 1800, its appearance much like it must have been prior to the American Revolution."

This unintentional and mostly unnoticed renewal of the rural and mountainous East—not the spotted owl, not the salvation of Alaska's pristine ranges—represents the great environmental story of the United States, and in some ways of the whole world. Here, where "suburb" and "megalopolis" were added to the world's vocabulary, an explosion of green is under way, one that could offer hope to much of the rest of the planet. The forests, as a recent federal study pointed out, will still take centuries of care before they recover their original grandeur. And backsliding is always a danger, the regreening of the East faces many threats. But it is undeniably real. In his journal Thoreau listed the species gone from

Concord by the middle of the nineteenth century: bear, moose, deer, porcupine, " 'rav'nous howling Wolf,' " and beaver. In 1989 environmental police had to kill a moose that had decided to make its home on the median strip of Route 128, famous as "America's Technology Highway." "We've never been faced with a moose ten miles from Boston," said one game warden, who donated the animal's carcass to a Salvation Army soup kitchen.

American heads turn west when the subject of nature comes up. I have before me the Sierra Club engagement calendar for 1995, with fifty-eight gorgeous pictures, most of them sweeping western vistas. Precisely two come from the thousand-mile sweep of the Appalachians—a patch of orchids in Tennessee and a picture from Maine titled, accurately, "Leaf in Stream." We are raised on what the writer Jose Knighton calls "eco-porn"—sunset-tinted photos of the Grand Tetons and other swelling bosoms of the West. But we might take as our emblem the pine: not towering white pines, marked by the first lumbermen in North America with a "King's Arrow" to reserve them for the Royal Navy, but the spindly pine that springs up when cows leave a pasture, the pine that begins the long process of reclamation. From the Pisgahs, the Unakas, and the Nantahals of the southern Appalachians to the Whites and Greens and Adirondacks of the North, the woods are coming back, and people are starting to notice. In the late 1980s Congress called for a study on how to protect the 26 million acres of forest in New York, New Hampshire, Vermont, and Maine—forest that in some cases wasn't there a hundred years ago. "Show me another twenty-six-million-acre chunk," says John Harrigan, a New Hampshire newspaper editor who sat on the study commission. "Outside of Seward's Folly, I don't think you can." Yellowstone Park, in contrast, covers 2.2 million acres.

. . .

The patron saint of the American West is John Muir. The ecstasy he committed to paper introduced a whole new grammar of wildness to the world, and just in time. Inspired by his passion, the first American environmental movement managed to save the last pristine corners of the West: Yosemite and Glacier national parks, the great wild lands of Alaska, the Grand and Bryce and Zion canyons. His hymn gathered a mighty choir.

In his day Muir had an East Coast twin: John Burroughs. They were known as "the two Johns," and in fact, Burroughs was the more famous writer. When he traveled with Teddy Roosevelt on one trip, witnesses said, it was hard to tell whether the writer or the president was more popular with the crowds that turned out to greet them. Generations of American schoolchildren read Burroughs in special educational editions.

Burroughs has pretty well disappeared from the national memory, mostly because the landscape he lovingly described has ceased to be of much interest. Burroughs was the bard of the birdfeeder, the poet of the small and homey. Under Muir's tutelage, and under a barrage of photos and calendars and coffee-table books from the West, we have been trained to prize grandeur, awe, spectacle. But Burroughs had little use for the sublime. When he finally did visit Yosemite, he spent his first paragraph extolling the robin, "the first I had seen since leaving home. . . . Where the robin is at home, there at home am I."

Instead of the vast and unexplored wilderness, Burroughs wrote about his native Catskills, where woodlands gave way to pasture and field, where small brooks ran into the placid Hudson. In *his* hymn people played a pleasing role. "Last summer," he recalled in an essay, he watched a farmer "take enough stones and rocks from a three-acre field to build quite a fortress; and land whose slumbers had never been disturbed with the plough was soon knee-high with Hungarian grass. How one likes to see a permanent betterment of the land like that!—piles of renegade stone and rock. It is such things that make the country richer."

If, as Barry Lopez has written, "one of the great dreams of man must be to find some place between the extremes of nature and civilization where it is possible to live without regret," then John Burroughs is as important a writer as Muir, and his vision, too, is essential. His message has been submerged as we have become urban and suburban people who escape to the national parks for relaxation, but perhaps it is beginning once more to be heard. A hundred college students a year apply for the four all-but-unpaid internships at Caretaker Farm, in Williamstown, Massachusetts. There, in the shadow of Mount Greylock, which was hiked by Thoreau and which retains some vestigial groves of old-growth forest, they learn the patient work of growing things by hand, supplying vegetables for 130 local families on a plot that might have supported one colonial farmer. Last summer I asked one apprentice, a good child of suburbia, if the world of the farm had come to feel like home. "It feels completely natural to be here by now," she said. "We're all wondering if the other world will feel as natural when we go back."

Michael Pollan is one of the few writers to have addressed these issues recently. His book *Second Nature* is partly an account of the greening of his Connecticut home and partly a spanking of environmentalists for focusing too much on wilderness. It argues that "the habit of bluntly opposing nature and culture has only gotten us into trouble, and we won't work ourselves free of this trouble until we have developed a more complicated and supple sense of how we fit into nature." He calls the gardener "that most artificial of creatures, a civilized human being: in control of his appetites, solicitous of nature, self-conscious and responsible, mindful of the past and the future." He is, I think, correct in pointing out that we misunderstand the middle ground even more than we misunderstand wilderness. It is there, in the places where we must grow food and cut trees, that we work out what it means to be a human animal. So far, so good; Pollan is a worthy successor to Burroughs. But the human animal is not the only animal, and huge swaths of the East are clearly able to support life both wild and tame.

Biologists often talk about "indicator species." If the well-managed woodlot and the organic carrot are indicators that human beings are living wisely in their place, then the wolf is an indicator that human beings can learn to accept real limits. The wolf avoids people; unlike coyotes, which adapt to suburbs with ease, wolf packs need many square miles—*empty* square miles—to roam.

Save for reintroduced populations of red wolves in coastal North Carolina and now the Smokies, the East is wolf-free. In 1630 Massachusetts enacted the first bounty in the New World—a shilling for every wolf carcass. Wolves were gone from Connecticut by 1837, from New Hampshire by 1895, from the farthest reaches of the Adirondacks by 1899, from Maine by 1909. Once the most widely distributed land mammal on earth, the wolf has been reduced to about 5 percent of its original range in the lower forty-eight states.

And yet its return is not impossible. Healthy populations still live in Canada, including in Ontario's Algonquin Park and Quebec's Laurentides Park. And perhaps wolves have begun the slow drift back down. Wolves might reestablish themselves voluntarily in New England and the Adirondacks, and perhaps even move farther south. But they may need help—the carefully monitored release of animals from Canada or Alaska, much like the release of wolves that is now under way in Yellowstone Park. Among other obstacles, the St. Lawrence Seaway is kept clear of ice all winter long, making overland migration nearly impossible. And government officials have shied away from reintroduction plans, fearing that a public raised on Little Red Riding Hood, and a hunting fraternity fearing competition from another predator, could not cope with the wolf. But when reintroduced in Minnesota and Michigan wolves have done little harm. They kill old or sick deer, culling the weakest animals from the herd instead of picking off the prime specimens, as human hunters do.

Stephen Kellert, a professor at Yale and an editor of the book *The Biophilia Hypothesis,* which proposes that there exists an ingrained human affinity for nature, has done surveys that show "a real fondness" for wolves, even among many hunters, as "a symbol of nature's wonder and beauty." John Harrigan has editorialized extensively in his small-town New Hampshire paper in favor of the return of the wolf and other predators, preferably, "on their own four feet" instead of through reintroduction. "Ninety percent of the response I get is positive," he said.

Even the lowing cows that Burroughs lauded could prosper alongside the wolf. A wolf is all but genetically programmed to chase deer and moose and such. Of the seven thousand farms within the Minnesota wolves' range, fewer than 1 percent have ever reported a wolf raid. Those farmers have been compensated by the state, which should easily be able to afford it—wolves have drawn ever more tourists to the north country, where they buy T-shirts and go on howling expeditions. In short, wolves belong here. The East will not be fully renewed until their packs wander its mountains again. That this is even a real possibility is a wonder, nearly a miracle.

Nature's grace in the East offers the most important kind of hope, not only to a region that has been given a second chance to decide how to inhabit itself, but to a world in terrible need of models. For the East is a real place—not a Yellowstone, with clear boundaries to separate people from nature. In that way it looks like the rest of the world—like Siberia and the vast forested stretches of Asia, like Central and South America, like Africa. Like them, too, it is real because of the devastation it has undergone. In Haiti forest cover dropped during the twentieth century from more than 80 percent to less than one; in parts of the Philippines, according to a 1993 article in the *New York Times,* a "chainsaw massacre of the regal hardwoods" has left erosion, silted streams, and weather that "veers from drought to flood." The same was true of much of Appalachia a century ago. Though other climates and soils may offer even greater challenges, the resurgence of forest in the East gives some distant promise that in other places in future days people may be able to depend on a replenished and revivified nature to provide them with a modest and reliable life.

Here, where a certain kind of exploitation begins, the fever has largely run its course. That fever still ravages most of the rest of the world; indeed, it finds much of its direction and capital in the financial and political centers of the American East. But not far away, outside the cities and suburbs, the ghost map of this place is reasserting itself—bear and turkey and moose are reclaiming their territory; trees are growing up around stone walls. The old frontiers have closed. That, we are told, is the story of American and indeed world history. A new frontier may be opening here—an expanding frontier of recovery that, given infinite human care and nurturing, might follow the waves of destruction across the continent and then around the world. On a hill in coastal Maine the body of naturalist Henry Beston is buried on the edge of a second-growth pine forest. His epitaph is from his classic book about Cape Cod, *The Outermost House*: "Creation is still going on, the creative forces are as great and as active to-day as they have ever been, and to-morrow's morning will be as heroic as any of the world." We have little choice in this hard-pinched world but to hope that he was right; and the region where he lived his life offers us at least a slender chance that it is so.

# THE TURN TO ACTIVISM

# 32

# Milken, Junk Bonds,
# and Raping Redwoods

*—Rolling Stone,* August 1989

It's always been pretty easy to understand how people acquire great fortunes, marvelous homes, beautiful paintings. John D. Rockefeller owned scads of oil wells; hence he was rich. Henry Ford sold a lot of motor cars, and Hearst a lot of newspapers. But the new wealth that flooded into Manhattan in the 1980s was more mysterious. The product of junk bonds, mergers and acquisitions, and leveraged buyouts, it seemed divorced from oil or coal or grain or cement. Instead, it was described as the product of "restructuring" or "management reshuffling" or other occult processes. The twenty-four-year-old MBAs were certainly working long hours, and the dollars they were making were real enough— they could buy fancy dinners with them, or join health clubs. But it seemed like play money, collected by passing Go, unconnected with real life.

If you stopped to think about it, however, it was obvious that the money that paid for all those co-ops and car phones and cocaine had to come from somewhere; you could restructure Nabisco nine times over, but someone someplace had to be buying cookies. A good story to explain the link between the unreal and the real—a parable for the Reagan decade—has been taking place over the last few years in Humboldt County, California, about 250 miles north of San Francisco. It is a story about Michael Milken, junk bonds, Ivan Boesky, Drexel Burnham Lambert, enormous conglomerates—and between ten thousand and twelve thousand acres of virgin redwood forest.

The two-thousand-year-old redwoods are part of a much larger tract owned by the Pacific Lumber Company. For generations, PL, as the company is known, had been logging trees in the area—but cutting them fairly slowly, at a rate that would allow them to grow back, and usually cutting them selectively instead of simply clearing huge areas. Though the company owned the world's largest privately held stock of redwoods, it had very little trouble with environmentalists. In fact, over the course of seventy years, Pacific Lumber gave the state of California twenty thousand acres of redwoods, helping the Save-the-Redwoods League at one point in the 1920s to acquire a huge parcel.

And Pacific Lumber seemed too good to be true in other ways as well. Wages were high; workers could rent cheap and tidy homes in the company-owned town of Scotia; every PL child got an $8,000 college scholarship. "This company was the elite of all companies," said Bob Younger, a lumber handler at Mill A in Scotia who has lived in the area all his life. "They took care of everything, they looked after you, they treated you like family." Cast Jimmy Stewart for company president; it was a pretty wonderful life.

In early 1986, however, a Los Angeles–based conglomerate called Maxxam took over Pacific Lumber. It was a deal that summed up the decade. For one thing, Maxxam and its chief, Charles Hurwitz, had no particular expertise in the timber industry. Hurwitz's first big move had come in 1973, when he took over McCulloch Oil. Selling off many assets, he soon acquired the Simplicity Pattern Company; there, according to the *Houston Chronicle*, he sold off the company's famous dress-pattern line.

The Pacific Lumber deal, though, was a particularly avant-garde move. Calling on the cash-creating power of the Wall Street investment bank Drexel Burnham Lambert, Hurwitz borrowed $754 million to buy the public company—borrowed the money with junk bonds, the high-interest notes that have fueled the takeover binge of the last ten years. The exact details of the transaction were murky, but they led to all sorts of revelatory allegations. A shareholders' suit, for instance, alleged that Hurwitz tempted the old board of directors with nifty golden parachutes. Complaints filed by the Securities and Exchange Commission (SEC) against Milken and Drexel Burnham alluded to the Pacific Lumber deal, though as Maxxam spokesman Donald Winks had been quick to point out, the company had not been formally accused of anything. There were even charges by some shareholders—denied by Hurwitz—that he illegally parked Pacific Lumber stock, in an effort to conceal his moves toward acquisition, with Boyd Jeffries, who admitted parking stock for Ivan Boesky.

The various charges probably did not bother Hurwitz too much—he had spent much of his professional life in the diverse legal wrangles that high finance so often entails. (According to *Fortune*, his first brush with the SEC came in 1971, not long after his graduation from college, when he, along with a number of his colleagues, was charged with plotting to inflate the price of a stock. He signed a consent decree without admitting guilt.) Amid the welter of briefs and depositions, a couple of numbers stand out. One is $12\frac{3}{4}$ percent, the annual interest due on some of the junk bonds that financed the takeover. Another is $83 million, the total interest due on the junk notes in 1989. And these numbers matter. Pacific Lumber was always profitable, but it never made the kind of money that would allow it to pay off a debt of that magnitude and still turn a profit.

Hurwitz, in other words, did not bring to Pacific Lumber some vast fund of knowledge about the woods, nor any great new ideas for cutting costs. He brought to Pacific Lumber a massive debt, which the company could pay off in only one way: cutting more trees. After Hurwitz took over, the rate at which Pacific Lumber cuts its trees doubled (as of 1989). Because Michael Milken invented this wonderful new tool called the junk bond, twice as many trees were crashing to the ground in Humboldt County.

Pacific Lumber contends that debt service is not the only reason for the accelerated cutting: a timber survey that Hurwitz commissioned soon after taking over the company showed that it had more trees than previously thought, and so, said Winks, the loggers are engaged in "taking off inventory." And indeed, there's reason to believe that even if Hurwitz had been given the company for free, he might have increased the rate of cutting. In a meeting with Pacific Lumber employees, he told workers his version of the golden rule: "Those who have the gold rule."

Company president John Campbell called Hurwitz's remark "unfortunate. He was trying to make a joke. It was an effort at making some humor." Public-relations man Winks said, "It was an ill-advised attempt to be humorous." But perhaps enlightening all the same: compared with "Do unto others as you would have them do unto you," it's quite a contemporary aphorism. Hurwitz, said Winks, is "puritanical," uninterested in the perks of wealth, adding, "He doesn't have a jet; he flies commercial," which seems to be the current standard for beatification. He's "an exercise addict," and though he inherited a sizable sum from his dad, a shopping-center pioneer, "he's just a guy who's driven by the need to succeed in business."

And succeeding in business means making more money. "What you had here was a company with an enormous amount of assets being undermanaged," said company president Campbell. "It was sleepy," said Winks. "It was like many American industries that operated that way and hence became targets." The slowpoke old company would eventually have chopped down the virgin groves (though environmentalists say there was at least a slightly better chance the pre-Hurwitz PL would have sold the land to the state or the feds). As a result of the invigorated Hurwitz management, everything was speeding up. Several hundred new jobs were created, new mills built, extra shifts added.

Surprisingly, not all company employees were overjoyed with the developments; a number banded together to try and buy out Pacific Lumber with an Employee Stock Ownership Plan, or ESOP. "They're cutting way too fast," said mill hand Younger. "Before, when you got a job at Pacific Lumber, you got a job for life. The timber was always going to be there. But now, if you ask me, it's all going to be gone in fifteen years. I'm twenty-eight—I'm looking ahead, and I see that I'm going to have to do something else."

Though Younger said as many as two hundred of the company's fourteen hundred or so workers have backed the ESOP, "most of the people still believe PL will take care of you, because that's the way it's always been. They don't understand times have changed." At the moment, he said, he's hoping that Hurwitz, who (the ultimate eighties guy) was involved in a busted Texas savings and loan, will decide to sell. "We'd just like to see it get back to sustained yield, to where we can have jobs in the future," he said.

Probably no one would have paid much attention to the labor woes of one lumber company, though, if it hadn't happened to have owned the last privately held groves of virgin redwoods in America. "If this was Douglas fir or southern pine, no one would give a damn," said Winks. Instead these trees are coastal redwoods, many of them born before Christ. Listen to Greg King, a local environmental activist: "There's one grove in there that epitomizes it all for me. We call it Headwaters Forest; it's on the Little South Fork of the Elk River, which is probably the finest redwood stream in the world. It's totally intact for about two miles; it's like a little microriver. There's a tree I just found in there recently that's between fifteen and twenty feet in diameter. One gets the feeling of being dropped into a world totally apart from this planet."

King and other local activists have gotten to know the redwoods pretty well. On several occasions, most recently in early

June 1989, members of the self-styled radical environmental outfit Earth First! staged sit-ins in the upper reaches of endangered redwoods; to fell the trees, loggers would have had to fell the protesters. Activists from Earth First! and other groups have won lots of publicity across the West in recent years by destroying bulldozers, pulling survey stakes to slow down road building, and other "ecotage" efforts. (They've also won the attention of the FBI, which arrested Earth First! founder Dave Foreman in the spring of 1989 on charges that he conspired to tear down power lines.) In Humboldt County, though, their protests have been nondestructive—classic civil disobedience. And their leaders are hardly wild-eyed mountain men.

Darryl Cherney grew up in the forests of Manhattan and first saw the redwoods the way almost everyone else first sees them— from the back of his parents' car. "I'd always had this romantic notion of moving back there to live," he said, "but I also had this New York notion that to live someplace that beautiful must cost several thousand dollars a month." By the time he finally returned to northern California in the mid-eighties, the Pacific Lumber groves were being threatened with destruction, and so he has spent at least as much time hiking through clear-cuts as idyllic forests. "In the places they cut old growth, they've announced that they'll leave a few trees," Cherney said. "So it looks kind of like a dirt parking lot with an occasional tree sticking out in the middle. No ferns, nothing—just a tree." Because of their isolation, Cherney said, many of the remaining trees have been toppled by the wind.

The Earth First! activists have joined a number of other environmental groups seeking to block the old-growth cutting not only in California but throughout the Pacific Northwest. In a series of lawsuits, environmentalists have argued that a number of wildlife species, including the spotted owl, the red tree vole, and a shorebird called the marbled murrelet, depend on the snagged tops and shady bottoms of old-growth forest. Maxxam spokesman Winks said that "since owls have wings, if the trees are gone, they can fly a few miles and find some more." But the courts, at least on a few occasions, have sided with the birds, temporarily halting some logging.

The environmentalists also dismiss the company argument that plenty of redwoods are already protected in state and national parks. "They say that there's eighty thousand acres of old growth protected," said Cherney. "But a lot of it is Winnebago park, hundred-foot-wide strips." In some places holes have been cut in the trunks of the redwoods so paying customers can steer through: drive-in nature. Overall, only about three percent of America's virgin forest remains unlogged. "That's just not enough," said Greg King.

And so some environmentalists are pushing for state ballot initiatives in 1990, calling on California taxpayers to save all the islands of old growth. If the propositions are passed, foresters won't be allowed to cut in a grove till a certain percentage of trees have reached 150 years of age.

At root, the dispute between Maxxam and the environmentalists is about different ways of looking at wilderness, different ways of thinking about man and earth. One view, just beginning to emerge, is expressed by King when he talks about hiking through an endangered grove. "It's hard to put into words what I feel except to say that it is life—it is reality," he said. "These trees are good friends of mine, as dear to me as any person."

The other, more conventional, view has been with us since some Stone Age fellow made the first ax. I asked spokesman Winks if Maxxam chief Hurwitz had ever seen these ancient groves, and if so, what he thought about them. "He's visited the facilities he now owns, but he hasn't made himself an expert," Winks said. "His interest is in seeing that the company set business goals and that they meet them. I think that he believes that there are lots of redwood trees, and that these are the ones he's paid for and now owns. . . . It's hard to argue with the emotional argument that an old tree is special. But there are more pragmatic arguments. An old tree takes up space that could be used by more and younger trees, a big tree produces good revenues. And it's like any other piece of property. What about his constitutional rights?"

Perhaps Hurwitz and Milken and the rest are correct—perhaps what really counts is that people keep building redwood decks and hot tubs (two of the prime uses of the lumber) and that jobs are created as quickly as possible and that men who are already rich grow richer. But I've seen both the canyons of Wall Street and the fog-hung cathedral forests of the Pacific Coast. And so it's hard for me not to wonder if King, the tree hugger, hasn't reached some profounder understanding: "We've degraded so much of the planet," he said, "that reality seems unreal."

# · 33 ·

## Court Jester

—*Mother Jones*, November/December 1991

This is very serious," I had to keep reminding myself. "Not a joke. Very serious. Lives at stake."

I arrived at the Arizona trial of Earth First! cofounder Dave Foreman and four local activists in late July 1991, three weeks before it ground to a halt in a series of plea bargains. The five guilty pleas to minor charges ended the trial, but not before a month of testimony revealed a good deal about law and order in the 1990s.

When I got there, the defendants' attorneys were just beginning to cross-examine the government's first important witness, one Ronald Kermit Frazier. The FBI had paid Frazier a salary and expenses in excess of fifty thousand dollars to record his conversations with the environmentalists, a stint that he testified represented "nice work if you can get it." Oh, and there was the twenty-five-thousand-dollar reward he might be able to claim if he could just convince the jury to convict. And, of course, the government had kindly paid him in cash so he could avoid the IRS lien he was under. But this was one case where it hardly paid to follow the money, because everything else was so delicious.

Frazier's pharmaceutical habits, for instance. A few days into the trial, the FBI's star witness apparently told the bureau, which had been in daily contact with him for more than two years, that he was a one-man Rexall. Which left the government in the interesting position of explaining to the jury why his intake of marijuana, peyote, psilocybin, amphetamines, barbiturates, heroin, and LSD had not hampered his ability to perceive or remember events. During the period of his heaviest LSD use, the prosecutor pointed out, Frazier did honors work in diesel technology at the local college, and won second prize in some statewide mechanics competition. He also peddled acid, and gave the drug to some of the defendants in the case. As soon as the government found out about his past, they granted him immunity from narcotics prosecution. This is your informant—this is your informant on drugs.

There was also Frazier's penchant for publicity. In the early weeks of the trial, he wrote a letter to the local paper, explaining how much he was enjoying its coverage of the case. "I'm looking forward to seeing my own testimony covered in a similar thorough fashion in your own indomitable style," he wrote. "You like sitting up there and being the center of attention, don't you?" one of the attorneys asked, and Frazier agreed.

And then there was his history. It turned out that he went to the FBI after one of the defendants in the case, Ilse Asplund, told him she wanted to cool off their relationship and just be friends. It also turned out that the last time a Prescott woman had spurned his advances, he had tried to turn her in to the authorities, too. And then there were what the prosecutor referred to as "unsubstantiated allegations" that he had abused children. And a sheepdog.

Or the hypnosis. The hypnosis was the really weird part. The FBI had flown Frazier to San Antonio for a daylong session with a psychologist, the tapes of which were played for the jury. A glassy-eyed Frazier was taught to "bridge in" and "bridge out" of a trance, so that he could recall any "peripheral" conversations he might have heard at Earth First! meetings. And it worked! Frazier remembered hearing a man discussing disabling a steam locomotive. Great stuff, if there were any steam locomotives left—this was Earth First! circa 1875.

But this was serious. Not a joke. People's lives were at stake. This loser-for-hire in his tasteful suit (the FBI had not only paid for it, they helped him pick it out) was point man in a multimillion-dollar federal attempt to destroy Earth First! And it worked. Through Frazier's constant cajoling, and the marginally more professional work of FBI undercover agent Mike Fain, the feds managed to lure these folks to cut down a power pole in the Arizona desert. A power pole that was connected at a great distance to a nuclear-power plant. The agent drove. It was the agent's truck. No one else had gas money, so the agent bought. Finally they went to work with a torch, at which point nine FBI agents clad entirely in black set off a flare and moved in for the bust. According to Michael Lacey, who covered the trial for Phoenix's *New Times,* the agents wore bulletproof vests and special anti-snake leggings. They carried walkie-talkies, nine-millimeter pistols, and fully automatic M-16s, and they peered through night-vision goggles. A Blackhawk helicopter waited nearby.

Thus equipped, they managed to take most of the terrorists, who were armed with a broken Swiss army knife. Take 66 percent of them, anyway. Peg Millett managed to walk away into the desert and hitch a ride home to Prescott, where she was apprehended later. That night the FBI also burst into Dave Foreman's Tucson home where, guns drawn, they caught him in the act of sleeping. He hadn't been out in the desert cutting down power poles. His crime was that he had given Mark Davis, flakiest of the Prescott desperadoes, a few hundred dollars. No tape existed of that conversation, but there were recordings of Foreman trying to argue Davis out of his obsession with nuclear-power plants. Still, it was enough for the arrest. Later the feds charged that Foreman had also provided autographed copies of his book *EcoDefense: A Field Guide to Monkeywrenching* to some of the defendants.

You think the days are past when the FBI targeted political dissidents and did whatever it took to get them? When you had to worry about writing books? You think they died with J. Edgar Hoover? With Cointelpro? That it's silly to spin conspiracy theories? Then explain this quote from agent Fain, which Fain recorded by mistake on his body wire while conversing with another agent: "[Foreman] isn't really the guy we need to pop. I mean, in terms of actual perpetrator. But this is the guy we need to pop to send the message and that's all we're really doing." The federal prosecutor, Roslyn Moore-Silver, opened her presentation to the jury with a flip chart outlining her theory of the case. TERRORISM, said one page. ANARCHY AND REVOLUTION, said another.

And it worked. No one in Prescott knew quite how to react to the news of the copped pleas, which ranged from counts of failure to notify authorities of illegal activity to conspiracy to commit property damage. Some said that Foreman, who had the strongest case, took a fall to aid his codefendants; others said that the FBI was eager to keep Fain off the witness stand. The defendants were now under court order not to say anything. Their spokesperson, Marty Lynne, said, "I've heard people say everything from 'This is really good' to 'This is a defeat.'" In a way, the short jail sentences expected for Millett, Davis, and Marc Baker, and the probation foreseen for Asplund and Foreman, are the least of the punishment. The government won when it launched the case, and turned the five into full-time defendants.

Throughout it all, Foreman, who in some ways was the most important American environmentalist of the 1980s, has had to occupy himself with stacks of depositions and mounds of tape. Not with reintroducing the wolf to Yellowstone. Not with saving the enormous desert wilderness of Utah, or the imperiled Adirondacks. Instead, he's been fending off the remorseless attack of the U.S. government, which is to say you and me, as represented by a sad sack named Ronald. Who told the jury that he turned informant because he was so angry and resentful that his only other choice was to go to an Earth First! meeting and "pull a Rambo." Meaning, he said, he would have "killed a bunch of people."

. . .

Ronald Frazier had to turn over his journals to the defense team. They contained all sorts of schemes. They expressed his hope that the FBI would relocate him to the Pacific Northwest to infiltrate environmentalists up there, and his elaborate and absurd plan for turning Asplund, the lover who had spurned him, into an informant. But the most revealing entry was only five words long. On March 14, 1989, he wrote: "Ed Abbey died today. Hooray!!!"

To understand what this trial was about, you need to know a little about Edward Abbey. Earth First! appalls the government—and, to a lesser extent, maddens a good many progressives—because it descended not from a rational plan or a conference with a manifesto or an international conspiracy or any of the other causes that rigid minds can understand. As much as anything else, it came from a book. The most controversial tactics of Earth First!—disabling bulldozers, pulling up survey stakes, and so on—came from Abbey's *The Monkey Wrench Gang*. Of course, but more importantly, so did the spirit. Abbey invented the approach that animated the group in its earliest years. Irreverent, mildly drunken, angry, funny. It was as if Mark Twain had written *Huckleberry Finn before* the Civil War and it had given rise to a very different sort of abolition movement.

It's important to recall that Earth First! arose at a moment when the environmental movement, and the Left in general, was moribund. It was the end of the Carter administration and the beginning of the Reagan years, and James Watt was not yet certified as an ecological Antichrist. No one was talking about global warming; the hole in the ozone was undiscovered. Before Earth First!—whose members dressed as endangered species, perched on platforms high up in giant redwoods and Douglas firs, and, yes, sometimes spiked trees—no one had ever been creative and angry and funny enough to make the public understand what the Forest Service was and how it operated. Now old-growth forest is high on every environmental agenda. And they did the same thing with cattle grazing on the public lands, "biodiversity," and a dozen other issues. They put them into play.

Earth First! changed the giant conservation groups, pressured them at the grassroots level, made them tougher. Malcolm X to the Sierra Club's Martin Luther King Jr. Wild, unpredictable, aggressive—too much. In her opening statement, the prosecutor accused the defendants not only of destroying property but of doing it in a "gleeful" way, of doing it "merrily." They "thought their acts of property destruction were *fun*!"

"At the beginning of Earth First!, virtually everyone involved was an Ed Abbey fan," said Foreman over lunch outside the courthouse. "When I realized, by late 1987 or so, that that was no longer the case, then I began making plans to leave." The split within Earth First! has been analyzed well past the point of boredom, but it is worth saying that Ronald Frazier got this part at least a little right. The death of Abbey mattered—not so much his literal passing, perhaps, as the almost inevitable turn away from his style. It's symbolic, said Foreman, that Earth First!'s very first public action was the Sagebrush Patriots' Rally in 1980, a counterpoint to Watt's Sagebrush Rebellion, which used the American flag as a symbol. "We were reclaiming America. By 1989, some people in the new Earth First! were burning the flag. Anger and alienation are all perfectly good emotions, but when they become your entire personality, they're self-defeating. How can you influence something you're constantly angry at?"

As the group grew and attracted new members, many of them less steeped in its original mythos, the contradictions got harder to contain. Which is not so bad—the post-Foreman Earth First! is doing lots of good work. It's a group for a different time. "Maybe Earth First! was like an early successional species of a bare slope," Foreman volunteered. "You need chaparral maybe to come in before you'll get any conifers. As they grow, they create new environmental conditions." If Earth First! was the chaparral, then what will be the next stage? What niche is open in the environmental movement for Foreman to exploit? "I think it's to infuse the ideas of conservation biology into the grassroots movement," he said—to drive home the message that species diversity and large habitat matter more than scenic vistas. Working with John Davis, the former editor of the *Earth First! Journal,* he's started an ambitious new magazine, *Wild Earth.* "I also want to spend a lot more time in the wilderness—the jury willing, of course."

• • •

The jury never got its say, as it turned out. Which is too bad in a way. The case had been spinning on for weeks in the old-fashioned courtroom on Prescott's central square, becoming more bizarre by the hour.

Mike Black, who was Millett's attorney, had the floor for the moment, and was interested in Frazier's drug use. Frazier had testified that Foreman appeared violent to him on one occasion; now it turned out that shortly before that occasion, Frazier had been gobbling acid.

"Did the FBI ever ask you to take a urine test?" Black asked, holding a Dixie cup aloft. No, it turned out they hadn't. "Tell us what it's like when you take psilocybin."

"Basically, it has a stimulant effect—a low dosage, so I didn't experience too many visual effects, except in the dark."

"Just as a matter of aesthetics, does taking a hit of acid and looking at the Grand Canyon enhance its beauty?"

"Not particularly."

As the day went on, it got no prettier. The political drama of a government cracking down on dissent gave way to the personal drama of a pathetic little man who would turn in the people who trusted him. It became clear that he resented Foreman because he was a wheel—under hypnosis Frazier recalled that he met Foreman for the first time around a campfire at an Earth First! encampment and that "everybody seemed so thrilled, really glad to see him." It became clear that Frazier wanted very badly to be accepted by these people, and felt as though he never quite was: "I felt like I was being used the way you'd use a reference book of a computer. You ask a question, it tells you the answer, you thank it, and you shut it off." It became clear that he was obsessed with his own self—he couldn't excuse Ilse or Dave or Abbey for focusing on something other than him. Though his motivation was pathological, he had correctly identified the real reason that Earth First! was so radical and so important. Because it was *Earth* First! and not me first, or people like me first, or people in general first. There's never been a movement like it, and now that the idea has been introduced, it will not go away. A trial or a plea bargain will not wipe it out.

In the courtroom, the tapes of Frazier's federal hypnosis droned on all afternoon. The government, of course, was convinced it was dealing with a conspiracy set up the way a government is set up. "Has anyone within that group ever told you what the ultimate purpose of that group is?" the friendly defense interrogator asked.

"Other than trying to save the earth," said Frazier, "no."

*as a wall* from the terrain so that one may stand straight and lean against it. I found this stretch long, long ago and, in my young girlhood I would walk secretly and *lean* against the mountain, sometimes facing it and putting my hands out on either side. There seemed to be a strong force passing through me, so untamed, wild and beautiful that there are no words for it. But I know this force remained with me, helped me manage my difficult life, sent me to 'five seas' if not the 'seven,' flowed as courage in my blood . . . and never left me—not even today."

A year or so ago, our county decided it needed a new landfill. Actually, it hired some consultants, and the consultants decided it needed a new landfill, and having hired them, the county would have looked foolish disagreeing. Three hundred and seventy-five acres, the consultants said, to store the ash from the hundred-million-dollar incinerator, which was the last thing they'd sold the county on. Three hundred and seventy-five acres of landfill lined with two giant rubber sheets, enormous landfill Trojans, to prevent unwanted leakage. Three hundred and seventy-five acres that would need to be kept free of trees, mowed twice a year for eternity, so no roots would ever rupture the rubbers. Three hundred and seventy-five acres—that's bigger than some golf courses. And of course the sodium vapor lights. Anyhow, the consultants were awarded a contract to figure out where in the county the landfill should go, and after a highly scientific search they announced their five final sites. And where were they? Not in the southern, urban part of the county, with 90 percent of the people and 90 percent of the waste. Four of the five were clustered forty miles from the city, at the very edge of the county, right around this particular mountain. The highly scientific consultants arranged for letters to go out to all the people who lived on the proposed sites, ninety families in all. Letters that arrived Christmas Eve and informed the residents that soon other highly scientific men would be arriving to drill holes in their land in order to make sure that if the condoms broke (but of course they couldn't, having been designed by men of science working in the public interest), the waste from the city wouldn't drop directly into a subterranean stream but would first have to travel a few hundred feet underground.

And we were not supposed to fight. Not supposed to fight because this is a poor backwoods place, and they were offering cash—a little tax relief, maybe some road funds. Not supposed to fight because we're not that kind of people. It's less apathy than a deep feeling of disempowerment, and what I mean by disempowerment is this. There was a meeting at the town hall, which is a sort of Quonset hut, where the impartial outside consultants were going to explain the mystery of why it was scientific to truck garbage forty miles in to the mountains. And it was winter, and still all the outside consultants were wearing suits and Italian loafer shoes without any laces. And if you are sitting there in your Sorels, you are allowed to get angry for a minute, but when the man in the loafers talks in his soothing way about the necessity of it all, you are supposed to sit down muttering and figure that it makes no difference, they'll do what they want, they always do.

But say you keep protesting a little longer. Say they suspect you too might have a pair of dress shoes home in the closet. They then say the magic word *NIMBY*, and you are supposed to be not disempowered but ashamed; you're just another of those people who say "not in *my* backyard." What if everyone was like that? It has to go somewhere, doesn't it. And so on. *NIMBY* is as powerful a mantra as *jobs*.

The NIMBY concept interests me. When I lived in New York City, I ran a small homeless shelter at my church, and before that I lived on the streets for a while in order to write about what people weren't even calling a crisis yet. (Nor are they calling it a crisis now. It was a crisis for a little while, but now it's a fact of life, and everyone would be amazed if there weren't people curled up in every subway station in America.) Anyway, the acronym was coined by people who didn't want homeless shelters in their neighborhoods because they might get mugged by people who lived in them, and even if they didn't get mugged, their property values would surely decrease, because who would buy a house where you might get mugged? And for a while everyone felt self-righteously angry about NIMBYs, especially all the people in the better parts of Manhattan where there weren't any homeless shelters. It was—it still is—a deep and difficult question. How can you justify damaging a working neighborhood? But how can you justify instead herding fifteen hundred homeless men a night into cots lined up in endless rows on a Harlem armory floor? (When you sleep there, you take off your shoes and you plant the legs of the cot in them so that they'll be there at five in the morning when the overhead lights flip on.) The answer, of course, arrived at not by deeply scientific consultants but by various contemporary saints, was that you designed small, decent residences where people could return to something like normal and which didn't blight the community in which they were placed. The same goes for homes for the mentally ill, the mentally retarded, and all the other kinds of places people fear and detest and then ten months later tell reporters aren't so bad after all.

But this NIMBY idea has taken on a life of its own, and now any time someone wants to put a shopping mall or a highway or a chemical factory or a radioactive waste storage facility someplace, they try to shut you up by calling you one. Happily, we are a few years behind up here. Most of my neighbors didn't understand that they were supposed to roll over paralyzed at this chunk of verbal kryptonite, and so they were undeterred in their organizing against the dump. We carried signs, we mailed letters (our upper school has two hundred and fifty kids, and two hundred sent letters; the little kids drew pictures), we assembled statistics, we met once a week to talk to each other.

The anger was about some of the usual concerns, like big trucks day and night, like noise, like odor. But an awful lot of it came from loving the land on which we live—not loving it in an abstract sense, but knowing it, gathering berries on it, cutting some logs on raise our eggs, meat, and vegetables, tap the sugar maples, harvest firewood, and rear our pets and children on the land. They told us we shouldn't worry because they weren't actually taking our homes. But my home doesn't just go to the walls and then stop. That land is my home." And then the Reverend Daisy Allen stood up. She is a Pentecostal Holiness minister, one of nine children (all named for local flowers) who grew up on one of the proposed dump sites, and though she is not feeling as well now as once she did, she has made a life's work of attending the dying, comforting the sick, providing for the hungry. She writes a weekly column for the local paper, the comings and goings on her road mixed with the new flowers in bloom or the birds that have arrived. "There's a beaver dam there," she said, "that's played a large part in giving beauty and a place for fish. Will the beaver lose their home? Will the fish die? . . . There's no florist in Baker's Mills, but will we lose or find endangered our trillium, our wild oats, our yellow, blue, and white violets? Will we lose our mayflowers and buttercups, and daisies and dandelions, cowslips, and adder's-tongue? Will the beauty of the apple blossom and pear trees be gone forever? Where will we pick our northern spies, our maidenblush, crabapples, yellow transparents, dutchesses? I just wonder how many people even know these apples." In this dark place, she said, "I can walk the country roads at midnight, able to see by moonlight. I study the Bible, and I'd like to give you an illustration from it. Naboth had a vineyard close to the palace of Ahab, king of Samaria. Ahab said to Naboth, 'Give me thy vineyard that I may have it for a garden of herbs. It's near my house. I'll give thee a better vineyard, or I'll give you money for it.' Naboth refused, because his father had had it. But Ahab pretended sickness, and his wife came in and said, 'Why don't you eat?' He said, 'I can't, because Naboth won't let me have the land I want.' And wicked Queen Jezebel said, 'Why are you so sad? Isn't it within your power and jurisdiction to take whatever you want, no matter whose it is?' And she wrote letters in Ahab's name—sealed with his name. And Naboth was stoned to his death.

Jezebel heard of his death and said to Ahab, 'Go take possession; Naboth is dead.' And he went to take possession, but God spoke through his prophets and said, 'Where Naboth's blood has been licked by the dogs, so will yours be licked.'" And the $150-an-hour guys sitting in the back of the room in their loafers didn't say a word.

And we won. What do you know. It turned out that once the regional agency rejected the landfill, the county found out it needed a lot less space—ten or twenty acres, maybe. And the county next door was already building its own oversized monstrosity of a dump, and it turned out they were desperate to rent space in it for a fraction of what it would have cost to build our own, and the consultants went to work on that. And the mountain is more or less fine.

Not totally. Smaller things happen all the time. A new summer house here, a shabby logging job there, and things are always harder to fight when they aren't so clear-cut. But basically we won. There is *nothing* ignoble about protecting your backyard as long as it's the backyard you're protecting, as long as you're part and parcel of your backyard. Not once that whole long winter of debate did I hear anyone use the phrase "property values." (Not true. I used it, thinking it might summon us some allies. But of course I didn't grow up here.) The chance to protect your own ecosystem, your own watershed, your own navel of the world—that's ten times more awesome a thing even than the chance to protect the rain forest.

Here's a poem from Jeanne Robert Foster about this mountain:

> *How can I lift my mountain before your eyes,*
> *Tear it out of my heart, my hands, my sinews,*
> *Lift it before you—its trees, its rocks,*
> *Its thrust heavenward;*
> *The basic cliffs, the quartz of the outcrop,*
> *The wide water in the cup of the lower summit,*

*The high peak lifting above the timberline*
*Gathering the mist of fifty lakes at sunrise;*
*The waterfall tumbling a thousand feet,*
*White with foam, white with rock-flower in summer;*
*The wreathing of dark spruce and hemlock,*
*The blood splashes of mountain ash,*
*The long spur to the north golden with poplars;*
*A porcupine drinking, bending without fear*
*To his image?*

*When darkness shall be my home,*
Eternal mountain, do not leave my heart;
Remain with me in my sleep,
In my dreams, in my resurrection.

It did not feel to me like we were taking care of the mountain, protecting it. It felt like the mountain had nourished us when we needed it, and we were doing only what was natural—as if the boundaries between people and mountains were not so rigid; as if the real divide had us and the mountain and the trillium and the beaver on one side and the guys in the loafers on the other.

As we were leaving that meeting, one of those fellows snapped shut the locks on his briefcase, looked up at me, and said, "We think it would be more mature if you guys didn't deal with this on such a personal level. We try to keep things on a professional basis." Of course you do, I thought. But for once in my life I'm not going to be cowed by the abstract. Tonight I'm glad it's on a personal level. Tonight, in the neighborly shadow of the mountain, I'm reasonably proud of being a person.

## · 35 ·

# Taking to the Streets:
# Report from the WTO

—TomPaine.com, November 30, 1999

The metaphor is irresistible. Between eight and ten this morning in downtown Seattle, Washington, the protesters owned the streets. Later in the day, they vied with police, back and forth; but as the day began the cops were back inside their perimeters, and the few thousand drumming, singing demonstrators were firmly in control. And so, as delegates began to arrive for the opening session of the WTO summit, they found the usual order of things completely reversed.

These people—elites from almost every nation on the planet—couldn't get through the cordon of linked-arm demonstrators blocking every intersection and entrance. When they tried, they were politely refused: "the WTO is closed today." A platinum card didn't help, nor an official title, nor the self-assured manner of those born to power. People beating on drums, people dressed like butterflies, simply turned them away.

The delegates huddled in small knots along the street, easy to pick out by their clothes: they were the ones in suits, ties, dresses, not the ones in ponchos, war paint, bandanas. They couldn't get where they were going, they couldn't do their work, and they couldn't quite believe it. A few of them panicked; "protect us at once," a man demanded of a police officer at the edge of the crowd, and indeed he was hustled away in a police car. But most of them just stood, bewildered or bemused, and eventually drifted away.

They'll be back tomorrow, of course, and they'll eventually have their meeting. However, and it's a big however, the era when global trade decisions get made without anyone noticing is officially over. That's the metaphor this day provides: in just the same way that activists managed to shut down the work of this summit, so too activists around the globe are learning to use the Internet and many other tools to slow down and confuse the rush to globalization.

Late last week, American agricultural organizations warned U.S. farmers not to plant genetically modified crops next spring, for fear they'd have no markets; they have no markets because the very same people who were marching through Seattle today have managed to convince most Europeans to demand actual food. It's a different world. At least a little different, anyway.

At 10 A.M., the regular order tried to reassert its authority. The police had grown tired of people blocking the intersection of Union and Sixth. And so they converged from two sides. From behind, looking Vaderish in black ponchos and gas masks, they shot tear gas and rubber bullets. From in front, looking storm trooperish in riot visors and full body armors, they wielded batons. People retreated before the charge; one of the few uses of serious force against unarmed, peaceful civil disobedients in recent American history.

A small tank rolled in to claim the corner. But the police were left with an intersection and not much more. Delegates couldn't make it through the clouds of pepper spray which lingered in the air, burning eyes and filling lungs. And before long the protesters were back, this time with arms chained through PVC pipe. And that was just one intersection; there were half a dozen other corners where the same kind of battle was under way.

A few bands of balaclava-clad anarchists did circulate up and down the street, causing mild mayhem: broken windows here and there. But most of the crowd was peaceful, brave, and remarkably upbeat even after the police charges. There was little anger, and little fear—and a wave of good feeling when word began to spread that indeed the few delegates that had gotten through to the convention center were packing up and going home for the day.

Posters and T-shirts celebrated a hundred related causes: the redwood groves of northern California, the people of Tibet, the sea turtles whose slaughter the WTO had officially condoned, the Zapatista rebels of Chiapas, the Industrial Workers of the World. "Eat Local Organic Food," "Stop Nigerian Genocide," "Visualize a World Full of Soul-Sucking Parasites," and best of all: "Wake Up, Muggles!"

Easy enough to dismiss them as a disparate group of unlikely campaigns, but easier still to see how they fit together—to sense a celebration of the local, the particular, the magic, the democratic, here in the shadow of a giant Niketown, a glass headquarters for sweatshop wages and homogenized taste. As corporations and bureaucracies get bigger, they simultaneously get more powerful and more vulnerable. That's the gut feeling I'll take home from the pepper-sprayed streets of Seattle. Here's a way to understand what I mean: ask yourself what city is going to volunteer to host the next meeting of the WTO.

I talked to a delegate from Jamaica early this morning, in the hours when the police had vanished, leaving them alone to face the demonstrators. He was on the steps of the Sheraton, where a line of singing young people had blocked his access. What do you make of it all, I asked him. He thought for a minute, thought hard, groped for a word, then for another. "I find it very interesting," he finally said. Exactly right, I thought. The world is a more interesting place than it was yesterday.

# · 36 ·

## Patriotic Acts

—*Mother Jones*, November/December 2000

Because the town common stood athwart the route toward the colonial militia's arms dump; because John Hancock and Sam Adams were staying in the town's parsonage; because the redcoats were slow leaving Boston and hence lost the cover of darkness— because of these happenstances, Lexington, Massachusetts, the town where I grew up, never quite manages the pure and untainted self-satisfaction of other modern American suburbs. Mini-mansions crowd its subdividing lots, and its luxe schools register ever higher test scores. But the Battle Green, a few acres of lawn near the town center that you pass on the way to the Stop & Shop, poses a quiet question about that suburban comfort. Eight men died here. A war that gave birth to a new nation with a new idea began here. It is the same gentle yet insistent interrogation that American history in general poses to the rich, smug moment in which we live. It has something to do with what it means to be a patriot. And after a year that's seen major disruptions in Seattle, outside the World Bank in Washington, D.C., and in the political convention cities, it's a question worth trying to hear through the noise of the now.

When I was eleven, and my dad was forty-two, the Vietnam Veterans Against the War announced plans to camp overnight on the Battle Green—"the birthplace of American liberty"—as part of their campaign to end the fighting in Southeast Asia. Local law prohibited late-night loitering on that hallowed ground, but on the evening of the demonstration the town's selectmen scheduled a meeting to decide whether the rule would be enforced. I remember driving to the meeting in the back of the family Plymouth—downtown was oddly deserted and quiet, except for the ominous rumbling pops from the motorcycles of vets arriving early for the encampment. They were hippies, most of them, or so I believed—I had seen a number of hippies hanging around Harvard Square, and these looked about as hairy and unauthorized.

Town Hall was jammed. The good liberal residents, who had moved to Lexington in the last decade in search of schools for their children, were out in force, hissing at the town selectmen, mostly lifelong Lexingtonians who sold real estate or funerals or nursing home beds. By a bare majority the selectmen voted to authorize the arrest of the demonstrators, and when they did, those good liberals flooded out of the hall and down the road to the green.

Night had fallen by now. In the dark, circles of vets and residents coalesced, lit by cigarette glow or flashlight. Rumors swept through: The police were coming. No, the National Guard was coming. The night crackled.

At ten or eleven, Mom took me and my brother home to bed—school the next day, after all, and that is why we were in Lexington too—but Dad stayed behind. A mild, churchgoing business reporter, he had made up his mind to stay. He might not have traveled somewhere else to protest the war, but the strife had come to his town, and he—and hundreds other of those good local liberals—were willing to make a stand. By the time we woke up, he was back home, with stories of the holding pen where they'd been taken, booked, fined, released. I don't remember the details, but I do remember how proud I was—am still—of his decision. And I remember the glamour of that evening. Something untoward—angry, sexy, zealous, tough, righteous—had happened in this place that, like all suburbs, devoted itself to keeping the untoward at bay.

The following summer, wearing a tricorne hat, I took my own place on the green. Along with mall clerking and Kentucky frying, Lexington offered its youth a unique opportunity for summer earnings: conducting tours of the green for the tourists who arrived, busload after busload, all day long. A kindly old Episcopal priest administered the test and signed your guide's license, offering you the right to sit on the guide's bench and play endless rounds of Risk while waiting for your turn in the rotation. When it came, you needed to spiel speedily or else your busload might be summoned back aboard its coach before you had the chance to pass your hat and collect your pay. As a result, the normal singsong drone of a tour guide was married to the slightly desperate rush of an auctioneer. Most of the tourists really wanted to know the location of the nearest toilet. Most of the time I really wanted to flirt with the girl guides, who looked cuter in their tricorne hats than could reasonably be expected.

Still, four or five times a day, summer after summer, I'd tell the stories: the oldest man on the green, Jonas Parker, who knelt over his hat full of musket balls, bayoneted before he could get off a second shot; Jonathan Harrington, mortally wounded in the first volley, who crawled a hundred yards to his front doorstep where he died in the arms of his wife. These were not isolated, cranky, ideological Ruby Ridge don't-tread-on-me outcasts: about every man in Lexington belonged to that company of minutemen; almost every family in town suffered some casualty. When news of the fight spread, similar companies poured in from every surrounding town. The Lexington militia had a captain—John Parker—but he was an elected captain, who consulted with his neighbors. They all believed in the most basic ideas of democracy: that power could grow big and remote. They were proto-Americans.

And so my sense of what it might mean to love your country

formed on that Battle Green, equal parts fatigue-clad Vietnam vet and musket-toting farmer. Community, courage, rebelliousness, adolescent lust, all bled together in my head.

As of the year 2000, even through the novocaine of prosperity, most Americans can feel that something is out of kilter. Most clearly, money now drives politics in more fundamental ways with each election, each legislative session. That feeling underlies the general enthusiasm for, say, John McCain, and the general lack of enthusiasm for politics in general. Flush and busy, we've not yet gotten angry, but we will. And we'll do something about it eventually, take one of those strides in the direction of democracy that mark our history. It's starting. We're stirring.

Granny D tells this truth better than anyone else at the moment. In the spring of 1999, not long after she'd finished her solo march, at age ninety, across the nation to demand campaign finance reform, I listened to this New Hampshire grandmother. We were outside the Capitol in Washington, and some of the schoolkids waiting in line recognized her—her picture had just been in *Time for Kids,* with her reflective orange vest designed to protect her from traffic and advertise her Web site (www.grannyd.com). In a flash she had gathered perhaps a hundred high schoolers around for an impromptu teach-in on what was wrong with our politics (corporate control) and how it could be fixed (public financing of campaigns). The kids listened transfixed. "She could have finished that walk in nine months," her son Jim said as he watched. "But it took fourteen because she never walked away from a question."

The reason Granny D and I were outside the Capitol that morning is that we planned on getting arrested. Along with a couple of dozen other people organized by the Alliance for Democracy, we wanted to protest the links between campaign finance corruption and environmental destruction. Our plan was to wait in line, get tickets, blend in with the crowd until we were inside the rotunda, and then unfurl our banners. A savvy plot, except that the protest organizers also wanted us to hold a press conference on the Capitol lawn before we went indoors, which sort of blew our cover. Fortunately, the Capitol Hill police, who seemed interested in order above all, took matters in hand, and after we'd preached for the cameras they marched us into the rotunda for an on-time arrest. There, in short order, we pulled out our sign that said "Stop Global Warming: Ban Campaign Contributions from Global Warmers," shouted a few spirited sentences that were lost in the room's lofty acoustics, and then were arrested and led out in handcuffs to a waiting bus. The high schoolers still waiting in line chanted, "Don't Arrest Granny D," as we drove away, their heroine waving her cuffed hands cheerfully out the window. It took a few hours to process us, and then we were back on the street, clutching slips of paper with the date and courtroom for our trials. C-Span aired our demonstration, and *All Things Considered* carried a nice piece, but all in all it was no big deal. The world retained its composure.

Still, the demonstration and arrest meant a good deal to me, my first official legal trouble at the age of thirty-nine, right about the same age that my father too had decided to lay down his cloak of journalistic objectivity and take a stand. This scene was almost as good as the Battle Green—we had been arrested directly in front of a splendid painting, one of four huge canvases of the Revolutionary era that dominate the rotunda. There were obvious scenes: the Continental Congress signing the Declaration of Independence, Burgoyne surrendering at Saratoga, and Cornwallis giving up at Yorktown. But the painting that served as our backdrop was less dramatic at first glance. It showed Washington resigning his commission before Congress in December of 1783, once the war was safely over.

To understand the great significance of that scene requires a little lore, mostly forgotten now. When hostilities with Britain ceased, Congress kept the army intact. But the loose confederation of states lacked the authority to levy taxes and hence couldn't pay the troops. Many of the officers faced ruin if they returned home—their affairs had been neglected during the struggle, and debtor's prison was a possibility for some. In such a dangerous vacuum, little wonder that many officers grew restive, almost treasonous. In the fall of 1783, some of them held a meeting to try to draft Washington as a sort of military emperor. The mutineers were numerous, and they gathered in a hall in Newburgh, New York, one evening to advance their plot. Washington attended, and told them he was dead set against such sedition. But his address failed to completely turn the grim-faced tide. He reached into his coat pocket to fish out a letter from a congressman, hoping it would sway sentiment. He held it at arm's length, twisted and turned it—and then reached into another pocket for a pair of glasses. "Gentlemen, you will permit me to put on my spectacles, for I have not only grown gray, but almost blind, in the service of my country," he said. That small aside from a man not given to self-pity was sufficient to remind his listeners of the hardships they had nobly endured together, none more than their general, and it reduced many of the officers to tears. They barely listened as he read the letter, so eager were they now to vote a repudiation of the whole scheme.

"This was probably the most important single gathering ever held in the United States," historian James Thomas Flexner wrote. Indeed, for had it gone the other way this nation would have been founded on different principles in a different spirit, a mutation of our political chromosome in the direction of concentrated power that would have warped everything that came after. Later that year Washington resigned his commission, in the great scene before which our tiny, echoing drama now played out.

The onescore and twelve of us gathered again a few weeks later in D.C. Superior Court for our trial. Judge Eugene Hamilton, chief judge of the court, presided—he was an African-American, and his very presence was something of a testimony to the tides of the nation's history. But he appeared stern—the case before ours involved a local woman who failed to appear because, according to her lawyer, she needed to take care of her children. The judge studied the probation report, noted no mention of her children, and issued a bench warrant for her apprehension.

Then he turned to us, all white, well scrubbed, and ready to plead guilty. Did we understand, he asked, that the charge of "demonstrating inside the Capitol" carried a possible penalty of six months in jail and a $500 fine? Yes, we said, somberly. Had we been promised any deals by any prosecutor? No, we said truthfully. And then he invited us to say what we would—to "make our allocutions"—before he rendered a sentence.

Granny D led us once again, speaking in the clearly enunciated tones of someone who took her schooling in a different era. She'd reached her tenth decade without legal trouble, she said, adding, "I do care what my neighbors think about me." But, she declared, "this old woman who stands before you was arrested for reading the Declaration of Independence in America's Capitol building. I shudder to think what might have happened had I read from the Bill of Rights." Perhaps, she continued, the judge was concerned that "we might have been blocking the halls of our government. Let me assure you we stood to one side of the rotunda where we would not be in anyone's way. But the halls are indeed blocked over there. They're blocked by the shameless sale of public policy to campaign contributors." She called it bribery—said she hoped to see the day when "lobbyists and elected officials were dragged from the Capitol building and the White House, their wrists tied, not ours. If that happened, I would be home in New Hampshire, happily applauding the television news." Piss and vinegar, in other words, completely firm but always polite.

And what was anyone going to say to her? She was ninety years old, she'd walked all the way from Los Angeles, and she was right. And what was anyone going to say to those who followed her? To Anna Hargis, a cheerful registered nurse who had run for Georgia public service commissioner to expose corrupt deals allowing unsafe gas pipelines, and along the way managed to collect 45 percent of the vote. To John Friedrich, who runs a nonprofit in D.C. that grows organic food and opens farmers' markets in poor areas, but who was sick of watching environmentalists outgunned by industry in one congressional vote after another. Or to Gayle Davidson, from rural western Massachusetts, who works with abused children one by one but would like Congress to do something about the fact that a fifth of our kids live below the poverty line. Or to the three or four of us there who had been working on global warming issues for a decade—writing books, making speeches, organizing movements. In Europe such efforts had begun to work, but here, even though scientists had long since reached a consensus on the scariness of the problem, any action was blocked by the power of the coal and car lobbyists on the Hill. Our impotence—the impotence that led us to stand in the rotunda with a cheesy vinyl sign—could be measured in every cubic meter of air.

The new political rhetoric of the mainstream is entirely about individuals, about our individual prosperity. When the right wing took Congress, what did they propose? A *contract* with America. The night of our sentencing, a few blocks down the street at the basketball arena, President Clinton was hosting his last big fundraiser, raking in over $26 million from corporations and lobbyists. And pretending, by wearing blue jeans, eating barbecue, and listening to country and western stars, that the evening was about real people.

But this phase of, in essence, using the country for our own individual ends, allowing ourselves to be bought off by economic prosperity, is passing already, the first symptoms of its mortal illness appearing in the streets of Seattle. The problems are too real for it not to: the encroaching power of global corporations, the looming questions of environment and health and justice that can't be solved within the politics that now exists. The pull of American history—the pull against concentrated power—is too strong. Or so one must hope. There are fledgling movements to control corporations so the next generation of American kids doesn't take up smoking, to keep half of Africa from dying of AIDs in the name of drug company profits, to stabilize the temperature of the planet, to free our campaigns from the taint of private cash. And right now they fall under the category of patriotic duty.

When we'd finished testifying in court that day, Judge Hamilton, who had paid close attention to everyone's words, cleared his throat. "All right," he said. "As you know, the strength of our great country lies in its Constitution and its laws, in her institutions and in her courts." Our hearts sank just a little; he sounded fierce.

But, he continued, "more fundamentally, the strength of our great country lies in the resolve of her citizens to stand up for what is right when the masses are silent. And unfortunately sometimes it becomes the lot of the few, sometimes like yourselves, to stand up for what's right when the masses are silent because not always does the law move so fast and so judiciously as to always be right. But given the resolve of the citizens of this great country, in time, however slowly, the law will catch up. So it becomes my lot to apply the law as it is at this time. Perhaps not as it should be but as it is. With every confidence that to the extent that it is lacking in righteousness, it will reach that point eventually given the resolve of her citizens to make it right."

We were sentenced to time served—our afternoon in the police station—and we were sent home, back out into our various Americas. A very small part of the very long chain that stretches back at least to the Battle Green, and—with any luck—forward into the always murky future.

# The Muslim Gandhi

—*DoubleTake*, special edition, December 2001

The story that follows may be no more than a curiosity—an outlier in the data. Since I am not a scholar of Islam or Afghanistan, I cannot judge, although it fits with little else we've heard in the news recently. I first came across it many years ago, and had forgotten it until the events of September 11, but since that time it has rattled around in my brain. The story concerns the Muslims of the Afghan-Pakistan border, a people with whom we suddenly find ourselves intimately engaged, but who are more remote to us than almost any other on earth.

In 1890, in the village called Utmanzai, not far from the Khyber Pass, a boy named Abdul Ghaffar Khan was born. The son of a prosperous landowner, he grew to be six foot three, a powerful and proud Pashtun tribesman, a devout Muslim. And he also grew to become, along with his dear friend Gandhi, one of the greatest nonviolent leaders of the twentieth century. At one point, his unarmed Islamic "army," the Khudai Khidmatgars, or Servants of God, numbered one hundred thousand men. Many of these "soldiers" died at the hands of the British rather than resorting to violence. In doing so, they contributed enormously to the breaking of the imperial powers' will.

Though we've often heard lately that the British and the Soviet empires both came to grief in Afghanistan, the fact is that the British ruled the region they called the Northwest Frontier for more than a century. Their reign was always uneasy—the Pashtun, or the Pathans as the British called them, were tough, and the British were nasty. The commander of the Punjab Frontier Force sent this dispatch back to London in 1859:

> To have to carry destruction, if not destitution, into the homes of some hundreds of families is the great drawback of border warfare, but with savage tribes, to whom there is no right but might, the only course open as regards humanity as well as policy, is to make all suffer. . . . In short, civilized warfare is inapplicable.

Punitive expedition after expedition burned valley after valley, year after year, but never managed to stamp out resistance.

This was the world into which Ghaffar Khan was born. His father, though devout, sent him to a Christian mission school, where the boy did well. The young Khan was about to join the Pathan Guides, an elite infantry corps with a long history of service to the empire. In short, he was going to attain the highest position he could in his colonial world. But the day before his enlistment, according to his biographer Eknath Easwaran, he heard a British officer insult one of the enlisted Pathans, disrespect he could not tolerate. He also decided against traveling to England to study engineering, turning down a scholarship offer from the missionaries. Instead, he opened a small school in his village, farmed his family land, and began to circulate in progressive Muslim circles, meeting with others who wanted to modernize Pashtun life.

Evading British checkpoints and patrols, he began wandering in the hills to the north—a district under such strict military rule that any Pathan who didn't bow low enough before an Englishman was locked in stocks. He walked from town to town, reopening schools closed by the British, meeting always with village elders and with the poorest people in town. Easwaran also insists that at some time in these years, after a period of fasting in an isolated mosque, he had some kind of religious experience akin to Francis's awakening at San Damiano:

> Islam! Inside him the word began to explode with meaning. Islam! Submit! Surrender to the Lord and know His strength.

Something gave him enormous drive. Between 1915 and 1918, he visited each of the five hundred villages in the settled districts of the frontier. As he learned more about the nonviolent campaign that Gandhi had begun in India, he began to see his work as a campaign for freedom as well as moral and material uplift. And just as the Hindus had begun to call Gandhi "Mahatma," the Muslims of the frontier started to proclaim Ghaffar the "Badshah Khan," or "King of Khans." Thus it wasn't long before the British arrested him for the first time, a practice they continued throughout the next decades with predictable results: with each release, his reputation grew greater.

By 1929, he had met Gandhi for the first time and heard him speak about the need for a "nonviolence of the strong." Khan returned home to urge more social reforms on his fellow Pashtun. "You have all heard of America and Europe," he told them. "The people in those countries may not be very religious, but they have a sense of patriotism, love for their nation, and social progress. And look at the progress that has been made there. Then take a look at ourselves! We have hardly learned to stand on our own feet yet!" But those could have been the words of any reforming nationalist politician of the age. Khan was much more—a deeply spiritual man who thought Gandhi's nonviolence resonated strongly with his own Islam, especially the orthodox understanding of a "jihad" against one's own weaknesses and temptations. To his mind, the great weakness of the Pashtun was their obsessive attention to honor and revenge between different clans, producing an endless cycle of revenge killing that the British easily exploited. In response, Khan formed the Khudai Khidmatgars—a real army, with uniforms and officers and flags and even a bagpipe corps, and perhaps the strangest oath any army had ever taken:

> I promise to refrain from violence and taking revenge.
> I promise to forgive those who oppress me or treat me
> with cruelty.

They began by wearing simple white overshirts, but drilling and marching soon dirtied them. The residue from the local tannery turned out to be perfect for turning shirts a deep brick red, however, and so the Red Shirts, as the British called them, were born. Aside from being unpaid, the army's members also pledged to volunteer at least two hours a day building schools and helping with community projects. Women joined as well as men. Units took long treks into the hills, and as they marched they sang:

> We are the army of God,
> By death or wealth unmoved.
> We march, our leader and we,
> Ready to die.

As it turned out, they had organized just in time, for in 1950 Gandhi touched off history's most massive campaign of civil disobedience when he made salt at the beach in Dandi. Almost immediately, people across the subcontinent joined the salt satyagraha, a Boston tea party multiplied by a million. The British went berserk at this open contempt for their rule—they arrested a hundred thousand people, eventually including Gandhi, shut down newspapers, raided Congress Party offices, beat unarmed crowds. But in the Northwest Frontier, far from the attention of the world, things were darker still.

In April, Ghaffar Khan, in a mass meeting in his hometown, urged Pashtuns to join in the civil resistance sweeping India. He set off for Peshawar to make the same plea, but was arrested en route. Thousands of demonstrators surrounded the jail, remaining nonviolent while their leader was sent off to a three-year jail sentence in India.

Khan's lieutenants in Peshawar were arrested as well, and again a large crowd formed there too, in the Kissa Khani bazaar. According to all accounts, they had begun to drift away when two or three British armored cars arrived and drove into the throng, killing several. Instead of dispersing, the protesters paused to gather their dead. Annoyed, the British began firing. Gene Sharp, a longtime nonviolence researcher at Harvard's Center for International Affairs, perhaps tells the story best:

> When those in front fell down wounded by the shots, those behind came forward with their breasts bared and exposed themselves to the fire, so much so that some people got as many as twenty-one bullet wounds in their bodies, and all the people stood their ground without getting into a panic. . . . The crowd kept standing at the spot facing the soldiers and were fired at from time to time, until there were heaps of wounded and dying lying about. This state of things continued from eleven till five o'clock in the evening. When the number of corpses became too many the ambulance cars of the government took them away and burned them.

Imagine Kent State, but not just for thirty seconds. For the whole damn day. And remember that this restraint came after a lifetime of savage repression by the British—year after year of fear and humiliation on a scale that we can hardly imagine, even in the wake of September 11.

At one point, the British ordered native soldiers, the Garhwal Rifles, to open fire. When these crack troops refused to shoot unarmed people, the entire platoon was court-martialed—and a chill went down the spine of the empire, for the system could not tolerate mutiny of that sort. The British themselves had fewer scruples, and set themselves to breaking the nonviolent campaign with a series of fierce provocations, carried out in complete secrecy since all journalists had been banned from the province.

The same commander who had opened fire in the bazaar led eight hundred troops on Khan's hometown, where they beat the nonresisting Khidmatgars and then stripped the red shirts off their bodies before burning and looting the village. In Easwaran's account, after all the volunteers had been beaten and arrested, the commander bellowed, "Any more Red Shirts?" One old man ran home, daubed paint on his clothes, and ran back into the street. "Here's one," he shouted. And he was not alone. By summer's end almost a hundred thousand had taken the oath, even though they were routinely flogged, stripped, even tossed into cesspools. An American tourist who passed through noted that "gunning the Red Shirts" was a popular pastime for the officers.

And yet the nonviolence held as it did throughout India, and against it, British will quickly crumbled. In a matter of months, the colonial authorities officially recognized Gandhi and his movement for the first time, inviting him in for negotiations that led to the Gandhi-Irwin Pact. (In the words of Winston Churchill, it was "the nauseating and humiliating spectacle of this . . . seditious fakir striding half-naked up the steps of the viceroy's palace, there to negotiate and to parley on equal terms with the representative of the king-emperor.") Among other concessions, this agreement granted a limited self-rule to the frontier for the first time; in retrospect, the pact really began the decade-long countdown to independence for all of British India.

That decade gave Khan and Gandhi time to become close friends. Whenever the British, who remained very much in power, exiled him from the frontier, Khan would settle at Gandhi's ashram. Picture after picture shows them sitting side by side, Gandhi chanting from the Gita at prayer meetings, Khan following with passages from the Koran, sometimes borrowing Gandhi's glasses when he had forgotten his own. And in a period of relative calm, when the British allowed it, first Nehru and then Gandhi came to visit Khan beneath the Khyber Pass.

Gandhi, in fact, recalled his visit as one of the most moving trips of his life, for instead of the thronging, screaming crowds that greeted him in India, tens of thousands Pashtuns lined the streets of Peshawar in their red shirts, smiling but absolutely silent. In talk after talk he urged them to carry their nonviolence even further. He told them not just to control their anger, but to aim for "the complete eradication of anger from the heart," adding, "A person who has known God will be incapable of harboring anger or fear within him, no matter how overpowering the cause for it may be."

It is hard to imagine this tiny Hindu exhorting the Pashtun to even greater toughness, but then the whole business is hard to imagine. Clearly Gandhi felt as if he was among the few people in the world able even to begin to absorb his message, and the fact that they were from different civilizations seemed to matter little. At each stop, says Easwaran, "some Pathan would stand before the assembly, red-shirted and eager, and tell the Mahatma what he meant to the Pathan nation. 'We can never forget the debt we owe to you,' one burly Pathan said at Mardan, 'for having stood with us in our stricken plight. We are ignorant, we are poor—but we lack nothing because you have taught us the lesson of nonviolence.'"

Their nonviolence did not flag in the last years before independence, not even when Khan was beaten and arrested one last time. In some ways, the greatest tests came as the end of British rule drew near and communal violence wracked the country. Gandhi and Khan wandered the entire subcontinent, sometimes apart and sometimes together, pleading with people to stop the killing. In India's Bihar province, they drove from village to village, Gandhi napping with his feet on Khan's lap. At prayer meetings they would read from each other's scriptures—locally it worked to suppress the hatred, but everywhere around them violence kept flaring up.

And when independence arrived, partition came with it. Both Gandhi and Khan boycotted the celebrations; for them, the price of freedom was too high. Pakistan, for Gandhi, meant an end to his dream of Muslim-Hindu unity. For Khan it meant not only that—it meant that the Pathans had traded British rule for rule from Karachi. Their territory was divided between Pakistan and Afghanistan, despite his pleas for some kind of Pashtun autonomy. Within a few years, the new authorities had placed him in jail; indeed, by the time he died, in 1988 at the age of ninety-seven, he'd spent as many years in Pakistani jails as British ones.

I have no idea what residue remains of the Khudai Khidmatgars—it's even harder to spot from a distance than the residue of Gandhi's life in the politics of India. Certainly Khan's ideas on the emancipation of women—"In the Holy Koran you have an equal share with men. You are today oppressed because we men have ignored the commands of God and the Prophet. . . . If we achieve success we solemnly promise you that you will get your rights"—seem to have withered instead of grown. The nonviolent creed didn't survive the Soviet incursion, or the other events of the years that followed.

Khan and the Khudai Khidmatgars may all be mere anomaly, suggesting nothing in the way of strategy or approach. "That such men would have laid down their arms and accepted nonviolence as the superior weapon sounds almost like a fairy tale," wrote Gandhi once. And yet it did happen. It is, at the least, a curious piece of data to add to our stock about Islam, about Afghanistan and Pakistan, and perhaps about human nature as well.

· 38 ·

# Speaking Up for the Environment

—*The Washington Post Book World,* April 22, 2001

I'm writing these words on a plane home from Washington, D.C. From a Washington press conference, to be precise, where I was answering questions, making arguments: drilling in the Arctic National Wildlife Refuge must be prevented, we desperately need a new energy policy, and so on. It didn't knock hoof-and-mouth disease off the evening news, but I was giving it my best shot. And all the while I was wondering, have I turned from a writer into a hack?

In an earlier life, I was on the other side of the microphone. As a newspaperman, as a "Talk of the Town" reporter for the old *New Yorker*, I went to hundreds of press conferences and held my tape recorder up in the air, shouted my share of questions. In a slightly later life, I wrote books and long essays—alone in my study, alone in my thoughts, slogging my way through the long, silent process of putting words to paper. That's still my "job," I guess, and I relish it. I savor the chance to read and ponder and most of all to set words down and make my own stabs at beauty and meaning. The trouble is, my books are about controversial topics, in particular the largest environmental problems like global warming. My reporting and reflecting have left me with a definite point of view. And more and more that point of view seems to lead me out of my study and into another world that operates by different rules.

I knew how it was supposed to work: people would read my words and demand change from their leaders, and that would be that. (I was, perhaps it's worth mentioning, twenty-seven when I wrote my first book.) The model, I suppose, was Rachel Carson and *Silent Spring*. And in fact, people did read my books. *The End of Nature* was translated into twenty languages, excerpted in dozens of magazines and newspapers. But things didn't go according to plan. The world didn't change. In fact, for the last decade, even as the science of climate change has grown endlessly more robust, our country in particular has done next to nothing about it. We burn more fossil fuel than we did a decade ago, we block international treaties, we are nothing short of a rogue nation when it comes to global warming. Yet nobody seems too exercised about it all. We go on going on—in the years since I published *The End of Nature* we've transformed our everyday fleet from cars to semimilitary vehicles. So what is a writer supposed to do? What are any of us who write about the natural world supposed to do, at a moment when it is under constant and sapping siege from every direction? How loud are you supposed to shout?

It's a hard question for a writer, and not just because of the time and energy that any crusading takes, time and energy most of us would rather devote to, well, writing. More, there's the worry about what will happen if you start to take a public role. Will it cost you the crankiness and whimsy real writing demands? Will you start writing press releases or editorials when you think you're writing short stories or essays? Will you sacrifice the particular, the small, the funny, the idiosyncratic? Will you gloss over your misgivings, subscribe to some party line, listen only to the people whose side you're on? Add to that the worry that you'll lose your credibility with your readers (or your editors).

I came to Washington last year, too, came with the express but apprehensive purpose of getting arrested. It was late spring, and the Alliance for Democracy was sponsoring a small protest in the rotunda. A couple of dozen of us—including the wonderful Granny D, the ninety-year-old woman who had walked across the nation for campaign finance reform—were supposed to hold up signs demanding action on environmental issues. We had a training session the night before in a church basement, and everyone gathered into small groups to talk about what was making them most nervous. There might be violence, said one person. I might not be able to handle jail, said another. When it was my turn, I said: What if people decide I'm a hopeless partisan and stop taking seriously my writing about these subjects? What if they decide I'm a propagandist, not a real writer?

At root, we think of writers as observers. Activists can write, of course, but they're activists using writing as one tool in their kit. Real, serious Writer Writers look on—whether it's from novels or from newspaper columns. They can hold strong opinions, write powerful op-eds, but they tell us what is happening, what should happen. They themselves aren't supposed to "happen." The subspecies "journalist," from which I am descended, is in some fashion not supposed to become engaged in the world around him.

For a long time, though, I've found my literary fellowship among the nature writers. This genre may be America's strongest suit in contemporary letters, our most distinctive gift to world literature. (And it grows stronger all the time: the more our forests and fields and even our genes come under assault, the more the fresh voices emerge to tell a story.) It is a distinctive literary community, in part because it is tight-knit (and even loosely organized, through groups like the Orion Society); in part because it exists mostly outside the academy and hence is less divided by dialectic than other literary tribes. But it stands apart most profoundly because it and its members don't just write about the natural world; they vote with their words—they defend it.

There's Rick Bass, the novelist, essayist, and champion of Montana wilderness, working to save the Yaak Valley. Wendell Berry, the Kentucky farmer and chronicler of the fictional town of Port William, who has been working to save family farming for decades. Terry Tempest Williams, the Utah writer and wilderness activist. W. S. Merwin, the Hawaiian poet and rain forest protector. Richard Nelson, the Alaska writer who has worked for years to save the Tongass National Forest from clearcutting. And so on and on and on.

First and foremost they are writers—people who sense the world and describe it, as powerfully as they can. Or maybe first and foremost they are guardians of the places and communities they love. Or maybe—very likely—the roles flip back and forth, enriching each other. For in the act of trying to save something—a forest, a mountain, the climate—you need to communicate with others, and to do that you need to look as hard and as carefully as you possibly can. The greatest of this writing is neither sentimental nor obvious—instead, it is very nearly shamanistic, allowing the natural world to translate itself into English in all sorts of ways. Emotional ways, taxonomic ways, descriptive ways, intimate ways, Olympian ways. It is a community of writers, with all the particulars of their upbringings, tastes, genders, mental states, seeking faithfully to serve as some sort of connection between people and the rest of the world. That faithfulness demands the most scrupulous accuracy—you have to know the tree's resilience, the coyote's circling route, the carbon molecule's structure. But it also demands that you care, which is the highest form of objectivity.

There is no way, in this kind of relationship, to escape a deep political involvement. If you make a visceral connection, one that takes you beyond the solipsism that is a writer's normal friend and enemy, then the defense of those places, those communities, is no longer optional. Not only would you lose the right to write about them, you'd lose the ability. That connection cannot be maintained at an emotional distance. You can defend a place without understanding it—that is sentimental hackwork, and there's plenty of it around. But you cannot understand a place without defending it. And if you understand one place . . . well, suffice it to say that everyone in the community of nature writers comes to each other's aid.

The press conference that brought me to D.C. marked the launch of a book of essays about the Arctic National Wildlife Refuge, assembled in six weeks' time by Alaskans Hank Lentfer and Carolyn Servid. The collection *Arctic Refuge: A Circle of Testimony* includes pieces from Barry Lopez and Scott Russell Sanders, John Haines, and Mardy Murie, a long, long list. Some of us had seen the wide coastal plain of the refuge, and some of us hadn't, but all of us were ready to write in its defense, and to talk, and perhaps do more if more was called for. Without that kind of commitment, my writing life wouldn't make much sense.

# A Last Best Chance for Baby Boomers

—*Orion Magazine*, November/December 2006

It's one of those givens that young people are determined and hotheaded and radical, whereas their elders have cooled off, made their compromises. Activism comes from college campuses, and that kind of energy disappears once kids and jobs are the order of the day.

Fair enough as a caricature. It's not always true, though. Gandhi was thirty-seven when he launched his first civil disobedience efforts in South Africa, and a good deal older than that before he began challenging the British in India. Rosa Parks was forty-two when she refused to give up her seat on the Montgomery bus. Martin Luther King Jr. was much younger when he agreed to lead the resulting boycott, but he was already pastor of a big church. Heck, Jesus was apparently in his thirties before he hit on his radical message and launched his organizing campaign.

I'm thinking this way because, for my money, the time has come for Americans to get much more insistent about climate change. And it seems to me that those of us with more gray hair and less gray matter may need to lead the charge.

The science couldn't be clearer: everything on earth is melting, and fast; sea level is threatening to rise far faster than earlier expected. We're sweating through the warmest year in American history. And after Katrina and the Gore film *An Inconvenient Truth,* polling shows that almost everyone not directly on the payroll of ExxonMobil now agrees that we've got a problem.

Which is not as encouraging as it might at first sound. Because most of political Washington is on the Exxon payroll, sucking contributions from all corners of the fossil fuel universe. If the GOP maintains control of Congress past November, House whip Roy Blunt (R, MO) has already promised that the 110th Congress will not do "anything meaningful" about climate change. But even if the Democrats unseat him, it's far from clear that they'll do very much. They could—there's actually good legislation in both houses, introduced by Representative Henry Waxman (D, CA) and Senator Jim Jeffords (I, VT). Far more likely, though, is some form of political erectile dysfunction—the McCain-Lieberman half-a-Kyoto bill, say, which was pretty limp when first introduced and which, in light of the ever darker science, now seems pointless. Worse than pointless, in fact, because if we sign on to a weak strategy now, all political will is likely to disappear for another few (fateful) years.

So the climate movement, which is what the environmental movement has mostly morphed into, needs to figure out how to push the pace of change.

Normally, as I said, you'd expect the youth to be the most militant activists. But that may not be the case here. It's not that they don't care—indeed the college movement against climate change is among the most sophisticated parts of the environmental effort at the moment. Late in summer 2005 its leaders convened at a New Hampshire prep school for the biggest summit yet, and it was truly impressive, albeit somewhat disorienting for people used to stereotyping student activists. These folks were as clean-cut and earnest as any high-achievers at good colleges across the country. There was almost no ego on display. Billy Parish, a Yale dropout who, as the organizer of Energy Action, is as close to a national leader as there is, doesn't even really give speeches; he just organizes breakout sessions, asks for comments, knits together the network. It's an Internet-age aesthetic, more chat room than political dais. Everyone has a MacBook; almost the first order of business is signing releases so that photographers can upload videos of the discussion sessions to YouTube. There's very little anger, almost no sarcasm. One organizer gets out his guitar, fires up his Dell laptop so he can see his lyrics, and says: "The only thing I like more than strategy is playing music that communicates strategy." His song, "Want Carbon Gone," includes the refrain:

> *School by school we'll set the way*
> *Clean energy future starts today.*

And indeed that's their plan. The Campus Climate Challenge, starting in the fall of 2006, aims to take a thousand college and high school campuses and point them toward zero emissions. Lightbulbs, carbon offsets, biodiesel shuttle buses—you name it, students will set the agenda, boards of trustees will agree, and before long there will be a thousand examples that everyone can see are working. "And when we're done," said one of the organizers, "we'll turn to the White House, the state capitols, and say, we've led the way, now you guys follow."

They're acting, you could say, like adults. Indeed, infinitely more like adults than our various political and corporate leaders who have just pushed this problem under the rug for twenty years now. And their approach clearly makes sense, both as a honey-not-vinegar tactic, and because, at least until the next president takes office, there's little to be done in Washington.

But I have a feeling that by itself it's only half the strategy. To win change I think we're going to need to speak out loudly enough so that politicians will have to listen. We'll have to raise the political cost of giving in to Exxon. And it's possible that we'll need to force the issue: to march, to sit in, to make it not just comfortable to do the right thing but morally uncomfortable to do wrong. One student at the gathering said, "Maybe we need a Malcolm X to make us look reasonable." In fact there's not even a Martin Luther King–level of outrage on this issue. We need the equivalent of lunch counter sit-ins, even as we need a plan to make the kitchen itself carbon neutral.

Militancy—even the nonviolent and entirely peaceful kind I'm talking about—carries risks. Say religious activists were sitting in at congressional offices, or college professors picketing SUV dealerships: it would scare, alarm, and anger some onlookers; it might polarize opinion that's trending in the right direction; it could seem nostalgic; it might become an end in itself. But it would say, "We're simply not going to stand by and watch you wreck the planet. We're going to stop you if we can, and by the way we'd like you to meet our young colleagues, who have the blueprints for the windmills and the specs for the high-efficiency boilers."

It would be entirely fitting if the angry troublemakers came from the ranks of those of us who are older. For one thing, we're the ones who caused the problem—if someone has to sit down on the tracks of the coal train and get arrested, it should be grandparents who've been pouring carbon into the atmosphere for half a century. In addition, many of us aren't as good at the details of the problem as the college kids—we don't know as much as they do about carbon offsets or tradable permits. But there's something else, too: the greatest moments in the lives of the baby boomers were precisely those times when they raised their voices, when they declared their selfless devotion to peace or civil rights. For too many, the decades that followed have made a quiet mockery of that earlier idealism. It turns out that we've excelled, most of all, at consuming. Now is the boomers' chance to reclaim their better, bolder natures and to end their run as it began.

# · VII ·

---

# TIME,
# MOVING,
# AND
# MEANING

# · 40 ·

## Homeless Men

—*The New Yorker,* December 27, 1982

The unnaturally balmy weather that New Yorkers so enjoyed in early December gave way suddenly about two weeks ago to a brittle, gusty cold snap. On Thursday, December 9, a series of three frontal systems, all from Canada, pushed across the city. By four o'clock that afternoon, the temperature had dropped below freezing—to thirty degrees—and, with the wind whistling in from the north-northwest at twenty-two miles per hour, it felt to anyone looking for a cab, or walking to a subway, or slumping drunk in a doorway, as if the temperature were just two degrees above zero. And by four o'clock that afternoon, as the light outside began to fail, New York's main intake center for homeless men, at 8 East Third Street, on the Bowery, was crowded to the point where men greatly outnumbered chairs.

Up the front steps of the shelter and to the right—past a man reading aloud from a Gideon New Testament and a man peddling loose Lucky Strikes for a nickel, and over two men sprawled asleep on the linoleum—was the end of a line that led, after a half-hour wait, to the records room of the shelter operation, known to the staff as "the five-by-eight office," for the size in inches of the index cards on which its data are kept. This is where men come who need meals and lodging at the city's expense. Those who came to the five-by-eight office window on December 9 traded some basic biographical information for a "ticket," as it is known, good for food and shelter through the nineteenth of the month—ten days. Then they joined another, more crowded line, which was slowly making its way fifty feet across a dayroom and down some stairs to the basement cafeteria. Seven men wide, the queue was tightly packed and anticipatory. At one point, where it narrowed to four abreast going around a corner, jostling turned to shoving, and the anonymous tight contact of, say, a rush-hour subway became much more personal, to the point where taking a breath was a conscious act. "At Camp LaGuardia—that's up in Orange County—the lines are a lot more orderly," said a soft-spoken man, who had to strain to make himself heard over the shouting, radio-playing racket that dominated the dayroom. "They have a lot of supervisors there. They wouldn't stand for a situation like this—not there," added the man, who wore both a grubby green parka and an antique brown corduroy overcoat. A number of the men had on more than one coat. They need the extra insulation on chilly street corners, but inside, in a hot room made hotter by the dense line, sweat collected on many faces. One man, who had been mumbling nothing much at steadily increasing volume, started to take off his gold windbreaker and toss it aside, but the man next to him made him put it back on. "This is the only coat you got, man," he said. "Everyone in here would like to have your coat, but it belongs to you. Now, hold on to it."

As the line left the dayroom (where paint flaked from every corner) and entered a dark stairwell that led to the basement, it thinned to a single file and then moved more quickly. All in the space of ten minutes, meal tickets were checked and dinner dished up and eaten. Warm, filling, and good, the meal consisted of two slices of white bread with two pats of margarine; rice;

diced beets; a stew with a few pieces of meat and a good many beans; oversweetened coffee; and, for dessert, three stewed prunes. Several Human Resources Administration security guards patrolled the cafeteria, and diners who sat too long in front of empty trays were told gently that it was time to move along. The exit from the cafeteria led outdoors, onto East Third, past a sign that asked shelter clients—that is the official term—not to disturb the neighborhood. It was twenty-seven degrees outside, and most of the men walked straight back in at the front door to begin the process of getting housing.

Of a total of 3,744 homeless men who were sheltered by the city on December 9, only ten actually got beds at East Third Street, and they were in the infirmary, on the second floor. The rest went to one of five shelters—Camp LaGuardia (where 945 men slept), Ward's Island (816 men, in two buildings), an armory in the Fort Washington section of Manhattan (520), an old school on Williams Avenue, in Brooklyn's East New York district (381), and a former school on Eighth Avenue at 157th Street, in Harlem (129)—or to one of six Bowery flophouses, ranging in population from the Palace (453) to the Stevenson (65). Most of those who had arrived at East Third Street around four o'clock and finished their dinner at 5:30 chose to "put their tickets in" immediately. They handed their tickets to a man in a glassed-in booth in the center of the shelter's main floor, and he told them to go wait on the second floor until their names were called for the bus to the Brooklyn school.

On the second floor, as in the rest of the Third Street facility, there were many more men than chairs, so there was a lot of sitting on the stairs and slouching against the walls. A few of the men on the second floor looked like the world's picture of Bowery bums: one stumbled and fell down seven stairs, hitting his head against a radiator, and another, irascible old Izzy, shook his crutch at those who came too close, exchanged cheerful and immensely profane insults with his friends passing by to other floors, and finally fell asleep and toppled out of his chair. When some of the other men hoisted Izzy back into his seat, he awoke and swore at them; they just laughed. But the bulk of those waiting for the Brooklyn bus were under forty and were black or Hispanic, and seemed more down on their luck than derelict or deranged. They all looked groggy and bleary-eyed—some apparently from drink or drugs, some from lack of sleep, many from both. One man left the waiting room, went to a nearby grocery store, and returned with a quart of Miller High Life concealed under his coat—for drinking is not permitted in the shelter. He and a friend debated risking confiscation of the bottle by drinking it then and there but decided to wait for the dark safety of the bus. Inside ten minutes, though, the man had deftly opened the quart and managed several long pulls. His friend, meanwhile, was trying without luck to sell a small Instamatic camera for three joints.

The second-floor waiting room, with its joined-at-the-waist plastic chairs, looked like a small-city Greyhound bus terminal, and there was the same air of nothing to do but sit (or stand). The few distractions included a visit from the cook, who poked his head in at the door on the way to an office upstairs. Several of the men complimented him on the meal he had just prepared; almost all the dealings between clients and staff people were, like this one, friendly—or, at least, polite in both directions. The salesman of loose cigarettes happened by twice, and many of the men bought one or two, some counting out pennies in payment. The only real spectacle was provided by the men on the third floor. Told to report downstairs for their bus, they did, only to find that the order had been premature; the bus had not yet arrived. Without complaint, they paraded back upstairs. A few minutes later, though, they left for good, and not long afterward a staff member climbed to the second floor carrying two bundles of about forty tickets each. He rounded up the men in the stairwell and herded them into the main waiting room, and then began to read off the names on the cards. As each was called, its owner replied "Here!" or "Yo!" and claimed his ticket. Then he walked downstairs to a yellow school bus that was idling in the street. It was now nearly 7:45 P.M., with the temperature at twenty-four degrees and the wind whipping at twenty-one miles per hour.

The bus trip to Brooklyn—it didn't begin until old Izzy had been bundled aboard, swearing happily—took perhaps twenty minutes, and the men sat placidly, some talking with their seat-mates. "The night before last, I went to the new shelter," said one man, who was unshaven but owned a nearly full pack of Salem Lights. "They said, 'Who wants to go to the new shelter on Ward's Island?' and no one was going, so I didn't know what was up, but I put my ticket in. And it was *so* nice! They had some individual shower stalls there, where you could pull the curtain, and you could change the temperature of the water to suit you, and there was a real TV room, just like in jail. And they assigned you a bed, so you could go to the bathroom or wherever and not have to worry some guy would be in your bed when you got back. Last night, I got to East Third too late to go back there, so I put in for Fort Washington, but when the bus hadn't come by 1:30 A.M. I got my ticket back and left. There's an abandoned building just across the Williamsburg Bridge that I have a mattress in, and I went there. It's good in the summer, but last night was *cold*. And you can't sleep when you're cold. I got to find some work, but I don't know enough people here. I'm from upstate, and I'd go back there if I had a place to stay, because I think there's construction work there. But for the time being I'm going to keep trying to get the new shelter. It's *nice*."

Shortly after eight o'clock, the bus pulled up in front of the former school in East New York, which was opened as a shelter on October 21, 1981, the day after a judge ordered the city to find four hundred more beds for homeless men. A security guard now directed the men up a central flight of stairs to an auditorium, where a lot of others were already sitting in row after row of uncomfortable wooden seats of the sort found mainly in high-school auditoriums. Some of the seats were splintered, and others were missing altogether. Food wrappers and a few bottles littered the floor. A color television set on the auditorium stage was turned to *Magnum, P.I.*, which featured criminals shooting at good guys in a helicopter; the volume was set so high that the sound was a virtually unmodulated blare, hard to understand. It was so loud because behind the television set three tables of shelter regulars were playing cards and talking, also at high volume. The new arrivals from East Third sat like lumps in their seats, either looking at the TV (but not laughing at the jokes, or seeming to notice much when commercials came on) or staring at the wall. When *Magnum, P.I.* ended, a security guard yelled, "Downstairs, everyone! They're handing out sheets!" Everyone got up and went downstairs and waited in a long line, which eventually led past a smiling, matronly woman passing out clean sheets. Then everyone went back up to the auditorium, where a show called *Simon & Simon*, about two detectives tracking a scuba-diving kidnapper, had come on the TV.

The bathroom down the hall from the auditorium was decrepit; not all the toilets flushed, and not all the stalls had doors. In the corridor outside, a bulletin board listed some of the daytime activities at the shelter: a "pool-shooting" room operated until 5 P.M. daily, and something called a "mood-changers group" met Thursday at 3 P.M. There was also a note on the board from a man who had lost all his possessions—most notably, his ID card—and was offering a "bonus" for their return. Between nine o'clock and eleven, the main thing that happened was that *Simon & Simon* ended and a man switched the set to Channel 4 for *Hill Street Blues*. When that show, which had a subplot about lapdogs, was over, the television was turned off, and the men who had put their tickets in five and a half hours earlier at East Third Street lined up single file, all clutching their clean white sheets, along the left side of a corridor. The line climbed two staircases, to the fourth floor, and then went down one, to the third. Most of the classrooms it passed had crudely lettered cardboard signs on the doors that read, "Full Up. No Beds." (One continued, "Thieves will get their do!!!!!") Under the rules of the shelter, men who come regularly to the Brooklyn site have reserved beds, which they can claim simply by arriving at an appointed hour. Any empty beds are then distributed to the nightly arrivals from East Third Street. This night—and many other nights as well—there were not nearly as many beds as bodies; most classrooms, each of which had about twelve beds pushed close together, really were "full up" with regulars. Two security guards picked those from Third Street who would get to spend the night in the few remaining beds. "We're not discriminating on anything except cleanliness," one of them told the line. "Brooklyn Men's Shelter is a *clean* shelter, and we don't want any lice or dirt."

Once the few men were picked, the line returned to the silent auditorium (the TV had been locked away) and waited. Nobody complained. Fifteen minutes later, a shelter employee came in to say that he was trying to find buses to take the men to the Fort Washington armory, where there were beds. He counted fifty-four men sitting or slumping in the auditorium but missed a fifty-fifth, who was lying facedown between two rows of seats. Very few of the men talked while they waited; some tried to sleep, but most looked straight ahead. One man shouted to himself in Spanish every few minutes.

After almost an hour—at about 12:30 A.M.—the staff member came back to announce that two vans were waiting outside to take men to Fort Washington. Each of the vans seated fourteen people, so twenty-eight of the fifty-five men were allowed to leave; twenty-seven, including the man asleep on his face, stayed behind to wait for more vans. On their way out, the twenty-eight men dropped their clean sheets in a big pile by the stairs. The driver of one of the vans had both the radio (playing a song called "Bad Boy") and the heater running full blast, but though the back seats were scorchingly stuffy none of the men said a word about that, or anything else. The trip down the traffic-free Interborough Parkway to the Grand Central Parkway, past the World's Fair Unisphere and LaGuardia Airport, and then over the Triborough Bridge took not much more than twenty minutes, and it was shortly after one when the van reached the armory, on 168th Street. The temperature had dipped to nineteen degrees, but the wind had dropped as well, to twelve miles per hour, so the wind-chill factor was just about one degree below zero—not quite as icy as it had been two or three hours earlier.

Inside the armory doors, the men lined up. Attendants told ten of them at a time to strip and leave their clothes and belongings in piles on the floor. Each of the ten tossed his dirty underwear into a garbage can, grabbed a chunk of yellow soap, and entered a room with ten showerheads in a row along one wall. "Be as quick as possible, but get really clean," said a businesslike but courteous attendant. The men got the showers good and hot, and lathered up. After a few minutes, they all rinsed, turned off the showers, and walked back into the hall, where a staff member handed each a towel. Rolled up inside the towel were a clean pair of briefs and a clean T-shirt, each stamped "MENS SHELTER" in black ink. After drying themselves and putting on their new underwear, the men collected their clothes and belongings and walked barefoot down a long hall, leaving room for the next ten men to strip and shower. At the end of the hall was a stairway, and at the top of the stairs was the armory floor.

During the winter, the armory is used for high-school track meets, and hurdles were stacked in some corners. The room is vast: far down at the other end several automobiles were parked, and they looked tiny. A sea of metal-frame beds stretched out across the wooden floor, in a grid of eighteen rows by thirty rows. Even though it was past 1:30, only about 200 of the 520 who would eventually sleep here had arrived. The men, who had put their tickets in at East Third Street and gone to Brooklyn and been in the first vanload back to Fort Washington, walked down the rows until they came to the first empty beds—about under a sign that said, "Finish, 300 M." On each bed were stacked a mattress, two sheets, a good soft pillow, a pillowcase, and a warm blanket. The men put their belongings under their beds (some chose to keep their clothes under the blankets with them), made them up, and crawled in. About a quarter of two, after waiting a little over eight hours in various lines and holding rooms, and travelling upward of twenty-five miles by bus and van, they had got a bed for the night—what was left of it. They would be awakened at six, so they could get about four hours of sleep.

Or four hours of trying to sleep. Many of the regulars nodded right off, but there were plenty of distractions to keep others awake. New men kept arriving for the next two hours or more, until almost all the beds were filled. (Obviously, these men slept an even shorter time.) Though the lights that hung from the ceiling were dark, bright lights ringed the walls of the vast room. Many of the men coughed all night, and two or three were deranged and sometimes rose to wander down the aisles saying things. ("I paid my taxes," one man mumbled over and over. "Beg pardon. Beg pardon. I paid my taxes.") From the men who were asleep came the sound of at least a hundred snores.

Early risers in the armory began to get up at about 5:30, and after that it was again hard to sleep. They dressed, pulled the sheets and pillowcases off their beds, and carried them to waiting garbage bags. One man stumbled off leaving his bed still made; after asking him several times to retrieve his linen, a staff member gave up and shouted, "You're sleeping on plastic tonight! Just remember that!" At precisely 6 A.M., the rafter lights came on, north to south across the armory, as switches were thrown. "It's that time again!" one of the workers sang out over and over. "It's that time again, gentlemen!" Slowly, the men collected their gear, stripped their beds, and walked out of the room, down the stairs, down the hall, and through the cold morning to a waiting bus, which carried them, via the F.D.R. Drive, back to East Third Street. The first bus from Fort Washington got to the Bowery at 6:30. It was eighteen degrees outside, and the sun wouldn't rise for half an hour. There was already a pretty good line waiting for breakfast.

# 41

# Growing Old Gracefully

*—The Boston Globe Magazine,* May 10, 1998

In a weedy grove on the east side of the Sacandaga River, in New York's Adirondack Mountains, where the blacksmith must have had his forge, I found horseshoes, hinges, angles, corners, chains, flanges—all the essentials of the early Industrial Revolution, rust flaking off them in brown sheets. An old woodstove with fancy ironwork stood under a birch tree, berry cane growing up through the belly. It's mostly blackberry there now, and birch and hemlock, with just the odd topography of old cellar holes remaining to mark the factory and the town. Deer scat, trillium, barrel hoops.

Griffin, this old ghost town, lies maybe eight miles from my house in the Adirondacks. A century of humidity, of snow and rain, of trees grown big with roots strong enough to crack stone, has turned the settlement into a barely discernible memory. If you walk the land with John Teachout, the sole remaining resident, he'll show you where the hotel stood, and the school; with his guidance, you can just about imagine it all. But if you walked the land by yourself, you'd more or less think you were in the woods.

Which is not to say that Griffin left no trace. John Teachout can also show you pictures—photographs that his father left him. He sits at the picnic table in his dooryard and flips the photos to you, one by one. Here's a picture of some serious-faced men at the mill, and here's one of twenty-seven kids on the schoolhouse steps. "This one's from around 1900—already you can see the mill falling in," said Teachout.

We know about this town not just from old photos but also from the work of several historians. Barbara McMartin, the pre-eminent chronicler of the Adirondack woods, has written about life in these hamlets, which were built on hemlock—on the tannin in the bark of the hemlock, to be precise, which for a while cured the leather gloves of half the world. Stephen Griffin, for whom this place was named, controlled thirty thousand acres; his was one of the nation's largest glove-tanning operations.

Some of the people who lived in Griffin when it boomed set down their memories in writing. So we know, for instance, that when Henry Girard wanted to marry Nellie McCarthy, he sent to Glens Falls for a wedding ring, but that the mailbag was carelessly tossed out at North Creek and landed in front of the train's wheels, which flattened the ring. (The railroad paid for a new one, and it got there in time for the wedding.) We know that, some-times, everyone would pitch in and hire a band from Northville, twenty-three miles away, and that one time some lumberjacks who were listening to the music "started boxing, which was quite a hobby in those days. When [the band] stopped playing, all the men stopped boxing; when they started playing again, most of the lum-bermen started boxing again. The musicians had a hard time to keep from laughing."

And we know this, too: at the end of the nineteenth century, some scientist figured out a synthetic tanning process, and so the hemlock bark was no longer needed. The mills caved in or burned down. The people moved away.

· · ·

We need to talk about economics and Social Security and demographics—all the things that would inevitably be affected if many of us decided to have smaller families. But before we get to those pragmatic issues, I think we need to deal with the intuitive fear of getting smaller, of *decline*. Of the human mark receding from certain places, as it will certainly recede if our population shrinks somewhat. That's why I've begun with these shards of local history.

This fear of decline comes from an old place inside us, so old that it's hard to pull out and examine, except to say that an abandoned cellar hole with a birch tree growing up out of the middle of it gives many people the willies. "The more educated people are, the spookier they find such ruins," said John Stilgoe, a Harvard professor who studies such places. "For people who worship a God called progress, such places are a confession of failure. When they come up against a landscape that's failed, they can't bring themselves to look at it."

But that spookiness rarely haunts me anymore, certainly not on this blue-sky spring day in Griffin, hearing the roar of the melting snow as it pounds through the little gorge. The human presence here was good—not environmentally benign by our current standards, not safe in the way an OSHA inspector would calculate it, not particularly cultured. But good—filled with love, hard work, fistfights, and the other things that make us human. *And the forest that fills in the cellar holes is good, too.*

It's not a failure, it's a change. First one thing was here, and now something else has come, or come back. The last moose was spotted in Griffin in 1852, and the boy who saw it was scared enough by the sight of those big antlers that he lay down in the creek bed and hid. Now, nearly 150 years later, the woods are back and so are the moose.

It's a complicated business, deciding to get smaller. But if we took up a little less space, the rest of creation would expand to fill that gap. And if we did it *confidently*, if we *chose* to, then there might be something kind of lovely about it.

· · ·

Having fewer babies might trigger problems, of course. A stable population is such a new idea that it would doubtless have ramifications, including changes in the economy. One big reason, after all, that our economies keep growing is that our numbers keep growing; 1 percent more Americans means 1 percent more toothpaste, more or less. And so a stable, or even slowly declining, number of Americans means a very different, probably less gung-ho economy.

It's true that the maturing of our economies will no doubt feel weird at first. As eighteenth-century economist Adam Smith himself said, "The progressive state is in reality the hearty state to all the different orders of society; the stationary is dull." But he was really just guessing. We don't know what stability might feel like. Perhaps, like the end of any exuberant adolescence, it will be equal parts bitter and sweet.

As an example, let's look in depth at one of the few economic impacts of lower birthrates that we know enough about to discuss intelligently. The biggest effect on our society of a drop in fertility would be to make the nation slightly grayer around the temples. There would be fewer young people, and plenty of senior citizens; America would be "older." Eventually, of course, we'll be in this situation no matter what we do, and, in fact, it's already starting to happen as the baby boomers age. But with fewer babies, it would happen more quickly—the population would stabilize, and our average age would creep up. That can't be helped: simple mathematics dictates that a population can't be stable, long-lived, and young at the same time.

Viewed one way, of course, our aging population constitutes a wonderful achievement. If you were born in 1900, you could expect to live forty-seven years; if you were born in 1991, you can expect about seventy-five years. That's 60 percent longer, twenty-eight more years, ten thousand more sunrises and newspapers and glasses of orange juice. We embrace these statistics for ourselves, for the people we love, indeed for just about every individual we can imagine; they've changed the way the world feels to us. And yet, for that organism we call "society as a whole," the same facts make us somehow gloomy. This aging process, former U.S. commerce secretary Pete Peterson suggested, "will challenge the very core of our national psyche, which has always been predicated on fresh beginnings, childlike optimism, and aspiring new generations."

Which leaves us a choice: Either we get an enormous bunch of new babies, and the generation after that an even more enormous bunch, and the generation after that a truly stupendous number, until very rapidly we're as densely populated as India. Or we figure out new ways to think about ourselves and our nation that turn this demographic inevitability of aging from a disaster into a commonplace, a given, even a kind of gift.

· · ·

"We have met the financial 'enemy,' and he is the elderly 'us,'" writes MIT economist Lester Thurow in his book *The Future of Capitalism*. It's hard to get much blunter than that. So let's begin with the bottom line: Will an aging society truly impoverish us? The argument goes something like this: old people are unproductive, and they demand government handouts, hence they're extremely expensive to keep around. Like most caricatures, this argument contains a certain amount of truth, and, like most caricatures, it also hides a good deal.

For instance, remember that as a society ages, the number of children it must take care of will shrink as the number of old people grows. The aging of the baby boomers will mean we need many more nursing homes and gerontologists. But the percentage of "dependent" people will be about the same as it was when they were born—when they needed nursery schools and pediatricians.

The trade-off between kids and the elderly is not perfect; many studies indicate that children are less expensive to care for. On the other hand, many elderly people remain productive working a part-time job or calling their broker at Fidelity, which is more than you can say for most five-year-olds.

But one fact about the elderly is beyond debate: every month, the government sends them checks. And as a population ages, there are going to be more checks, and fewer people paying the payroll taxes that support them. If you don't count the national debt, half the federal budget now goes to the elderly, a proportion that would rise to 100 percent sometime in the next century if the retirement laws remain unchanged. It's one of those crises that we can see coming a long way away and that we so far seem powerless to stop.

One reform proposal after another has popped up in recent years; a lot of them focus on getting individuals to save more. The government should make this easier, say advocates such as Peterson, by setting up incentives to save. But Peterson argues that we also need to shift our thinking and to rescue an old word: thrift.

Even with thrift, though, it's unlikely that the government will be able to sustain pensions and benefits of the size it promised, and it's unclear if the government really should. Since Social Security pays out to everyone, regardless of need, young low-income workers are essentially subsidizing upper-income elderly: if you work at Burger King, you're helping someone pay for that Winnebago with the "I'm Spending My Kids' Inheritance" bumper sticker. And even though the benefit formulas are supposed to give the poorer elderly a little more than their "share," studies have found there is no real redistribution of wealth—largely because rich people live (and hence collect) longer than poor people. It is, in other words, a disgrace.

It's a disgrace, because there *are*, in fact, plenty of poorer old folks. Social Security accounts for more than half the total income of retirees living on less than $20,000 a year, and these people in turn make up about half of all recipients. It's these people—visit any trailer park in America—whose lives will be trashed if the system goes kaput. So why doesn't the government simply set a "means" test and figure out who actually needs Social Security? Because there's a bloc of committed voters that so far won't allow it. The American Association of Retired Persons, the nation's biggest lobby, insists that Social Security is an "entitlement"; furthermore, say many supporters, if it isn't a universal program, voters won't support it. In other words, if you don't subsidize a lot of Winnebagos, the Winnebago owners will make sure that no one subsidizes the people in the trailer parks. Employed by muscular young men on street corners, this argument would rightly be called a protection racket.

· · ·

So far, we've been talking less about *aging* than about *funding*—that's how politics defines the issue. It's far more interesting, though, simply to think about what it means to grow old now, about whether there are new ways we might want to live, even if we weren't worried about Social Security.

Consider retirement, for instance. We get ready to retire at about age sixty-five, not because of some signal from our biological clock but because of a signal from Otto von Bismarck, the nineteenth-century German prime minister. He wanted to give pensions to civil servants, but he didn't want to pay out very much, so his actuaries calculated that seventy would be a good choice; when there was protest, he backed down to sixty-five. But though we live 60 percent longer than Bismarck's bureaucrats, he still rules our thinking about when to give up work; it makes no more sense than if we still wore monocles because they were fashionable in Bismarck's day. As a result, we live increasingly weird and unintegrated lives. In our earlier years, we're time-starved; people want more hours for themselves, for their families. Polls show we'd even take salary cuts in exchange for a few more hours a week. But when retirement comes, we have far more time than we know what to do with.

We keep, all of us, a mental calendar of our lives: we know when we're in our spring; we know when autumn approaches. But, all of a sudden, that calendar is out of whack. Summer lasts far longer than it used to; the fall is gentler. Plan your life by the old schedule, and you'll put up storm windows on your life long before the first snow.

It's not just retiring at sixty-five that doesn't make much emotional sense; it's also working like a dog at forty-five, when you need to be spending more time with your family. The physical fact of our longer lives should change our thinking, change it in significant ways. But, so far, it hasn't really sunk in. For the most part, we still look on those years past age sixty as a foreign country, as something separate from the rest of life. "You get a lot of hand wringing about how expensive it's going to be to have a society where everyone's walking around with canes," said Lincoln Day, a demographer. "But that turns out to be a small fraction of even the oldest people in society." The same wave of medical technology that has increased life expectancy has also made older people healthier. Only 15 percent of Americans older than sixty-five are frail or sick—only 15 percent.

This is vital information. If you don't know it in your bones, you'll make decisions about your life that don't make sense, decisions that made sense in nineteenth-century Germany. If you are middle-aged, you can expect twenty or thirty more years of life, and those twenty or thirty years have been added not to the end but to the middle. This new stage in adult life implies all sorts of changes, for social institutions even more important than pensions. Exiting school when you're twenty-two may have made sense when you only had another twenty-two years to live, for instance, but when you're likely still to be hard at work half a century later, you need new models, new notions.

· · ·

What I'm trying to say is this: we approach the "problem" of aging by carefully keeping our thinking inside this box constructed by Otto von Bismarck. The Bismarck "solution" to old age is that everyone cease work on or around his sixty-fifth birthday and start getting a government check, needed or not. We will distort our economies and our politics trying to keep his particular vision alive; worse, we will distort our lives. And perhaps worse still, we will miss a huge chance as a society to change some of our basic institutions in ways that would not only make life easier for a larger elderly population but also help with our environmental troubles.

What slows down as people age? Not minds, necessarily. But reflexes, muscles. Which means that thinking about the *how* of living becomes more important. Often that means something as simple as being able to cross the street. In Canberra, Australia, 613 older residents were surveyed. The report found many things, but one of the most specific, as reported by the *Canberra Times*, "is that the green 'walk' period at intersections should be longer, because it seems to cater for young things, who will gambol across the road, rather than for the aging, who may take longer and who, at the moment, are often forced to scuttle to make it."

What all this means is that the baby boom generation, as it ages, has the chance to finally change America in remarkable ways—to change its very shape. Always before, the self-interest of the boomers has been at odds with their oft-professed concern for the world: the environment may have mattered to them, but not, on the whole, as much as making a pile of money. As they age, however, the generation that launched Earth Day can make a difference *every* day. With enough will, you can change your surroundings pretty fast. Consider Curitiba, the city of several million in the south of Brazil where the local government built the world's best bus system from scratch in two decades. It's a wonderful place not to own a car—old and young walk and ride the bus everywhere. And, as a result, residents use 25 percent less fuel than other Brazilians. Twenty-five percent is a big number, big enough to begin to address some of the problems, like global warming, now threatening us. And it didn't even take that much money, just a certain amount of imagination translated into political will.

It's the next generation of elderly people that will decide the question. As MIT's Lester Thurow points out, "long before they are a technical majority of the population, the elderly will be unstoppable politically, since those under eighteen can't vote and those between eighteen and thirty tend not to." All those powerful old people could build new bus lines, rezone suburbs, accomplish all the mundane but mammoth tasks that would reshape the country, or they could screw the grandkids to guarantee every red cent that they've got coming.

If they cling to the pension, then the boomers will die as they lived: big talkers. But if, instead, they choose to invest much of their money in things that will make their own lives easier and also ease some of the planet's strains, then they will finally have realized the great ambition of their youth and turned the world upside down.

It's not such a long distance from talking about having a single child to talking about making the country elder-friendly. Not only are they linked by demography, they're also connected by the realization that we could, if we decided to do so, change what seems inevitable. We don't need to expand our population 50 percent; we don't need to grow old scuttling across intersections. We can make choices.

Getting smaller, backing off a little—those notions have their own quiet glory. And since I live in a place where people have backed off some, I know that it's possible, that it's not synonymous with decline and deterioration and decay. From the window where I write, I can see the remains of a seventy-five-year-old sawmill, where the man who built my house once spent his days cutting boards. It was a good living, and, by every account, he was a good man who still lingers in local memory.

But the sawmill has been gone for several generations. The forest has come rushing back in, and behind the forest have come the bears and bobcats. And now we're talking about the wolf coming back, too. Seventy-five years ago, that would not have been possible; it was too crowded here, too dense with small subsistence farms. It's not that the farms were wrong and the wolf right, nor the other way around. It's that there are all sorts of sweet things in this world, many of which are us, and many of which are not.

In a sense, what we face is the test of a simple proposition: does age bring with it maturity? Let's define maturity this way: as the understanding that you're not the most important thing in the world. It's hard for anyone succored by a consumer culture to mature. But it's maturity we need, maturity that must undergird any sustainable world. Only mature people might utter the two words our civilization most desperately needs to hear: "That's enough."

# 42

## Cross-Country Ski Your Way to Shining Health, Renewed Vigor, and Everlasting Happiness!

*—Outside,* February 1999

January 1, 1998: The first new person I met in the New Year was sitting across the cafeteria table from me in a tie-dye shirt at a yoga center in western Massachusetts. He looked over at me and said, quite casually, "You know, if you're generating mucus from one membrane, you're generating it everywhere." I wiped my nose and looked around for some better omen for the twelve months to come.

Which is when I saw Rob Sleamaker for the first time sitting apple-cheeked and grinning amid the leotard-clad ascetics, almost as out of place in this ashram as I was. He'd come to this "holistic center" to teach a weekend course on yoga and cross-country skiing. I'd come to listen in—but more than that, to see if he was the sort of guy I wanted to turn my life over to. Rob had agreed to coach me for the next year, to help me take my mediocre body and turn it into that of a cross-country ski racer. Not a champion, obviously, but a competitor. And something I'd never been: an athlete.

Rob looked normal enough—indeed, before the day was out we were sneaking away from the ashram cafeteria, with its seitan burgers and spinach stir-fry, to visit a decidedly unholistic local bar for an unorganic beer. Still, I wasn't sure I wanted to marry the guy. For the next 365 mornings when I climbed out of bed, Rob would be there, in the form of his personalized training gospel, telling me how long I was going to cardiovasculate that day and at what heart rate I was going to do it. If he said 228 minutes, that was how many I was going to do—not 227, and not 229. When he said run, I would ask how fast. I might actually see him only once or twice a month, but I would spend, he said, about 650 hours in his company. He would become a mental member of my family.

And so I had to make sure he understood. What I wanted was not just fitness, certainly not trophies. I wanted a break from myself. Call it early midlife crisis, call it silly, call it vain. I'd spent my whole adult life as an environmentalist and writer (and my weekends as, yes, a Sunday school teacher), preaching sacrifice, voluntary population control, the idea of Saving the Earth through Humility and Restraint. When my last book came out, one reviewer called me a "yuppie Gandhi." She meant to be stinging, but I didn't really mind—at the end of the twentieth century there are worse things to be called. Still, I could feel myself slipping into a kind of insipidity; one entire possibility of my life—the fiercer, physical possibility—was slipping away for good. I mean, Gandhi had *concave* pecs.

Rob seemed the perfect guru for my transformation. For one thing, he was as much psychologist as exercise physiologist. "You're going kind of hard," he said one morning as I huffed and puffed up hills to impress him. My pretense punctured, I could just relax. And the last night of the workshop, as we sat again in the bar mapping out the year ahead, he turned to me and summed up my project better than I could have myself. "You have a mind, a body, and a spirit," he said. "If you want to use your intellect for one long period, that's OK. But you're born whole, and you can get back to that."

Bring it on! When he leaned over and lent me his heart rate

monitor, it felt almost talismanic, as if I were leaving on a quest. I had to nasally generate some mucus to cover my emotion.

. . .

I grew up with no cruel disadvantages. A loving family, enough money but not too much, I was a victim of nothing. Except, in certain ways, myself. I was, in fact, a weenie. That is to say, when I was a boy, I hated the president of the United States for two reasons. One, the carpet bombing of southeast Asia, which as the child of a good liberal home I felt to be excessive. Two, the 600-yard-run, the final event of the annual President's Physical Fitness Test. The pull-ups were easy enough; I'd simply hang on the bar until it was abundantly clear to whatever sadist taught gym that year that I was not actually going to be able to chin myself. But the 600-yard-run had to be completed, albeit at a walking stagger, whole minutes after the rest of the class. What a jerk, Nixon.

But if it hadn't deeply damaged me, my weeniness, it had left scars. My picture of myself as a pale dumpling never really changed. As time went on I moved to the woods, spent many long hours in the wilderness. I climbed high mountains. I rescued lost hikers. The rack on my car was worth more than my car. More than anything else I cross-country skied, out in the woods every day of the long Adirondack winters.

Still, I had never *really* challenged my body, not in competition. And so, at thirty-seven, at the age where age seems about to start, I thought I'd give it a shot. A year of living strenuously. I had no real idea what would happen—I knew there were thousands of training guides, dozens of magazines with recipes for stronger abs, Internet sites where you could discuss your $VO_2$ max until your fingers ached. But I wanted to know what came between the before and after pictures. I wanted to know what happens when a normal human being goes all out.

To my mind, nordic skiing offered the perfect test. It summons every muscle, every emotion. It's a mix of dash and endurance, long thigh-burning ascents followed by swooping downhills, the most profoundly aerobic sport on earth. The physiologists, when they rank athletes by cardiovascular exertion, always come up with the same champions: rowers, Tour de France bikers, and, above them all, nordic skiers.

Besides, it's my favorite sport: gliding through the woods is the only time in my life I've ever felt graceful and speedy.

Of course most Americans could care less about cross-country skiing. Since Bill Koch's silver in the 1976 Olympics (still the only American cross-country medal ever) gave the sport its late-1970s popularity spike, the number of cross-country skiers has dwindled from roughly 12 million to below six. U.S. retailers sell only about 150,000 pairs of cross-country skis each winter. And at Nagano, CBS decided not to even show the sport's premier race, the men's 50k, so they could feature a figure skating *exhibition* the night *after* the actual medals were awarded.

· · ·

Whatever else you can say about it, cross-country is a sport that works best when it's snowing, and on this day in Vermont's Northeast Kingdom, it was not. It was, in fact, raining—soaking into the several feet of snow like grape juice into a paper towel, when I left the ashram and drove north to train for a week at the Craftsbury Outdoor Center. Nevertheless, I skied every day, trying to eke some glide out of the softening base, experimenting with my heart rate monitor, and getting used to my new regimen of going slower, not harder. Rob, in his work with American biathletes and in his book, *Serious Training for Serious Athletes*, had been one of the first to push the now widely touted idea that mileage counts less than intensity, and that most of the time easier is better. Much of my year's work would be this long, slow slog—an hour, two, three, sometimes four, at a heart rate of about 140—on the theory that it would literally change my plumbing, make the network of capillaries in my muscles more dense, the better to drain away lactic acid.

My training was undramatic, like punching a clock. But it was justified by the promise that in a year I'd be fitter. Faster. That in the winter of 1999 I would be a competitor. Rob suggested I enter a few races that first winter, for the experience, and since I'd never been in a formal race of any kind—not a marathon, not a 5k, not a 100-yard dash—it seemed like good advice.

Craftsbury had a 20k competition scheduled at the end of that rainy first week. The trails filled with spandex-clad sylphs rocketing by on skis, including several Olympians tuning up for Nagano, and that morning the temperature suddenly dropped, turning what snow was left into bulletproof ice and shattering my confidence. Choosing the right wax in conditions like these is about as easy as performing thoracic surgery, so I twitched nervously around the start area, looking for tips. Finally the Rossignol team manager, glaring at me as if I'd asked for his wife's telephone number, mumbled something about purple klister, an evil, taffylike wax that I desperately applied.

Then we were off, with me at the tail of a pack of several hundred skiers. Halfway through the first 10-kilometer loop, I was reduced to herringboning up every hill and double-poling across every flat, my purple klister scraped clean by the ice. My glasses fogged and one lens fell into the snow, and I was on my knees hunting for it as everyone else zoomed past. Oh, and I took a wrong turn near the finish.

In Ottawa a few weeks later, I was better prepared. A friend had blowtorched my skis with some exotic fluorocarbon in the parking lot. I had a brand-new spandex suit. I was sleek, all systems go. And then someone started telling a story about the time he'd forgotten to wear his wind briefs on a cold day just like this one and how it had taken him hours of excruciating pain to thaw himself out. "What are wind briefs?" I asked.

It turns out that on cold days, since Lycra does little to cut the wind, ski racers wear fleece-lined jockstraps, or underwear with a plastic panel on the fly. As it also turns out, I wasn't the first one to make this error. Months later, reading John Morton's biathlon novel *Medal of Honor*, I came across a classic description of "hooter freeze" ("athletes were moaning in pain, rocking back and forth on the cots"). But even if I'd known it, that would have come as very cold comfort. Already I could feel things shriveling.

Before I could worry any more, the horn sounded for the start, and my wave of several hundred skiers headed out through a field and then up a series of hills. My wax worked, the trail was fast, but I was lost in a series of conjectures about my reproductive organs. Normally I don't spend too much of the day thinking about my member, but now I could think of little else; on the downhills, when the wind would whistle even faster, I'd pull my fanny pack around in front and crouch behind it like a shield, sacrificing a second or two of speed for a degree or two of windchill factor. I remember stopping for a quick shot of hot lemonade halfway through the twenty-kilometer course, and, I remember, as seemed to be my habit, taking a wrong turn near the end. I got back on track, flew across the finish, and headed straight for the men's room, where I spent the next half hour whimpering.

The World Masters Championships were next. It is true that by then I had acquired a fleece-lined jockstrap. Still, I had no more business racing against these guys than I did offering stock tips to Alan Greenspan. There are plenty of slow masters racers, but the World mostly attracts those Norwegian team members who never bothered to stop training, hard-core types with suitcases full of wax and quivers full of skis. I was racing the sport's elite.

And race them I did, for about thirty seconds, as my thirty-five to forty age group wave burst out of the starting gate. After the first of the 30 kilometers, I'd lost sight of the pack; by the 10-kilometer mark, the next-older age group was starting to catch up. I felt like what I was—a wannabe, a different and lower species. I took a long, sprawling fall on a downhill, and I might as well have been back in gym.

And then something strange happened. I noticed another racer from my age group: number 2009. He was ahead, but I slowly gained on him, and when he stopped so a friend could hand him a drink I went on by. Galvanized by the idea of not finishing dead last, I refused to let go when he caught up on the next downhill. My mouth was cotton, my bootstraps had come loose, but for five kilometers we powered on in our own little race, hardly noticing as others zoomed by. He finally pulled up for a rest with three kilometers left, and though I too began to bonk a few minutes later, he never caught up. The winner of my age group, a German former Olympic medalist, finished half an hour ahead of me, but I didn't care. I'd beaten 2009. I'd discovered some other guy inside me. Gandhi wouldn't have much cared for him, but I thought he was kind of cool.

· · ·

By April I was in a world of pain. I had an ugly bit in my mouth, a valve that let me breathe in but trapped all my exhalations and sent them to a computer. A clip pinched my nostrils, and I was running, faster and faster, until I couldn't go any more. On the wall a sign read, sure enough, WORLD OF PAIN.

Rob and I had come to Lake Placid to test my mettle at Dr. Ken Rundell's sports science lab at the Olympic Training Center. The lab's centerpiece is the largest treadmill in the country, 8 feet by 10 feet, capable of achieving a 30 percent grade. For the first quarter-hour or so it's manageable—the treadmill never gets too fast, and they stop you every three minutes to measure how fast your body is accumulating lactic acid. Then, when you've reached your aerobic threshold and your body is starting to fill with lactate, they stop taking the blood samples, speed up the treadmill, and force you to run until you drop.

My transformation so far had been like my wife's pregnancy five years ago—subtle at first, hard to discern from the outside. But I wanted confirmation. I wanted numbers. My number in April: a $VO_2$ max of 54.42 ml, meaning that my body could consume that many milliliters of oxygen each minute per kilogram of body weight. Enough, said Rob, to let me hope for "the top third of my age group" in races. It was mostly a matter of genetics, he warned—it wouldn't go up much, maybe 5 to 10 percent by the time I returned to the treadmill in November. For a thirty-seven-year-old my score could be worse, but eight-time Olympic gold medalist Bjorn Daehlie, the Norse god of frosty propulsion, reputedly tests out at 96.

There was one number left to calibrate. After tweezing my thighs and hips and belly and back and arms with a set of calipers, Dr. Rundell announced that my body fat percentage was 11.73. Not bad, he said, but the elite athletes he usually tests run 3 to 6 percent.

Afterward Rob and I went to lunch. I was digging into my chips and salsa when I noticed he'd grown quiet. "We all like chips," he said finally, "but they do have quite a bit of fat." By week's end I had overhauled my diet completely. I read cans like a lawyer, searching for hydrogenated oils; I convinced myself that toast tasted fine without butter; I ordered low-fat meals on airplanes, which is like asking for extra whacks at the S&M parlor. I managed a fourteen-city book tour subsisting almost entirely on bagels and lox, no cream cheese. By day I answered questions about world population, global warming, child-rearing. But all the time I was itching to get back to the hotel treadmill. I watched so much CNN working out that Bernard Shaw interrupted my dreams. And my body had changed. The technical description would now be gaunt. I slid from 170 pounds to about 160, spread over a six-foot-three frame.

It's not that I stopped eating—I ate four meals a day, oatmeal and spaghetti and raisin bran and salad, plus Gatorade, Clif Bars, Gu, Newtons. But I came to understand, I think, some of the anorexic's impulse. There are things you can't really control—how finally smart or attractive or athletic you are—but you can control what goes into your mouth. Part of being an athlete, I was coming to understand, involves an intense self-absorption, lovely and scary both. One night in Lake Placid I had dinner with Rich Kenah, the great American middle-distance runner, who told me, "To be an Olympic-caliber runner is basically to be selfish, to live within your own inner circle, without much room for anyone but yourself. I have to protect my time, my resources, my energy."

That's sort of how I found myself feeling; I didn't stint my daughter or my wife, but my friends must have found me changed. I went out for a hike one day with an old friend, but I was wearing my heart rate monitor, and we weren't staying in my zone, so I kept breaking into a trot, and soon his friendly ragging turned into sotto voce expletives, and he didn't call again all summer.

. . .

Who needs friends, anyway? Forget conversation—differentiation was my watchword, my obsession. Most days I went long and slow; others I sprinted. I worked just on the edge of what Rob calculated my body could stand. A week of my training schedule, chosen at random, looked like this:

Sunday: 205 minutes of what Rob called "overdistance," running or roller skiing at a heart rate between 135 and 146, with a thirty-second burst of speed every 20 minutes or so.

Monday: 61 minutes of endurance training, moving fast enough that my heart beat 150 times a minute. Then 80 minutes of strength training—in my case, climbing aboard one of Rob's inventions, the Vasa Trainer, a sliding-seat contraption that mimics cross-country's poling motions.

Tuesday: 102 minutes of overdistance.

Wednesday: 164 minutes of overdistance, another 80 minutes on the Vasa Trainer.

Thursday: 41 minutes of overdistance and 61 minutes of uphill intervals, run right at my aerobic threshold of 165 beats per minute.

Friday: 82 minutes of overdistance, more time on the Vasa Trainer.

Saturday: Blessed rest.

In the middle of all this, I went to Rob's wedding—an epic of fitness. The parking lot looked like a convention of Thule roof-rack dealers, and a huge bowl on the buffet table held not shrimp or caviar but hundreds of Clif Bars. Thanks to Rob, though, I now felt at least slightly at home in this tribe. More guide than coach, more Yoda than drill sergeant, Rob listened to every new account of my aches and pains, my small triumphs and setbacks.

The enemy was less exertion than boredom—I now know every word you can spell with the letters "Fischer," and am capable of prodigious feats of mental calculation. If I'm roller skiing for 178 minutes, for example, then by the time I've gone six, I have figured what percentage of ground I've covered and, at fifty strides a minute, how many more it will take to bring me back to the car.

But I was starved for snow, for the glide that first seduced me into this sport. And so in midsummer, ostensibly to cover the unveiling of some new Salomon gear, but mostly to meet the great nordic skier Ben Husaby, I flew off to Mount Hood in Oregon. Ben and I did a little technique work, but mostly we talked about the rigors of the sport. Neither of us was inclined to exertion on that hot day, and while the rest of the press junket dutifully hiked with a naturalist to the lodge where we'd spend the night, Ben and I rode the chairlift. It made me feel perversely athletic to do so.

Cross-country skiing is such hard work because it's mostly uphill—the average World Cup loop climbs six thousand vertical feet in the same distance as, say, a running marathon, and 30 percent grades are not uncommon. Husaby, a two-time Olympian, told me that in his best years he could go for a full half hour within three percent of his maximum heart rate, 192 to 195 beats per minute. Now that's extreme, about as extreme as the human body gets, a lot more extreme than, say, street luge. Which makes cross-country today, with its old-fashioned emphasis on effort over attitude, an oddly countercultural sport. "In the nineties some of us were trying to make the sport a bit cooler," Ben said. "We were listening to the right music, wearing the right sunglasses. No one was paying any attention."

Perhaps they would have if the athletes had talked more about the pain. Cross-country is not about cool—it's about drool. Most World Cup racers sport little goatees of frozen saliva, the result of sweat, hyperventilation, and Gatorade tossed down at forty miles per hour. In the early weeks of my training, on the night before the longest race of the winter, I'd eaten dinner with a fifty-two-year-old ultradistance cyclist named John Spas Jr., who had lots of advice. ("In the morning, be certain to evacuate your colon.") What stuck with me most was this: "In every endurance event there is a time when you'll say, 'What the fuck am I doing here?' And you'll just have to say, 'This is what I do.'"

The next morning, I found myself up against four middle-of-the-packers on the last 17-kilometer lap of the 50-kilometer race. Passing me with 10 kilometers to go, one called out cheerfully, "Good luck." That was it. I got good and pissed, jumped on the tails of his skis, and passed him on a hill half a mile from the finish. It wasn't like me, this surge of aggression, strong enough to override my own blurring vision and pounding heart. I knew, all of a sudden, that I didn't have to stop when it started to hurt.

I was coming to understand that mental training—those gooey "visualizations" and "affirmations"—was every bit as real as my banging heart. One summer afternoon former University of Oregon track coach Bill Freeman told me about a story he'd seen in a running magazine, in which marathoners were asked what they thought about as they raced. "They interviewed dinks," he said. "People were saying, 'I mentally build a house.' That's pretty much how you define an unimportant athlete. He may forget his pain, but he's just hopping around out there. Rest assured that Frank Shorter was not building a house. He was thinking about his heart rate, his breathing, what the other athletes were doing."

Back at Mount Hood, Ben Husaby had referred me to a book called *Endless Winter*, an account of a World Cup season by his former teammate Luke Bodensteiner. And indeed, in retirement, with no need to keep his game face on, Bodensteiner made remarkably clear how it felt. Describing an Olympic race in which he'd spilled neon-red energy drink down his skinsuit, he wrote, "Sweat was running in rivulets down my face, and red juice was frozen solid onto my chest. My brain felt like it was imploding, being squeezed by my rushing, acid-filled blood. My vision was turning tunnel, fading from light gray to black in the periphery."

I hadn't pushed myself *that* hard, not yet. But Bodensteiner had also put his finger on something else: how different, how slightly better, I was starting to feel than "normal" people. After finishing thirty-seventh in that race, he wrote, "a weak-looking guy from the *New York Times* asked me a question, shoved a mike into my face, and then turned away, paying no attention to my answer whatsoever. I explained to his tape recorder that a soft, large mammal like himself, who's been on no larger a mountain than the Empire State Building, would have no understanding of this sport anyway, and I left."

• • •

Mentally and physically, by August this large soft mammal was getting hot to race. Like a man with an addiction, I was craving snow. Australia suffers the drawback of being a very great distance away, but it has the good marketing sense to stage its winter when the rest of the globe is mired in the friction of pavement and grass. So I headed to the Australian Alps, skiing on trails past gum trees, the smell of eucalyptus in the air.

But who had time for tourism? I'd signed up for a race at the end of my stay, a 25-kilometer event on the shoulder of Mount Kosciusku, the continent's highest peak. I thought about it every day of my trip—every hour, probably. I was wildly eager to check out the new engine housed beneath my ribs. Too eager: I hit the first hill at a manic clip, passing almost everyone in my wave, my legs moving like steel springs. I was very nearly giddy. But not for long. Before the race was a third gone, I felt leaden. I fell on a downhill. And I lost nearly all my will. I was reduced to a plodder. I started designing a house.

And so, as fall wore on, it was back to my never-ending schedule of exercise. As Mark McGwire hit homers, I roller-skied. As the stock market crashed and rose, I rode the Vasa Trainer. Forget Linda Tripp—I was watching videos of Vegard Ulvang striding up Scandinavian tracks. After a decade of full-time environmental writing, I was suddenly thinking more about the carbon dioxide load in my blood than about the carbon dioxide heating up the atmosphere.

Finally, in November, I went back to the World of Pain. I was ready for the bit this time, and the printouts showed mostly good news. My $VO_2$ Max had gone up about 7 percent, to 58. My muscles produced a quarter less lactic acid. My aerobic threshold was about the same, but I was running half-a-mile-per-hour faster when I reached it. Oh yes, and my body fat had dropped almost in half, down to 6.69 percent. Those numbers were my new physical identity.

But there was one last station of the cross. And that was West Yellowstone, which in November is to nordic skiers what New Hampshire is to presidential candidates in March. Over Thanksgiving, the most serious cross-country skiers in the country descend on the town to train, and this kingdom of Winnebagos and T-shirt shops turns into a republic of the lean.

I was rooming with Ben Husaby, back for one last season with the Factory Team, an elite squad sponsored by Fischer skis, Salomon boots, and Swix waxes, the industry's dominant brands. For two days it felt awfully sweet to be back on snow, and then it felt awfully awful. "West," as the locals call it, lies at 6,666 feet, and the altitude nailed me: slight hills trashed my lungs; walking up the Holiday Inn stairs involved gripping the rail with both hands.

Ben knew what to do. "Watching bad TV is a very important skill for an endurance athlete," he counseled, ordering me to bed. "We had one guy on the national team who could do it twelve or thirteen hours a day." Even without altitude problems, he and the other serious athletes spent an enormous amount of time prone— two training sessions a day leaves enough energy to shovel down food and to nap. A man who doesn't even own a TV, I took his advice. Training was training.

Out on the trails, greats were swooshing past hopefuls. There's Carl Swenson, who won last year's Wisconsin Birkebeiner. There's Laura McCabe, twice an Olympian. Here's Husaby, stopping to help a fifteen-year-old kid from Casper, Wyoming, who is wearing a T-shirt and whose wax is icing up. Husaby melts the wax by licking it (with his *tongue*), and then rewaxes the kid and sends him on his way. It's as if spring training and Little League happened simultaneously on the same fields.

I flailed away on the groomed trails until, on Thanksgiving morning, Husaby told me we were heading into Yellowstone itself. A few park vehicles had left behind iced-over ruts on the closed road, so we could double-pole the entire way. For 25 kilometers I didn't move my feet, just crunched my stomach and pushed with my triceps and thanked heaven I'd done my sit-ups. It wasn't particularly painful, just endless, and I was used to endless.

We finally arrived in Madison Junction, deep in the park, to find ourselves surrounded by a herd of three hundred bison. Husaby and veteran coach Rick Kapala and I headed off through the woods, skiing slowly around a deadfall. From a ridge we watched a coyote sitting serenely in the sun, surveying us and the bison. And then, because we wanted to see a particular hot spot, we forded the thigh-deep Gibbon River. Before long we were dressed again, double-poling another 25 kilometers back down the road as the sun bent behind the ridges.

We weren't going at racing speed—good nordic skiers cover 50 kilometers in two hours, and that's with hills to climb. But a year ago I couldn't have done anything like this. "You showed me some mettle," said Husaby as we finally clicked out of our skis. He didn't even need to say it. For once I knew it myself. I knew that in the year just past I had evolved, ever so slightly, in the direction of bison and coyote.

So now come the races—a couple of ski marathons in January and February, the epic Norwegian Birkebeiner in March. That'll be me, the skinny one, somewhere around the middle of my age group. If the drool is freezing to my chin, you'll know that I'm winning my own private race.

# 43

# Across the Disappearing Finish Line

—*Outside,* November 2000

Barring the odd world war or depression, being a man was once a fairly simple task. My grandfather, for instance, lived to be a well-adjusted ninety-five—he visited Costa Rica on a banana boat at ninety—by walking a few brisk miles every morning and avoiding between-meals snacks.

But it's not so easy anymore. Here are some things you need to know if you're going to be a healthy man, according to a recent issue of *Men's Health*: chronic, day-to-day work stress can lower your sperm count by a third; a diet rich in garlic keeps your aorta flexible; vitamin $B_2$ fights off migraines; shrinking your waist from forty inches to thirty-seven inches cuts diabetes risk in half; you can build your triceps by doing dips off the edge of a swimming pool; if you're determined to have sex in an elevator, a spokesman for the American Elevator and Machine Corporation recommends using a freight elevator ("Many lack security cameras, but check the ceiling to make sure"). Not only that—but negative sit-ups can build abdominal muscles faster than crunches.

None of this would surprise women. For a long time—say, three or four million years—being a woman was hard work. But sometime around 1985, when men in their underwear began reclining on Times Square billboards, manhood became nearly as time-consuming. A sampling of *Men's Fitness* covers over the past year promises "24 Ways to Customize Your Physique," "6 Dangerous Foods," "12 Instant Nutrition Fixes," "7 Best Biceps Builders," "Better Sex—10 Ways to Drive Them Insane," "7 Super Shakes for Peak Energy," "5 Awesome Back Wideners," "5 Ready-Made Seduction Dates," "20 Hospital Survival Tips," "6 Moves for Bigger Arms," and "50 Ways to Improve Your Life—Guaranteed."

I'd never paid much attention to this kind of thing before the winter of 1998, when at the age of thirty-seven I embarked on, well, my quest to spend a year training pretty much full-time to be a cross-country ski racer—I knew I wouldn't win any races, but I wanted to understand my mind and body in new ways, before age closed certain doors. Maybe I was tired of living mainly through my head; maybe I was just freaked to be growing old. In any event, I found my coach, Rob Sleamaker, who drew up a yearlong program that called for more than six hundred hours of training— daily two-, three-, four-hour runs and skis, long bouts of uphill sprinting, my heart-rate monitor bleating softly all the while. Add to that endless sets of crunches and biceps curls and triceps extensions, and before much time had passed, muscles—not underwear ad-size muscles, but still—actually began to appear on my formerly smooth body.

And vanity began to infect my formerly oblivious consciousness. I found myself posing in front of the mirror as I shaved— flexing my pecs so they'd pop up and down, tensing my butt (my glutes, I mean) when I showered, feeling the indentations in my upper arm that marked the birth of my triceps. You couldn't really make out my washboard abs, but I could count the ridges of riblike muscle whenever I tightened my stomach. I read Arnold Schwarzenegger's 1977 autobiography, *Arnold: The Education of a Bodybuilder*, with new understanding.

Unlike Arnold's, however, the veins in my arms bulged like phone cords, not tug lines; my forearms bloomed from celery stalks to broccoli stalks. My wife, Sue, was the only one to notice I was sprouting muscle mass, and even she, in my opinion, paid far too little attention to the details of my emergent triceps. Of course, endurance athletes are not supposed to Popeye up—more muscle takes more blood to feed it, eventually reducing your efficiency. Still, self-image matters, I was finding out. As a boy, resolutely unphysical, I supposed I should exercise in order to get girls. I got girls anyway; eventually I got married and fathered a child and so fulfilled my genetic mandate, and the fact that I couldn't reliably open pickle jars did not prevent my DNA from passing down yea unto the generations.

And yet did I measure up to my forebears, those sturdy small-town westerners, on the manliness scale? My father, growing up, had spent his summers at a log cabin on the edge of Mount Rainier—a place without lights or running water, in the shadow of the great Douglas firs. We'd visit the cabin every few years on some vacation driving trip, and usually we'd find my cousin Craig there. A mountaineer, Craig was forever heading off to Pakistan or Baffin Island or some other place with high icy cliffs to conquer. Sometimes he'd open his pack to show us his collection of carabiners, pitons, and ropes. Dad loved it—this was his fantasy life, long before Everest-mania. But he'd reared us in the cushy suburbs of the East, where SATs counted more than sit-ups, and sometimes it seemed to me as if I was devolving, defying Darwin.

That summer, as I roller-skied and ran and lifted and interval-trained in preparation for the winter race season, Mom and Dad celebrated their fortieth anniversary. Dad had recently retired after a lifetime as a journalist, and the whole family joined them at a slightly down-at-the-heels resort in the White Mountains that offered a shaggy nine-hole golf course out back. It was a great pleasure that summer to head out onto the green with my dad and my younger brother, Tom. I'd never played before, and I had no swing;

they had to show me how to grip the club. But when I connected I had power—the ball would sail away into the middle distance. It didn't bother me that it went left or right or onto the neighboring fairway. I just liked the idea that it went long and strong.

. . .

The more I trained, and especially the more I began to race, the more I understood that my mind needed toughening at least as much as my body—that endurance was about going until it hurt, when the natural impulse was to slow down, and then deciding whether to listen to that impulse or not. When I came back from a few weeks of summer skiing in Australia, I began the longest, hardest month of my training schedule, an endless September that peaked one Saturday morning with a 238-minute run. My parents were visiting our Adirondack home, and they offered to watch my six-year-old daughter, Sophie, while I worked out. I ran and ran and ran some more, finally stumble-charging up the last rise, congratulating myself that from now on the whole year was downhill. I was peeling off my T-shirt and savoring the smug aura of finishing something hard when I noticed Dad. He was about a hundred yards away from Mom, walking back and forth, and he was lurching a bit. "He's testing himself," she said, with a frantic edge in her voice.

Slowly the story started to come out. In August he'd been hiking hard in the Cascades, feeling fine. But when he got home he'd begun stumbling a bit—and once fell right over. Some days, Mom added, he slurred his words. Dad had chalked it up to the late-summer humidity, or perhaps a sinus infection, and had rallied (and reassured) himself by walking faster, working up a sweat. But when I took him aside that afternoon he confessed that his right side felt weak. Could I have had a small stroke? he asked me. As soon as he said it, I felt myself starting to panic—it had never even entered my mind that at sixty-eight he'd start to decline. But I knew it must be true; it would explain the balance, the speech, even a few recent mild displays of uncharacteristic temper.

I bade my parents good-bye with a sour taste in the back of my throat. The next day Dad phoned from home in Boston to say that his doctor was convinced that indeed he'd had a very mild stroke. He'd scheduled an MRI for later in the week just to make sure, but he told Mom and Dad to go ahead planning a trip to Mexico; I could tell from his voice that Dad was immensely relieved.

And I was too. I spent a little time thinking about the Meaning of It All—how your body would eventually betray you no matter how fit you got—and then I went back to work, because racing season was coming into distant view. The weather began to change; a front came through one of those early autumn nights, dropping temperatures down into the low thirties, threatening the tomatoes. The weatherman talked about "the possibility of sleet or snow on the high ridges." The S word hadn't been heard in these parts since early May, and it made me quiver inside.

I started stacking firewood in earnest that week, and while I was working Friday afternoon I looked up to see our dog, Barley, trotting toward me with something in her mouth. At first I thought it was a shoe, but when she dropped it for me I saw it was a hawk—dead, but utterly unmarked, a broad-wing, all strength and sinew. Sophie and I spread its strong, gray feathers, examined its powerful beak and talons, and then wrapped it in plastic and put it in the freezer so that she could take it to school. I went back to the woodpile.

When I looked up a few minutes later, Sue was standing there in the fading light with tears running down her cheeks. My mom had just called. Dad had a brain tumor, "an aggressive nonbenign tumor." They were operating on Tuesday. Just like that.

I hugged her for a long time, and then headed straight out into the woods, cursing and crying and carrying on. Mom said the doctor had told them that even with the operation "the long-term average survival" was twelve months, which put a new spin on the whole idea of long-term. For me, twelve months was a "training cycle." I was still sobbing when Dad came on the phone. "This is ridiculous, isn't it?" he said with a rueful chuckle. He'd been shaving when I called, and for some reason that made me even sadder. How do you manage to look in the mirror when someone has just told you that in a year you won't be there?

A couple of weeks before, I'd visited some actuarial Web site that let you calculate your likely life span. Didn't smoke, long-lived relatives, plenty of exercise, low cholesterol—when I tapped the final button it told me I was going to die at ninety-three. I'm certain that Dad would have gotten the same result. He was strong and active; he'd just written his first book. But there was no little button on the actuarial table for something called glioblastoma, the most virulent form of brain cancer.

When we got to Boston the next day, the change was obvious. Six days earlier his speech had been a little slurred. Three days earlier he'd driven to church and chaired a meeting. Today, Saturday, his triumph had been walking the twenty yards to the Adirondack chairs in the backyard. His world was shrinking with incomprehensible speed. He told us about finding out the bad news: the surgeon had pronounced his death sentence, and then said he should choose. "I could get a big bottle of Scotch and have a wonderful last night before going into a coma, or I could have this surgery and that would keep me going a little longer."

. . .

The night before Dad went to the hospital, as I was taking off his slippers to put him to bed, I could see the hard, veiny calves that only a month ago were powering him up high mountains in his native Northwest. They were useless now. Was he useless? What did it mean to lose your body in a week? And what would it mean, twenty-four hours hence, to lose some large chunk of your mind?

That next morning, at the hospital, Dad passed into another, yet-smaller world, where his abilities meant nothing. When the surgeon finally came for his pre-op visit, Dad asked only one question: "Will my personality change?"

"I hope not," the doctor said.

We watched as they wheeled him out of his room to the operating theater. It was after lunch before the doctor appeared to give us the news. Dad had come through surgery OK, but the pathology was exactly what he suspected: glioblastoma, grade four. The worst grade. He couldn't get it all, it had already spread to both lobes. Sorry. The next few months, the doctor said, would be "the good time," a phrase that would come to haunt us.

When they finally let us up to see him, Dad looked . . . beautiful. A turban of bandages wrapped his head, but beneath it his face was eerily young, as if he were in his twenties. The sparkle was back in his eyes. When we turned on the TV the Red Sox were leading the Indians in game one of their playoff series behind seven RBIs from Mo Vaughn. Dad was making jokes—he whose head had been sawed open and then the two halves pulled apart by traction. This much was clear: his personality had not changed, not one whit. Doubtless it would darken when the tumor recurred, when the swelling built up again. The hope, though, was that we'd bought ourselves a few months, a window of time to make peace with his passing. Nothing more.

And so we settled into the pattern of small victories and somewhat larger defeats that must mark most terminal illness. They shifted Dad to a "rehabilitation hospital" in the suburbs, where after daily morning trips by ambulance to the radiation ward he would return for afternoons of physical therapy. The therapy rooms reminded me of the world where I'd spent much of the last year—they were filled with weight machines, parallel bars, treadmills. But here, in place of the ersatz philosophy of the gym, real struggle prevailed. Dad's workouts, as tightly scheduled and as exhausting as mine, involved batting a balloon back and forth with the therapist, folding washcloths, unscrewing a jar top, kicking a ball. He could swing his right foot perhaps an inch, enough to nudge the ball along the floor, but no more. When he tried to steer his wheelchair, it inevitably drifted to the right till he hit a wall, reflecting the now-distorted architecture of his brain. His major triumph: learning to apply and disengage the wheelchair brake.

Through it all I kept running. I suppose I should have stopped, if only because it seemed in such poor taste, calibrating my body's improvement as Dad's withered away. But Dad had been the most interested in my project from the beginning. And there was nothing else to structure my life. No one expected me at an office. I was commuting between the Adirondacks and Boston, between my adult and boyhood homes (I was sleeping on the bed I'd slept on as a boy, the same bed Dad had slept on in his youth). There was no way I could write—when I tried to still my mind enough to string two thoughts together, I invariably began to weep. Only motion seemed to relax me.

I'd begun this compulsive exercising on the premise that I was at the tail end of my youth. Now it was all too easy to calculate that if I lived as long as my father was going to, I was already halfway used up. But I could feel the second half of my life starting in more complicated ways too. Identities long fixed shifted back and forth. Sometimes I was still his son. But then the next morning would dawn, and we'd need yet again to make some impossible decision: more radiation, say. Dad would doze off while the doctor was explaining the options, and we'd be left trying to figure out what he might want, what we might want. The goal of all the physical therapy diminished. Instead of teaching him to regain real function in his muscles, the single aim became training him to help in the process of transferring himself from bed to wheelchair, and vice versa. If he learned that, he could go home and Mom could take care of him by herself. The technique, as detailed and precise as a good cross-country skiing kick, involved lifting his butt an inch up off the bed and then sliding himself in two stages about a foot and a half into the wheelchair. He would push himself up on his knuckles, slide ten inches, rest thirty seconds till the panting subsided, then make the next assault. Each time he'd forget the sequence and need to be reminded; each time it left him red-faced and tired.

All this training, and for what? It wasn't like my training. I knew I was getting steadily stronger and fitter. Not Dad. He worked all afternoon stretching his rubber bands, lifting his tiny dumbbells, and yet his body decayed faster than he could build it up.

I went in to the rehab center one morning and found him in an uncharacteristic rage. Some doctor had wandered through that morning (one of the glories of managed care was that unknown doctors constantly drifted in and out of our lives) and remarked to him, on the basis of a handshake, that he was getting weaker. Dad was outraged, agitated. He didn't want to go to therapy that afternoon, but I talked him into it.

You followed your schedule no matter what; sometimes that seemed about all my year had taught me.

· · ·

If I needed a metaphor for my autumn, it came in early November. Back in the Adirondacks for a week, I noticed some fresh new pavement on a back road on the far side of the Hudson River. Fresh pavement, to a roller-skier, exerts a nearly gravitational pull—smooth and fast, it's the next best thing to snow. What I hadn't noticed was just how steep the hills were. I was, as always, wearing a bike helmet, but I'd forgotten my knee pads, and the light was fading. Predictably, I went for it. For an hour I skied the hills, tucking for fast descents, powering up with short, choppy kicks, feeling pretty damn strong. And then, predictably, a dog ran out at the bottom of a hill just as a car passed on my left—and I was down in a second.

Predictably, I jumped up, in the way that guys do when they've fallen, as if to say, Oh, I meant to do that. I waved off the stricken driver—and as soon as he was out of sight I sat right back down to consider. True, my knees were bleeding dramatically, soaking my shredded tights, but on the other hand I had ninety minutes left in my workout. I'd snapped a pole, so I clearly wasn't going to keep skiing, but I had my sneakers in the car. And so—predictably?—I ran, knees bleeding and stiff. It was clearly stupid. Perhaps I just wanted to hurt, and to keep going through the hurt.

My road-scraped knees healed just in time for me to return to Lake Placid and the giant treadmill at the Olympic Training Center for the final readout on my year's training. I'd passed through this particular crucible in the spring, establishing my baseline numbers and learning just how much the test could hurt—you ran until you couldn't run anymore, or at least until you thought you couldn't. This time, rubber bit clenched in my mouth to catch my exhalations, I lasted two minutes longer than I had in April, but it didn't cheer me up. Because I knew I'd had another minute in me, if only I'd fought the pain a little harder. But when the treadmill tilted toward the gut-check stage, I couldn't keep going. It hurt, that's why.

My coach, Rob, professed delight. "You've had a forty-five percent improvement in body fat, your lactate threshold is twenty-five percent better—your engine is burning hotter at a lower lactate production. It means you can ski at a faster pace longer." Part of me did feel exhilarated. It had worked the way it was supposed to, all those hours and miles. Mine was not the physique of a champion, but what I had done was maximize my genetic potential, grown about as powerful as my ancestry would allow.

But the day left me feeling unsettled. When things had gotten really tough, I had looked for a way out. My heart might have become more efficient, but my *heart* seemed no stronger.

Maybe it was because I was beginning to question whether endurance was such a grand goal anyhow.

From the moment I'd learned of Dad's first conversation with the surgeon—Scotch or scalpel—part of me had been wondering whether we should be keeping him alive. We'd press the specialists with questions about whether his condition would improve, and all we'd get was the Ph.D. equivalent of shrugs. In the meantime, he was home, enduring, and Mom was, too. The HMO professed to believe that a couple of hours of nursing assistance a day was all Mom needed; never mind that Dad outweighed her by eighty or ninety pounds. She hired extra aides to come in the evening and help her get him out of bed; the next-door neighbor's son slept upstairs now just in case he rolled out of bed and she couldn't get him back in. New pills piled up almost daily; dosages changed with every visit to the doctor; Mom was awake by six to give him his first medicines, and still up at midnight to feed him the final batch. When I thought about the burden she was under, I doubted I could handle anything like it. And yet she kept going forward, forward, forward, like—well, like an elite athlete. In her case, though, it wasn't uphill intervals and mental imagery that had laid the base. It was year upon year of loving, so consistently that the giving had become instinctive.

As for me, if watching someone die could perform the same kind of magic, I wasn't sure I was ready for it. When the treadmill got steep enough, I started looking around for someone to turn it off.

Whenever we were with the doctors, no matter how much of a fog he seemed to be in, Dad would ask that they treat his cancer "aggressively." But one night, when I was talking to him very late, he said, "If it's going to be like this all the time, then there has to be a cutoff somewhere." Amen, I thought. Where's the guy with the switch?

. . .

We made it to Thanksgiving, and I spent the week in West Yellowstone—my longest absence from his bedside so far, a guilty vacation—at the annual cross-country training camp that fills the town with gaunt, wax-obsessed nordic racers trying to cope with the 6,600-foot altitude. I flew home on Friday, though, for a delayed turkey dinner, where we managed to convince ourselves that we had much to be thankful for and that, with Dad propped up at table's end, all was joy. After the pie settled, I went for a run and instantly understood why athletes are so eager to train at altitude. My body had compensated for the thin Montana air by adding extra red blood cells. I ran through suburban Boston on a high—no matter how hard I pushed, I couldn't make myself hurt. My heart-rate monitor showed I was working reasonably hard, but I could have been out for the lightest of jogs. I felt out ahead of my body, as if I was outrunning my feet.

Sadly, the corpuscles quickly disappeared, and with them the sense that I had become a minor deity. Worse than that, the East was still warm and bare as December began. The temperature hit the seventies on the first of the month. The pond by our house was filled with summery ripples. No need for the woodstove; we slept with the windows open.

It bothered me on many levels. For ten years I'd been a nearly full-time student of global warming—worrying, tracking the rising sea temperatures that were bleaching coral reefs, writing about the increase in the strength and frequency of hurricanes. But I felt it most personally come winter. Always my favorite of seasons, it had become deeply unreliable. As the man from Fischer Skis had told me in West Yellowstone, global warming had already damaged their business, interrupting every winter with long stretches of mud and thaw. Business would doubtless carry on; in fact, I'd just come across a series of economic forecasts proving, in the smug fashion of economists, that increases in the greens fees from golfers would outweigh the losses from declining ski sales. But I didn't want to play golf—I wanted to speed sublimely through the woods, riding on an outstretched ski, pushing with every muscle in my body. I wanted the annual remission from friction.

Rob had been pushing me to pick a final race to aim for, something grand enough to be worthy of this whole experiment—and he'd been urging me to think about the Norwegian Birkebeiner, the mother of all cross-country races, held each March on a course that runs over the mountains from Rena to Lillehammer. Open to all comers, it attracts thousands of Norwegians, and most of the world's best marathon skiers. As they race, they commemorate the pivotal event in Norway's thirteenth-century civil war. The Birkebeiners—Birchleggers—were the underdogs, "often in such dire need that they had nothing but the bark of birch trees as footwear." But they were determined that the rival faction, the Baglers, not capture Haakon Haakonsson, the toddler son of their dying king. So on Christmas Day 1205, two Birkebeiner skiers spirited him away on an epic journey across the mountains. The boy grew up to be King Haakon and to finally rout the Baglers, raising Norway to its medieval glory. And hence, each year in late March, racers pound those same grueling 58 kilometers, about 40 miles, mostly uphill, each carrying an eight-pound pack to match the weight of the young king.

I doubted I could go. With Dad dying, the prospect of a transatlantic trip seemed unlikely. And I wondered if I could even finish the race. But I still logged on to the race Web site and clicked the button for an application. Maybe Dad would get better for a while—maybe the "good time" would arrive. I knew I wanted to go; it sounded crazy, hard enough to justify this crazy year.

This crazy year in which winter seemed never to come. By mid-December we'd set up the Christmas tree at church and gone caroling in shirtsleeves. Finally, December 17 brought a little snow to the Adirondacks, and a few phone calls established that the Olympic trails at Lake Placid were partially open. They were barely covered, but it was skiing, and I kicked around and around the same short loops with the junior biathletes, guns strapped to their backs, and the local masters skiers, all of us desperate for snow. The next day warm, foggy air melted big tawny patches in the snow, and it was back to the damn NordicTrack. December was shot.

We got through Christmas Day in Boston just fine—a lot of the ornaments hung at wheelchair height, testament to Dad's pleasure in the work—but then, tired from the strain of this last big celebration, Dad was all but comatose for a couple of days. "Were it my dad," said the surgeon, "I wouldn't do much more."

At which point Dad emerged from his fog for the first time all day to ask yet again that he be treated "aggressively." Which annoyed the hell out of me—some part of me wanted him to go away and stop bothering us. Stop making me feel guilty for not being more help to my mother; stop pulling me away from my family; stop stop stop being so damn needy, so unlike my father. Which, of course, left me feeling twice as guilty as before.

A snowstorm might have righted me. It usually does. A couple of hours alone in the woods, gliding along, pushing up hills and carving down them, breaking out into the open on Adirondack lakes and tucking back into stands of hemlock, reminding me of the proper order and scale of things.

• • •

By late January the ground was still bare, and Dad was setting off on a major journey. Each day he seemed to grow a bit more abstracted from his shrinking world. He was never short with any of us. If his grandchildren were on hand, he would watch them playing around his bed with deep delight, and he never ceased following Mom with his eyes.

Sometimes the world he was visiting seemed inscrutable. Once I asked him what he was thinking so deeply about, and he replied, in a loud voice, "Insects!" But he did tell Mom several times that he constantly saw a white line in front of his eyes. One morning, when he was more alert than usual and when we had the house to ourselves, I asked him if he could describe the line to me. He asked for a pencil and, gripping it tightly in his shaking hand, drew a wavering line about two-thirds of the way across the page and labeled it R. On the edge of the paper, he drew a wavering circle and with great effort wrote "W. Ocean" across it. (In a lifetime of writing, they were the last words he ever wrote.) The picture represented, he said, a "typical Western river" leading to a "Western ocean."

"And what does that ocean mean?" I asked.

"Infinity," he said. "Completeness."

He nodded off for a few moments and then woke back up. Why didn't the river connect to the ocean? I asked.

There were, he said, necessary tasks still to be done, but he couldn't find the words to say what they were.

"Is death more scary to think about or more peaceful?" I asked.

"More peaceful," he said emphatically, and then drifted back to sleep.

That night at dinner he seemed happy—we'd been discussing "ultimate truths," he told Mom, with just a little smile to let us know he knew how unlike him it was to discuss ultimate truths. But a new man was clearly taking shape before our eyes.

· · ·

My own journey seemed all but irrelevant, dull even to me, but by now the training was so ingrained that I kept with it almost automatically. And Rob, the one person besides my wife whom I'd trusted with my resolve to mount a supreme effort in some race, kept trying to help me find the right venue.

The trip to Lillehammer seemed less likely than ever, but I came across a brochure for the annual Keskinada races in Ottawa, in late February. The theme for 1999 was Norway; they were trying to duplicate parts of the Birkebeiner in Canada, including sending off one wave of racers carrying eight-pound backpacks. Ottawa was only a quick trip from Boston; this one I figured I could make. And so the images that filled my mind on training runs were suddenly Canadian: the pine forests of the Gatineau Park, the 50-kilometer trail. There was finally a little snow on the ground, and Rob told me to prepare with a four-hour time trial two weeks before the race. Four hours is a long time, especially with none of the adrenaline of a race to distract you; I headed to the ski tracks and did the same five-kilometer loop eleven times, till I knew every soft spot in the snow. Every lap brought me by a pigpen filled with noisy hogs; I'd stop there and choke down some energy gel. When the clock finally stopped, I'd gone 55 kilometers, and proved to myself that at the very least I could manage the distances in the race ahead. And I'd done it with my pack on my back, like a true Birchlegger.

Almost in spite of myself, I could feel my body starting to peak. As the really long workouts of the fall dwindled in number and distance, and the brutal intervals built up my speed, power began to accumulate. I imagined that I knew what a racehorse felt like in the gate, pent-up energy ready to express itself. Long, hard uphill skiing left me feeling spent but not wasted; my body craved fuel and burned it evenly; I was eager for a test, impatient for the Ottawa race to arrive. I was, in fact, in the best physical shape of my life.

In the middle of all this, my friend John Race came to visit. We'd met when he guided me up Mount Rainier five years before. Intellectually curious the way I was physically curious, he'd nonetheless spent almost all his energy on things of the body and the spirit. He'd spent months on Mount McKinley, gotten within five hundred feet of the top of Everest, climbed 26,000-foot peaks like Cho Oyu. Now he was hungry for intellectual growth, and he wanted to write about his experiences. He was playing on the path I'd been following since I could first remember, and I was playing on his. It made me think of the first notion Rob had taught me when we'd started working together a year before—each of us born to be balanced physically, intellectually, and spiritually.

It hadn't taken me long to figure out how linked all three could be. If exercise was about being physical, then racing—being willing to hurt, to go harder than you wanted to—had an obvious spiritual quality. But the neat progression of my idea ran into trouble when Dad got sick. He was clearly operating at some higher level now, but it wasn't because he was trying. Instead, it seemed to be because he was letting go. Not giving up, not dropping out, but slowly, methodically, patiently letting go of his life. Every so often, I kept trying to ask serious questions, to find out what was going on inside. Partly it was just my curiosity, but I sensed, too, that he enjoyed talking about it, liked the fact that someone acknowledged he was dying and that it was an interesting process. One day he muttered that he was trying to figure out if there was something beyond this "make-believe" world, if there was something beyond "next week." His metaphors, like the drawing of the river, tended always toward the outdoor, the concrete, toward the joys of the Western boyhood that had filled his imagination ever since. "I feel like I'm climbing," he told me slowly one day. "Like I'm climbing up a cliff."

"Are you near the top?" I asked.

"Getting there," he said, with a grin.

I thought of all the climbs we'd taken when I was young, in the mountains of Maine and New Hampshire; of the pleasure he'd taken in the Adirondacks when I moved there; of the long trip we'd taken with his brother and my brother around Mount Rainier. Every time I'd looked at him in those weeks on the Wonderland Trail, he'd been grinning. Climbing wasn't a struggle for him, didn't represent a battle or even a test. It was a great joy, because it carried you higher, to where the view was clearer. And more than that—though the grand view may have started you slogging in the first place, no one kept hiking for years unless they came to like the slog. Sometimes it's bittersweet to reach the top, because there's nothing to do but linger for a while and go back down. This time, however, he wouldn't need to descend.

I'd started this exercise of exercising in an effort to try on a new identity, the way a high-school boy might try on meanness, or a college boy might grow a goatee. But now, watching Dad, I realized what a solid thing an identity is. He was unchanged even by this catastrophe—he remained as decent and egoless a man as I'd ever met. As for me, I'd examined my core from a different side, or placed it under light of a different wavelength, and found it to be much as I'd always known it: curious, eager, tempted by deep commitment but afraid of the effort and pain.

I could live with that—it had served me well so far—but now I wondered if I could die with that. Wondered if I could go as gracefully as my father was going, as bravely and yet as peacefully. What would it be like to reach the end of my life without regrets?

Dad took one last trip into the hospital, for one last MRI. The tumor had fired up again, the doctors said, started once more to grow. Don't even bother calling the ambulance if something happens, they advised—you don't want them sticking a tube down his throat. Mom listened, asked Dad if he had anything to say.

He looked up, and in a clear, conversational tone announced, "I have this fascinating vision of a white line along the edge of a riverbank."

. . .

So there was Dad, cheerful in the face of a brain tumor. And here I was, gloomy because I'd caught a cold two days before the big race in Ottawa, and was reduced to obsessively guzzling tea, sucking on zinc tablets, and fretting about compromised respiratory efficiency. But on race morning I was up at 5:45, and I was the first to arrive at Gatineau Park. I splurged thirty dollars at the ski-waxing booth and watched the ski techs patiently iron on purple and red and then a coat of klister because the tracks were icy. I took my skis outside, tried them for a few strides, and instantly felt my mood soaring—I had rock-solid kick and lustrous glide. They felt like perfect extensions of my legs, each twitch converted into forward momentum.

The starting pen for my wave filled with other backpack-carrying skiers, about forty of us among the hundreds of more conventional racers. An official weighed the rucksacks, making sure they topped the infant-king-Haakon line on the scale. We shuffled back and forth in the tracks for a few minutes, trying to stay limber, until the Norwegian ambassador to Canada sounded the ceremonial horn and we took off.

Because of the packs, it was easy enough to keep my competition in sight. We hit the first long uphill, and my legs felt so strong I had to consciously rein myself in a little, remind myself I'd be out on the course for a good three hours. One by one I picked off the guys in my wave—a fellow carrying a blaze-orange knapsack, a fellow in camouflage Lycra, a fast-looking skier who somehow managed to fall on the first small downhill. Twenty minutes into the race, a fellow in a brown rucksack was in front of me, and I was pretty sure he was either second or third in my wave—in other words, if I passed him I'd be in the money. I stayed on his tail for a few minutes, pulling abreast occasionally, even chatting for a while to let him know the pace wasn't hurting me. And I passed him.

After that I was skiing by myself. The hills just kept on coming, and my form began gradually to erode; by the halfway point I was laboring. I stopped for a drink of water and a ClifShot, and the people manning the table seemed concerned. "You're shivering," said one. "Are you hypothermic?" Before they could ask again, I skied off.

At some point along the course, a photographer crouched, taking pictures of everyone coming by so that he could try to sell them at the banquet that night. Through his lens, I was just one more tired-looking guy stuck somewhere in the middle of an unimportant race. And yet for me it was an epic. I crouched down in my tuck and let my muscles recover for a few minutes as the trail tilted downhill. Then came a long flat. Finally, at about 40 kilometers, the trail turned back on itself, and for about 500 yards you could see the skiers right behind you. Oh, God—one had a brown backpack, the same fellow I'd passed nearly two hours before, now right on my tail, maybe forty seconds behind. Worse, my limbs were slowing down—I couldn't muster more than a sluggish kick.

I could feel myself about to give up, about to be passed, about to turn normal.

And then I didn't. I made it up one hill and coasted down the other side; after that, though I was shaky and absolutely drained, I managed to go hard. Not fast. But fast enough, because I was still passing people. Fast enough, because every time I looked over my shoulder, the tracks were clear. Eventually there was a sign by the trail and it said: "Finish 1,000 Meters." Did a thousand meters mean a kilometer? Ten kilometers? My hypoxic brain fuzzed the question around until suddenly the trail spit out onto an open field, and the finish was only a few hundred good old English yards away. I sprinted, I fell across the line, someone picked me up and wrapped a wool blanket around me. They said I'd come in second in my wave.

· · ·

My father's race finished on March 3. Though his sickness had lasted barely six months, half the impossibly short "long-term average survival" the doctors had given us at the start, he had endured. He'd kept going.

I had spent a year thinking about endurance. Trying to understand it as a function of physiology, of lactic acid and capillary networks. Trying to understand it as the ability to fight through the drama of pain. But now I understood it, too, as a kind of elegance, a lightness that could come only from such deep comfort with yourself that you began to forget about yourself. Something no heart monitor would ever measure.

Dad died in time to let me go to Norway for the Birkebeiner. Once I'd thought that this would be the epic end of my saga, but now I knew that whatever epiphanies I'd been allotted had come at the edge of his sickbed. Now there was just the pleasure of enduring in a great crowd of others doing the same—old men, some of them eighty and eighty-five, a little stiff in their Lycra, but still elegant. They'd been skiing these hills fifty years ago, tracking down

Allied airdrops in the woods, and they did so still, for the sheer joy of it.

The course was brutal as advertised, and I was in no danger of letting loose another epic performance. But never mind. I went deep inside, kept track of my weakening calves and my tightening chest, measured my resources against the distance left to go. And it all came out just fine—a little over four hours of hard skiing, ending with a series of sharp downhills into the Olympic stadium filled with brass bands and cheering crowds. I finished just above the middle of my age group, which I declared a great victory, considering they were all Norwegians. But I took my conquest as quietly as everyone else—there was no whooping or hollering on the bus to the showers, just satisfied and tired smiles. The year was over, and it was time for a smoked salmon pizza and a bottle of Ringnes and some Tiger Balm to rub on my aching thighs.

The next morning dawned clear and cold, and Sue and Sophie and I went for another ski. And for the first time in a long time, it meant nothing at all.

# · 44 ·

## Mr. Natural

*—Outside*, May 2003

It was 7:15 on a gray winter morning, and I was walking across an icy parking lot at the Lahey Clinic, outside Boston, when I slipped and went down hard. Banged but not broken, I jumped up in the cartoon-quick way that guys do, as if to imply that I hadn't actually fallen but was just making a planned reconnaissance of the pavement. It was precisely the kind of accident that I'd had my share of in my first forty years. A fluke, an outlier, unpredictable.

I was headed in for a full-day battery of tests. Lahey is a vast medical city, its walls filled with posters reminding patients that *U.S. News & World Report* ranked it one of America's top hospitals, a Harvard of healing. Partly I was there as a reporter, finishing work on a book, *Enough*, about the efforts of technoscientists to use genes, nanotechnology, and other new disciplines to keep us alive and young forever. But mostly I was there as a recent arrival at that milestone that is forty, ready for my first real overhaul—an "executive physical," they call it. Looked at another way, I was there for my entrance exam into a statistical universe I'll inhabit for the rest of my life.

Your first four decades are the random decades. Maybe you slip on that patch of ice, maybe your SUV rolls into a ditch. But nothing medically serious happens to a large enough group of people to amount to a statistic worth knowing; the leading causes of death are still things like accidents, homicide, suicide, infectious disease. But slowly, subtly, sometime around midlife, your particular data points start to arrange themselves on the larger human curve. Flukes settle into probabilities, percentages. The doctor wants to start tracking your good cholesterol, your bad cholesterol. If you are a male, this new world hits home the first time someone in a white coat puts a glove on and tells you to bend over. ("Mildly enlarged," my Lahey doctor, internist John Przybylski, told me. "You have to get up at night to pee? That's your prostate knocking at the door.") By the end of my day at Lahey, after I'd been through half a dozen tests—from X-ray (obvious signs of arthritis around my lowest vertebra) to colonoscopy to allergy (lung capacity starting to decrease)—the avuncular Dr. P. promised we'd be able to calculate how likely I was to die of a heart attack by the age of fifty.

My results were not all that startling, or all that bad, just the first inexorable signs of what could only be termed decline. All on schedule—but that was the point. My body was now on a schedule. "We're here to talk to you about the next forty or fifty years of your life," the doctor said as he picked up my chart. Looking a little more closely at the dates, he corrected himself subtly: "The next thirty or forty or fifty years of your life."

• • •

This, of course, is the great boomer bummer. Most of us alive today can reasonably expect to live to seventy-five, while at the turn of the last century the average American dropped dead at forty-seven. But that great leap in life expectancy won't repeat itself in this millennium—it came with revolutions in sanitation and antibiotics. Even if we wiped out cancer, we'd add only a couple of years to the average life span. But that doesn't mean we're going quietly into the good night. Not us—we're entitled; we've got technology. Never mind Viagra. It gets way, way weirder than that.

A confluence of new technological developments has suddenly led some from this generation to imagine that there might be an escape clause, a way out of mortality altogether. It doesn't take much poking around the techie Web sites to find people dreaming hard about physical immortality. And their dreams sound increasingly more like science fiction than science.

Consider, for example, Dr. Michael West, the head of a Massachusetts company called Advanced Cell Technology, which in 2001 (a year before the Raelian UFO cult's Clonaid claimed to have done so) cloned a human embryo. West didn't grow it into a baby, partly because he has other things in mind. Some of those things involve curing diseases—he'd like to harvest stem cells from cloned embryos to see if they're of use in the fight against, say, Parkinson's disease. But right about there, West parts company with what we normally consider medicine. He has told one interviewer after another that what he's really interested in is keeping humans alive—and young—forever. A team of biologists who worked for him at another corporation managed to synthesize telomerase, the enzyme that keeps cells from dying off after so many divisions. Now he's imagining "making body components one by one," each of them "made young by cloning. Then our body would be made young again segmentally, like an antique car is restored by exchanging failed components."

Such sentiments are not uncommon. At a conference on advanced technology in 1999, University of California at San Francisco molecular geneticist Cynthia Kenyon explained how she had dramatically extended the lives of a class of worms. It was, she told her fellow researchers, as if a nonagenarian suddenly looked fortysomething. "Just imagine it: I'm ninety," said the forty-five-year-old scientist. And if genes won't do the whole trick, researchers are ready with a wide array of other plans. Nanotechnologists—who manipulate matter at the atomic and molecular levels—believe that their tiny machines will soon be able to patrol the bloodstream, constantly repairing damage and eventually replacing all the functions of the circulatory system. When a nanotechnologist was asked in a recent *New York Times* article if he would miss the beat of the unneeded heart, he said no: "The noise in my ears keeps me up when I try to go to sleep."

A few years ago, Alcor Life Extension Foundation, the Scottsdale, Arizona–based cryonics company that is reportedly storing Red Sox legend Ted Williams's frozen carcass, was investigated for freezing the head of an eighty-three-year-old woman before she was declared legally dead. Alcor's attorney called in depositions from top scientists; Eric Drexler, the father of nanotechnology, asserted that "future medicine will one day be able to build cells, tissues, and organs to repair damaged tissues." Hans Moravec, head of the Mobile Robot Laboratory at Carnegie Mellon University's Robotics Institute, in Pittsburgh, took the idea further. "It requires only a moderately liberal extrapolation of present technical trends," he said, "to admit the future possibility of reversing the effects of particular diseases, of aging, and of death, as currently defined."

It is at least possible, in other words, that we stand somewhere near the dawn of that great human dream, life eternal. So why does it sound a little . . . nasty?

· · ·

Always before, life has meant passing through. Making way for those who will come after. Coming to terms with decline. Living intensely in the moments we get. Accepting that the day will come when, instead of telemarking off the icy cornice, we'll rock by the fire and *remember* telemarking off the icy cornice. Understanding that, like everything before us, we will rot our way back into the woof and warp of the planet. That's what humans are: animals that can anticipate their demise.

And being human has always meant being, in some irreducible

way, yourself. Not a genetically programmed machine designed for maximum performance, not an interface with silicon or with nanomachines giving you more power by orders of magnitude. That basic identification—I am me—is the reason that, in the end, activities like sports have real meaning. Otherwise it doesn't mean much to accomplish anything, because who is it doing the accomplishing?

Think I'm exaggerating? The same theorists working to get rid of the human heart are also busy imagining sports the new breed of humans—or semi-robots—might want to play. "This could be an especially interesting prospect for highly dangerous activities you might not otherwise have the nerve to try," writes nanotech pioneer Robert Freitas in his essay "The Birth of the Cyborg." Boxing, parachuting, mountaineering. In such a world, people could "feel reckless," Freitas says, "without risking personal harm." Without, in other words, it meaning a thing. You could be Super Mario.

· · ·

Or you could choose otherwise and be yourself. As the afternoon at Lahey wore on, there was one exam left: the stress test. I stripped down to my shorts while a pretty nurse shaved my chest and hooked me up to a set of monitors. I climbed aboard the treadmill and began to walk, in accordance with the standard Bruce protocol for the Treadmill Exercise Stress Test, beginning at 1.7 miles per hour on a 10 percent grade and getting steeper and harder every three minutes. But—and this will amaze health club athletes—you get to hold on to the front bar. It's true that by the time the twenty-one minutes were up, my forearms were cramping. But it's also true that I was going six miles per hour up a 22 percent grade. And I was still able to wheeze "No problem" every time the nurse asked me how I was doing. I aced the test—me, my own out-the-door-every-afternoon-for-a-run-bike-ski self.

"Now I'll be able to say yes when people ask if anyone's ever gotten all the way through," the nurse said. Could one impress pretty nurses with a nonbeating nanoheart? Could one impress oneself? When I sat down with the doctor, we looked over all my numbers and calculated that there was a 3 percent chance I'd die of a coronary before the decade was out. Three percent's not nothing, and in the next decade it will get higher, and the decade after that, and then, by God, it will someday happen. But I'll take it. I can deal with being a real human.

# Acknowledgments

The pieces collected in this book represent not only my work but also the efforts of the large number of people required to put a magazine together. I'll mention the editors with whom I've worked, but behind them is a small army of fact-checkers, proofreaders, and others who make writers seem better than they really are. I learned this early on, working at the *New Yorker* with Mr. Shawn but also with people like Eleanor Gould, John Bennett, Martin Baron, Peter Canby, Sheila McGrath, John Murphy, and a great many others.

At *Orion*, I'd like to thank Aina Barten, Jennifer Sahn, Chip Blake, Laurie Lane Zucker, Hal Clifford, and many others; at the *New York Review of Books*, Robert Silvers and Barbara Epstein; at the *Utne Reader*, Jay Walljasper; at *Outside,* Hal Espen and Elizabeth Hightower; at *Adirondack Life,* Betsy Folwell and Galen Crane; at *DoubleTake,* Robert Coles; at *Mother Jones,* Monika Bauerlein and Roger Cohen; at *Grist,* Chip Giller and Lisa Hymas; at *OnEarth*, Doug Barasch and George Black; at *Christian Century,* Debra Bendis; at *Gourmet,* Jane Daniels Lear; at the *Atlantic,* Corby Kummer and Cullen Murphy; at *Sierra*, Bruce and Joan

Hamilton; Mel Allen at *Yankee;* and at *Harper's,* Lewis Lapham and Luke Mitchell, who worked long and hard on long and hard pieces.

Thanks as well to the commissioning editors of the various anthologies in which some of these pieces were first published: William H. Shore; David Rosenberg; Hank Lentfer and Carolyn Servid; Roger Rosenblatt; Michael Katakis and Russell Chatham; Emilie Buchwald; and a special thanks to my dear friend and colleague John Elder, who edited *The Return of the Wolf* and who has taught me an enormous amount about the forested East that we both love.

Robin Dennis and Lindsay Ross put this book together at Henry Holt; thanks also to Paul Golob and John Sterling, Maggie Richards, Justin Golenbock and Tara Kennedy, and Nick Caruso. Gloria Loomis, as always, made the deal happen. And Sue and Sophie gave encouragement and love throughout—when I had to travel for my work I missed them mightily!

# Permissions

10. "Of Caribou and Carbon" first appeared in *Arctic Refuge: A Circle of Testimony*, edited by Hank Lentfer and Carolyn Servid, and published by Milkweed Editions (2001).

11. "Year One" first appeared in *Sierra*, vol. 91 (January/February 2006).

12. "What's On: 11:30 A.M." is excerpted from "What's On," which first appeared in *The New Yorker* (March 9, 1992).

13. "Out There in the Middle of the Buzz" first appeared in *Forbes ASAP* (December 2, 1996). Reprinted by permission of *Forbes ASAP Magazine* © 1996 Forbes LLC.

14. "Covetousness" first appeared in *Outside* (June 1997).

15. "The Cuba Diet" copyright © 2005 by *Harper's Magazine*. All rights reserved. Reproduced from the April 2005 issue by special permission.

16. "A Grand Experiment" copyright © 2005 Condé Nast Publications. All rights reserved. Originally published in *Gourmet*. Reprinted by permission.

17. "The Great Leap" copyright © 2005 by *Harper's Magazine*. All rights reserved. Reproduced from the December 2005 issue by special permission.

18. "Pie in the Sky" first appeared in *Orion Magazine*, www.orionmagazine .org (March/April 2006).

19. "Hype vs. Hope" first appeared in *Mother Jones* (November/December 2006).

20. "(Tod) Murphy's Law" originally appeared in *Yankee*, YankeeMagazine .com (September/October 2007).

21. "Job and Matthew" originally appeared in *Communion,* edited by David Rosenberg, and published by Anchor Books, a division of Random House, Inc. (1996).

22. "State Fair" first appeared in *DoubleTake* (Fall 1996).

23. "If You Build It, Will They Change?" first appeared in *Toward the Livable City*, edited by Emilie Buchwald, and published by Milkweed Editions (2003).

24. "High Fidelity" copyright © 2004 by the *Christian Century*. Reprinted with permission from the March 23, 2004, issue of the *Christian Century*.

25. "The Christian Paradox" copyright © 2005 by *Harper's Magazine*. All rights reserved. Reproduced from the August 2005 issue by special permission.

26. "Will Evangelicals Help Save the Earth?" copyright © 2006 by Bill McKibben. First published in *OnEarth* (www.onearth.org), Fall 2006. Reprinted by permission.

27. "God Within the Shadows" first appeared in *The New Yorker* (April 6, 1987).

28. "The Desert Anarchist" is reprinted with permission from *The New York Review of Books*. Copyright © 1988 NYREV, Inc.

29. "Prophet in Kentucky" is reprinted with permission from *The New York Review of Books*. Copyright © 1990 NYREV, Inc.

30. "Getting Warmer" first appeared in *Outside* (May 1993).

31. "An Explosion of Green: The Bard of the Birdfeeder" is excerpted from "An Explosion of Green," which first appeared in *The Atlantic* (April 1995).

32. "Milken, Junk Bonds, and Raping Redwoods" first appeared in *Rolling Stone* (August 1989).

33. "Court Jester" first appeared in *Mother Jones* (November/December 1991).

34. "Not Here" first appeared in *Sacred Trusts*, edited by Michael Katakis and Russell Chatham, and published by Mercury House (1993). Jeanne Robert Foster's poem "Crane Mountain," from *Adirondack Portraits: A Piece of Time*, edited by Noel Riedinger-Johnson, is reprinted by permission of the publisher. Copyright © 1986 Syracuse University Press.

35. "Taking to the Streets: Report from the WTO" first appeared on TomPaine.com (November 30, 1999).

36. "Patriotic Acts" first appeared in *Mother Jones* (November/December 2000).

37. "The Muslim Gandhi" first appeared in *DoubleTake* (December 2001).

38. "Speaking Up for the Environment" first appeared in *The Washington Post Book World* (April 22, 2001).

39. "A Last Best Chance for Baby Boomers" first appeared in *Orion Magazine*, www.orionmagazine.org (November/December 2006).

40. "Homeless Men" first appeared in *The New Yorker* (December 27, 1982).

41. "Growing Old Gracefully" first appeared in *The Boston Globe Magazine* (May 10, 1998).

42. "Cross-Country Ski Your Way to Shining Health, Renewed Vigor, and Everlasting Happiness!" first appeared in *Outside* (February 1999).

43. "Across the Disappearing Finish Line" first appeared in *Outside* (November 2000).

44. "Mr. Natural" first appeared in *Outside* (May 2003).

# Index

# About the Author

BILL MCKIBBEN is the author of more than a dozen books, including *The End of Nature, Enough: Staying Human in an Engineered Age,* and *Deep Economy.* A former staff writer for *The New Yorker,* he writes regularly for *Harper's, The Atlantic Monthly,* and *The New York Review of Books,* among other publications. He is a scholar in residence at Middlebury College and lives in Vermont with his wife, the writer Sue Halpern, and their daughter.

*Books by Bill McKibben*
*available from Holt Paperbacks:*

*Deep Economy*—In this powerful and provocative manifesto, Bill McKibben offers the biggest challenge in a generation to the prevailing view of our economy. For the first time in human history, he observes, "more" is no longer synonymous with "better"—indeed, for many of us, they have become almost opposites. McKibben puts forward a new way to think about the things we buy, the food we eat, the energy we use, and the money that pays for it all.

*Enough*—McKibben turns his eyes to an array of technologies that could change our relationship not with the rest of nature but with ourselves. He explores the frontiers of genetic engineering, robotics, and nanotechnology—all of which we are approaching with astonishing speed—and shows that each threatens to take us past a point of no return. This wise and eloquent book argues that we cannot forever grow in reach and power—that we must at last learn how to say, "Enough."

*Fight Global Warming Now*—McKibben and the Step It Up team of organizers, who coordinated a national day of rallies on April 14, 2007, provide the facts of what must change to save the climate and show how to build the fight in your community, church, or college. They describe how to launch online grassroots campaigns, generate persuasive political pressure, plan high-profile events that will draw media attention, and other effective actions. This essential book offers the blueprint for a mighty new movement against the most urgent challenge facing us today.